北方民族大学民族学自治区"十三五"重点学科

北方民族大学教研项目"民族学专业课程教学行动研究"
（2019JY0028）资助出版

时间：快与慢

（汉英对照）

[挪威] 托马斯·许兰德·埃里克森◎著

马建福　周云水◎译

黄河出版传媒集团

宁夏人民出版社

图书在版编目（CIP）数据

时间：快与慢：汉英对照 /（挪威）托马斯·许兰
德·埃里克森著；马建福，周云水译. -- 银川：宁夏
人民出版社，2020.6
　　ISBN 978-7-227-07228-7

　　Ⅰ.①时… Ⅱ.①托… ②马… ③周… Ⅲ.①生活方
式 – 通俗读物 – 汉、英 Ⅳ.①C913.3-49

中国版本图书馆 CIP 数据核字(2020)第 092350 号

时间：快与慢（汉英对照）　　[挪威]托马斯·许兰德·埃里克森　著

馬建福　周云水　译

责任编辑　闫金萍　赵学佳
责任校对　陈　晶
封面设计　魏　佳　姚欣迪
责任印制　陈　哲

黄河出版传媒集团
宁夏人民出版社　出版发行

出 版 人　薛文斌
地　　址　宁夏银川市北京东路 139 号出版大厦(750001)
网　　址　http://www.yrpubm.com
网上书店　http://www.hh-book.com
电子信箱　nxrmcbs@126.com
邮购电话　0951-5052104　5052106
经　　销　全国新华书店
印刷装订　宁夏凤鸣彩印广告有限公司
印刷委托书号　（宁）0017099

开本　　787 mm×1092 mm　1/16
印张　　23.75
字数　　350 千字
版次　　2020 年 6 月第 1 版
印次　　2020 年 6 月第 1 次印刷
书号　　ISBN 978-7-227-07228-7
定价　　68.00 元

中文版序言

自从这本书第一次用英语出版以来已经过了 19 年，我很高兴也很荣幸看到它现在被翻译成中文。近 20 年来世界发生了很大变化，尤其是在信息和通信技术领域。请允许我介绍一些最重要的变化。

1.社会媒体在 2001 年几乎不存在。我的空间、推特、脸书、视频网站、微信和大量其他网络平台都是在接下来的几年里建立起来的，直到 2010 年才在全球蓬勃发展。

2.互联网的使用在很大程度上是我所说的全球中产阶级的领域；相对富裕的人多集中在欧洲和北美。如今，对互联网使用最多的是中国人，以及数以亿计的印度人、非洲人和南美人。

3.互联网主要通过计算机访问，而智能手机自 2007 年首次推出以来逐渐占据访问的主导地位。

4.网上几乎没有服务，除了书，几乎没有商品出售。今天，似乎有一个应用程序可以应用于从预订理发或出租车到付账单、买衣服和杂货的所有方面。很多商品和服务贸易已经从实体商店转移到了网上世界。

5.物联网还没有形成。我指的是诸如冰箱、扩音器或割草机之类的物体，它们连接到互联网和彼此之间，并且在没有人类直接干预的情况下不断地相互交流。

总的来说，自 21 世纪初以来，全球的互联网络得到了极大的增强。关键词是社交媒体、智能手机和基础设施的改进。

这些快速的变化意味着，《时间，快与慢》的许多例子都是过时的。同时，我也会坚持认为，书中所提到的问题，如果不是更多的话，在今天和当时一样重要。由于网络和通信方式越来越快速和高效,时间的加速正在继续,而其他人的注意力正变得越来越稀缺,这仅仅是因为我们现在彼此都可以使用,这意味着被排除在重要的网络之外不仅很容易,而且也很容易被注意到。被别人遗忘是我们这个时代最大的社会焦虑之一。此外,长期专注于一件事的能力,对文化发展和个人发展同样至关重要,目前这种能力被广泛认为受到互联网和快速通信(现在主要由智能手机介导)的威胁。

最后,我冒昧地说,尽管近几十年来信息和通信技术发展迅速,尤其是智能手机的变革效应,但这本书的主要论点仍然值得认真对待。我不希望每个人都同意我所说的话,但我希望读者会发现参与这场讨论是值得的。

2019 年 9 月于奥斯陆

托马斯·许兰德·埃里克森

Preface for the Chinese edition

Nineteen years have already passed since this book was first published in English, and it is a pleasure and an honour for me to see it translated into Chinese presently. Much has changed in these almost two decades, not least in the realm of information and communication technology. Allow me to mention some of the most important changes.

1. The social media barely existed in 2001. MySpace, Twitter, Facebook, YouTube, WeChat and aplethora of other networking platforms were all established in the following years, and have flourished worldwide only after 2010.

2. The Internet was largely the domain of what I call the global middle class; relatively affluent people concentrated geographically in Europe and North America. Today, the far largest nationality on the Internet are the Chinese, and hundreds of millions of Indians, Africans and South Americans are also online.

3. The Internet was mainly accessed via computers, while the smartphone has gradually taken predominance since it was first introduced in 2007.

4. Services were barely available online, and apart from books, few goods were sold. Today, there seems to be an app for everything from booking a haircut or a taxi to paying one's bills and buying clothes and groceries. A lot of trade in goods and services has migrated from the physical shop to the online world.

5. The Internet of Things had not yet come into being. By this I mean objects, such as refrigerators, loudspeakers or lawnmowers, which are connected to the Internet and to each other, and which increasingly communicate with each other without the direct intervention of humans.

In general, connectivity has been enhanced enormously worldwide since the early 2000s. Keywords are the social media, the smartphone and improved infrastructure. These rapid changes imply that many of the examples in Tyranny of the Moment come across as dated.At the same time, I would argue that the problems addressed in the book are just as relevant today as they were then, if not more so. The acceleration of time owing to the ever faster and more efficient modes of networking and communication has continued, and it remains a fact that the attention of others is becoming an ever scarcer resource, simply because we are all now available to each other, which means that being

left out of significant networks is not only easy, but it is also easily noticed. Being forgotten by other people is one of the greatest social anxieties of our time. Moreover, the ability to concentrate on a matter for a long time, crucial for cultural growth and personal development alike, is by now widely seen as being threatened by the interruptions, distractions and fast communication of the Internet (now mainly mediated by smartphones).

I would, in conclusion, venture the claim that in spite of the fast development of information and communication technology in the last couple of decades, and notably the transformative effects of the smartphone, the main argument of this book still deserves to be taken seriously. I do not expect everybody to agree with what I am saying, but I hope that the reader will find it worthwhile to engage with the argument.

Oslo, September 2019

Thomas Hylland Eriksen

前　言

　　这本书的构思源于一种不安的感觉，多年以来，这种情绪不断滋长，在我的心里一直挥之不去。这种含糊的不安间接地告诉我，有些事情可能会越来越糟糕。最近的 20 年见证了各种各样省时技术的迅速发展，从高级的多功能时间管理人员到电子邮件、语音信箱、移动电话和文字处理软件；过去我们从未像现在这样缺乏空闲的时间。我们似乎不知不觉地成了科技的奴隶，而我们本来是想用科技来获得自由。信息革命使人们获得信息的渠道成倍地增长，影响了全世界几十亿人，当然也包括每一个读到这一行话语的人；我们享受或承受的信息量，在前一代人那里是不敢想象的。然而，宽泛得令人惊讶的信息渠道，或者说完全自由获取的信息，并没有让人们变得更加明智，恰恰相反——人们越来越困惑。

　　这种双重的悖论伴随着改变了表面的效率和创造力的令人不安的怀疑，实际上适得其反，这恰是本文讨论的出发点。有一种很强烈的预警，表明我们将要创造一种社会，在其中几乎不可能提出超过几英寸长的想法。细小的碎片——信息的线头——弥漫于间隙之中，侵入知识的连贯体，并使其分裂，逐步替换有点老旧、庞杂和萧条的事物。50 岁以上的人，很难在劳动力市场上找到工作，除非他们假冒成年轻有活力、思想开朗又灵活的人。前一周的时尚很快就会绝望地变成过时品，凡此等等。我不是一个浪漫主义者，也非一名勒德分子(Luddite，勒德分子在 19 世纪英国纺织技术工业化时，破坏因为工业革命而改变的织布机，他们认为是这些机器让他们失去工作，改变了他们的生活。现在引申为反对机械化和自动化的人)——如同其他任何人一样，我没有耐性等待一个像样的公司为我提供超速、便宜和稳定的网络连接——但也不可能为当前的潮流喝彩，这种潮流转型速度极快，正在朝向一个万事皆休的社会转变。

　　1999 年，我暂时放下挪威奥斯陆大学的工作，开始外出休假。出于某些原因，我未能开展很多的研究，但我的确是很勤奋地工作，这让桌面异乎寻常的杂乱——到处堆满了论文、校订稿、报告和电子邮件稿等。无论我何时清理好桌面，之后都会到走道上取一杯咖啡，在我再次回到房间打开房门时，混乱的景象会重新出现。我没有别的选择，只能冷静地坐下来，分析完全无法继续工作和减缓主要计划的原因。最后，我以自己为何不能完成研究工作为题，做了一项研究。最简单的原因是总会有许多其他的细小任务要完成，以至于我永远也不能持续地推进缓慢而繁琐的学术研究工作。认识到这一点之后，我就开始写作本书，最终呈现为目前的模样，暴露并批评了信息科技带来的某些不可预料的后果。单单看本书的标题，很容易使人陷入文化保守主义或者文化悲观主义的情绪之中。这自然远离了我的初衷。在我先前出版的著作中（其中大部分还未被斯堪的纳维亚半岛之外的人所知），我尚持世界主义和反民族主义的政治激进观点；我深信文化与政治全球主义最终会导致真正的全球人道主义，同时也相信新的工作——这对于信息社会来讲是典型的工作方式——将会改进在工业社会中占主导的苦差事和严格的等级制度。换句话说，《时间：快与慢》这本书不是要表达对一种没有互联网的社会的渴望，对生锈的工厂铁门的怀旧式渴望，对农业生活的向往，或"停下一切，让我远离世界"的其他各种观念。本书的目标不是也不可能是废止信息社会，而是要让人们理解它所带来的不可预料的后果。

信息社会的加速特征拥有一段很长的历史背景，伴随时间呈现出强有力的回响混合。它直接与电报机和蒸汽机有关，并不断影响我们生活的各个方面——从家庭、思维方式到工作、政治和消费。可以使用几千种方式描述它，而且至少要几千页纸才够用。我在这本书中处理这一话题的动机涵盖了作区分的可能性——简言之，我的目标是对我们不经意创造的社会进行批判性反思。过去几年来，我一直在谈论时间、技术和人类生活的关系，其中融合了听众对此的反应。在 IT 部门或其他行业工作的人们，包括记者和官员，往往对我所描述的加速与匆忙深有同感，并承认他们在工作日中满负荷运转，闲暇时间被切断，无法按计划进行一个稳定周期的工作，这反过来影响到他们的家庭生活，等等。而其他人则没有这么大的热情。在我小孩就读的幼儿园里，明智的管理人员对于他的职员以及其他类似行业中的人不可能减少他们的工作速度和压力水平的提法表示反对。地方政治家和非政府组织的代表对于我那相当仓促和充满事实的谈话,给出的反应是"听你讲话是一种享受"——我已习惯了这种具有嘲讽性的奉承,所以一直在等待"但是"后面的句子——"但是这仅仅是你们自己这一类的少部分人,活动水平才会反常得高"。这难道不是难以回答的反驳吗?事实上并非真的如此。就像本书所呈现的那样,这个话题与我们大家都有密切关系。

本书首版于 2001 年春季,由阿斯切荷格出版社(H. Aschehoug)以挪威文发行。在准备出版英文版期间,我曾经考虑尽力去除本书内明显源自斯堪的纳维亚的痕迹,转而使用英美人士喜欢的案例予以代替,但很快我就想到了更好的路子。我选择妥协与折中,替换掉一些对上下文没有意义的斯堪的纳维亚的案例,避免让读者一味地陷入游记式写作。我邀请英语世界的读者朋友,一起来看看挪威奥斯陆的全球化状况,只此一次应该无碍大局。问题是普遍的,或许曼哈顿的视角并不比奥斯陆的视角更广阔。

托马斯·H.埃里克森于奥斯陆

2001 年冬

Preface

This book began with an uncomfortable feeling, which had grown steadily over the past few years and refused to go away. It seemed that this vague discomfort indirectly tried to tell me that something was about to go terribly wrong. The last couple of decades have witnessed a formidable growth of various time-saving technologies, ranging from advanced multilevel time managers to e-mail, voicemail, mobile telephones and word processors; and yet millions of us have never had so little time to spare as now. It may seem as if we are unwittingly being enslaved by the very technology that promised liberation. Concomitantly, the information revolution has led to a manifold increase in the public's access to information, which affects hundreds of millions worldwide, certainly including everyone who reads these lines; we enjoy, or suffer from, an availability of information that was unthinkable a generation ago. Yet the incredible range of information freely or nearly freely available has not created a more informed population, but—quite the contrary—a more confused population.

This double paradox, along with a nagging suspicion that changes which ostensibly boost efficiency and creativity may in fact do the exact opposite, is the starting-point for the exploration that follows. There are strong indications that we are about to create a kind of society where it becomes nearly impossible to think a thought that is more than a couple of inches long. Tiny fragments—information lint—fill up the gaps, invade coherent bodies of knowledge and split them up, and seem certain to displace everything that is a little old, a little big and a little sluggish. People in their fifties find it difficult to sell themselves in the labour market unless they masquerade as young, dynamic, open-minded and flexible people. Nothing is more hopelessly dated than last week's fashion. And so on. I am no romantic or Luddite—like everyone else, I am impatiently waiting for a decent company to offer me a superfast, cheap and stable Internet connection—but it is impossible to applaud the current drift towards a society where everything stands still at enormous speed.

In 1999 I was on a sabbatical from my job at the University of Oslo. For some reason I did not get much research done, but I did work diligently and indeed got a lot of desktop clutter out of the way—articles, proofs, reports, e-mails... Whenever I had cleared my desk, I might go down the corridor to fetch a cup of coffee, and just as I opened the door to re-enter the office, the mess had already begun to reappear. Eventually there was no option other than to sit down calmly to analyse how it could be that it seemed completely impossible to work continuously and slowly with a major project（at last, then, I got some research done, namely on why I couldn't get any research done）. The short answer is that there were always so many other little tasks that had to be undertaken first that I never got going with the slow, tortuous work that is academic research. This realised, I began to write what eventually grew into the present book, which exposes and criticises some unintended consequences of information technology. Given the topic, there is a danger that the book will be filed under cultural conservatism or, worse, cultural pessimism. That would be very far from my intentions. As in my previous work （most of which is unknown outside of Scandinavia）, I still hold cosmopolitan, anti-nationalist, politically radical views; I am convinced that cultural and political globalisation may ultimately lead to a truly global humanism, and I also believe that "new work" —the style of work typical for information society—is an advance on the routine drudgery and rigid hierarchies dominating industrial society. *Tyranny of the Moment* does not, in other words, intend to give voice to yearnings for a society without the Internet, a nostalgic longing for rusty factory gates or, for that matter, the sturdy pleasures of the agrarian life, or any other view of the generic "stop the world, let me off" type. The aim is not and cannot be to abolish information society, but to create an understanding of its unintended consequences.

The acceleration typical of information society has a long prehistory with powerful reverberations through time. It is directly connected with the telegraph and the steam train, and it increasingly affects most aspects of our lives—from family and style of thought to work, politics and consumption. It can be described in a thousand ways and, not least, on several thousand pages. My motivation for treating the topic in a short book of this kind consists in the possibility that it might make a difference— the aim, in a word, is to contribute to a critical reflection about the kind of society we are unwittingly creating. Over the last year I have given many talks on the relationship between time, technology and human life, and audience reactions have been mixed. People who work in the IT sector or other service professions, including journalism and the bureaucracy, have generally reacted favourably to my descriptions of acceleration and hurriedness, confirming the assumption that their working days are overloaded, their leisure time is being chopped up, they are unable to work for a sustained period on a project, which in turn affects their family life, and so on. Others have been less enthusiastic. The very sensible manager of my children's kindergarten objects that it is impossible for her staff, and for others in similar professions, to reduce their working speed and stress level. A group of local politicians and NGO representatives reacted to one of my rather hurried and fact-laden talks by saying, by way of introduction, that "listening to you is enjoyable" I am used to this kind of mock flattery, and was by then waiting for the "but" clause and indeed, "but this is only about a handful of people of your own kind, whose level of activity is unnaturally high". Difficult objections to respond to? Not really. As this book hopefully shows, its topic is relevant to all of us.

A different version of this book was published in Norwegian by H. Aschehoug in spring 2001. In preparing the English version, I considered the possibility of trying to erase every visible trace of its Scandinavian origin, replacing all examples and all local flavour with UK or US equivalents. I soon thought better of it. Instead, I have opted for a compromise, replacing those Scandinavian examples which do not make sense out of context and thereby avoiding involuntary lapses into travel writing, but keeping others. Inviting an English-language readership to see the world in globalisation （or glocalisation）with Oslo as a vantage-point, just this once, will not do any harm. The issues are universal, and a Manhattan perspective is no less provincial than an Oslo perspective anyway.

Oslo, 2001 T.H.E.

目 录

CONTENTS

目 录
CONTENTS

第一章 警惕空隙

早　上

8:21　在奥斯陆街头,浏览《挪威邮报》第一版,上面仅印了一幅图片,是人们正在等待交通信号灯的转变。半页的广告用了一行标语"观看挪威最快的电视节目"吸引读者,然后是谢谢。

8:35　在小卖部买了一份小报,可以在等待电梯时阅读。

8:43　进到办公室,打开电脑。自昨天下午到现在,总共收到21封电子邮件。我将外套挂在衣帽钩上,然后去取了一杯咖啡。

8:48　期望能开始写作,但才开始就不得不接了几通电话,并在互联网上核对些东西。

8:53　我没找到有用的信息,只好开始回复邮件。

9:03　以一种极其少有的真实反思,理解这些不得已的事情,然后关掉电脑,拔掉电话线,开始使用手写笔做记录。

1　Introduction: Mind the Gap!

08:21　Scan the first page of Aftenposten, the Oslo broadsheet, while waiting for the traffic lights to change. A half-page advert entices readers with the one-liner: 'Watch Norway's fastest TV programme'. Thanks anyway.

08:35　Buy a tabloid in the canteen. Got to have something to read while I'm waiting for the lift.

08:43　Enter the office. Turn on the computer. 21 new e-mails since yesterday afternoon. Hang my coat on a peg and fetch coffee.

08:48　Looking forward to starting to write. Just have to take the phone and check something on the web first.

08:53　Cannot find the information I'm looking for. Start replying to email instead.

09:03　Understand, in a rare glimpse of genuine reflexivity, that something has to be done. Turn off the computer, pull out the phone cord and begin to take notes in longhand.

但是，这次我不得不承认表达欠妥。无论如何已是最后的条目。除了一开始用掌上电脑和几片碎纸记录的涂鸦之外，这本书几乎完全是在文字处理机上完成的。与那些将电脑键盘作为第四个指关节的人一样，让我用手写一张比明信片更重要的东西，就会是个大问题。实际上，从那些令我感到愉快的在线网友那里和曾经谈话的电子笔记中，我得到了许多主要观点和关键词。然后，我开始修订整理一系列的短篇随记，同时为了书的体裁需要，尽量使其整体上具有不同的轮廓。这些初稿的内容，几经令人沮丧的放弃、重拾、砍削、粘贴和增删，逐渐呈现出线性发展的雏形，当然这个过程太过漫长，以至于很难控制（就我而言，最多能顺畅地写出30页，列出12个要点，也就8万字左右）。我起初将其分成7个独立的部分，每一部分作为一个主要的章节。一开始我写出了第三章的初稿，然后又写了第二章。然而，我很快就感觉陷入了困境，第二章读起来怪怪的，就像一个巨兽，有3个头却没有尾巴，只好转而写作第五章的中间部分。在写作时，我不时会插入关键词，并把注意力分散到其他打开的文档中。直到出版社截止交稿日期来临之前，整本稿子还有脱漏的标点、残缺的段落、需要补充的参考文献，以及标注的问题和不完整的句子。

But this, I have to admit, is a misrepresentation. The last entry is anyway. Apart from the very first, fumbling notes made on a Palm handheld computer and on scraps of paper, this book is in its entirety written on a word processor. Like others who have grown up with the keyboard as their fourth finger joint, I have enormous problems writing anything more substantial than a postcard by hand. In reality, it happened like this: I had a few general ideas and keywords, some electronic notes from talks I had given, and a few one-liners I was pleased with. I then began to re-work the notes into a kind of continuous prose, while simultaneously trying out different outlines for the book as a whole. When the content of this initial document, after a frustrating period of abortive attempts and nonstarters, cutting and pasting, adding and deleting, began to show the rudiments of a kind of linear progression, it was too long to be manageable (in my case, the limit is about 30 pages in 12 point, that is about 80,000 characters). I then divided the file into seven separate files, one for each main chapter. I wrote the draft version of Chapter 3 first, and then began work on Chapter 2. But then I painted myself into a corner, left Chapter 2 as a troll with three heads but no tail, and embarked on the middle section of Chapter 5 instead. While writing, I continuously entered keywords and scattered ideas into the other open files. Until a very short time before the publisher's deadline, the whole manuscript was punctuated with lacunae, missing paragraphs, missing references, question marks and incomplete sentences.

过去，文本的草稿与最终稿之间存在严格的区分。作者本人在誊抄稿件时，需要明白自己的前进方向，而不用关心稿子的写作风格。比较理想的情形是，作者自己在动笔写第一个句子时，就有一个长而连贯的推理，或者在脑海中有一幅设计好的蓝图。文本初稿写完之后，需要一个专业的打字员。但现在已经不是前面所讲的那样了。如今，写作者往往是协同工作，各种事情交杂在一起，有奇思妙想和无意识的念头，文本的结构也会在写作过程中发生变动，这犹如在海中重新建造船只。文字处理对我们的思想和写作所产生的影响，或许会超过我们所关注的事物，但确切地来说，还没有人系统审视过它如何影响我们处理信息的方式。例如，就像马克思这样的天才，在写资本论时，要是有文字处理软件，恐怕就不会出现或长或短、或简单或复杂的凌乱文本。我想，他的文稿可能会更加整洁，不会那样的复杂，其长度至少会增加 25%。由于文字处理和支持思考及写作的方式，组成《资本论》

的章节和书目看起来更像互相摞在一起的砖块，而不是互相连接并深度贯穿论证的有机联系。

本书讨论时间与科技，以及科技影响人类当代生活的方式。这似乎是一个很大的哲学问题，需要用极大的敬意向康德、柏格森和海德格尔鞠躬膜拜。然而，最近这些问题已经进入人们的日常生活，表明它们行将迈过我们的门槛。在 20 世纪 90 年代后半段，这一新的时代已经开启，后面的章节会讨论这一问题。因此，需要采用一种具体并更具常识性的方式看待这些问题。

In the old days, there was a rigid distinction between a draft and a finished text. When one began to copy out a manuscript, one ought to know where one was heading, irrespective of genre. Preferably, one should have a long, coherent line of reasoning or a well-structured plot present in the mind when one wrote the first sentence. When one had copied it out, the text was finished and went to a professional typesetter. This is no longer the case, as the above description indicates. Nowadays, writers work associatively, helter-skelter, following whims and spontaneous ideas, and the structure of a text is changed under way; the ship is being re-built at sea. Word processing has probably affected both thought and writing more than we are aware, but exactly how it has affected the way we deal with information has not yet been subjected to systematic scrutiny. Would a messy work of genius such as Marx's Capital, for example, have been shorter or longer, simpler or more complex if its author had had access to word processing software? It would, I suspect, have been tidier and less complex. Probably at least 25 per cent longer. Because of the very style in thought and writing word processing encourages, the chapters and 'books' that make up Capital would have seemed more like blocks stacked on top of each other than organic links in a long, interconnected chain of deeply concentrated reasoning.

This is to do with time and technology, and the ways in which technology affects the way we live in time. These may seem large philosophical questions that ought to be treated with great deference and deep bows in the direction of Kant, Bergson and

Heidegger. However, the issues have recently announced their arrival right at our doorstep by entering everyday life. The actual take-off of this new era was in the second half of the 1990s, and this will be demonstrated in later chapters. For this reason, the issues can should be treated in a concrete and largely commonsensical way.

　　本书的核心主张是，当今时代大量无阻碍流动的信息，将要填满所有的缝隙，其结果是任何事情都可能成为一系列歇斯底里的饱和时刻，没有"前后彼此"之分。实际上，由于下一个时刻很快来临，"此时此地"已经受到威胁，以至于活在当下已经很难。这种极度匆忙的结局势不可挡，作为心理范畴的过去和将来，已经受到时间的专横的威胁。当今是计算机、互联网、通信卫星、多频道电视、短消息、电子邮件、掌上电脑和电子商务的时代，无论何时，只要一方处于发送状态，最稀缺的资源是其他各方的注意力。当某方成为接受者时，最稀缺的资源是迟缓而持续的时间。这里存在着当代社会的张力。

　　A central claim of the book is that the unhindered and massive flow of information in our time is about to fill all the gaps, leading as a consequence to a situation where everything threatens to become a hysterical series of saturated moments, without a "before" and "after", a "here" and "there" to separate them. Indeed, even the "here and now" is threatened since the next moment comes so quickly that it becomes difficult to live in the present. We live with our gaze firmly fixed on a point about two seconds into the future. The consequences of this extreme hurriedness are overwhelming; both the past and the future as mental categories are threatened by the tyranny of the moment. This is the era of computers, the Internet, communication satellites, multi-channel television, SMS messages （short text messages on GSM phones）, email, palmtops and e-commerce. Whenever one is on the sending side, the scarcest resource is the attention of others. When one is on the receiving side, the scarcest resource is slow, continuous time. Here lies a main tension in contemporary society.

请允许我举个这样的例子：在我还是孩童时，我属于儿童这个亚文化群，其成员对于太空旅行和恐龙充满强烈的好奇心。到了青春期末了，我才明白现代社会有数千万的孩子，处境几乎与我一模一样：他们厌倦学校刻板的作息时间，在体育运动中往往低于平均水平，很容易受到各种逃离现实的虚构形式的诱惑，常常花费整天的时光，想象中世纪奢华社会中的武士，最近则幻想在仙女座星系或月亮上创立殖民地，抑或关注其他神秘宇宙的自然科技。

Allow me also to put it like this: as a boy, I belonged to that subculture among children whose members are passionately interested in space travel and dinosaurs. Only late in puberty did I realise that there were thousands upon thousands of children, spread thinly across the modern world, who had been in exactly the same situation as myself: they were bored by the tedious routines of school, they were below-average performers in sports, and were for these reasons easily tempted by various forms of imaginative escape from reality, frequently spending their days among knights and dragons in societies of the generic J.R.R Tolkien kind, or at recently founded space colonies in the Andromeda region or on the moon, or else in the no less marvellous universe of natural science and technology.

面向这类青少年的通俗科幻小说，往往描绘两个互补的未来。其中之一在20世纪80年代中期突然被取消。1986年1月，"挑战者号"太空飞船爆炸，全体机组人员罹难，一个时代就此结束——同样，一个可能的未来突然变得完全不可能：太空时代彻底流产。今日，距离阿波罗4号载人飞船登月已经30多年，然而登上火星却成了未来更遥远的事（如果真会发生的话），比1969年那个令人难忘的夏季所预期的遥远得多——在那个夏天宇航员尼尔·阿姆斯特朗第一个登上了月球。

The popular science fiction literature directed at an adolescent readership of this generic kind depicted two complementary futures. One of them was abruptly called off in the mid-1980s. When the Challenger space shuttle exploded and the crew was killed in January 1986, an era was over or, rather, a likely future had suddenly become extremely unlikely: the space age had been abolished. Today, more than 30 years after the Apollo XI, passenger shuttles to Mars are much further into the future （if there at all）than they were on that unforgettable summer day in 1969 when Neil Armstrong was the first human to set foot on the Moon.

我们设想的另一个未来是计算机时代。对于那些在 20 世纪六七十年代中成长起来的人,电脑似乎比太空时代更加遥远抽象。较之于第一代虚拟地址扩展器,我们对亚瑟王、弗罗多和雷克斯霸王龙会多几分友好的态度。当时,计算机甚至难得一见,但我们知道它是巨型机器,有很多错综复杂的线路和闪烁的灯泡,还需要安放在宽阔、无菌的空调房里,一些工程技术人员各司其职,连续供应的打孔卡片和纸带不断运行。几年前,国际商用机器公司(IBM)的市场总监,说了一句不朽的话语,他认为世界总共只需要 10 台电脑。

The other future that was envisaged for us was the computer age. For most of those who grew up during the 1960s and 1970s, it seemed more remote, and much more abstract, than the space age. We were on friendlier terms with King Arthur, Frodo and Tyrannosaurus Rex than with Vax-I. Most of us had hardly even seen a computer, but we knew that they were enormous machines with a maze of thick wires and blinking bulbs, which required a large, sterile and air-conditioned room, a small army of engineers and a steady supply of punch-cards and paper strips to function. A few years earlier, the marketing director of IBM had uttered the immortal words, that the world needed a total of about ten computers.

20 世纪 70 年代开始,苹果、金宝多和施乐等品牌的微型计算机开始出现在消费市场。1981 年,IBM 制造的个人电脑开启了一个主战场,其目标是非计算机痴迷者市场,仅仅 3 年之后,苹果公司开发了第一代苹果机,装备了鼠标和图形界面,这两者后来被微软公司(以及包括阿姆斯查德在内的其他公司)复制。目前,大部分个人电脑的显示器与第一代苹果机的桌面极为相似。当 IBM 生产出第一台计算机突然袭击市场时, 计算机专家认为几年之内每个办公室将有一台电脑,甚至许多家庭也会有一台电脑。当时许多人对此摇头质疑。数年之后,果真每一个办公室都有了电脑,许多家庭也有了个人电脑。

From the late 1970s, microcomputers began to reach the consumer market, from producers such as Apple, Commodore and Xerox. In 1981, the "PC" from IBM was launched in a major campaign aimed at a non-nerd market, and only three years later, Apple developed its first Macintosh, a computer equipped with a mouse and a graphic interface, both of which were later copied by Microsoft (and by a few other companies including Amstrad). An image which is very similar to the original Macintosh 'desktop' forms the display of most personal computers today. When IBM made their first major, ultimately ill-fated, assault on the market, computer gurus stated that within a few years, there would be a computer in every office, and many would even have one at home. People shook their heads in disbelief. A few years later there was a computer in every office, and many had one at home.

大约个人电脑出现 10 年之后,互联网有了重要的突破。就像我所写的那样,另一个 10 年已经过去,今日可以很容易看出在这两个互相补充的未来中,如果其中之一从未传递它的东西,另一个总会报复:它来得更快,带来的后果更多,超出 20 年前任何人的想象。

About ten years after the personal computer, the Internet had its major breakthrough. As I write, another decade has passed, and today it is easy to see that if one of our two complementary futures never delivered its goods, the other came with a vengeance: it arrived faster, and with much larger consequences, than anyone could have dreamed of a little more than two decades ago.

这不是一本关于计算机的书籍。这与即将到来的问题远非毫不相关,但是谴责科技本身,就像拍摄钢琴演奏家一样无济于事。本书讨论信息社会以及它带来的社会文化的奇怪副作用,其中许多与计算机化只存在转弯抹角的关系。经济增长、节省时间和推进效率的技术,使我们日益富有,并越来越有效率,这让我们可以有更多时间从事自己的活动,但是有充分的理由怀疑——甚至会在更大的程度上——这会导致完全相反的结果。更多的弹性使我们的柔韧性越来越少,越来越多的选择让我们更不自由。为什么我们没有时间去休闲? 这与人们的期待完全背道而驰。为什么信息接收得越来越多,理解包容却在减少?在一个迷恋目前及不久之后的社会中,为何没有良好的、政治上的明智愿景? 为什么我们依然觉得微软Word 软件的加载时间太长? 这些答案与变迁节奏的周转率增加有关,也与错误类别的过度复杂有关。

This is not a book about computers. They are far from irrelevant to the issues at hand, but blaming technology as such would be tantamount to shooting the pianist. The book is about information society and the strange social and cultural side-effects it has entailed, many of which are only obliquely related to computerisation. Economic growth and time-saving, efficiency-boosting technology may have made us wealthier and more efficient, and it may have given us more time for activities of our own choice, but there are sound reasons to suspect that it also maybe even to a greater degree-entails the exact opposite. More flexibility makes us less flexible, and more choice makes us less free. Why do most of us have less time to spare than before, contrary to what one might expect? Why does increased access to information lead to reduced comprehension? Why are there no good, politically informed visions for the future in a society infatuated with the present and the near future?And why do we still feel that the loading of Microsoft Word takestoo long? The answers are to do with too much complexity of the wrong kind and the increased rate of turnover in the rhythm of change.

现在有几个好的理由，可以感觉生活的满意（当然也有几个不好的理由）。我们活得越久，就有越宽泛的机会，总体上比上一代人拥有更多的选择。在发达国家尤其是这样，但许多第三世界的国家，在这方面也有很大的进步。在20世纪，许多国家的人均寿命和识字比例急剧升高，尽管非洲现今的情形依然受阻。然而，一些事情即将偏离正轨，这是本书的主题。不过我要强调——以免还是不太清楚——作者本人既不是老式的浪漫主义，也不是梦想往事的怀旧主义——或者想当然地认为现代社会具有连贯性和整体性。大体上，我与新信息科技的关系是积极和热切的，我认为信息时代是工业时代有价值的继承者。这些观点如何与我们当今时代流行的基本批判达成和解，我将在本书中予以指明，并在最后一章中简要阐述。但是，首先我要声明，我自己不提倡读者直接核查最后一章的内容。这种纤维素类的产品适用于那些受到威胁的文化类型：它是线性的和累积性的。本书各章节具有特定和非随机的次序，各章之间并非简单地堆叠在一起，而是有机的连接体。按照特定的顺序写作是本书给读者的印象，这是模仿文字处理软件之前的时代。本书讨论的主题是当前大家的兴趣，但是在形式上——这种缓慢展开式的、推理的随笔——对于习惯信息消费的下一代来说，恐怕有些老掉牙了。

There are several good reasons to be pleased about living right now (and certainly a lot of bad reasons). We live longer, we have a wider range of opportunities and, on the whole, more options than earlier generations did. This is particularly true of the rich countries, but there have been advances in this direction in many "Third World" countries as well. Both longevity and literacy rates rose dramatically in most countries during the twentieth century, the current setbacks in Africa notwithstanding. Yet, something is about to go awry. That is our topic. Let me nevertheless stress in case it should still be unclear that the author is neither an old-fashioned romantic nor a nostalgic who dreams of a preor early modern age when coherence and wholeness could still be taken for granted. My relationship to new information technology is in principle active and enthusiastic, and I regard the information age as a worthy successor to the industrial age. How these views can be reconciled with a fundamental critique of a prevalent pattern in our age, I shall have to indicate in the course of the book, chiefly in the final chapter. The reader is not encouraged to cheat and check the contents of the last chapter first. This cellulose product is true to just that cultural style which is threatened: it is linear and cumulative. It has a particular, non-random order, and the chapters are not merely blocks stacked on top of each other; they are connected organically. The book thus gives the impression of having been written in a particular sequence; it imitates the era before word processing. The topic is of current interest, but the form the slowly unfolding, reasoning essay may well be judged as old-fashioned by the next generation of information consumers.

在开始讲述专横的时间这一故事之前,我们先简要回顾冷战之后这个时代的主要特征。这个时代来得太匆忙,以至于最好的研究方案也得追赶当前的时代脚步。后续各章节从一些经过挑选的路径追溯文化的历史,强调信息科技的历史,尤其是那些未曾预料的后果。第四章名为《速度》,讨论了20世纪世界历史中特别重要的方面:几乎一切事情都在越来越快地变化,新产品尚未占领阵地就已经被淘汰,而我们却还未回过神来。时间被敲成片片碎屑,几乎没有留下任何东西。第五章名为《指数级增长》,是要唤起人们注意一种特别的数学函数。指数曲线的主要特征是:每隔一定区间,函数值就要翻番;如果数字小,增长似乎并不剧烈。最终,曲线会类似垂线,由 X 轴代表时间,这意味着时间变化接近零。令人奇怪的是,当今社会能发现许多类似的曲线。在第六章,我要讨论加速度和指数级增长带来了令人新奇的副作用,我称之为堆垛现象:各种事情互相堆叠在一起,而不是成线性排列。两个明显的案例是万维网和多频道电视如同漏斗过滤的信息,不那么明显的例子是那些较不重要的情形。第七、八两章表明我们日常生活蕴含的一切都在文化的类别之中;无论是当代人的风俗习惯或一夫一妻制,还是年轻人对"灵活就业"与消费习惯的崇拜,都展现了时间的专横性。

The story about the tyranny of the moment is about to begin, with a short overview of some characteristics of this era, the period after the Cold War. This era came about so fast that the best research still consists in trying to catch up with the present. The following chapter pursues some selected paths back in cultural history, emphasising the history of information technology and not least its unintended consequences. The fourth chapter introduces a particularly important aspect of the history of the last century or so, namely acceleration: nearly everything changes faster and faster, and we are only millimetres away from the point where a new product is obsolete before it hits the shelves. Time is hacked up into such smallpieces that there is hardly anything left of it. The fifth chapter calls attention to a particular kind of mathematical function, namely exponential growth. The main property of exponential curves is the doubling of their values at regular intervals; so long as the numbers are small, they do not seem to grow dramatically. Eventually, they take off and begin to resemble vertical lines, which indicates since the x axis represents time that time approaches zero. Surprisingly many such curves can be identified nowadays. In the sixth chapter, I discuss a curious side-effect of acceleration and exponential growth, namely the phenomenon I call stacking: the strange fact that more and more of everything is stacked on top of each other rather than being placed in linear sequences. A couple of examples are information as funnelled through multi-channel television and the World Wide Web, but there are other, less obvious cases which may be no less consequential. The next and penultimate chapter shows what all this implies for everyday life in our kind of culture; how contemporary mores, ranging from serial monogamy and the cult of youth to "flexible work" and new consumption habits can be seen as expressions of the tyranny of the moment.

本书尽管采用了通俗的风格和适中的长度，但并非一本毫不显眼的书籍。我们谈论的不是一种新的模式和代码，也不是一套行将控制人类社会的新组织原则。因此，本书结束于某些政治的考量，是比较中肯的。若以"我们必须重新控制时间"作为结论，显然过于简单化并容易误导读者；相反，我建议大家应该重新学习对特定时间形式的评估。为了发现在各领域内与时间相像的东西，知道时间的重要及其遭受威胁的原因，我认为只能设定一套标准的时间，此外别无他法，因此也就不能按照线性的和积累的模式来阅读本书。

In spite of its popular style and modest length, this is not an unambitious book. We are talking about nothing less than a new pattern, a new code and a new set of organising principles that may be about to dominate our kind of society. For that reason, it seems pertinent that it should end with some political considerations. It would be both simplistic and misleading to conclude that "we must regain control over time"; instead I suggest that we must re-learn to value a certain form of time. In order to discover what this kind of time is like, in which domains it rightly belongs, why it is important and why it is threatened, there is no other solution I can think of than setting a few slow hours aside to read the entire book in a linear, cumulative fashion.

第二章 信息文化与资讯崇拜

"信息时代"这一词汇已经提了很多年了。20世纪70年代,当托夫勒(Alvin Toffler)在写作他关于未来的冲击和第三次浪潮的畅销书时,可能只是碰巧使用了这一词汇。但作为一个概念,它却可以追溯到诸如麦克卢汉(Marshall McLuhan)之类的媒体理论家,他在20世纪60年代出版了他最重要的著作;若再往前推,就可以追溯法兰克福学派的文化批判,比较突出的有阿多诺和马尔库斯。在第二次世界大战之后的数年间,他们给那些对西方文明充满感激之情的学生提出了预警。然而,"信息时代"这一概念或术语,在20世纪90年代有了重大的突破,这恐怕不是巧合。正如包括"全球化"和"认同"在内的其他时髦术语一样,这个术语在政治家的口中很快会失去意义,这些人会采取油嘴滑舌的方式使用这个术语,目的是要证明自己能够与时俱进,而不是要谈论信息社会与工业社会或"机器时代"的差别。这是一个令人悲伤的事实,一个极好的词语在最需要的地方,却变成了最无用的陈词滥调;因为这些词语常常能够讲述当前最重要的事情,因此可以被每一个人占为己有。另一方面,这些词汇正日益下降的边际价值——它们正在降低的价值以及被缩短的寿命——本身就是信息社会典型问题的征兆。

2 Information Culture, Information Cult

The phrase "information age" has been around for some years now. It might well have been coined by Alvin Toffler when he wrote his bestselling books about future shocks and third waves in the 1970s, but as a concept it can be traced to media theorists like Marshall McLuhan, who wrote his most important books in the early

1960s, and further back to the cultural critics of the Frankfurt School, notably Adorno and Marcuse, presenting their apocalyptic visions for Western civilisation to grateful audiences of masochistic students in the years following the Second World War. It is no coincidence, however, that the term （and concept）of the information age had its major breakthrough in the 1990s. Like other fashionable terms, including globalisation and identity, the term easily becomes meaningless in the mouths of politicians, who may be tempted to use it in a rather glib way to prove that they are abreast with the current situation, not in order to say anything substantial about the differences between this kind of society and the industrial society, or "mechanical age", which preceded it. It is a sad fact that perfectly good words become useless clichés just when they are needed the most; the reason is that these words tend to say something important about the present and are therefore appropriated by everybody. On the other hand, the falling marginal value of words their decreasing value and shortened lifespan is itself a symptom of the problems typical of information society.

换句话说，"信息社会"这个词语因为信息社会而失去了其本身的意义。信息社会是一种现实，假如一个人要认真地理解当今的时代，没有什么方式比考虑工业社会向信息社会的过渡更有用。

Put differently, the phrase "information society" has lost its meaning because of information society. The latter is a reality, and if one is going to make a serious attempt at understanding the contemporary age, there are a lot less useful ways to begin than by looking at the transition from industrial to informational society.

然而，需要注意的是，最近几十年来，出现了许多其他的变化，而且大部分都朝着同一个方向变化——变得更加复杂和不稳定，以及更具个人主义。1980年，在奥斯陆只有一家印度餐厅。至2000年，距离我的公寓步行不到10分钟就已经出现了六七家的印度餐厅，有快餐店（有番茄酱和咖喱粉）、禁烟的印度教克利须那派素食餐厅，以及五星级美食店。在亚当斯1988年出版的小说中，因为在奥斯陆没有比萨的送货服务，故事的主人公极为恼怒。现在这已经不再是问题了；如果有问题，恐怕就是通过电话或互联网订餐时，如何在比萨、中餐、印度餐和其他各种烹调方法制作的食物中进行选择。过去的二三十年里，在富裕国家，影碟机和个人电脑已经很常见，就像更早的电视一样普遍。因为顾客量少，银行分支机构纷纷关门或重新设计，支票也成了过时的支付方式，而网上银行正如雨后春笋般涌现。在年轻人中间，网聊与手机短信成了标准的交流方式。

It should nevertheless be kept in mind that the last couple of decades have seen a great number of other changes as well, many of them pulling in the same direction towards greater complexity, uncertainty and individualism. In 1980, there was not a single Indian restaurant in Oslo. In 2000 there were more than half a dozen within less than 10 minutes' walking distance from a flat I used to live in, ranging from fast food ("Curry & Ketchup") to a non-smoking, vegetarian Hare Krishna place and one offering five-star gourmet fare. In Douglas Adams's novel Dirk Gently's Holistic Detective Agency from 1988, the hero is exasperated at the lack of pizza delivery services in Oslo. This would not be a problem now; if anything, the problem consists in choosing between pizzas, Chinese, Indian and other cuisine available for home delivery via phone or the Internet. Everywhere in the rich countries, video recorders and personal computers have, during the last couple of decades, become as common as television became a little earlier. Bank branches have been closed down or redesigned with a view to keeping customers out; the personal cheque is becoming an obsolete means of payment, and Internet banking is rocketing upwards. Internet chat and SMS messages （short text messages transmitted between mobile phones）are becoming standard means of communication among teenagers. Until mid-1999, the SMS（Short Message System）technology for GSM phones was virtually unknown; it was initially meant to notify people that they had voicemail. It was then discovered by young people, who began to use the inexpensive service to keep in touch. The number of SMS messages sent in Norway in October 2000 was of the same order as the numbers sent in all 1999, indicating a twelve-fold increase in a year.

21 世纪始于 1991 年

21 世纪始于 1991 年。这些有趣的例子像水面上的涟漪一样,但与深层次的结构变化有关。事实上,这种变化不仅可能,而且很有必要讲述。言归正传,21 世纪不是在 2000 年或 2001 年才开始,而是始于 1991 年。可能除了霍布斯鲍姆以外,没有人会间接地支持这种奇怪的观点,他认为 20 世纪是从 1914 年到 1991 年。

The Twenty-first Century Began in 1991

These anecdotal examples are naturally mere ripples on the surface, but they are connected to deeper structural changes. As a matter of fact, such changes make it not only possible, but necessary to state, without any further ado, that the twenty-first century began, not in 2000 or in 2001, but in 1991. This perhaps idiosyncratic view is indirectly supported by none other than Eric J. Hobsbawm, whose "short twentieth century" begins in 1914 and ends in 1991.

这种分期的合理性,可以通过 1991 年发生的三个主要的全球性事件来证明。第一件大事是苏联的解体。我们都知道,这件事的政治后果是苏联就此消失。但是,仍然有两个超级大国或多或少地分割着世界,在政治上也有一个清晰可见的左右分歧。美国提出的意识形态建立在大量的个人自由和少量的安全之上(实际上这种安全少得可怜,以至于美国公民很多人为了能够对付威胁自己安全的人,不得不配备手枪)。苏联提出了恰恰相反的意识形态——大量的公共安全保障但很少的个人自由(个人自由少到这样一种程度——只要一个人按照自己的想法乱说话,就会被发配到西伯利亚劳改)。这两种对立的意识形态进一步衍生出一系列二元对立的范畴:国家规定与个人创新,集体与个人,团结一致与自私自利,等等。

虽然在西方社会，很少有人热切地喜欢苏联的制度（郝伯特·乔治·威尔斯可能是最后一个赞赏苏联的知识分子，萨特也只是为苏联的战略依据辩护过），但它具体表现了人类生活组织方式的另一种方式，也是对人类本性的另一种看法，以及对美国流行的社会规划的另一种考虑。世界上大部分的政治运动，都是试图在美国的极端个人主义与苏联的极端集体主义之间定位；在批评者看来，这种对立标志着政治辩论宽广空间的界线。早在布莱尔与吉登斯提出"第三条道路"的选择方式之前，全世界就已经积极地推出了多种方案，比如从瑞典式的社会民主到无政府主义，还有从印度的贸易保护主义到南斯拉夫的经济民主。在冷战时期建立的可预测又令人恐惧的空间内，逐渐产生了政治的可选择性，然而当其中一个超级大国消失时，这些可选择性几乎烟消云散。最后，美国呈现的价值标准在全世界占据主导地位。20世纪90年代，意识形态基本上孤掌难鸣。

This periodization may be substantiated through three major global events which took place around 1991. The first was the breakdown of the Soviet Union. As a result politics, as we used to know it, disappeared. When there were still two superpowers more or less dividing the world between them, there was also a clear, visible distinction between left and right in politics. The USA represented an ideology based on a lot of individual freedom and little security (so little, actually, that a large proportion of the country's inhabitants owned handguns in order to be able to kill persons who threatened them). The Soviet Union represented its opposite a great deal of security and very little personal freedom (so little, in fact, that one could be sent to a labour camp in Siberia if one spoke one's mind). The contrast between these two systems was translated into a series of related dichotomies; state versus free initiative, community versus individual, solidarity versus selfishness, and so on. Although there were very, very few in the West who earnestly liked the Soviet system (H.G. Wells may have been the last intellectual to do so; Sartre defended it on purely strategic grounds), it embodied an alternative way of organizing human life, another view of human nature and another view of social planning than that which was prevalent in the

USA. Most political movements in the world tried to position themselves between the extreme individualism of the USA and the extreme collectivism of the USSR; seen through the eyes of their detractors, these opposites marked the boundaries of a wide space for political debate. Long before Blair and Giddens, there were many "third ways" actively being promoted around the world, ranging from Swedish-style social democracy to anarchism, Indian protectionism and Yugoslav economic democracy. The plethora of political alternatives that grew within the predictable, but frightening space created by the Cold War, all but vanished when one of the superpowers disappeared. As a result, the values embodied by the USA have become globally hegemonic. Ideology in the 1990s has largely been unself-conscious, the sound of one hand clapping.

第二个主要的事件是南斯拉夫的解体及其之后发生的战争。20 世纪 90 年代巴尔干半岛的悲剧间接地提醒人们,族群的民族主义和激进主义可能是抵抗美国的霸权及全球化的一股强势力量,至少在短期内会是如此。战争也使研究者开始注意这样一个事实,那就是现代性并不能促使族群及其他"原生性"认同消失;相反,随着人们受教育的程度增加以及电视频道的增多等,以亲属关系和地域空间为基础的认同会得到强化。当人们意识到自己是全球化的受害者,并被排除在全球化之外时,这样一些复归传统的形式将不是什么稀罕的事情。

The other major event was the dissolution of Yugoslavia and the ensuing wars. The tragedies of the Balkans in the 1990s were an indirect reminder that ethnic nationalism and fundamentalism could be a very strong countervailing force to the US hegemony and globalization, at least in the short term. The wars also revealed a fact that researchers had been aware of for some time, namely that modernity does not lead to the disappearance of ethnic and other "primordial" identities; on the contrary, identification based on kinship and place can be strengthened as an indirect result of increased education, moretelevisionchannels and so on. These and other forms of "re-traditionalisation" are not uncommon reactions when people see themselves as being victimized and excluded by globalization.

另外，南斯拉夫的解体表明集体认同并非一劳永逸的事，国家的主权与不可分割性在未来将不可预测。在战后国际关系研究方面，比较武断的意见认为，国家之间的边界变化令人无法接受。南斯拉夫剧变的事实表明，社区的巨大需求与现有国家所能提供的条件完全不一样。在这方面来看，南斯拉夫的族群冲突和认同话语具有的不确定性与认同的偏移性，与当今美国和西欧的特征一样，主要表现为激进主义与少数族群之间关系的紧张。后面将对此再做分析。

Further, the dissolution of Yugoslavia showed that collective identities are not given once and for all, and that the sovereignty and indivisibility of the state cannot be counted on in the future. One of the post-war dogmas in the study of international relations has been that changes of national boundaries could not be accepted. The case of Yugoslavia showed in dramatic ways that there is a great demand for communities that are both larger and smaller than those offered by existing states. In this, the identity discourses and ethnic conflicts in Yugoslavia are comparable to the uncertainties and shifting of identities presently characteristic of the USA and Western Europe, as well as tensions between purism （or fundamentalism）and mixing（or hybridity）among minorities. To this issue I shall return later.

最后，巴尔干半岛的战争是一系列战争的开始，不存在孰好孰坏的分野。迟至20世纪80年代，西方人文主义者和伦理学者都认为战争已经远去。通常，他们支持解放运动，并赞成少数人反抗政府的压迫和超级强权。但是，在索马里内战中，同样的人道主义者会支持谁呢？在卢旺达的胡图族与图西族之间，他们又会去同情哪一方呢？对于斯里兰卡持续的内战，他们又该如何看呢？即使是在巴以冲突中，与以往的情况相比，20世纪90年代出现的矛盾看法要多得多。

Finally, the wars in the Balkans were among the first in a long line of wars without obvious good guys and bad guys. As late as the 1980s, humanists and moralists in the West could easily take a stance regarding wars in far-flung places. Usually, they would support struggling liberation movements and small peoples against oppressive states and superpowers. But who did the same humanists support during the civil war in Somalia? Who did they sympathise with in Rwanda; the Hutus or the Tutsis? And what is their view of the ongoing civil war in Sri Lanka? Even in the case of Israel/Palestine, there was considerably more ambivalence during the 1990s than had earlier been the case.

暂且不提海湾战争中,是谁在 1991 年 1 月份首先开战,哪一场战争是鲍德里亚所描述的从未真正发生的呢? 又是谁通过美国有线新闻网(CNN)每天向世界播报战事的实况? 海湾战争标志着美国开始实施"新的世界秩序",这在十年之后北大西洋公约组织反对米洛舍维奇领导的南斯拉夫时得到了验证,虽然当时这并不是一种"自由左派"的观点,但至少包括两部分:一半左右的欧洲左派分子支持军事行动,另一半则持反对意见。随着全球两极对峙的消失,在后冷战时代,同床异梦的事情接连发生,比如当时《经济学家》杂志就建议联合国出于人道主义的原因制裁伊拉克——过去这种主张与社会主义及反对北大西洋公约组织的观点有关。

Not to mention the Gulf War, which broke out in January 1991 and which was famously described by Jean Baudrillard as a war that never really took place, but which was broadcast in daily instalments to the world, courtesy of CNN. The Gulf War marked the inauguration of the USA's "new world order", confirmed nearly a decade later in the NATO campaign against Milosevic's Yugoslavia, where there was not one "left-liberal" view, but at least two: about half of the European left was all for the military operations, the other half was against them.In the strange post-Cold War era that followed the evaporation of global bipolarity, strange bedfellows are being made continuously, as when The Economist strongly advised the UN to lift sanctions against Iraq for humanitarian reasons an opinion that would formerly have been associated with anti-NATO and socialist views.

对于 21 世纪而言，互联网将是一个模板

1991 年发生的第三件事直接与本书的主题有关，因而需要被更彻底地看待——尽管政治腐败、作为稀缺资源的认同和地缘政治的模糊性，理所当然也是 21 世纪的特点。

The Internet is a Template For The Twenty-first Century

The third major event that may be located to 1991 is more directly relevant to the theme of this book and will accordingly be treated more thoroughly although the collapse of politics, identity as a scarce resource and geopolitical ambiguity are certainly also constituting features of the world of the twenty-first century.

从 20 世纪 60 年代后期开始，直到 1983 年阿帕网的出现，互联网一直作为军事通信网络存在。但是作为一个封闭的系统，除了军职人员以外，互联网使用者还包括学者和计算机网络爱好者，他们通过所谓的"BBS"（电子布告栏）交换信息和游戏程序。直到 1991 年左右，互联网才开始商业化并彻底平民化，因而老百姓可以在家里获得互联网的账号，也就在这一时期欧洲学术界开始常规地使用电子邮件。

The Internet had existed as a military communication network since the late 1960s, until 1983 as ARPANET, but it was a closed circuit eventually including, apart from military staff, academics and networks of computer enthusiasts who exchanged games and information through so-called BBS （electronic bulletin boards）. It was only around 1991 that the Internet became commercialised and thoroughly civilianised, so that Mr and Mrs Smith could get an Internet account at home; and it was around this time that even European academics began to use email routinely.

几年之后,具有图形界面的万维网,也就是许多人所讲的互联网产生了。我是在 1993 年的春季学期首次遭遇网络,当时我们的电脑工程师要我更新软件。那时,奥斯陆大学的教职工已经使用电子邮件好几年了,但是对于这一新兴的全球网络的其他用途,我们大部分人依然只有模糊的概念。

A couple of years later, the World Wide Web, that graphic interface which to many people is the Internet, was launched. My first encounter with the web took place in the spring semester of 1993, when one of our computer engineers called on me to update my software. Employees at the University of Oslo had already been using email for a couple of years by then, but most of us only had vague notions of other uses for this emerging global network.

电脑工程师双击了一个称作"马赛克 1.0"的图标。他解释说"这种新东西就是万维网"。然后切换到了一个预先的模式:这将进入一个庞大的资源系统。他浏览了一下基本的原则——全球资源定位器、超文本传输协议、图形界面和超文本标记语言——然后接着给我演示了几个网站。其中两个网站分别是阿德雷德大学和美国国会图书馆。我当时想:这下好了,我可以阅读澳大利亚南部的参考书籍,还可以在全世界最大的图书馆查找书目了。这真是进步? 电脑工程师接着说:"目前还没有那么多资源,但等待就可以了。"

The computer man double-clicked on an icon called "Mosaic 1.0". "This is something new called the World Wide Web", he explained, and added, switching to a prophetic mode: "It's going to be enormous." He ran through the underlying principles "URL", "http", "graphic interface", "HTML" and then went on to show me a few web sites. The University of Adelaide and the Library of Congress were two of them. Oh well, I thought, so here one may eventually find reading lists from Southern Australia and inventories from the world's largest library. Is this progress? "There isn't that much out there yet", the computer man said apologetically, "but just wait."

诚如我们所知的那样，剩下的已成历史了。在当年的秋季，网站（或"主页"）的密度开始显著增加。计算机公司都建立了自己的网站，其他诸如唱片公司和出版社之类的企业也紧随其后，大学与学院的大部分主修专业及少量辅修专业也开始上线，而且网站布局不断改善，内容也日益丰富。到 1994 年，加利福尼亚州极其追赶时髦的《连线杂志》（WIRED）也开始建立自己的网页。同时，很多致力于晦涩主题的网站如雨后春笋般出现，无政府主义、前卫摇滚、科幻小说和宗教神秘主义等纷纷粉墨登场。整个 20 世纪 90 年代，不管规模大小，也不管是否主流，各种网站在万维网上不断涌现，这在很大程度上加快了我们这个时代的信息堆垛。

The rest is, as we say, history. Already in the autumn of the same year, the density of web sites （or "home pages"）began to increase noticeably. The computer companies established their sites, other companies such as record labels and publishers followed; most major and quite a few minor universities and colleges went online, with improved layout and thicker content from one week to the next. The then extremely trendy California magazine WIRED wrote in 1994 that the coolest thing to do this week, was to make one's own home page. Many did. At the same time, a thick undergrowth of websites devoted to arcane topics began to flourish: anarchism, progressive rock, science fiction, religious sectarianism... The large and the small, the mainstream and the underground; they all went on to the web during the 1990s, adding in no small measure to the acceleration and stacking of information typical of our age.

万维网的发展突飞猛进。新的网络标记语言经过改进提高，开发出了超文本标记语言和相关的技术，包括太阳公司推出的一种应用程序开发语言 Java，使得声音、图像和任何格式化文本等都可以出现在网络。网络的传输速度或频带宽度不断增加。没有人知道这个月有多少网页存在于网络上，就在我写作的时候，网站的数量已经接近 1 个亿。每个网站都包含了很多网页。

The WWW took off nearly immediately. New, improved versions of the web "mark-up language" HTML and related advances, including Java, a new programming language for the web, made it possible to include sound, animations, any kind of formatted text, reply coupons and so on. The transmission speed or bandwidth increased and continues to do so. Nobody knows just how many million web pages exist out there this month, but at the time of writing, the number of sites is approaching 100 million. Each site contains anything between one and a huge number of pages.

万维网代表了一些品质全新的事物。用作家吉布森的话来讲，网站堪比永不停歇的期刊和巨大的图书馆，但是即使我们不考虑网站上的广告数量，它也不同于图书馆。首先，网站上的信息并不是我们订购的，也不是按照字母顺序或其他顺序排列。不同的主题根据不同的原则连接在一起，这些原则往往异想天开。网页没有等级资历之分，一个技术娴熟的学生开发的网站，也可以像微软公司的网页，拥有相同的空间，同样具有吸引力。

The WWW represents something qualitatively new. The web can perhaps, in the words of author William Gibson, be compared to a never-ending journal, or a large library, but it is distinct from a library even if we do not take the amount of advertising into account. Above all, information on the web is not ordered, either alphabetically or in any other way. Different topics are linked together according to varying, often whimsical principles. The web is not hierarchical either, and a site belonging to a skilled student can be just as attractive, and take just as much space on the screen, as Microsoft's home page.

换句话说，网络具有非常民主和权力分散的特点，这是权力部门为何要费尽心机加以管制的原因。众所周知，网络上具有海量的色情文字与图片，还有各种政治宣传口号、仇恨的言论、违法的劝告和古怪的话语——自然还有大量的广告。一些悲观主义者担心网络将退化为另一个市场竞争的舞台，不幸的是他们错了。就像旧的媒介那样需要以木质纸浆为基础，网络在某种程度上可以视为一种媒介，一个可以盛装各种实际事物的空容器。然而，这个容器也能为内容塑形。这是一种更加快速的媒介，而不是皮革包边的禁欲主义哲学文集。与麦克卢汉的观点相反，媒介不是信息，但媒介可以塑造信息。哲学的历史与一本不带插图或超链接的500页书籍的差异，不仅仅是在只读光盘驱动器，或者小说或电影的形式。它是不同的。一种思想也许不只用德语才能表达（正如海德格尔相信的那样），但是这种思想不再是一个网页，而一定要与其他思想互相关联，不是通过超级链接而是按照连续的方式。

In other words, the web is incredibly democratic and decentralised, and this must be the main reason why the powers that be take such great pains to try to regulate it. As is well known, pornography of all kinds exists in large amounts there; if one looks, one will also find political propaganda and hate speech of every kind, exhortations to break the law, eccentric utterances and naturally terabytes of advertising. Some pessimists fear that the web will degenerate to just another arena for marketing; they are, fortunately, wrong. Like the old media based on wood pulp, the web can up to a certain point be seen as a mere medium, an empty vessel that can be filled with practically everything. However, it also contributes to shaping the content. It is a much faster medium than, say, a leatherbound volume of Stoic philosophy. Contrary to McLuhan's view, the medium is not the message, but the medium docs shape the message. The history of philosophy does not just look different on a CD-ROM, or in the shape of a novel or a film, from a 500-page book with no illustrations or, for that matter, hyperlinks. It is different. It may not be true that certain thoughts can only be worked out in German （as some Heidegger specialists seem to believe）, but certain thoughts are longer than a web page and are necessarily interlinked with other thoughts in a sequential way and not through hyperlinks.

此外,不像印刷媒介那样,网络上的内容可以不断变化。有自尊心的公司不仅仅拥有自己的网站,还能够持续地改进网站质量。昨天还能获取的网站资源,到了今天就可能没办法再获得了。链接也会每个月更新一次。改变不是一种紧急状态,而是日常生活的特点。

Further, unlike print media, content on the web changes continuously. Self-respecting companies no longer merely have web sites; they are about to improve their web sites. There can be no guarantee that a page that was available yesterday will be available today. Links must be updated monthly. Change is not a state of emergency, buta feature of everyday life.

互联网的用户数量增长迅速。到 2000 年年底,全球约有 4 亿人在线。这些用户分布在全球各地,每一个国家都有互联网的使用者,但分布状况呈现曲线。在一些国家,因特网用户人数与国家大小有关,而不是与物质生活水平有关(不像私人轿车的分布特征)。在挪威,2000 年就有 230 万人在线。而仅仅 3 年前,在线人数只有 50 万。整个非洲的互联网用户人数只比挪威多一点点(可是总人口却是挪威的 100 倍以上),如果去掉技术相对先进的南非不算,整个非洲的互联网用户人数,比欧洲最小国家的互联网用户数还少一半以上。

The number of Internet users has grown very fast （see Figure 2.1）. At the end of 2000, nearly 400 million people were online. Their geographical distribution is truly global there are Internet users in every country but skewed along the familiar lines. The number of Internet users in a given country nevertheless varies along dimensions other than material standard of living （unlike the distribution of private cars）. In

Norway, half the population （2.3 million） were online in 2000. Only three years earlier, the number was just half a million. All of Africa had slightly more Internet users than Norway（and a population that was more than 100 times larger）, but if one subtracts relatively technologically advanced South Africa, there are less than half as many Internet users in the entire African continent than in one of the smallest European countries.

世界上拥有最多"互联网线"的是美国、加拿大和北欧国家，至 2000 年年末，这些国家几乎一半多的人都能上网。在英国，有 35% 的人可以自由地获得互联网资源（在 1997 年时仅仅只有 2%），斯洛文尼亚（25%）和爱沙尼亚（22%）实际在线人数都比法国（15%）多。

The most "wired" countries in the world are the USA, Canada and the Nordic countries, where roughly half of the population had Internet access at the end of 2000. In Britain, about 35 per cent have access to the Net （in 1997, the figure was 2 per cent）, while both Slovenes （25 per cent） and Estonians （22 per cent） are actually more online than the French （15 per cent）.

现在还有人在说没有人能够离开网络挣钱，但是他们的期望值还是很高。在 1998—1999 年冬季，网上书店亚马逊公司挣到的钱，几乎等于北欧一座中型城市的价值，比如挪威中部城市特隆赫姆。尽管之后票面价值有所下降，但如果考虑到公司继续在挣钱，而且万一破产，公司没有多大的价值出售，这个名义价值依然是个天文数字。就像其他以网络为基础的公司一样，亚马逊公司的主要资产存在于一种期望之中。

It is still being said that "nobody" makes money off the web, but the expectations remain high. In the winter of 1998/99, the Internet bookshop Amazon.com had a price-tag that was roughly equivalent to the total value of a medium-sized

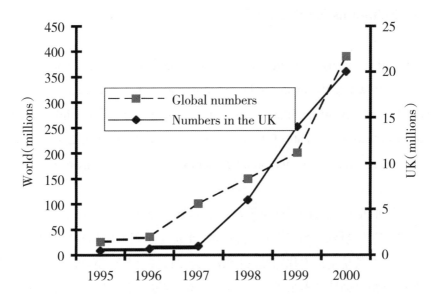

Source: www.nua.ie

Figure 2-1　Number of Internet users, 1995—2000

图 2-1　互联网用户数量

Scandinavian city like Trondheim. Although the nominal value has fallen since then, it is still astronomical, considering the company has yet to earn money and has little of value to sell in case of bankruptcy. Like most Internet-based companies, its chief asset is expectation.

养猪都要信息技术

在信息社会中，甚至猪都可以与信息技术兼容。信息社会并非某些人所说的后工业社会——这个社会的主要产品是信息，不是工业或农业产品。美国是一个信息社会，但其传统工业仍占国民生产总值的一半以上。德国和日本也是如此，对于国内经济的基础而言，丰田公司远比索尼公司重要。

In Information Society, Even the Pigs Are IT Compatible

Information society is not the same as "post-industrial society", which some talk about a society where the main product is information, not industrial or agricultural products. In the USA, which if anything is an information society, traditional industry still represents more than half of the GNP. This is also the case in Germany, and in Japan, Toyota remains a more important cornerstone for the economy than Sony.

另一方面，信息社会的特征是信息技术的整合，这是各种产品的关键因素。就连超市的收银员也得完全依赖计算机技术，要是光学条形码扫描设备坏了，她就将无能为力，尤其是她记不住商品的价格时会更糟糕。温室、挤奶机和给猪喂料的机器，都依靠微电脑处理器来工作。实际上，在一些国家，就连牲畜的交配也完全电脑化。母牛与公牛精子的配对也要通过网络，依赖大型数据库的管理，将储备中心冷冻状态的精液分配到各个地方。公牛的身体不再是必不可少的附件。所以，当千年虫病毒可能会使电脑系统崩溃时，各种焦虑迅速传开也就不值得惊奇了——不是作家、会计师或其他计算机痴迷者，而是欧洲的农民感到焦虑。人类不管是爆破一座山、建一艘船、卖一包薯片、调查一桩纵火案或做一个心脏搭桥手术，还是搞一个社会人类学的讲座，都日益依赖于计算机技术。这就是为什么1999年的千年虫问题会变成一个力量强大的神话的根本原因。尽管很多人的直觉都认为问题能够解决，但是虚构的迫在眉睫的崩溃是一个奇异的故事，反映了当代世界的脆弱性，这偶尔能够比得上作为头条新闻素材的克林顿总统和辣妹组合。如果所有的大型计算机都崩溃，后果会怎样？猪就无法定时喂食了，饲料的数量也是多少不一，电梯可能停在楼层之间，微波炉就要彻底见鬼，而银行自动取款机也无法存取现钞了。一些人预料那时唯一可以依赖的只有电脑了，因为在千年虫爆发之前，他们已经一再地检查过重要的软件。

On the other hand, information society is characterised by the integration of information technology as a key factor in all kinds of production. Supermarket cashiers are totally dependent on computer technology; if the optical bar code reader collapses, they are helpless, especially since they no longer know the prices by heart. Greenhouses, milking machines and feeding machines for pigs are run by microprocessors. Indeed, the mating procedure for cattle is now entirely computerised in several countries; the coupling of cow and semen takes place via the Internet by way of a large database, and the semen is distributed in a frozen state from central stores. The physical bull is no longer required. It should come as no surprise, then, that the anxieties associated with possible computer breakdown at the transition from 1999 to 2000 (the "Y2K" syndrome) were particularly widespread not among writers, accountants and other regular computer addicts but among European farmers. Whether one is about to blast a mountain, build a ship, sell a bag of crisps, investigate a case of arson, perform a heart bypass operation or give a lecture in social anthropology, people in our kind of society are increasingly dependent on computer technology. This is why the Y2K problem became such a powerful myth during 1999. Although many had a gut feeling that things would work out well, the myth of imminent breakdown was such a fantastic story about the vulnerabilities of the contemporary world that it was occasionally able to rival Clinton and Scary Spice as headline fodder. Suppose all mainframe computers broke down, what would happen then? Well, the pigs would be fed at erratic times and/or in strange quantities, lifts would stop between floors, microwave ovens would drop dead and ATM would no longer be able to distinguish between deposits and withdrawals. Some even foresaw a situation where the only reliable thing in society would be ... the computers, since all serious software for microcomputers had been checked and double-checked for Y2K compliancy well before the great transition.

有一个现代神话讲述一个人发明了一件耸人听闻的新式武器,这种装备杀不了任何人,也破坏不了任何建筑物,甚至连窗户也不能损坏,能损坏的只是一些纸张(这只是人道主义的武器——与中子弹武器恰恰相反)。当他申请专利时,专利局的官员满脸狐疑，建议他先回家去，并要他在申请专利之前考虑清楚。然而这个发明者依然坚持要申请，最后专利局官员只好非常厌倦地说："那行，先去拿表，填好以后再回家去。"这个人耀武扬威地嘲讽道："你明白了就好！"显然，千年虫的神话就是这个故事的变种。

A modern myth tells of a man who had invented a sensational new weapon, an instrument which killed nobody, destroyed no buildings or even windows; all it did was to destroy paper. （A humanistic weapon it was the opposite of the neutron bomb.）The bureaucrat in the patent office was sceptical, and advised him to go home and think it over before applying for a patent. The inventor nevertheless persisted, and finally the bureaucrat said, wearily: "All right then, take that form and fill it in, and then go home." The inventor quipped, triumphantly: "You see?" The Y2K myth is a variation of this story.

信息除了渗透到商品与服务的生产过程之外，还逐步变成了一种重要的原材料。当然，信息一直以来都很重要，在某种意义上，每一个社会都是一个信息社会。如果一个人能有效地杀掉猛犸象而自己安然无恙，或者能够放一把火而不留任何活口，那么他就是欧洲冰河时期最强大的人了。然而实际上，最近这种面向信息的转变，已经把它作为经济的主要稀缺资源。传统的原材料已经降低了其相对价值，额外的价值越来越依赖信息。例如，在微处理器的价值中，原材料的成本只占两三个百分点，剩下的全部是信息技术。20 世纪 90 年代最成功的微软公司，其附加值最高的电子产品，外包装的质量还不到一克。相比之下，在微软之前的通用汽车公司，其产品的包装重量达到了 4 吨。

Apart from permeating the production of goods and services, information has grown steadily in importance as raw material. Of course, information has always been important, and, in a certain sense, every society is an information society. Anyone whoknew how to kill a mammoth efficiently and （reasonably）safely, or howto make a fire without live embers, was a powerful person around the last Eurasian Ice Age. Yet it is a fact that there has been a shift towards information as the main scarce resource in the economy recently. Traditional raw materials have fallen in relative value; added value increasingly consists of information. For example, the cost of raw materials accounts for only 2 to 3 percent of the value of a microprocessor. The rest is information. The most successful company in the world during the 1990s, namely Microsoft, makes its profits off products that can be transported electronically in packages with a weight of less than 1 gram. The Microsoft of the previous generation was called General Motors. Their packages had a gross weight of 4 tonnes.

不过很明显的事实是,信息处理的从业人员越来越多。最近 10 年来,对于那些依靠谈话、写作和阅读谋生的人来讲,这是一种不证自明的事实,而且这些行业的人口正在逐步增加。时至今日,在任何国家中,学者、网页设计师、作家和记者都只是少部分人。20 世纪 90 年代,信息顾问突然间增多,但是每一个国家的农民依然多于信息顾问。另一方面,西欧有许多农民业余还兼任教师或地方政府雇员,他们工作的一部分就是纯粹处理信息。与信息有关的工作任务已经潜入这些人的工作时间之内,在这之前他们采用其他方式打发时间,有时候只是发出噪音来消磨时光。很多人花费大量的时间开会、回电话、发送传真和电子邮件、写作和阅读、归档文件、开会消磨时光、填表或写报告,等等。一篇来自挪威国家健康中心的报告显示,20 世纪 90 年代中期的财政预算有 60% 花费在各种信息处理之上。计算机专家和科幻小说家乔宾评论道:"这个数字应该是 4% 或 5%",但是没有人知道如何才能达到这个标准。

A more familiar aspect is the fact that a growing part of the working population spend most of their time processing information. This is self-evidently the case with people who make a living talking, writing and reading, and our numbers have grown rapidly during the last decades. However, even today, academics, web designers, copywriters and journalists make up only a small proportion of the population in any country. The proliferation of "information consultants" has been explosive in the 1990s, but there are still more farmers than information consultants in every country. On the other hand, many farmers in Western Europe work part-time as teachers or local government employees, and thus process pure information part of their working time. Information-related work sneaks into the working hours of groups who formerly used their time in other ways, sometimes simply as noise. A growing number spend a growing amount of their time in meetings, responding to telephone calls, faxes and e-mails; writing, reading, filing or destroying minutes from meetings, filling in forms, writing reports and so on. A report from the Norwegian equivalent to the National Health Service revealed that in the mid-1990s, an astonishing 60 per cent of the total budget of the national health service was spent on various forms of information processing. Computer specialist （and science fiction author）Jon Bing commented: "The figure ought to have been, say, 4 or 5 percent", but he added that nobody knew how to get there.

信息被看作当前西方经济的驱动力，正越来越多地通过互联网传输。当 1999 年"美国在线"与"华纳兄弟"合并时，实际上是互联网公司"美国在线"接管了娱乐公司"华纳兄弟"，而并非是其他的合并方式。尽管与"华纳兄弟"相比，"美国在线"的赢利只是很小的部分，但它的股票价值却接近"华纳兄弟"的两倍。

Information can be described as the driving force of the present Western economy, and more and more of it is being channelled through the Internet. When America Online and Warner Brothers fused in 1999, it was in practice the Internet company AOL that took over the entertainment company WB, and not the other way around. Although the profits of AOL were minuscule by comparison with those of WB, its stock value was nearly twice as high.

得不到信息才稀奇

在信息社会里,得不到信息反倒成了一种稀缺的资源。即使那些没有工作的人,也会受到快节奏信息处理的影响,而且作为消费者和普通市民,他们还要深受新技术的制约。与其他类别的社会不同,信息社会的主要特征是嘈杂和冗余:信息充斥在每一个角落,每一个人都可以获得足够的资讯,这与工业社会或其他类型的社会不同,那些社会经历过真正的信息短缺(比如过去大家习惯的说法"求知欲"等)。

In Information Society,
Freedom From Information is a Scarce Resource

Even people who do not have a job affected by the accelerated rhythm of information processing are deeply affected by the new technologies, by virtue of being consumers and ordinary citizens. Unlike in other kinds of society, life in information society is characterised by redundancy and noise: there is far too much information around, and there is certainly enough for everybody, unlike in industrial and other kinds of society, where people experienced real information shortages (as witnessed in common metaphors such as "thirst for knowledge" etc.).

我的父亲出生于 20 世纪 30 年代,他成长在一个工人阶级家庭里,能够获得的书籍很少。父亲在中学时为当地一家报纸撰写电影评论,挣到了平生的第一笔钱。拿到薪酬后他立刻去购买书籍,并且很快就爱上了买书。当他去书店时,总会带上一两个背包,带着愉悦的心情把买来的书籍背回家,并按照书名的字母顺序将每本书摆放在书架上,然后坐在摇椅上开始阅读第一本。这些活动体现了他是一个有教养的现代人,具有较大的个人乐趣。现在,该讲一下我这个出生在 20 世纪 60 年代的人。前面提到过,我的父母属于中产阶级,所以在我成长的家庭里,已经拥有一个规模可观的小型图书馆了。当然，因为生长在信息时代，我也泡在各种各样的资讯里。每当我经过大型书店时，至少会在里面待上半个钟头或一个小时，即使没有购买任何书籍，也总会带着一种满足感离开。广泛地翻阅而没有购买书籍，表明个人发挥了自己对信息的过滤功能。因为当前的信息太多，而不是太少，而且信息的总量还在增加。挪威最偏僻、人口最少的摩城靠近北极圈，每年它向挪威国家图书馆提交的材料，包括各种出版物——广义上涵盖电影、图书、杂志、明信片和光碟，其中大部分由挪威的大众传媒机构生产。在 20 世纪 90 年代的 7 年里，其所提交的材料条目数量翻了一番。1991 年，还只有 48400 条，而到了 1998 年已经增加到 100008 条。请注意，我们谈论的是一个不到 500 万人口的国家。

My father was born in the 1930s. He grew up in a working-class family with few books. When he first began to earn money as a film reviewer for the local paper during secondary school, he immediately started buying books, and quickly became adept at it. Whenever he walked into a bookshop, he invariably emerged after a while with a bag or two, went home in a very good mood, stuck most of the books into their appropriate alphabetical places in the shelf, sat down in an easy chair and began to read the first one. That kind of activity embodied his view of the enlightened, modern person as well as offering considerable personal enjoyment. Now, I was born in the 1960s. My parents were middle-class, and for reasons already mentioned, I grew up in a home with a rather good-sized library. I am also, by virtue of living in the information age, pickled in information. Whenever I walk through a large bookshop, therefore, I regard it as a respectable achievement to be able to spend at least half an hour there without buying anything. Wide-ranging browsing without buying indicates that the personal information filters are functioning. There is too much information, not too little. And the amount increases. The figures for submitted materials to the Norwegian national library, which for reasons of domestic politics is located in a remote and depopulated place near the Arctic Circle called Mo i Rana, include all publications, widely defined films, books, magazines, postcards, CD-ROMs; that is, most non-electronic mass communication produced in Norway. Over the course of seven years in the 1990s, the number of titles submitted per year more than doubled, from 48,400 in 1991 to 100,008 in 1998. and this in a country with fewer than 5 million inhabitants.

在信息社会，一项重要的技巧是让自己免受那些不想要的信息的干扰，这些信息占了总信息量的 99.99%，剩下 0.01% 的信息自然需要采用冷酷的方式利用了。

A crucial skill in information society consists in protecting oneself against the 99.99 per cent of the information offered that one does not want（and, naturally, exploiting the last 0.01 per cent in a merciless way）.

有关信息社会的无意识后果，我最喜欢的一篇文章是在 30 年前写的，其作者直到 20 世纪 90 年代中期仍不愿意对文字进行处理。作者的名字是布琳斯维尔德（Tor Age Bringsvrd，读起来有点像意大利文），他是挪威一名多产的小说家，很受大家的重视，他所讲述的故事是《收集 1973 年 9 月 1 日的男子》（按照原文，应该是 1972 年）。这个故事的主角认识到世界上的信息太多。不管如何努力，他永远都无法有启发性地回顾历史、政治和科学等。一天，他做出了一个重要决定：发誓在未来几周和几个月内紧张地工作，以便完整地回顾 1973 年 9 月 1 日这一天。他估计自己能够处理好，所以挽起袖子，开始了收集工作。他购买挪威和北欧所有的报纸，并订购了无线广播录音带，还收集其他语言印刷的报纸与出版物。但他很快就认识到，对于俄语及其他自己不懂的重要语言，他需要参加密集的培训课程学习。在数年精心的收集之后，一场大火烧毁了故事主人公的公寓，那些有关 1973 年 9 月 1 日的简报、磁带和剪贴簿化为了灰烬。故事的主角被轻度烧伤，躺在医院的病床上，嘴里毫无条理地嘟囔着尼克松总统与毛泽东主席的事情，还有 1973 年秋季举行的足球赛，等等。很自然，他被护士诊断为严重的精神病人。

One of my favourite texts on the unintended consequences of information society was written three decades ago, by a writer who declined to take the leap to word processing until the mid-1990s. His name is Tor Age Bringsværd (pronounciation roughly as in Italian; "?" = the "aw" in "raw", "?" = the "a" in "man"), a prolific and highly regarded novelist in Norway, and the story is "The man who collected the first of September 1973" (in the original, the year was 1972). It tells the story of a man who realises that there is too much information in the world. No matter how much he tries, he will never arrive at an enlightened overview of history, politics, science and so on. One day, he takes a momentous decision. He makes a vow to work intensively the coming weeks and months to obtain a full overview of this single day, 1 September 1973. That much, he reckons, he can handle. So he rolls up his sleeves and starts collecting. He buys all the Norwegian and Scandinavian newspapers, he orders recordings of radio broadcasts, then moves on to newspapers and other publications in foreign languages, and soon realises that he will need to take intensive courses in Russian and other important languages he does not know. After several years of collecting material, a fire destroys our hero's flat, which is by now filled to the brim with clippings, tapes and scrapbooks about 1 September 1973. From his hospital bed, our hero, who has suffered minor burns, babbles incoherently about President Nixon and Chairman Mao, reports from football games in late August 1973 and so on; and he is naturally diagnosed as a dangerous lunatic by the nurses.

几年之后，布琳斯维尔德从不同角度探讨这一主题。在他那本名为《沉睡者悲伤的早餐》的小说中，作者开篇就让读者看到了巴特霍尔蒂先生。他站在纽约的一家书店门口，背着一个大包，口袋里装着现金支票。他掂量了一下包的重量，并快速地计算着，嘴里还向旁人嘟囔："今晚我买了一大包书。但是谁能告诉我，何时我才能找到时间来阅读这些书籍呢？"

A few years later, Bringsvard approached the topic from a different angle. In the opening sequence of his masterful, but untranslated novel The *Oversleeper's Sad*

Breakfast, we encounter Mr Felix Bartholdy, standing outside a bookshop in New York with a heavy bag in his hand and a cashier's slip in his pocket. He considers the weight of the bag and makes some rapid calculations, while muttering, to passers-by: "I have bought all this stuff this evening. But can anyone tell me when the hell I am going to find time to read all of it?"

巴特霍尔蒂继续放声地说着:"我已经有一万多册书籍,其中大约4000册还没有阅读。通常我每周阅读两册,一年就可以读完104册。要读完4000册书,我需要将近40年的时间。现在我已经43岁,在读完我所购买的书籍之时,我已经83岁了。但是这也没什么……"此时他感觉一阵晕眩,然后斜倚在墙边,嘴里继续嘟囔着:"我还要继续买书。我要收藏书籍。我要抓住我所看见的一切书籍。我是一个执着的人。我购买的书籍数量需要达到我所阅读数量的5倍。"

Bartholdy continues, thinking aloud: "I have more than 10,000 volumes already. About 4,000 of them are still unread. Usually, I read two books a week. Two books a week equals 104 books in a year. In order to plough through 4,000 volumes, I shall need around 40 years. I am 43 years old. Before I have finished readings the books I already have bought, I shall be 83. But that is not all..." he begins to feel dizzy and leans against the wall as he concludes, whispering: "I continue to buy. I stockpile. I grab everything I see. I am a sick man. I buy at least five times as many books as I read."

正如小说所言,对巴特霍尔蒂来讲,事情越来越糟糕,但他是他那一代人的典型。在某种意义上,他超前于他那个时代几十年(这本小说是20世纪70年代出版的)。他生活的年代没有互联网和数字电视,当时全世界每年出版的书籍总共只有55万册,20年之后已经翻了一番。但是,他是信息过载的典型受害者。面对信息海洋的惊涛骇浪,他没有学会在里面自由地"游泳"。相反,在把信息海洋中的海水喝干之前,他感觉不到满足。

As it happens, things only get worse for Felix Bartholdy, but he is a true-born child of his age; in a sense, he is a couple of decades ahead of his time (the novel was published in the mid-1970s). He lives in an era with no Internet or digital television, an era when a mere 550,000 books are published annually in the world (he is aware of this figure), compared with nearly twice as many two decades later. But he is a typical victim of information overload. Facing the enormity of an ocean of information, he does not learn to swim. Quite the opposite, he will not be satisfied until he has drunk the entire ocean.

物以稀为贵

在现代社会,工会和雄心勃勃的政府机构组织社会主义读书会,搞巡回演讲(妇女与工人是其最钟爱的目标群体),目的是要教导人们远离吸烟的危害。一种普通的观念认为大多数人都急需知识的增长,因为知识就是力量,至少可以改变自己的生活状态。这个口号仍然有效,但是发生了一个重要的变化,那就是信息不再是稀缺资源。重要的不再是尽可能多地参加演讲会,或者多去看电影,也不是在自己的书架上陈列尽可能多的书籍。相反,对于富裕国家的任何一个受过教育的人来说,首要的目标是要对信息进行过滤,选出需要最优先获取的信息。

Less is More

In the classic modern era, with its itinerant lecturers (women and workers were favourite target groups), socialist reading groups organised by trade unions and ambitious state programmes to "educate the people" about anything from contraception to the dangers of smoking, it was a common notion that most people were in dire need of increased knowledge. For knowledge was power; at least, power over one's own conditions of life. This slogan is still valid, but there has been a major shift in that information is no longer scarce. The point is no longer to attend as many lectures as possible, see as many films as one can, have as many books as possible on the shelves. On the contrary: the overarching aim for educated individuals in the world's rich countries must now be to make the filtering of information a main priority.

在信息极度冗余的社会中，人们如果想要理解社会文化或其他任何事物，都无需获取尽可能多的信息。这就像不能同时阅读全世界的电话簿和一万卷的词典一样，两本书从第一页起都需要勤勉地阅读。在阅读的事情上，任何人都不可能超过亚伯拉罕森与阿米巴，即使他愿意用一生的时间去阅读。这正是巴特霍尔蒂的问题，信息时代如何避免这样的问题，将是人类面临的最重要挑战。

In this situation of extreme informational redundancy, a person who wants to understand his or her society, culture or anything else, cannot aim at obtaining as much information as possible. That would be tantamount to reading two books simultaneously the telephone directory for the whole world and a 10,000 volume dictionary and begin, diligently, on the first page in both works. One would never be able to advance beyond Abrahamson and Amoeba, even if one went on for a lifetime. This is Felix Bartholdy's problem, and avoiding it may well be the most important human challenge in the information age.

有时候会有这样的说法，认为我们这一代人消耗的事物，是我们祖父母那一辈人从未听说过的。而现在我们消耗的东西，似乎正是信息的短缺。

It is sometimes said that our generation runs out of things our grandparents had never heard of. What we now seem to run out of, is lack of information.

在这种情况下，我们就迫切需要一种机制。当任何事情的供应不再存在限制时,我们需要采用什么样的标准,区分信息的好坏,判断哪些是知识或干扰自己的噪音? 当我夜晚休息时,如何才能过滤掉我所接受到的99.99%的信息? 又如何确定剩余的0.01%的信息是我实际所需要、不会让我嗤之以鼻的?

In this situation, an acute need for a sorting mechanism appears. What are the criteria for distinguishing between good and bad, knowledge and noise, when the supply of everything is limitless? How can I sleep at night knowing that I have filtered away 99.99 per cent of the information I have been offered; how can I be certain that the 0.01 per cent that I actually use is the most relevant bit for me, in so far as I haven't even sniffed at the rest?

过去,这些问题的答案要么是一种教化和个人的认同,要么就是独特的兴趣。现在,信息的丛林已经如此茂密,以至于我们为了充分了解所有的事情,不得不顽固地一门心思去对待这些问题。即使政府花钱雇你搞研究,比如说混沌理论,你也不可能阅读完该领域内所有的东西,即使限于英语文献范围之内。扫一眼标题、摘要和内容目录是可行的,但对接下来的文本怎么办呢?忘记它,还有其他任务等着你呢! 下一刻将会抹杀当前这一刻的事情。

In the old days, the answer to this kind of question was either a sound education (Bildung), a secure personal identity or distinct interests. Today, the jungle has become so dense that one needs to be both stubborn and single-minded in order to be well informed about anything at all. Even someone paid by the state to do research on, say, chaos theory, cannot possibly read everything that is being written within the field, even if one restricts the scope to the English-language literature. It is viable to scan titles, summaries and tables of contents into the brain, but continuous texts? Forget it. Other tasks are waiting. The next moment kills the present.

对知识而言,过滤、探索和组织的原则,已经是压倒一切的需要。那么,该如何去做呢？或许,越来越多的人习惯于这样的世界——随时掠过色彩斑斓的信息碎片,却缺乏方向与凝聚力,人们为何看不到这个问题呢?我怀疑大家都有这样的经历,如果是这样,信息革命就会出现未曾预料的结果,这可能会使知识的概念发生根本的转换。

The need for filters, pathfinders, organising principles for knowledge becomes overwhelming. Or does it? Is it perhaps rather the case that growing numbers of people become accustomed to living in a world where colourful fragments of information flit by, lacking direction and cohesion and do not see this as a problem? I suspect this is happening to many of us, and if such is the case, an unintended consequence of the information revolution may be a fundamental transformation of the notion of knowledge.

消除差异的快节奏

在信息社会,快速的节奏正在将差异抹平。从日常可获取的统计数字来看,可以说,人们的早餐更愿意选择玉米片而不是稀饭,同样,人们更喜欢浏览一张报纸而不是阅读整篇论文。更多的人使用手机,他或她更习惯使用传真和电子邮件,在办公室或家中使用录音电话或语音信箱,在已过的几周内通过按电梯按钮,使电梯门比以往能早几秒钟关闭。如果按下这个键后,每次可以赢得 5 秒钟的时间。按照一天坐 4 次电梯计算,一周就有 20 次。这表明每周可以节省下 200 秒钟,一个月就可以节省 6.5 分钟,一年就可以节省一个多小时。这些额外的时间可以干些什么呢?

不妨参考一下这些建议:

In Information Society, The Gaps Are Being Filled With Fast Time

Extrapolating from commonly available statistics, it is possible to state that the person who is reading this right now is more likely to eat cornflakes than porridge for breakfast, and that he or she is also more likely to skim a newspaper today than to read an entire journal article. It is more likely that the person in question has a mobile telephone than not, it is highly likely that he or she has grown accustomed to using both fax and email, has an answering machine or voicemail at work and at home, and several times during the past week has pressed that lift button which makes the doors close a little earlier than otherwise. Suppose the net gain of pressing this button is 5 seconds at a time. Suppose, further, that one takes the lift four times a day, five fimes a week. This implies 100 seconds of saved time every week. In a month, one will have saved six and a half minutes, and during a year with perfect conditions, one will have saved more than an hour! What to do with this extra time? Allow me to make some suggestions:

玩电脑游戏或观看电视节目；
等待延误的航班；
阅读 5 份小报或 1 个版面的海报；
从伦敦驱车前往布赖顿；
做 1 次慢跑；
与孩子们讨论未来或与父母谈论过去；
学习 10 个西班牙语动词的形态变化。

·Relax with a computer game or a television programme.
·Wait for a delayed flight.
·Read five tabloids or a broadsheet thoroughly.
·Drive from London to Brighton.
·Jog.
·Talk to one's children about their future or with one's parents about their past.
·Learn ten Spanish verbs in all conjugations.

当然，一个小时可以做很多事情。如果把这些事情列成清单，恐怕很容易变成一大卷。不太可能准确地讲清楚人们节约的时间，因为我们使用机械时钟记录的时间，具有空洞和抽象的特点。我仍主张把节约整块的时间作为原则问题，比如等候电梯时，时间被蚕食的速度惊人，尤其是电梯在达到一楼之前，如果层层都要停下来，就更是如此了。

Of course, an hour can be used for anything. A list of this kind could easily have filled several volumes.It is impossible to say exactly which time this saved time is, since our mechanical, clock-driven time is empty and abstract. I still contend that the entire hour saved is, as a matter of principle, spent waiting for the lift, and the saved seconds are eaten at a frightful rate when one is waiting for a lift which insists on stopping on every floor before reaching the ground floor.

时间的密度在增加，间隙正在消失。各种各样的事物日益增多，这种环境或许让我们觉得特别满意，认为我们能够控制时间预算，比如通过按电梯里小小的按钮，又比如办公室的白领在听到会议被取消时，为突然间获得的 1 个小时兴奋得热泪盈眶。因此，很多人一眼就能认出萨特，据说他为了节省系鞋带的时间，总是习惯穿一双无鞋带的便鞋。

The density of time increases. The gaps are being filled. There is more and more of everything, and given this context, it does perhaps give us a particular satisfaction to feel that we can control our time budgets by pressing that little button in the lift, just as few office workers shed tears when they suddenly get a full hour as a present because a meeting has been cancelled. It has become easier for a lot of people to identify with Jean-Paul Sartre, about whom it has been said that he habitually wore moccasins to save the time he would otherwise have used tying his shoelaces.

在信息社会，对于那些关注经济供给的人来说，最稀缺的资源既不是铁矿石，也不是用麻袋盛装的粮食，而是他人的关注。在信息领域工作的人员——从天气预报员到教授，都在同样的分秒之间与其他人的生活竞争。不像其他的物体那样，信息的总量不会因为某人放弃或出售而减少。假如吉姆有两个苹果，他把其中一个给彼得之后，他就只剩下一个苹果了。但是如果吉姆有两个主意，他把其中一个主意给彼得，或许最终他能够拥有 3 个主意，因为彼得可能会添加自己的评论。由此看来，任何提供知识或信息的企业，都不可能出现空仓的情况。商品可能会过时并且滞销，信息经济就如空仓库一样，任何时候都可能出现淘汰和滞销，并且速度越来越快。

In information society, the scarcest resource for people on the supply side of the economy is neither iron ore nor sacks of grain, but the attention of others. Everyone who works in the information field from weather forecasters to professors compete over the same seconds, minutes and hours of other people's lives. Unlike what happens to physical objects, the amount of information does not diminish when one gives it away or sells it. If Jim has two apples and gives one apple to Peter, he has one apple left. But if Jim has two ideas and gives one of them to Peter, he may well end up with three, since Peter probably adds his comments. Be this as it may, any enterprise which supplies knowledge or information has a warehouse that can never become empty. The goods can only become obsolete and unmarketable the informational economy's equivalent to empty stores and this happens all the time and at increased speed.

对于居住在这一类社会中的人来说（有时候外界称他们为"客户"），主要的稀缺资源并不是桌椅、熏火腿和牛头之类的事物（尽管这些东西还像以前那样买卖），而是控制和管理我们自己的时间。信息从外部迫使我们更多地依赖它，而且攻势日盛，使我们更难回避。信息的来源也越来越多。争夺自由时间的战争已经上演。

For people who live in this kind of society （sometimes identified by the outside world as "customers"）, the main scarce resource does not consist in, say, tables and chairs, smoked hams and stuffed buffalo heads （although such things are naturally sold and bought as before）, but control over our own time. Information is forcing itself upon us from the outside, more aggressively and this is more difficult to resist than, say, stuffed buffalo heads. There is always more where it comes from. The war over the free seconds is on.

这不仅仅是无绳电话和互联网无线接入。那些只是这个画面的一部分,重要的是这些新媒体正在以极快的速度发展,没有人能够准确地知道网络看起来将会是什么样子, 也不知道在三五年内又该如何使用它——或者是否像现在这样,通过电视、掌上数码设备、电脑或手机接入。但是信息具有流行性,能够扩散到所有领域。20 世纪的最后 15 年,不仅见证了互联网和相关技术的提升,而且见证了语音通信、出版物和电视频道的巨大进步。

This is not just about WAP （Wireless Application Protocol） telephones and cordless access to the Internet. That is part of the picture, and it is important: these media are new, they grow at a terrific rate, and nobody knows exactly what the Net will look like, or how it will be used, in three, four or five years or whether it will chiefly be accessed through television, hand-held computers or mobile phones, or via the desktop computer as is the case today. But information is epidemic and spreads across all fields. The last ten to fifteen years of the twentieth century saw not just the rise of the Internet and related technologies, but also considerable growth in voice telephony, books published and television channels.

没有任何技术变革能够按照预料的结果出现

同样，技术、社会和文化的关系也是如此。关于这种关系已经说了很多——也依然在谈论——但是现在我们只能限于这样的表述，认为它是复杂的。技术创新的效果，很容易也的确会引诱人做出简单的结论，认为这无非就是打字机、电视或一些其他事物。这样的假设往往是错误的：技术变革在许多方面都有可能产生。大部分优秀的科幻作家，包括富有才气的空想主义者，比如吉布森和巴拉德，都专注于技术的副作用：罪犯或坏人如何开发技术，技术导致文化灾难，或者以任何人都难以预料的方式改变人的思维模式。这些作家熟悉自身的文化历史，关注早期技术变迁引起的其他变化，这些变化通常更加剧烈，超出发明者当时的预想。

No Technological Changes Turn Out as Anticipated

This is to do with the relationship between technology, society and culture. A lot can be said and is being said about this relationship; for now, we must restrict ourselves to stating that it is complex. It is both easy and tempting to reach simple conclusions about the "effects" of technological innovations, be it the typewriter, television or something else. Such assumptions are always wrong: technological change always points in several possible directions. Most good science fiction writers, including brilliant visionaries such as William Gibson and J.G. Ballard, focus nearly exclusively on the side-effects of technology; how it is being exploited by criminals or evil people, or leads to cultural disasters, or changes the human mode of thought in ways nobody had predicted. These writers know their cultural history, and are aware that earlier technical changes led to other, often more dramatic, changes than the inventors had envisioned at the time.

例如，就拿电话来说。撇开一些人把电话当玩具、认为其实用性很有限的事实不谈，很少有人预计到它能够迅速地改变城市的居住模式。但这恰恰发生在那些与同事、客户和其他人定期频繁联系的群体身上。20 世纪初，中产阶级普及电话以前，职业政治家倾向于住在特定的小区内。这具有实用价值，因为他们工作的重要组成部分是协调关系以及工作时间以外的政治游说。后来他们有了电话，就可以住到自己想住的地方，许多人因此搬离了城市中心。

Take, for instance, the telephone. Apart from the fact that some people regarded it as a toy with a limited practical applicability, few predicted that it would rapidly alter urban residential patterns. This is exactly what happened with respect to groups who depended on regular and frequent contact with colleagues, customers and others. Before the telephone became common among the middle class at the beginning of the twentieth century, professional politicians tended to live in certain neighbourhoods. This was practical, since an important part of their job consisted in coordination and lobbying outside office hours. Then they each got their telephone; suddenly they could live wherever they wanted, and many moved out of the city centres.

另一个例子是打字机。第一台机械式打字机是由丹麦牧师马林在 1867 年发明的。当时发明这台打字机的主要目的是帮助盲人和视力受损的人，让他们更容易书写。尼采是较早使用这种打字机的人，因为他的视力很差。有些评论人士认为，尼采的信仰和哲学警句，以及被削减的"晚期风格"，都是使用新式书写科技的直接后果。尽管这有点夸张，但尼采在 1882 年所写的一封书信中却说道："书写工具影响了我们的思维。"

Another example is the typewriter. The first mechanical "writing machine" was Malling's Writing Ball, invented by the Danish priest Hans Rasmus Johann Malling Hansen in 1867. Its main purpose was to make it easier for blind and visually impaired people to write. One of its early users was Friedrich Nietzsche, who suffered from poor eyesight. Some commentators have retrospectively gone so far as to argue that Nietzsche's brief, aphoristic, chopped-up "late style" was a direct result of the new writing technology. Although this may be an exaggeration, he himself wrote in a letter dated 1882 that "the writing implements affect our thoughts".

　　打字机的发明，除了可能对思维和推理产生作用之外，还在短期内彻底改变了文本的生产方式。在成熟的工业社会中，女秘书成了办公效率的标准形象，出版也更加快速和容易。排字工人要花大量的时间与精力，辨认那些模糊的手写体文字。同时，打字员还要处理许多过去未曾见过的字符，就像现在人们发送电子邮件致歉一样，他们在使用打字机时也有同样的困惑。我们使用的电子邮件在速度和可靠性方面，可能会言过其实，而打字员也认为他们通过回避难以辨认的字体，保护了阅读者的视力。

Apart from its possible effects on thought and reasoning, the introduction of the typewriter revolutionized the production of texts in a matter of a short time. Armies of female secretaries became a standard image of efficiency in the matured industrial society, and publishing became faster and easier. Hitherto, typesetters had spent a great deal of time and energy deciphering hopeless handwriting. At the same time, the typewriter rendered texts more anonymous in character, and just as people may nowadays apologise for sending personal letters as e-mails, they had similar misgivings about using the typewriter in the same way then. And just as we may defend our exaggerated email usage by referring to its speed and reliability, typewriter converts argued that they saved the recipient's eyes by avoiding illegible longhand.

　　打字机带来的或直接引起的变化还有很多。它使妇女大批量地进入办公室，拉开了作者与书稿的距离，提高了抄写与排字的速度与精度——甚至可能导致了思维模式的变化。保罗·维利里奥属于坚持手写的作家群体的一员。他所有的书籍都是用钢笔写成的。因为只有降低书写的速度，才能够配合他推理的节奏。

The changes brought about or directly inspired by the typewriter were thus many.

It brought women into offices in large numbers, it created distance between the writer and the text, it led to greater speed and precision in copying and typesetting, and arguably it led to changes in the mode of thought. The most important living theorist of speed, Paul Virilio, belongs to that select group of authors who insist on writing by hand. All his books are written by pen. Only thus can he reduce the speed of writing to match his rhythm of reasoning.

那么,文字处理会有什么副作用呢? 20 世纪 80 年代之前,在视窗操作系统和文字处理软件逐步消除不同的主导操作系统之间的差别之前,苹果机与微软 DOS 系统的用户已经习惯了计算机的不同操作方式。(安东尼·伯吉斯以前有一台苹果机,但他却犹豫是否使用,因为他发现当他打开电脑时会有问候和笑脸,这就降低了书写的功能。)苹果机显示了风格化的桌面图像,可以使用鼠标按照自己的方式点击。在文字处理器中,显示的是令人愉悦的黑白两色,以及所见即所得的满足感,还有字体矫正和页面边距调整。传统的计算机使用微软 DOS 系统,问候用户时往往使用保留指令"A>",如果是硬盘驱动则用"C>"。背景是黑色,文字是琥珀色或绿色。文字处理器常常叫作"完美文书",显示的是色彩较为暗淡的标准字体,只有在打印时才能看到其他附加的效果(比如 12 点大小的海维提卡字体,调整右边距,行间距为 1.5 倍)。对当时北美的大学生进行的研究表明,个人电脑的用户提交的书写作品,比苹果机的用户更好。因为苹果机很容易完成印刷体文本,使用苹果机的学生在没有真正完成作品之前,往往误以为自己已经可以提交了。这项研究还表明使用技术的种类也可以影响选题。个人电脑的用户钻研严肃的学科领域,比如法律、政治和经济,而苹果机的用户则偏重有个性的学科,从娱乐产业到体育赛事都有涉及。一组对比测试表明,苹果机用户很少有理解文本的问题,但无法看透个人电脑的复杂语言。不幸的是,这项研究还是没有解决"蛋与鸡"的问题,也就是说,它无法解释在选择书写技术之前,苹果机用户是否比个人电脑的用户更肤浅和幼稚(或者可以说,更具有创造性)。

What are the side-effects of word processing? In the 1980s, before Windows and

Word gradually erased the major differences between leading operating systems, Macintosh users and MS-DOS users were accustomed to very different ways of relating to their computers. (Anthony Burgess once got a Macintosh, but hesitated to use it because he found it debasing to write on an instrument that greeted him with a smile and a welcome when he turned it on.) The Macintosh display showed a stylised image of a desktop, and one used the mouse to click one's way around. In the word processor, the display was pleasantly black-and-white and WYSIWYG (What You See Is What You Get), with correct fonts, adjusted margins and so on. A classic MS-DOS PC, on the other hand, greeted its user with the more reserved statement "A>", possibly "C>" if one had a hard drive. The text was amber or green on a black background. The word processor, which was usually called Word Perfect, displayed only a sordid standard font; any added effects (such as Helvetica 12 points, adjusted right margin, line spacing 1.5) were visible only in the print-out. A study of North American college students from this period indicated that the PC users generally submitted better written work than Mac users. Since it was so easy to make typographically "finished" products on a Mac, these students were seduced into believing that they were ready to submit their work long before it was actually finished. There were also indications to the effect that the kind of technology used also influenced choice of topics. While PC users delved into serious fields like law, politics and economics, Mac users preferred to write about personalities from the entertainment industry and sports events. A test panel of 13-year-olds had generally few problems in understanding the Mac texts, but could not penetrate the more complex language of the PC users. Unfortunately, the study does not solve the chicken-and-egg problem; that is to say, it does not reveal whether the Mac users were more childish and superficial (and, perhaps, more creative) than the PC users before they chose their writing technology.

文字处理软件增加了打字机的逻辑性。它进一步减小了技术的内在阻碍，使得文本的生产成为一个无关痒痛的问题(因而很少出现信息过载)。它在拓宽作者与文本的鸿沟之时,又缩小了作者与排字工人的距离。

The word processor takes the logic of the typewriter further. It reduces the inherent resistance in the technology even more, making the production of texts a painless matter （and thereby in its way contributing in no minor way to the information overload). It widens the gulf between the writer and the text, and shrinks the distance between writer and typographer.

马克思曾经说过:"手工磨产生的是封建主为首的社会,蒸汽磨产生的是工业资本家为首的社会。"在这句经常被人引用的话中,马克思似乎推崇技术决定论,认为技术的变化必然会自动地推动社会的变迁。对于这个问题,大部分作家——包括晚年的马克思——都比较谨慎。技术会产生不可预料的副作用,而且往往会陷入一种文化背景之中,以至于很难准确地预料其使用方式。例如,过去 10 年来,发达国家的生活实际足以适度地概括互联网与廉价航空旅行的后果。但是,如果走到另一个极端,认为技术变化没什么影响,就和相信互联网即刻会翻转这个世界的想法一样愚蠢。有清楚的证据表明,网络正在产生持久且非常重要的变化,本书的观点接近于技术决定论,而不赞同与其相反的观点。大范围内的技术变化能够控制特定方向的活动,却减少了社会整体的灵活性。就像下一章要讲的那样,没有时钟、印刷和金钱的世界,将会完全不同于我们现今生活的世界;当前电子通信革命最终也会按照这道水流的顺序发展。换句话说,如果不信,就不妨拭目以待。

Marx once wrote, infamously, that "the hand mill creates a society with a feudal lord, while the steam mill creates a society with an industrial capitalist". In this often quoted sentence, he seems to promote technological determinism, the belief that technological changes inevitably and automatically entail particular societal changes. Most of the writers who deal with these issues, including the later Marx, are more cautious. Technology has unintended sideeffects, and it is always enmeshed in a cultural context where it is difficult to predict exactly how it will be used. There is thus good reason to be modest in one's generalisations about the consequences of, for example, the Internet and cheap air travel for the lived reality in the rich countries during the past decade. But going to the opposite extreme, and arguing that technological changes make no difference at all, would be just as silly as believing that the Internet immediately turns the world as we know it on its head. There are clear indications that the Net is already generating lasting and highly consequential changes, and the position defended in this book is closer to technological determinism than to its opposite. Technological changes that are implemented in a wide range of instances, reduce flexibility in society as a whole and steer activities in particular directions. As the next chapter will show, a world without the clock, printing and money would have been an entirely different world from the one we live in; and the current revolutions in electronic communications are ultimately of the same order as these watersheds. You ain't, in other words, seen nothin' yet.

21 世纪的自由等于脆弱

在 21 世纪，自由与脆弱将是同义词。20 世纪 90 年代，变迁的综合过程获得了动力，信息技术的变革是其驱动力之一，也是主要的组成部分。这一点在冷战结束之后的这些年，已经变得扑朔迷离，令人很难理解。至少有两种方式与通信革命相联系，其中最明显的联系方式是加速与堆垛，这在后面将深入讨论。比较不明显的联系是冷战后的秩序。事实上，有人主张无形屏障的消失直接与信息技术有关，这种观点值得严肃对待。跨区域的通信有了新的可能，这在 20 世纪 80 年代的东欧逐渐实现，独裁政府发现在他们的国家内同样很难控制信息的流动。政府主导的单向宣传设备，几乎很难与双向通信的全球电信网络兼容（单向的商业宣传设备更容易应对全球通信的挑战）。当电视广播取代木质纤维成为主流媒介时，持不同政见的群体获得外部信息和进行内部交流就会更加容易和安全。1989 年春季，整个欧洲的人很快就知道了奥匈帝国边界的开放，还有当年夏天保加利亚共产党的自由化,以及苏联戈尔巴乔夫激进改革的趋势。当 1989 年 12 月 9 日柏林墙的大门敞开时,东欧政体就像多米诺骨牌一样,以令人惊讶的速度发生变化。

In The 21st Century, Freedom And Vulnerability Are Synonyms

The revolution in information technology is an integral part, and a driving force, of a more comprehensive process of change which gained momentum in the 1990s. This, the years immediately following the Cold War, has been an odd and often confusing period. Oblique. Difficult to understand. This is connected to the revolution in communications in at least two ways. The obvious link is to do with acceleration and stacking, which will be discussed at length later. The less obvious link is with the very establishment of the post-Cold War （dis-） order. Some actually argue that the disappearance of the Iron Curtain is directly connected with information technology, and this view deserves serious treatment. Given the new possibilities for communicating across borders, which were increasingly available in Eastern Europe during the 1980s, authoritarian governments found it difficult to control the flow of information in their countries. A one-sided, state-run propaganda apparatus is hardly compatible with two-way communication over the global telecom network. （A one-sided, commercial propaganda apparatus is clearly better equipped to meet the challenges of global communication.） Both access to external information and internal networking among dissident groups became easier and safer when the airwaves replaced wood pulp as a dominant medium. People all over Eastern Europe quickly learned about the opening of the AustroHungarian border in spring 1989, about the liberalisation of the Bulgarian Communist Party the same autumn, and about tendencies towards radical change in Gorbachev's Soviet Union. When the checkpoints of the Berlin Wall were opened on 9 November 1989, the East European regimes fell like so many dominoes, surprisingly fast.

东欧共产主义政体的解散异常复杂，这里不宜详细分析。但是，毋庸置疑的是，政体改变的速度的确可以被看成信息技术变革的速度。

The causes of the fall of "Communism" are complex, and this is not the appropriate place for a detailed analysis. But there is little doubt that the speed of the regime changes has to be seen in the light of changes in information technology.

柏林墙被推倒之后，世界进入了20世纪90年代，但是按照我的时间表来看，这是21世纪初。电视、电话和互联网的连接越来越快地遍布全球各地。

With the fall of the Wall, we have entered the 1990s, that is the early twenty-first century according to my timeline. Television, telephones and Internet connectivity are becoming rapidly more widespread everywhere (see Figure 2.2).

只有少数几个古怪的国家，比如缅甸和朝鲜，竭力封锁那些未经审查的信息，以保护本国公民。毛里求斯的年轻人结成帮派，在电影《第一滴血》的鼓动下到处捣乱，一些对社会不满的团体看了有关巴勒斯坦和北爱尔兰的电视报道后，也想获得变革的主意。这些想法扩散得越来越快。基本上，世界各地的人们互相了解的程度远远高于以前，每天交换的信息都在变化。世界格局快速变化，冷战时期的稳定性和可预测性已经远去。政治左右派别的差别变得日益模糊。例如，欧洲社会民主党与传统的右翼党派一样，也强烈地反对外来的移民。这些年来，左派显示了保守和怀旧的趋势，甚至促使两百多年来的历史任务发生变化。布莱尔综合征——形式重于内容——在这一时期成了许多国家的政治特征，保守党与社会民主党的实际差别，远不如以前明显。政治分区遵循着还不明显的界线，历史上的左翼正在寻找一个有说服力的新定义。

Only a few, curious states such as Burma and North Korea seriously try to protect their citizens against uncensored impulses from the outside. Youth gangs in Mauritius

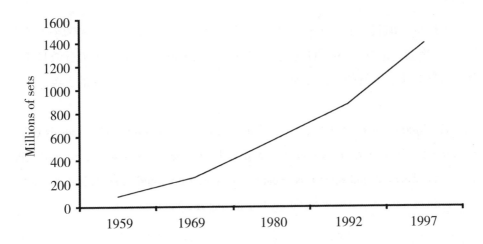

Source: Held et al. 1999, p. 358, www.unesco.org

Figure 2-2   Number of TV sets in the world, 1959—1997

图 2-2   电视机用户增长曲线

get into mischief, inspired by the Rambo films, while discontented groups everywhere get ideas for change by watching television reportage from Palestine and Northern Ireland. Ideas spread faster and faster. On the whole, people all over the world know more about each other than ever before, and the information on offer is changed daily. The scene changes fast, the stability and predictability of the Cold War are gone. The left/right divide in politics has become fuzzy. The resistance to immigration, for example, is just as strong in Europe's social democratic parties as on the traditional right. The left has in these years shown a tendency towards nostalgia and conservation, even if its historical task, for the past 200 years, has been to promote change. A concern with form and style rather than substance has been symptomatic of politics in many countries during this period, and the actual differences between conservative and social democratic parties have become much less obvious than ever before. Political divisions follow lines that are not yet clearly demarcated, and the historical left is in search of a new, persuasive definition of its project.

单极世界取代了过去的两极世界。这一极被称为市场自由主义和个人主义的，打着诸如灵活性、自由和开放之类的标语摇旗呐喊。对它的阻力分散且不协调。信息的获取不再是稀缺资源，但是信息的分类机制却成了稀缺的资源。

The bipolar world has been replaced with a unipolar world. That pole is called market liberalism and individualism, and it beats the drum with catchwords like flexibility, freedom and openness. Resistance is scattered and uncoordinated. Access to information is not a scarce resource, but sorting mechanisms are.

在描述新时代时，开放和多元主义是两个模棱两可的关键词。在主流意识形态中，这两个词具有积极的内涵，但事实可能完全不同。开放的典型后果是不稳定的认同。越来越多的人不敢确定早晨镜子中看到的人是谁。国家认同也不再是往日那样，对许多人来说，在谈论自己时，国家认同已经是一个过时的方式。性别认同似乎相对固定，但是没有人能讲清楚男人或女人意味着什么——这些角色的变化，已经超过了社会学能够监控的速度。甚至年龄也不再是一个可靠的指数，当今的个性化广告可能会有这样的台词："男孩，40岁，寻找……"这几年，贸易组织和政党也成了模糊的实体，不再能为人们提供一个安全的归宿。集体认同的新概念会定期地出现，而其中一些恰恰反对现有的集体观念——游动、混杂、都市和全球认同。这些标签无需记住，它们与其描述的现象一样短暂。

Openness and pluralism are two ambiguous keywords describing the new era. Their connotations are positive in the dominant ideology, but the reality may well be different. One typical result of openness is uncertain identity. More and more people are uncertain as to exactly who they are looking at in the mirror in the morning. The nation is no longer what it used to be; to many, national identity is an obsolete way of talking about oneself. Gender seems relatively fixed, but no-one is able to state what it means to be a man or a woman any more-these roles change faster than sociology is able to monitor. Even age is no longer a reliable indicator of who one is, in an era when personal ads may well begin with the words, "Boy, 40, seeks...". The trade unions and the political parties have, in the space of a few years, become fuzzy entities that no longer offer people a safe home. New concepts of collective identities are regularly being launched, some of which seem to contradict the very idea that collectivities exist nomadic, hybrid, urban, global identities. These labels need not be remembered; they are as ephemeral as the phenomena they describe.

新的时代既自由又令人沮丧,既使人着迷又令人恐惧。它创造了新的脆弱形式:全球集成的计算机网络表明,任何事物——从计算机病毒到化学毒品、致命武器和毁灭性思想,比以前更加自由地流动,通过大量的蝴蝶效应产生了不可预料的后果。如果计算机瘫痪,我们就会完全无助——我们不可能简单地再去使用羽毛笔,以及过去使用过的一切东西。在这方面,新的"适应"实际上造成了灵活性的丧失。此外,它还预示着新政治的到来,地方与全球力量、根源与脉冲、传统文化与多民族现实的关系,决定了没有现成的解决办法。对许多人而言,它也创造了一个现存的处境,人们必须日复一日地重新定义自己,在缺乏稳定性和可预测性的背景下,人们既要自由地选择,又不能不自由地选择。此外,对于很多评论员来讲,新时代实际上等同于新经济,以及新工作——信息处理、适应性、公司人员快速流动、产品与人事等流行语。一切都在改变,而且很明显还在继续产生影响。当我成年时,奥斯陆有1家大型造船厂和3家大的酿酒厂,城市中心的北边山谷里还有大大小小的工厂,包含了最古老的工业。今天,所有这一切都烟消云散,代之而起的是奢华的别墅、商店、饭馆、大学、电脑公司、读书俱乐部和无线电播音室等。最重要的是,新时代的特征是信息的流动具有连续性,令人眼花缭乱且容易疲倦,其可能性之丰富与内聚力之贫乏几乎程度相当。

The new era is liberating and frustrating, fascinating and frightening. It creates new forms of vulnerability: globally integrated computer networks imply that anything from computer viruses to designer drugs, lethal weapons and destructive thoughts flow more freely than ever before, bifurcate and result in incalculable effects through myriad butterfly effects. If the computers let us down, we are helpless we cannot simply return to the feather pen, pretending everything is as it used to be. (In this way, the new "flexibility" actually entails a loss of flexibility.) Further, it heralds the coming of a new politics, where the relationships between local and global forces, roots and impulses, traditional culture and a multi-ethnic reality set an agenda where there are no ready-made solutions available. It also creates a new existential situation for many people, who may (or have to) redefine themselves from day to day, in a context which lacks stability and predictability, where people are both free to choose and unfree not to choose. Further, the new era is, to many commentators, virtually synonymous with a new economy, that of "new work" information processing, flexibility and rapid turnover of firms, products and personnel being some of the catchwords. That there have been changes, and that these continue to make an impact, is obvious. When I grew up, Oslo had a large shipyard and three major breweries, and a valley north of the city centre (appropriately named Nydalen, "New Valley", in the nineteenth century) had a motley mix of small and large factories, comprising some of the oldest industry in the country. Today, all of this (but one brewery) is gone, replaced by luxury flats, shops, restaurants, colleges, computer firms, book clubs, radio studios and so on. Last but not least, the new era is characterised by a continuous, dizzying and tiring flow of information which is just as rich in possibilities as it is poor in internal cohesiveness.

　　要描述信息社会需要厚厚一大本书，但是也可以这样简单地描述：全球经济的重心已经从事物转移到了符号上。由于符号的散播比事物更自由，符号经济以惊人的速度发生变化，并且需要其他的组织形式和更大的适应性。要结束东欧政体的改变，需要的是观念而不是武器。想法和预期支撑着当前西方繁荣的经济，同时也鼓动了叛乱和移民。自由的同时获取多种观念，表明我们的大脑有自由的空间供各种观念竞争，最终导致混乱和不稳定的认同。

Information society can be described in thick books（this is naturally being done）, but it can also be described like this: the point of gravity in the global economy has moved from things to signs. The sign economy changes at astonishing speed, and requires other organizational forms and a greater flexibility than the economy of things, since signs float more freely than things. It was ideas, not weapons, that ended up changing the regimes of Eastern Europe. Ideas and expectations also underpin the current economic boom in the West, as well as motivating rebellions and migration. The free availability of ideas simultaneously implies that many of them compete for the free spaces in our heads, leading to confusion and uncertain identities.

文化马赛克时代

旧的张力未去,新的张力又来。我们这个时代具有两个革命性特征:电子的和多民族的。为了理解当代社会,我们的世界没必要像其中任何一个,但是我们没有别的选择,必须承认两者都是我们所呼吸的空气的一部分。而且,这两者是一个硬币的两面。电子革命和多民族社会是相互映衬的镜像:两者都把个人认同从传统与根基中挖了出来,作为主要的连续性叙事。多民族性的特征是文化马赛克,伴随着各种混杂的形式、悖论、冲突和紧张,而互联网和多频道电视的典型特征是碎片化的、色彩斑斓的、混乱不清的和不连贯的信息流。这两种趋势产生了流动、运动和不清楚的边界。它们把文化从地方中割裂出来,把人们从现成的故事中分离出来,这些故事讲述的是他们是谁以及他们能够成为什么。它们还使工作与工作场所、消费与程序、教育与标准模板、知识与已有模式发生分离。过去、整体和连贯性——所有的一切都受到了威胁。

New Tensions Supplement the Old Ones

Two revolutions characterise our age: the electronic and the multi-ethnic. In order to understand contemporary society it is not necessary to like either, but one has no choice but to admit that both are part of the air we breathe. Besides, they are two sides of the same coin. The electronic revolution and multi-ethnic society are mirror-images of each other: both disembed personal identity from tradition and roots, that is major, continuous narratives. The cultural mosaic typical of multi-ethnicity, with all its hybrid forms, paradoxes, conflicts and tensions, has its exact parallel in the fragmented, colourful, confusing and incoherent flood of information typical of multi-channel television and the World Wide Web. Both tendencies create flows, movement and unclear boundaries. They sever culture from place, people from ready-made stories about who they are and what they can become, work from the working place, consumption from routine, education from standard templates, knowledge from established models about what counts as knowledge... The past, wholeness, coherence all of this is threatened.

信息社会产生的新冲突，可以看作一组二分法：当左边占优势时，右边就会产生对冲反应。比如下面这些二元对立的实例：

熟悉与陌生

禁锢与自由

社区主义与自由主义

集体与个人

根源与脉冲

基要主义与矛盾情绪

过去与未来

连续性与变化

成熟与青春

The new conflicts that arise from information society can be depicted as a set of dichotomies, where the right-hand side dominates, while the left-hand side represents the counter-reactions.

familiarity	newness
security	freedom
communitarianism	liberalism
community	individual
roots	impulses
fundamentalism	ambivalence
past	future
continuity	change
maturity	youth

张力的种类很难适应左右之间的轴心,如同前面所提到的那样,2000年左右的激进主义似乎也抵制变迁,老左派担心的事情包括气候变迁、计算机技术、多民族的可能性和都市化。在此,我们暂且不谈此事。对于复兴的左翼而言,任何时候大部分人都会提出全球社会正义是压倒一切的问题。然而尽管如此,在我们的谈话背景中,还应该快速浏览一下信息社会稀缺资源的新形式。或许这些稀缺性可以这样表述:

慢节奏

安全性

可预测性

归属感(也就是稳定的个人认同)

凝聚力和对他人的理解

线性累积型有机增长

真实的体验(既不受大众媒体的挖苦也接受调停)

These kinds of tension fit badly within the right/left axis, and, as mentioned, "radicalism" in the 2000s seems to be tantamount to resistance to change; the old left is worried about anything, from climatic changes to computer technology, multi-ethnic possibilities and urbanisation. We shall leave this matter here; there is in any case much to suggest that global social justice will be the overarching issue for a renewed left. In our context it is nonetheless relevant to take a quick look at the new forms of scarcity that emerge from information society. Some of them may be described like this:

slow time

security

predictability belonging, stable personal identity

coherence and understanding

cumulative, linear, organic growth

real experiences (which are neither ironic nor mediated by mass media)

正如黑格尔所作的正确评述，现实是具体的。如果这看起来依然抽象，我答应很快再进入一个更加具有体验性的模式。

As Hegel correctly remarked, reality is always concrete. So if this seems abstract, I promise to go into a more experience-near mode very soon.

还有一些人坚持认为，这些主题并不新鲜，所有这些主题、矛盾和问题至少都有 100 年以上的历史，其中一些的古老程度堪比农业和都市社会。要回应这种批评，我觉得没有更好的观点能够胜过卡斯特［西班牙社会学家，主要研究信息社会，交流和全球化。社会科学引文索引（SSCI）2000—2009 年的数据显示，他是全世界被引用较多的 15 位社会科学学者之一。——编者］的著作，他为自己三大卷的《信息社会》写了一个很长的脚注：

Still, some will argue that all this is not really new; all these themes, contradictions and problems are at least a hundred years old, in some cases as old as agriculture and urban society. As an answer to this kind of criticism, I have no better option than to offer an answer culled from the massive work of Manuel Castells, who writes, in a lengthy footnote towards the end of his three-volume *The Information Age*:

　　在我的论文集中,这几年的讨论总会碰到一些周期性的问题,我认为把它们呈现给读者,可能会比较有用。这是有关新奇的疑问。所有这些有哪些是新的呢?为何这是一个新世界?我的确认为千禧年末正在涌现一个新世界。薯片和电脑是新事物,无处不在的移动通信是新事物,基因工程是新事物,电子综合性全球金融市场实时运作系统是新事物, 互相连接的资本主义经济撑起的整个星球都是新的,而不仅仅部分片段是新的,发达经济的都市劳动力对知识和信息的处理也是新的,都市的人口是新的,苏联的寿终正寝、共产主义的逐渐消退和冷战的结束都是新事物;亚太地区在全球经济中作为一个平等的伙伴出现也是新事物;宗法制国家受到的广泛挑战是新事物;对于生态保护的普遍觉悟也是新事物;基于空间流动和无时间序列的网络社会的出现,从历史的观点看也是新事物。

In discussions in my seminars in recent years a recurrent question comes up so often that I think it would be useful to take it to the reader. It is the question of newness. What is new about all this? Why is this a new world? I do believe that there is a new world emerging in this end of millennium. Chips and computers are new; ubiquitous, mobile telecommunications are new; genetic engineering is new; electronically integrated, global financial markets working in real time are new; an inter-linked capitalist economy embracing the whole planet, and not only some of its segments, is new; a majority of the urban labor force in knowledge and information processing in advanced economies is new; a majority of urban population in the planet is new; the demise of the Soviet Empire, the fading away of communism, and the endof the Cold War are new; the rise of the Asian Pacific as an equal partner in the global economy is new; the widespread challenge to patriarchalism is new; the universal consciousness on ecological preservation is new; and the emergence of a network society,based on a space of flows, and on timeless time, is historically new.

他喘了一口气接着说："然而，这不是我要说的观点。我的主要观点是，不管你是否相信这个世界或其未来是新的，我要分析的是这个世界本身。这是我们的世界，是一个信息时代的世界。"

He then comes up for air, and adds: "Yet this is not the point I want to make. My main statement is that it does not really matter if you believe that this world, or any of its features, is new or not. My analysis stands by itself. This is our world, the world of the Information Age."

由此看来，本书的分析框架大致也是如此。但是还差一些重要事项——技术、社会和文化的关系。这个话题比较新潮，但是我的重要观点之一在于，如果我们不认真考虑信息社会，就不可能理解目前的情形，我们必须将其视为定义相对明确的历史产物——这个观点在信息社会受到了严重的攻击，让人误以为通过模仿或复制就可以从历史中学习。因此，下一章要谈论文化的历史，以及从信息技术社会获得的一系列快照，借以揭示通往现在的一些路径。如果有些读者比较性急，愿意阅读速度、发展和堆垛，以及这些对你我的意义，也可以直接跳过下一章，当然于我而言就事与愿违了，因为这说明我还是没把问题的原因说清楚，这当然有点令人沮丧。

With this, the framework for an analysis of the tyranny of the moment should be roughly in place. But something important is still missing, and that is the relationship between technology, society and culture. The topic is very current, but one of my crucial points is going to be that it is impossible to understand the present without seeing it as the product of some relatively well-defined past an insight which is both under serious assault in information society and misunderstood as an inducement to learn from history through miming or copying it. For this reason, the next chapter is pure cultural history, a series of snapshots from the history of information technology indicating some of the paths leading to the present. If this book, contrary to expectations, has some extremely hurried readers who would rather read about speed, growth and stacking, and what this means for you and me, it is strictly possible to skip the next chapter, but I discourage it, for reasons that should already be clear.

第三章 印刷机才是灾难起源：
书本、时钟和货币的时代

如果把大自然的进化史压缩到 24 个小时，包括从第一个单细胞生物到当今结构学上的现代大象和人类(不要忘了结构学上的现代单细胞生物)的进化过程，那么人类只是在午夜 12 点的前 5 秒钟才出场。农业革命似乎在午夜前 1.5 秒才登场。那么互联网呢？只能忽略不计了。

3 The Time of the Book, the Clock and Money

If all of evolutionary history, from the first single-celled organisms to the present with its anatomically modern elephants and humans（and, lest we forget, anatomically modern single-celled organisms）, were to be compressed into 24 hours, modern humans arrived on the scene 5 seconds before midnight. The agricultural revolution appeared one and a half seconds before midnight. And the Internet? Forget it.

如果这个视角让人过于眼花缭乱，或许我们可以忘记三叶虫和雷龙，只把人类的历史范围看作一天一夜，用 24 小时代表 10 万年。当前考古学者倾向于认为现代智人比较古老，而他们的近亲则还要古老。那样的话，西亚农业的首次亮相，大约是在晚上的 9:30。大约 1 小时之后，出现了最早的楔形文字。德国古腾堡印刷机大约在午夜 12 时差 8 分出现，而欧洲战士与冒险家征服美洲则在几秒钟之后。电话和流水线生产几乎只有一分半钟的历史，而电视与商用空中运输则只有 30 秒的年龄。那么因特网呢？也只能忽略不计了。

If this perspective is too dizzying, we may forget trilobites and brontosaurus for now, and limit the scope to the history of humanity seen as a day and night. That 24-hour cycle would represent about a 100,000 years. (Leading scholars currently tend to agree that homo sapiens sapiens is about this old, while several near relatives are much older.) In that case, the first instance of agriculture appeared in Western Asia a little after nine thirty in the evening. The first kind of writing, Sumeric cuneiform, was adopted in the same part of the world an hour later. Gutenberg's printing press saw the light of day at 8 minutes to midnight, and the conquest of America was begun by European soldiers and adventurers a few seconds later. The telephone and assembly line production are nearly a minute and a half old, while television and commercial air travel have existed for a mere 30 seconds. And the Internet? Forget it.

从文化历史的视角来看，如果整个过程是一个故事，农业就是一个脚注，而现代性则是脚注里的补充说明。人类历史有90%以上的时间是狩猎采集阶段，在工业和信息社会显著发展之前的200年内，农业和园艺业逐步取代了采集狩猎，即使在与外界隔离的边远地区——北极荒漠、澳洲荒原和中非的雨林，人口密度也在快速增长。

Seen from a perspective of cultural history, agriculture is a footnote, while modernity is a footnote under a footnote, if duration is all that counts. Hunters and gatherers, who were humanity for more than 90 per cent of our species history, have gradually been displaced to the most isolated and marginal parts of the world the Arctic semi-desert, the Australian desert, the central African rainforest and have been replaced by horticulturalists and agriculturalists with rapidly increasing population densities, before the phenomenal growth of industrial and informational society during the last couple of centuries.

大型水域或分水岭在技术史上的时代差距已经日益减小。在使书籍普遍化的印刷机出现之前，书写方法已经存在了 4500 年。印刷术使用了 500 年之后，遭遇了电子文本的挑战；无线电广播流行数十年之后，就把主导地位让给了电视，因为后者能够提供更合适的产品。同样，人背马驮的历史已经延续了 5000 年，直到被内燃机驱动的汽车代替——罗马时代的旅行者如果在 1890 年参观皮卡迪利广场，应该不会为城市新发明的交通技术感到震撼——但是如果看到 20 年之后的飞机，定会目瞪口呆。

The time gap between the great watersheds, or divides, in technological history has been progressively reduced. Writing had existed for 4,500 years before the printing press made books common. Printing had only only just cleared the table after the celebrations of its 500th anniversary when it was seriously challenged by electronic text, and the radio was only allowed its dominant position for a few decades before television turned it into a supplier of niche products. Similarly, it took 5,000 years from the introduction of the horse carriage until its replacement by combustion-engine powered automobiles with pneumatic tyres a Roman time-traveller visiting Piccadilly Circus in 1890 would not have been shocked by innovations in urban transport technology but the first aeroplane was invented only 20 years after the car.

出版业的模式与产品更新速度之快，使得任何生产商都不愿意在最新模式面世之前规划下一个模型。理论上讲，任何产品在上架之后最终都会过时（在计算机领域，这实际上频繁地发生）。

The replacement of models and product variants today happens at such a speed that there scarcely exists a producer of anything at all who does not plan the next model before the latest model has been presented to the public. In theory, a product may eventually become obsolete before it reaches the shelves （in the world of computing, this actually happens every so often).

　　要描述最近十年、一百年、两百年或者一万年的文化史,只需屈指算算人类创造的世界具有多大的中心范围。这个视角是当前整个分析的基础。然而,在考虑加速度及其效果之前,我们应该观察自己生活形式的主要特点,当然是指现代社会。我认为,不需要对历史分期——现代社会或文化究竟何时开始——进行复杂的讨论,只需对现代社会与非现代社会进行简单的对比。学术界的人不喜欢这样做,理由如下:不仅现代性是一个相当麻烦的词语,并对赖以谋生的学术界人士产生了副作用,而且非现代社会也各有差别。换句话说,当有人要着手做我将要干的事情时,需要面对几个学术团体的反对。作为防御性借口,我要强调下面这些描述在一般层面上是正确的,能够从具体到抽象,清楚地说明文化史的方向。这很重要,当一个默默无闻的闪族天才发现身体符号可以代表口头语言时,专横的时间就成了漫长历史的最终产品。他或她就让语言摆脱了说话者的束缚。

A description of the latest 10, 100, 200 or 10,000 years of cultural history that concentrates on acceleration, puts the finger on a central dimension of the humanly created part of the world. This perspective underlies the entire present analysis. Before moving to a consideration of acceleration and its effects, we shall nevertheless look into some of the main characteristics of our form of life, by which I simply mean modern society. Instead of entering into a complicated discussion about periodization when did modern society or modern culture begin? I propose some simple contrasts between modern and non-modern societies. One is not exactly adored in academia for doing this, and for sound reasons: not only is modernity a notoriously difficult word which, among other things, has the side-effect of providing armies of academics with their daily bread but, in their way, non-modern societies are just as different from each other as they are from ours. One is, in other words, faced with opposition from several academic camps when doing what I am about to do. As a defence plea, I will stress that the description that follows is correct at a general level, and that it indicates a clear direction in cultural history, from the concrete to the abstract. This is important, for the tyranny of the moment is the end-product of a long historical process that began when an unknown Sumerian genius discovered that a physical symbol could represent a spoken word. He or she liberated language from the speaker.

写在白纸上的文明拐点

在说话和视觉艺术之后，书写代表着信息时代的主要转折点。任何人在给文化史罗列重要发明的时候，书写都排列在前面。自然，如果没有这项技术，我们的社会类别将会无法想象。甚至我们可能不是一样的人类。

After Speech And Visual Art,
Writing Marked a Major Watershed in Information Technology

Writing ranks high on anybody's list of the most important inventions in cultural history. Naturally, our kind of society would have been unthinkable without this technology. We would not even have been the same people.

书写作为一种工具，是思想、事实、论断和情感的外在化表现。它几乎采用与博物馆定格文化同样的方式，冻结了这一切。在4000—5000年前的西方农业社会，书写主要有两种用途：列表和宗教信仰。列表主要是记录库存、登记居民户口（为了征税和征兵）、清点粮食袋数和奴隶的数量。因此，统治者可以采用一种完全不同的全盘视角鸟瞰自己的帝国。若没有书写技术就不可能做到这一点。最终，读写能力扩展到了算数，并且，有人将古代地中海世界中腓尼基人熟练的簿记，描述为他们为贸易而带来的传奇礼物。

Writing is a tool for the externalization of thoughts, facts, assertions, emotions. It freezes them in approximately the same way as the museum freezes culture. In West

Asian agricultural societies 4,000 to 5,000 years ago, writing was essentially used for two purposes: lists and religion. One made lists or inventories of inhabitants (in order to be able to tax them and enlist them in the army), sacks of grain, slaves and so on. The rulers thereby got a very different kind of overview over their empire than would have otherwise have been possible. Eventually, literacy was extended to include numeracy, and the Phoenicians' legendary gift for trade in the ancient Mediterranean world is ascribed to their adeptness at book-keeping.

宗教信仰最初对书写的使用分为两方面：首先，书写本身具有巫术的成分，刻在石头上的咒语往往会在仪式中使用。有文化的人经常被人们赋予超自然的能力，就像对待铁匠一样（现在的报纸有时也会给网页设计师一个"技术奇才"的头衔）。其次，书写具有记录和定格作用，因而会被授予神秘的视角和道德准则。这样，书写也是现代宗教的基础，有时候谈到圣经时，会说圣经上的每一个字都是真实的，准确地描述了上帝造人、拯救堕落的人类并最终使人进入天国，等等。

The initial religious use of writing fell into two kinds: first, writing itself had a magical element, and incantations engraved into stone were thus used ritually. The literate were regarded as people endowed with almost supernatural powers, on a par with blacksmiths (today's newspaper incidentally features a web designer who has given himself the professional title "technical wizard"). Second, writing could be used to record, freeze and thereby authorise particular versions of myths and moral principles. In this way, the foundation was laid for the modern religions, which are sometimes spoken of as "religions of the Book", with their claim to verbatim authenticity, exact descriptions of creation, salvation, paradise and so on.

至少在世界上三个地方——也可能在四个地方——独立地发展出了书写技术：西亚、中美洲和中国，可能还有埃及。除了中文和相关的手稿之外，旧大陆所有的文字手稿——从阿拉伯语、希伯来语、古印度梵文到埃塞俄比亚的阿姆哈拉语——都可以追溯到楔形文字。不过，最早的象形文字适用范围有限，学起来也比较困难。最终，字母代替了文字家族——严格来讲，起初是代表音节的字音表，最终代表音素的符号普遍流行。然而，语音与书写永远无法达到完美的匹配，尽管许多受过教育的人都想使两者完美结合。有些手稿只有辅音，阅读者需要自己添加元音。即使把重读音节也计算在内，大部分西欧语言的语音还是优于书写。书写与拼读不同，而书面语又会影响口语。

The technology of writing was developed in at least three, possibly four places independently: West Asia, Central America, China and （perhaps）Egypt. Apart from Chinese and related scripts, all scripts in the old world from Arabic and Hebrew to the North Indian Devanagari syllabary and the Amharic script of Ethiopia can probably be traced back to the Sumeric cuneiform. It was rudimentary, pictographic （one symbol represented one word）, limited in its flexibility and could be difficult to learn. Eventually, this family of scripts was supplanted by alphabets strictly speaking, the earliest were syllabaries, where a sign stood for a syllable; but eventually, scripts where a sign stood for a phoneme or sound became common. However, the congruence between speech and writing is never perfect, although many who live in literate societies think so. Some scripts consist exclusively of consonants （the reader has to fill in the vowels personally）, and most West European languages have more sounds than letters, even if accented letters are included. Writing is distinctive from speech, and written language influences spoken language.

腓尼基字母是最古老的字母系统之一，公元前 8 世纪希腊就开始输入并采用腓尼基字母。换句话说，希腊文的创作至少使用过一种脚本，换句话说，他们在采纳新字母表之前，数百年内一直是目不识丁。已有的记载古希腊文明第一阶段的文本和碎片，具有清晰的痕迹反映这一中间时期的创造。例如，美索不达米亚史诗《吉尔伽美什》、最古老的《圣经》以及荷马史诗，都有口头形态的成分。这些书籍的基础，是在写作之前一代一代口耳相传的故事。与公元前 6 世纪开始的经典哲学相比，这些东西完全不同。在诸如泰利斯、巴门尼德和赫拉克利特之类的哲学家那里，书写首次作为思想的转化器形成。到了古希腊哲学成熟时期，特别是在柏拉图和亚里士多德时代（公元前 5 世纪至前 4 世纪），不用书写就能明确表达观点简直是不可想象的事情。柏拉图的对话和亚里斯多德的论述，包含了逻辑连贯性、冗长的推理链、清楚的定义和有关语言词汇的讨论，这一切的前提是概念与目标之间清楚的差别。换句话说，语言脱离了言语活动，得到了具体化和形象化。人们可以在文本中反复核查作者的写作文字，挑剔地评论作者的观点，有空闲时还可以检查其推理的逻辑连贯性。在亚里士多德的著作中表现的逻辑原则，很难在口语文化中形成。然而在亚里士多德的时代，还没有关于标点符号和字词空格的惯例。

The Phoenician alphabet is among the oldest, and it was imported and adapted by Greeks in the eighth century BC. At least one script had formerly been used to write Greek, namely, but it seems likely that they had been illiterate for centuries when they adopted the new alphabet. Known texts and fragments from the first period of the ancient Greek civilisation have clear traces of having been created in an intermediate period. Like the Mesopotamian epic Gilgamesh and the oldest books in the Bible, Homer's epics, for example, have elements of orality. They are based on stories that had been narrated for generations before being written down. With classical philosophy, from the sixth century BC onwards, it is different. In philosophers like Thales, Parmenides and Heraclitus, writing comes into its own for the first time as a transformer of thought. In mature Greek philosophy, particularly in Plato and Aristotle (fifth and fourth centuries BC), ideas are being formulated that would literally have been unthinkable without writing. Plato's dialogues and Aristotle's treatises consist of logically coherent, lengthy strings of reasoning, clear definitions and meta-discussions of the nature of language and words, all of which presupposes a clear distinction between a concept and its object. Language is, in other words, severed from the speech act, it is reified and externalised. The ideas can be subjected to critical examination, one may go back and forth in the text to check what the author said on the previous page, and one may examine, at one's leisure, the degree of logical coherence in the reasoning. The principles of logic, as they are presented and discussed in Aristotle's work, would have been difficult if not impossible to formulate in an oral culture. (However, as late as in Aristotle's time, there were still no standard conventions for punctuation and word spacing.)

人们常常把从神话到哲学思想的转变称为"古希腊的奇迹"。在神话思维中，言语行为、语言概念和外在现实性是统一的，而哲学在这三个方面进行了区分，因而可以批判地讨论语言与世界的关系。

The transition from mythical to philosophical thought is often described as "the Greek Miracle". In mythical thought, there is unity between speech act, linguistic concepts and external reality, while philosophy distinguishes between the three levels, and makes it possible to discuss the relationship between language and the world critically.

写作促使知识的积累式发展成为可能，这意味着人们获得了书写技术，就可以直接地获得他人已经写过的东西。人们之间不再依赖于面对面地交流。他们可以采用物质和凝固的形式，把自己的思想和发现留给后辈子孙。人类知识总量的增加，就是书写的结果，这将在后面的章节中讨论。在13世纪，阿奎那花费一生的时光，试图调和两种重要的文本——《圣经》与亚里士多德哲学——当时已经将其视为古老的东西。6世纪，前往黑海地区旅行的探险家，把自己观察到的东西与公元前5世纪时希罗多德的描述进行比较。数学家和科学家在开发新的见解时，可以把欧几里得几何学与阿基米德作为出发点。

Writing made it possible to develop knowledge in a cumulative way, in the sense that one had access to, and could draw directly on, what others had done. One was no longer dependent on face-to-face contact with one's teachers. They had left their thoughts and discoveries for posterity in a material, frozen form. The quantitative growth in the total knowledge of humanity, to be dealt with in later chapters, is a result of writing. A Thomas Aquinas could, in the thirteenth century, spend an entire life trying to reconcile two important sets of texts the Bible and Aristotle's philosophy which were already then considered ancient. Explorers travelling in the Black Sea area in the sixth century AD could compare their observations with Herodotos' descriptions from the fifth century BC. Mathematicians and scientists could use Euclid and Archimedes as points of departure when setting out to develop new insights.

书写可以使我们稳固地站在已故远祖的肩膀上，同时也为思想提供了一副拐杖，能够削弱记忆力。当人们浏览书写的文稿时，就不再单纯依靠记忆了。如果将此作为一般原则，对于信息社会人类精神的命运而言，这种洞见是一个不祥的预兆。

Writing makes it possible for us to stand firmly on the shoulders of deceased and remote ancestors, but it is also a pair of crutches for thought, which weakens the faculty of memory. When you can look it up, you no longer need to remember. Seen as a general principle, this insight seems to be a bad omen for the fate of the human spirit in information society.

在无教化的社会中，口传宗教一般能够流传几个重要的神话，但是口语传播的范围有限，这决定了宗教信仰的扩散程度，因而也就没有一套固定的教义需要遵守。相反，在有教化的社会中，成文的宗教（常常有具体的宗教文本）从理论上讲不受地域的限制，还有一套教规和原则，并有权修改神话和故事的版本。一般来说，这种宗教流行于阿拉伯半岛和摩洛哥（当然事实远没有这么简单，当地的情况往往是两种宗教互相碰撞，口传宗教永远也不会完全消亡）。源于西亚的三大宗教都具有这些特点，他们不可能与非洲的宗教共享单一的传统。

A non-literate society has an oral religion where several versions of the most important myths usually circulate, where the extent of the religion is limited by the reach of the spoken word, and where there is no fixed set of dogmas that the faithful must adhere to. A literate society, on the contrary, usually has a written religion（often in the shape of sacred texts）, with a theoretically unlimited geographic reach, with a clearly delineated set of dogmas and principles, and with authorised, "correct" versions of myths and narratives. Such a religion can in principle be identical in the Arab peninsula and in Morocco （although it is never that simple in practice; local circumstances impinge on it, and oral traditions never die entirely）. The three great religions of conversion from West Asia have all these characteristics, which they do not share with a single traditional African religion.

此外，无教化的社会有一套建立在习俗与传统基础之上的评判体系，而有教化的社会则有立法体系。无教化社会的道德取决于个人之间的关系——它能嵌入个体间的具体关系中——而在理论上讲，有教化社会的道德尊重法律，也就是说，它已经嵌入成文的法律之中。在我们现在的这一类社会中，即使父母与子女的关系，也要受到成文的法律的调整。

A non-literate society, further, has a judicial system based on custom and tradition, while a literate society has a legislative system. Morality in the non-literate society depends on interpersonal relations it is embedded in tangible relationships between individuals while morality in the literate society in theory is legalistic, that is, embedded in the written legislation. Even the relationship between parents and children is regulated by written law in our kind of society.

在无教化的社会中，知识传递的路径是从嘴巴到耳朵，每个人被迫训练自己的记忆力。当某些社会成员还活着，他以特定的方式保存的整个知识库，可供人们需要时使用。当小规模口传社会的这些成员离世后，知识的净亏损就相当大了。后面的章节中，我会在当代社会加速变迁的背景下讨论年轻崇拜现象。鄙视老年人而崇拜年轻人的原因，明显与老年人去世后老知识并没有失去的事实有关——只有他们的智慧，而在快速流动的社会中，这是一件交换价值日益减少的商品。

In a non-literate society, knowledge is transmitted from mouth to ear, and the people are forced to train their memory. The total reservoir of knowledge which is available at any particular point in time is embodied in those members of society that happen to be alive. When someone dies in a small, oral society, the net loss of knowledge can be considerable. Later, I shall discuss the youth cult of the contemporary age in the context of accelerated change. One cause of the disdain of old age and the worship of youth is obviously the fact that our elders' knowledge is not lost when they die only their wisdom, and that is a commodity with decreasing exchangevalue in a fast-moving society.

大部分无教化的社会都在亲属关系的基础上组织起来，而有教化的社会倾向于成为国家社会，其中的社区是一个抽象的思想意识，比如民族主义在功能上就是隐喻的亲属关系。在某些非国家社会中，部分宗教典籍在历史上也是按照这种方式产生的。

Most non-literate societies are organised on the basis of kinship, while literate societies tend to be state societies where an abstract ideology of community, such as nationalism, functions as a kind of metaphorical kinship. In certain non-state societies, religions of the Book have historically worked partly in the same way.

细心的读者可能会发现，我在这里将社会的类别简化到了极致，把古希腊的城邦与现代的民族国家并列在有教化的社会中。而在谈论无教化的社会时，也采用了同样模糊的方式。这没什么问题，对于那些有兴趣想更详细了解的人来说，还有很多有关教化与口承的专业文献，采用了历史和比较的分析视角。许多社会呈现出混杂的形式，可以被归入教化与口承之间的灰色地带。有些社会使用书写技术的程度很有限，而另一些社会是为了其他目的使用书写技术，而不是激励人们批判地科学地思考（例如宗教的律条强调对核心文本机械的学习），欧洲社会有很多是在19世纪才完全成为有教化的社会。这些详细情况对于研究固然很重要，但在分析本书的问题时关联性不大。此背景下的重要问题是历史发展的总趋势，以及在分析我们自身的社会类别时，这种描绘能在多大程度上提供相关的背景。

Observant readers will have noticed that I am simplifying to the extreme here, juxtaposing ancient Greek city-states and modern nation-states under the heading "literate societies", and similarly talking in a vague fashion about "non-literate societies". This is correct, and for those who are interested in the details, there is an enormous professional literature about literacy and orality in a historical and comparative perspective. A great many societies can be located in the grey zone between literacy and orality: they represent hybrid forms. Some have used writing to a limited degree, while others have used it for purposes other than stimulating critical, scientific thought （religious indoctrination through rote learning of core texts, for example）, and it is doubtless true that many European societies became fully literate only in the nineteenth century. These details, important as they are in research, are less relevant here; what matters in this context, is the general drift of history, and the point of this sketch is to offer a backdrop for an analysis of our own kind of society.

从政治层面上来看，总的趋势是无教化的社会呈现权力分散和平等的特点，首领的政治地位可以继承。相反，有教化的社会呈现权力高度集中的特征，具有职业的管理层，原则上官职的产生必须遵循一套正式的规则。较之于无教化的社会，一般来说，有教化的社会不管是在地理空间，还是在人口数量方面，都要大得多。在无教化的社会中，人们讲述的神话往往离不开他们是谁和来自哪里；在有教化的社会中，官方编纂的历史有着同样的功能，但其基础是档案和其他书面材料。

At a political level, the general tendency is that non-literate societies are either decentralised and egalitarian, or chiefdoms where political office is inherited. Literate societies, on the other hand, are strongly centralised, and tend to have a professional administration where office is in principle accorded following a formal set of rules.In general, literate societies are much larger, both in geographic size and in population, than non-literate ones. And while the inhabitants of non-literate societies tell myths about who they are and where they come from, literate societies have history to perform the same functions, based on archives and other written sources.

一个社会若是建立在亲密人际关系、记忆、地方宗教和口传神话的基础上，我们可以称之为"具体的社会"；如果一个社会建立的基础是正式的立法、档案、有典籍的宗教和成文史，我们可以称其为"抽象的社会"。现在可以清楚地看到，在具体社会向抽象社会的转变过程中，书写是一门非常重要的工具。除了书写之外，我还要提到另外四种技术革新，他们具有现代社会独有的特性，这是信息社会的先决条件。

It should be clear by now that writing has been an essential tool in the transition from what we could call a concrete society based on intimate, personal relationships, memory, local religion and orally transmitted myths, to an abstract society based on formal legislation, archives, a book religion and written history. I shall mention four other technological innovations which, together with writing, indicate those peculiar characteristics of modern society that are preconditions for information society.

刻在表盘上的时间片段

最初，时钟用来调节祈祷的时间；那么，现在的时钟调节什么呢？欧洲中世纪发明的时钟可能与修道院的祈祷有关（伊斯兰教报告祈祷时间的人与基督教堂的钟声，都是当代的提醒方式，履行了最初计时技术的功能）。日历比书写更古老，也在更多的地方独立发展。然而在非现代社会，一般来说，日历无法成为科学家制订五年规划及个人记录日程表和最后期限的技术性辅助手段，但与季节、仪式周期、天文学和农业年份联系紧密。与日历相比，时钟更准确，也划分得更细微。时钟测量时间的方法，是将其分割成可以计量的片段。尽管时钟最初是用来履行宗教的功能，但很快就扩展到了其他活动领域。荷兰思想家格劳修斯（Hugo Grotius，1583—1645 年）明确表达过的一条道德准则，可以用来说明这一点。格劳修斯对政治哲学贡献卓著，有时候他被列为第一个反对道德原则与宗教相背离的现代欧洲人，他提出了很有名的一句话："守时就是美德"（后来富兰克林将其提炼为"时间就是金钱"）。

The Clock was Introduced To Regulate Prayer Times;
What Does it Regulate Now?

The clock was developed in the European medieval age, probably to synchronise prayer times in the monasteries. （The calls of the Muslim muezzin and the Christian church bells are contemporary reminders of this initial function of timing technology.） Calendars are older, and were developed independently in many more places than writing. In general, however, calendars in non-modern societies were not a technical aid to help societies make five-year plans and individuals to keep track of their daily schedules and deadlines, but were rather linked with the seasons, ritual cycles, astronomy and the agricultural year. The clock is more accurate and more minute （literally） than the calendar. It measures time as well as cutting it into quantifiable segments. In spite of its initially religious function, the clock rapidly spread to coordinate other fields of activity as well. The Dutch thinker Hugo Grotius （1583—1645） formulated a moral maxim which illustrates this. Grotius is widely known for his contributions to political philosophy, but he is also sometimes mentioned as the first modern European to defend a moral principle completely divorced from religion: "Punctuality is a virtue!" （"Time is money" is a later refinement of this principle, usually attributed to Benjamin Franklin.)

时钟将时间具体化，这与书写将语言具体化的方式一样。时间成了独立存在的人类经验，成为一些可测量的具体事物。这绝对不是传统社会的事情，传统社会居民的日常生活是在事件驱动的时间结构之中。事件调节时间的流逝，而不是倒过来用时间调节事件。假如一位旅行者或民族志学者前往一个非洲村庄，当他询问某件事何时发生时，答案可能会是"当一切准备好时"，而不会出现别的回答，比如"五点差一刻"。但是，现在却没有清晰的区分。甚至在时钟与时间表已经使用很久的社会中，这两样东西也可能与人们的日常生活没有直接的联系。我的一个同事在爪哇岛的乡村从事田野调查，有一天他想要乘坐火车到邻近的市镇。因此，他向一位当地人询问火车何时到达。那个人用令人迷惑的眼神看了他一眼，指着火车轨道说："火车从那个方向来，在这里停一会儿，然后继续向另一个方向开去。"

In the same way as writing externalises language, clocks externalise time. Time becomes "something" existing independently of human experience, something objective and measurable. This was definitely not the case in traditional societies, where inhabitants lived within an event-driven time structure in their everyday existence. Events regulate the passage of time, not the other way around. If a traveller, or an ethnographer, to an African village wonders when a certain event will take place, the answer may be: "When everything is ready." Not, in other words, "at a quarter to five". But today, there are no clear-cut distinctions. Even in societies where clocks and time-tables have made their entry long ago, it may well be that they are not directly connected to people's everyday life. A colleague who conducted fieldwork in the Javanese countryside reports that one day, he needed to take a train to the nearest town. So he asked a man when the train was due. The man looked at him with the proverbial puzzled expression, and pointed to the tracks: "The train comes from that direction, then it stops here, and after a little while it continues in the other direction."

钟点把时间变成了一个自主的实体，这是一些独立存在的事件。在我们的脑海中，一小时可能是以一种抽象的方式存在，是一个可以填充任何事物的中空体。因此，可以把钟点界定为"空的、被量化的时间"。与长度单位"米"和容积单位"公升"一样，钟点也可以被切割成精确测量的片段。对每个人而言，这些预设的实体是完全一样的事物，不管是在什么地方或什么时候，都认同这些标准。生活在我们这个社会中的每一个人，自从他出生开始，就要签署一份合同，向钟表和日历的时间提交自己毕生的信任。（有时候这份合约还具有可操作性。比如，我那3岁的儿子总是强调，星期天是天线宝宝的时间，他可以和小妹妹在家无法无天地玩耍，而如果是星期二，他就要老老实实地去上幼儿园。）

Clock time turns time into an autonomous entity, something that exists independently of events. "An hour" may exist (in our minds) in an abstract way; it is an empty entity that can be filled with anything. Hence it is common to speak of clock time as "empty, quantified time". It is chopped up into accurately measured "pieces", like metres and decilitres. These entities are presupposed to be identical for everybody, anywhere and any time. Living in our kind of society entails that each of us signs a contract the moment we are born, committing us to lifelong faith in clock-and-calendar time. (The contract sometimes takes a while to become operative. My son, who is 3, thus often insists that it is Sunday and time for TV cartoons and a day of anarchic mayhem at home with his little sister, even if the calendar indicates that it is Tuesday and time for kindergarten.)

在当前的背景下，钟表时间的两个方面尤其重要：首先，它把时间变成了一个准确、客观又抽象的实体，能够约束个人体验时间的流动与衰落——因此这类时间流逝的速度总在变化。众所周知，5分钟可以表示很多意思，从一会儿到毕生之久，都可以用它来表示。对于专横的时间，哲学家已经发起过猛烈的批判，其中柏格森［亨利·柏格森（Henri Bergson，1859—1941年），重要的法国哲学家，在20世纪前50年影响力尤其大。他相信，在对现实的理解上，直接经验和直觉比理性主义和科学更重要。——编者]无疑是最有代表性的人物。在两次世界大战期间，柏格森是当时全世界最有名的知识分子，1928 年他获得了诺贝尔文学奖。柏格森在1889 年完成的博士论文《时间与自由意志》中，严厉地批评了量化又空洞的时间，认为它从外面调控我们，而不是让手头的任务从内部填充时间。

In the present context, two aspects of clock time are particularly important: First, it turns time into an exact, objective and abstract entity, a straitjacket for the flows and ebbs of experienced time perhaps for this kind of time will always pass at varying speed; as everybody knows, 5 minutes can be anything from a moment to an eternity. The philosopher who has developed the most systematic assault on this quantitative time tyranny, is doubtless Henri Bergson （1859—1941）. He was perhaps the most famous intellectual in the world in the interwar years, and received the Nobel Prize for literature in 1928. In his doctoral treatise from 1889, Sur les donné es immé diates de la conscience （"On the immediate givens of consciousness"）, rendered in English as Time and Free Will, he severely criticises the quantitative, "empty" time that regulates us from the outside, instead of letting the tasks at hand fill the time from within.

其次，每个被带入了时钟魔圈中的人，都认可钟表时间的同一性。当我们说晚上 8∶15 时，每个人都能明白其含义是什么。大家都晓得应该何时打开电视观看特别的节目，虽然每个人独自分开居住，但却可以同时做同一件事。当某人打开电视时，这个特定的节目已经开始了，这不是因为电视台没有坚守承诺，而是电视观众的时钟出了问题。（电视采用了相当强的同步技术，在 20 世纪后半叶的国家建构中起了重要的作用，有趣的是，电视从单频道变为多频道，时钟恰恰按照相反的方式工作。后面还会对此详细讨论。）工厂中复杂生产的协作和办公室环境也是如此，从公共交通到电影戏剧表演，如果没有时钟，任何事物都将不可想象。

Second, the clock synchronise everybody who has been brought within its charmed circle. Everyone who reads this is in agreement regarding what it means when we say that it is, say, 8.15 p.m. Everybody knows when to turn on the television to watch a particular programme, and they do it simultaneously, independently of each other. If the programme has already begun when one turns it on, it is not because the TV channel has failed to meet its commitments, but because something is wrong with the viewer's timepiece. (Television is a very strongly synchronising kind of technology and has played a major role in nation-building in the latter half of the twentieth century; interestingly, when the move is made from single-channel to multi-channel television, it seems to work in exactly the opposite way. More about this later.) Coordination of complex production in factories and office environments would also, naturally, have been unthinkable without the clock, as would anything from public transport to cinema shows.

钟表计量时间就像温度计测量温度。如果可以用温度计测量气温，当测量者获得了准确的度数时，仅仅说"感觉冷"就无法让人接受。假如温度计显示的温度高于20摄氏度，那显然挨骂的不是当时的气温，反倒是那个测量者，虽然曾经的人们会咒骂气温。

The thermometer does the same to temperature as the clock does to time. Under thermometer-driven regimes, it is not acceptable to state merely that it 'feels cold' when one can walk over to the thermometer and obtain the exact number of degrees. If it shows more than 20 degrees Celsius, it is not the air temperature, as it were, but oneself that is to be blamed.

藏在钱夹里的抽象社会

货币、书写和时钟属于同一个信息技术的家族。另外一种比温度计更重要的技术是货币的发明，它将追随者和受害者拉往同一个方向。传统社会存在语言与时间的观念，但没有书写和时钟。同样，任何社会都有类似货币的工具，但是我们现在的货币，作为"一般用途的货币"，是最近才有的事物，历史上受到文化的限制。货币作为支付、价值衡量和交换的手段，分别相当于时钟对于时间和书写对于语言的作用。这些技术使事务的处理抽象化，并在一个大的领域内提出了标准的网格（最终使整个世界网格化）。它们将单个的、常规的处理纳入到一个无形的抽象之伞底下。

Money Belongs To The Same Family Of Information Technologies As Writing And Clocks

A more consequential kind of technology than the thermometer is another invention which pulls adherents and victims in the same direction, namely money. In traditional societies, both language and time concepts exist, but not writing and clocks. Similarly, moneylike instruments exist in many kinds of societies, but our kind of money, "general-purpose money", is recent and historically culturebound. It does roughly the same thing to payment, value measurements and exchange as clocks and writing do to time and language, respectively. They make the transaction abstract and impose a standardised grid on to a large area (ultimately the whole world). They place individual, mundane transactions under an invisible umbrella of abstraction.

在各种传统社会里，贝壳货币、金币和其他小的贵重物品早已通行。或许，使用它们作为价值标准，可以让不同的商品相互比较——比如，1袋粮食等于1个金币，1只山羊等于半个金币，因此，就可以先把1袋粮食分成相等的两份，再拿其中半袋与1只山羊进行交换。货币可以作为交换的手段，例如使用1个金币购买两只山羊。货币甚至可以作为支付的手段——比如，某人杀了他的邻居，可以用3个金币作为补偿，赔给寡妇和孩子。然而，与传统社会相比，现代货币是一种更加强大的技术。首先，它具有普遍的适用范围。也许，列侬和麦卡特尼认为爱情不是一件可以销售的商品（当然很容易找到一些愤世嫉俗的社会学家，他们的观点恰恰与此相反），但是总的来说，货币的功能就是作为支付和交换的一般等价物。

西非的梭螺在离开特定区域之后就没有价值，即使在特定范围之内，也只能购买某些商品和服务。在一个拥有几百万居民的国家，具有一般用途的货币是一种法定货币，只要我们所属的国家可以自由兑换货币，这种货币在全世界都可以有效地使用。作为信息技术之一，货币有助于世界的创造，哪怕这只是人类方式整合而成的世界。货币使得全世界的工资和购买力可以互相比较，例如，新几内亚的1吨芋头可以与台湾的电子产品进行交换，货币成了世界经济的必要媒介。在许多社会中，交易和贸易依赖于信任及买卖双方的人际关系，我们熟悉的抽象与一般的货币，意味着经济交换的外在化。只要大家认可纸钞的经济价值，我就无需知道我的债权人和债务人。随着近年来货币进入虚拟空间，几乎在世界各地，和纸钞类似的塑料卡片都可以用于经济交换，这就变得更加抽象了。

Shell money, gold coins and other compact valuables are known from a wide range of traditional societies. They may, perhaps, be used as value standards to make different goods comparable a bag of grain equals half a gold coin; a goat equals half a gold coin; ergo, a sack of grain can be bartered with a goat. They may be used as means of exchange; I can buy two goats with a gold coin. They may even be used as means of payment I have killed my neighbour, and have to pay the widow and children three gold coins in compensation. However, modern money is a much more powerful technology than anything comparable that we know from traditional societies. Above all, it is universal in its field of applicability. It may be that Lennon and McCartney were correct in their view that love is not a marketable commodity (although it is easy to find cynical sociologists who argue to the contrary), but in general, one single kind of money functions as a universal means of payment and exchange, and as a value standard. West African cowries had no value outside a limited area, and, even there, only certain commodities and services could be purchased with them. General-purpose money is legal tender in an entire state of millions of inhabitants, and if we belong to a country with a convertible currency, it is valid worldwide. Regarded as information technology, money has truly contributed to the creation of one world, albeit a world into which only people of means are integrated. Money makes wages and purchasing-power all over the world comparable, makes it possible to exchange a tonne of taro from New Guinea with electronics from Taiwan, and it is a necessary medium for the world economy to be possible at all. Whereas transaction and trade in many societies depended on trust and personal relationships between seller and buyer, the abstract and universal money we are familiar with, implies an externalisation of economic transactions. As long as there is agreement over the economic value of the coloured bits of paper, I need not know either my debtors or my creditors. With the recent move of money into cyberspace, which entails that the same plastic card can be used for economic transactions nearly anywhere in the world, it becomes even more abstract.

标在五线谱上的乐曲声音

与书写、数字、时钟和货币一样，乐谱担当了同样的工作。现在我要谈的最后一个实例是乐谱。我们了解的大部分（可能是全部）社会，都有一定类别的音乐，但是乐谱的发明却有好几次，比如 9 世纪的欧洲、10 世纪的中国与日本。然而，只有欧洲是在一开始就把乐谱的表达目标作为沟通音乐内容的一门具有整体象征性的语言。最初，基本的音符只有升调和降调。后来变得越来越精确，到了 11 世纪，意大利阿雷佐的圭多引入了五线谱，使得特定音程的标记成为可能。同一时期，音符体系获得了标准化，并引入象征符号，用来描述音调的持续时间。在 16 世纪初，全世界大部分地方的人都已经熟悉五线谱。

The Sound Of The Music Notation Marked On The Staff

Music notation does the same kind of work as writing, numbers, clocks and money. My last example for now is musical notation. Most （all）societies we know possess some kind of music, but notation was only invented couple of times, namely in

Europe（ninth century AD）and China/Japan（tenth century AD）. However, it was only in Europe that an expressed aim of notation from the very beginning was to create an entirely symbolic language for communicating musical content the Chinese/Japanese system was based on pictographs proper to the written language. In the beginning, the rudimentary notes marked only ascent and descent of tone level. Eventually, they became more accurate, and in the eleventh century, Guido of Arezzo introduced the staff, which made it possible to mark specified intervals. In the same period, the notation system was standardised, and symbolic markers depicting tone duration were also introduced. At the beginning of the sixteenth century, the system with which we are familiar was largely in place.

本文与乐谱的几个方面有关。首先，乐谱对于音乐就像书写对于语言的关系。乐谱能使乐曲与表演者互相分离，也使得音乐的储存不再依赖于人，对于单个演奏者而言，他无需与其他演奏者接触，就可以学会一首乐曲。只有用书面形式描绘的音乐，才可能不断得到传播。在口语中，那些意义含糊的表述没法通过文本传递；同样，音乐亦是如此（情感与速度是其中的两方面）。其次，乐谱对于音乐的固化作用，就像历史对于神话以及时钟对于时间变量的固化作用。在一些欧洲国家，民俗音乐已经演化了数百年，到了民族浪漫主义时期，人们突然采用凝固的形式抄写和保存这些音乐。因此，现在演奏的乐谱在过去同样演奏过，比如说 19 世纪中期。第三，与其他条件相比，乐谱依赖的条件具有另一类复杂性。比如，在同一时期复调音乐得到了发展，而这种创新的音乐只可能出现在欧洲。如果没有精确的乐谱体系，就既不会有巴赫赋格曲[赋格曲，复调乐曲的一种形式。建立在模仿的对位基础上，从 16—17 世纪的经文歌和器乐里切尔卡中演变而成。——编者]的平均律，也不会有贝多芬交响曲的多声部。在经历了数百年的波动变化之后，A440 音调[A440 是 440 赫兹的声音音调，西方音乐上，此音为标准音高。西方乐理中，A440 乃是中央 C 上方的 A 音符。——编者]最终在 1939 年得以确定。这在音乐界的地位，可与金本位相媲美，就像格林尼治时间和巴黎的量杆一样。对于所有的人来讲，这个共享的、抽象的标准可以一直有效。

Several aspects of musical notation are relevant in the present context. First, notes do the same to music as script does to language; they liberate music from the performer, and make it possible to store music independently of people as well as for individual players to learn a piece without personal contact with another performer. Only those aspects of music that can be depicted in writing are transmitted. Just as there is an indefinite residue in speech that is not transmitted through texts, the same could be said of music （feeling and, for a long time, pitch and speed, are three such aspects）. Second, notes freeze music, just as history freezes myths and clock time fixes the variable flow of time. In several European countries, folk music that had evolved gradually for centuries, was suddenly transcribed and preserved in frozen form during national romanticism; as a result, it is played today note by note as it was played, say, in the mid-nineteenth century. Third, notation lays the conditions for another kind of complexity than would otherwise have been possible. Tellingly, notation was developed in the same period as polyphony, a musical innovation which appeared only in Europe. Neither the mathematical regularity of Bach's fugues nor the very large number of voices in Beethoven's symphonies would have been possible without an accurate system of notation. The standard tone A440 （a pure A is a wave with the frequency 440） was finally defined in 1939, after having fluctuated for hundreds of years. It is the equivalent in music to the gold standard, Greenwich Mean Time and the meter rod in Paris. A shared, abstract standard is assumed to be valid for all persons at all times.

社会变得日益抽象

书写技术的普及促进了语言的标准化。时钟的技术促成了时间单位的标准化，使庞大的人口可以做到同步行动。需要精确协调动作的人数越多，采纳新标准的区域范围就越广。1841 年 6 月，大西部铁路最后一截延伸段正式开通时，布里斯托尔与伦敦存在 10 分钟的时差。当时，两个城市的居民还不需要保持精确的同步性。随着铁路的开通，以及之后 10 年内电报的开通，两个城市对同步性的需求就凸显出来了。铁路开通后，伦敦到布里斯托尔的旅行时间，从原来的 24 小时减少到了 4 小时；但是，电报开通后，急电的派送时间几乎减少到了零。

Society Becomes Increasingly Abstract

The spread of the technology of writing led to the standardisation of languages. The technology of the clock led to both the standardisation of time units and the synchronisation of large populations. The larger the number of people who needed to coordinate their movements with minute precision, the larger were the regions that were comprised by the new standards. When the last stretch of the Great Western Railway was opened in June 1841, the clocks in Bristol ran 10 minutes behind clocks in London. There had been no need for an exact synchronisation of the inhabitants of the two cities until then. This need for synchronisation came partly with the railway, partly with the telegraph during the following decades. The railway reduced the 20 hours journey from London to Bristol to 4 hours, but the telegraph soon reduced the time required to send urgent despatches almost to zero.

当前，全球通行的 24 小时制建立于 1884 年。在此之前，各地时区的混乱造成了时间变换的困难。多年来，人们一直呼吁制定一个的共同标准，直到华盛顿会议召开之后，国际座谈小组才最终达成了一致的意见。

The present global system of 24 time zones was established in 1884. A maze of local time zones had made conversion difficult earlier, and the need for a common standard had been voiced for years when an international panel finally reached an agreement at a meeting in Washington, DC.

从亲属关系到国家认同，从习俗到立法，从"货贝"或相似的物品到一般用途的货币，从主观化的乐曲到乐谱，从地方信仰到成文宗教，从取决于个人的道德到普世性道义，从记忆到档案，从神话到历史，从以事件计时到时钟，这些转变都指出了一个同样的方向：从一个以具体社会关系和实践知识为基础的小规模社会，转向一个以抽象立法体系和逻辑科学知识为基础的大规模社会。

The transitions from kinship to national identity, from custom to legislation, from "cowrie money" or similar to general-purpose money, from internalised music to notation, from local religions to written religions of conversion, from person-dependent morality to universalistic morality, from memory to archives, from myths to history, and from event-driven time to clock time, all point in the same direction: from a small-scale society based on concrete social relations and practical knowledge to a large-scale society based on an abstract legislative system and abstract knowledge founded in logic and science.

在社会和历史科学中，这方面的比较一度盛行，但现在已经过时。当前，大部分学者专注于探索单个社会的特质，而不是研究社会的普遍原理。自然，其中有很多充分的理由。事实上，现代社会同样存在着传统的知识形式。例如，裙带关系、过时的宗教观念、相信一些非特定的"精灵"（比如不从楼梯底下行走、在家里不能打开雨伞）、直觉和无意识的创造，在现代社会中依然存在，和传统社会一样。至于亲属关系和取决于个人的道德则更不用说了。就我个人的著作而言，其中有很多研究讨论的是现代现象，与亲属或种族性具有共同的特点，另外，我写过一本小册子谈论神话与历史问题。因此，反对这种宏伟的普遍原理是有根据的，但只有坚持使用放大镜才可能真正实行。若将遥远的美拉尼西亚村庄与曼哈顿都市的生活进行比较，我相信可以确定几个维度，从而区分出它们的主要差别。

This kind of contrast has been popular in the social and historical sciences, but it has gone out of fashion. Most scholars are presently more preoccupied with explorations of the particularities of single societies than with gross generalisations. And naturally, with very sound reasons. In reality, traditional forms of knowledge exist side by side with the modern ones. Nepotism, anachronistic religious notions and faith in unspecified "spirits" (never walk under a ladder, do not open an umbrella indoors), intuition and spontaneous creativity continue to exist in modern as well as traditional societies, as do kinship and person-dependent moralities. In my own work, Ihave written a short book about the parallels between myth and history, and much of my academic research has dealt with a modern phenomenon which shares many features with kinship, namely ethnicity. So the objection to these grand generalisations is valid, but only if one insists on using a magnifying glass. I remain confident that the dimensions that have been identified do demarcate major differences between life on Manhattan and life in a remote Melanesian village.

另外两个历史性变化是印刷术和工业革命，这两者对于思想和生活方式都有重要的意义，需要在最后详加分析：印刷机里的信息蔓延。

Two further historical changes, with important implications for both thought and way of life, need mentioning at the end: printing and the Industrial Revolution.

在印刷业时代之前——从 1400 年到 1468 年使用古腾堡活版技术期间——许多社会开始出现受过教育的人，但是分布不是特别广泛。究其原因多种多样，但最主要是因为一本书的价钱相当于一小块土地。当时的书籍主要是由和尚用手抄写，除此之外就依靠职业的抄写员。古腾堡发明的活版印刷，可以说是近两千年以来最重要的发明，在此之后，书籍的价格就大幅下降了。1455 年，古腾堡印刷了最著名的 42 行《圣经》。然而，实际上当时书籍的价格依然不便宜。古腾堡印刷的《圣经》售价为 30 荷兰盾，而当时一名普通工人的年薪只有 10 荷兰盾。之后的几十年，新技术的传播很快就覆盖了欧洲的中心地区，书籍逐步开始变得廉价。1476 年，卡克斯顿在英国创立了第一家印刷店。卡克斯顿身兼数职，既是印刷工与编辑，也是业务员和发行人（这种结合方式在 19 世纪很普遍），他为英文正字法和语法的标准化作出了不小的贡献。印刷也使其他国家的标准化成为可能，同时有利于获得本国语言编写的书籍，减少了拉丁语的适用程度。较之于以往少数熟悉拉丁语的精英，市场大了很多。对于晚近新科学、哲学和文学的涌现，印刷术是一个至关重要的因素。同样，对于欧洲城市里公民社会的建造和大众教育而言，印刷业也很重要，其产生的后果是古腾堡永远不可能预见到的——他的主要理想似乎是印刷《圣经》和偿还债务。

Before the era of print Gutenberg lived from about 1400 to 1468 literacy existed in many societies, but it was not particularly widespread. There were several causes for this; among other things, the fact that a book could be as costly as a small farm. Books were always written by hand, largely by monks, but also by professional copyists. Then Gutenberg invented his printing press frequently seen as the single most important invention of the last 2,000 years and suddenly, books became inexpensive, from 1455 and onwards, to be exact (this was the year Gutenberg printed the famous 42 lines Bible). Books did not become really cheap immediately. Gutenberg's Bible cost 30 guilders, and the annual salary for a worker was 10 guilders. During the following decades, the new technology spread to cover the central parts of Europe, and books became increasingly inexpensive. The first printing shop in England was founded by William Caxton in 1476. Caxton was printer, editor, book salesman and publisher (a common combination as late as the nineteenth century), and he contributed in no small degree to standardising English orthography and syntax. Printing entailed standardisation in other countries as well, and facilitated access to books written in native languages, at the expense of Latin. The market was suddenly much larger than the small elite of Latin scholars. Printing was a decisive factor for the emergence of new science, philosophy and literature in early modern times. It was crucial for both mass education and the creation of civil society in European cities, and led to consequences Gutenberg could never have foreseen. His main ambitions seem to have been to print Bibles and pay his debts.

印刷业的特质有助于信息的惊人发展，在标准化方面也作出了贡献。廉价的印装书对于语言及世界观的标准化贡献良多。从奥格斯堡到不莱梅，整个中产阶级都可以收听到同样的广播，而且采用的是同一种语言。因此，国家公共领域首次出现，包括同样的作者、同样的政治与神学问题、同样的哲学和地理科学新事物。印刷业对于民主和民族主义的发展尤为重要，以至于安德森在他的著作《想象的共同体》中认为，当民族主义出现在历史舞台上时，印刷业扮演了主要的角色。如果没有印刷业的生产与销售体系，我们很难明白居住在马赛市区的人如何与里尔的市民具有共同的道义感情。若把印刷作为产生抽象社区的技术装置，那些素未谋面的人就在印刷王国中结成了一体，能够产生共同的感受。当然，我们要考虑的根本问题是：如果印刷业留下了民族主义和民主的遗产，那么互联网和数字卫星电视会给我们带来什么呢？

The features of printing that are most relevant here, are its contribution to the spectacular growth in information, and its standardising aspect. Cheap, printed books contributed to the standardisation of both language and world-views. An identical message,clothed in identical linguistic garb, could now be broadcast to the entire middle class from Augsburg to Bremen. Thus a national public sphere could emerge for the first time, consisting of equals who were preoccupied with the same writers, the same political and theological questions, the same philosophical, geographic and scientific novelties. Printing was so important for the development of democracy and nationalism that Benedict Anderson gave the leading role to print capitalism in his historical drama about the rise of nationalism, Imagined Communities. Without this formidable system of production and distribution, it is difficult to see how a person in Marseilles could even dream of having a morally committing feeling of community with a person in Lille. Seen as a technological device for creating abstract communities, that is solidarity and empathy between people who will never meet in the flesh, print capitalism is king. The underlying question for us is, naturally: if print capitalism bequeathed nationalism and democracy, what lies in store for us after a period similarly dominated by the Internet and digital satellite television?

在印刷技术出现之后，读写能力真正得到普及还需要一段很长的时间。在莎士比亚时代，英国与威尔士约有 1/10 的人接受过教育。现在甚至没有任何国家的文盲率会高于这个比例。即使在保守的宗法社会里，妇女接受教育的比率也高于莎士比亚时代城市居民的受教育率。

It took a long time for literacy to become truly widespread even after the rise of printing technology. In Shakespeare's time, perhaps 10 per cent of the population in England and Wales were literate. No country has an illiteracy rate even approaching this today. Even women in conservative, patriarchal societies have a higher literacy rate than the citizens of Shakespeare's England.

印刷技术和初等教育的普及，以及诸如报纸杂志（包括以按月摊付方式出版的书籍）之类的大众媒体，真正把普通人的思想拽入了新的抽象社会。这类社会由许许多多的人组成，他们组成了一部大型的机器，在生产过程中最终可以被其他人轻而易举地替代。他们的知识与技能并非独一无二，而是标准化的模式，因而可与其他人的知识技能相比较。随着 19 世纪的工业革命，这种可能性首次成为现实。

It was printing coupled with universal primary education and mass media like newspapers and magazines （including books published in monthly instalments） that truly pulled the minds of ordinary men and women into the new, abstract society. This society consisted of an enormous number of persons who were all cogs in a giant machine, and eventually they could easily be replaced by others in the productive process. Their knowledge and skills were not unique, but standardised and therefore comparable to others' knowledge and skills. With the Industrial Revolution in the nineteenth century, this possibility was turned into practice for the first time.

　　传统工艺直接从师父传给徒弟，然而工厂生产程序的标准化却是如此之高，以至于理想化状态下仅仅需要少量的一般技能。[同样，官僚阶层的产生几乎也遵循相同的模式，杜伦大学或苏塞克斯大学（杜伦大学位于英国杜伦市区附近的一个小城镇，苏塞克斯大学位于英国南部布莱顿镇附近，两所大学皆为英国享有盛誉的大学。——编者）的毕业生，在从政时几乎没什么差别。]早期的社会学家，从马克思到涂尔干，都注意到工厂将生产过程裂解成了不同的部分，每一个工人只承担整个生产过程的一小部分。在 19 世纪，不仅仅是马克思，还有很多观察家提出了批评，认为这会导致异化的效果。这在福特发明生产传送带前一两代就出现了，随后情况日益恶化。当然也有好的一面：例如书籍和工业产品变得更便宜，也更容易获得。

　　While traditional crafts were transferred directly from master to apprentice, production in a factory is so standardised that, ideally, it only requires a few, general skills. （The same thing may with some justice be said about the "production" of a bureaucracy; whether one has graduated from Durham or Sussex makes little difference.） The early sociologists, from Marx to Durkheim, were concerned with factory production, which entails splitting up the process so that each worker only produces a tiny bit of the whole. Criticisms to the effect that this led to alienation were made not just by Marx, but by a lot of concerned observers in the nineteenth century, that is, a generation or two before Henry Ford invented the conveyor belt. Things would, in other words, only get worse. Or perhaps better: Like books, manufactured goods became cheaper and more easily available.

　　工业生产不仅使各项工序可以同时进行，也使产品标准化。比如，一张小型磁盘与其他磁盘的构造和模型一样，假如它与众不同，则是因为它存在缺陷。相反，在手工艺生产的社会中，每个产品都需要单独制作，而且独一无二。

Industrial production synchronises work and standardises its products. An item, such as, say, a mini-disc recorder, is identical with all other items of the same make and model, and if it is unique, that is because of some defect. In the society of craftmanship, on the contrary, each object was individually made and unique.

计时器和工厂的时钟都属于工业生产模式，因此，从乡间的修道院到大规模的工业社会，精密计时器都可以发挥同样的作用。

The time recorder and the factory clock belong to the industrial mode of production. Thus the chronometer had finally gone the whole way, from the pastoral communities of monasteries to largescale industrial society.

现代社会的特征是其独特的复杂性。这并不是只有唯一的可能性。印度种姓社会和澳大利亚人传统的世界观，分别代表了社会复杂性与文化复杂性的两类实例。然而，在20世纪后半叶，现代性具有独特的位置，在它即将普及化之前，还具有霸权特征。现代性让芸芸众生被同步化和标准化，成为一部庞大机器上的一颗颗小齿轮。现代性按照一个共同的机械化时间结构，为经济交易提供一个全球性媒介，在共享的理论科学基础上，不断推进生产和破坏的技术。现代性将千千万万的思想与行动协调在一起，这在非现代社会中，既不可知也难以想象。时间、语言、经济、记忆、道德和知识的形象化，使得特定的个体成为多余。而且，它为一个几乎无限的复杂社会奠定了基础。通过这个简单的公分母，可以将数百万新人不断吸收进这个系统，而不需要改变自身的特征或使社会重组。

Modern societies are characterised by a particular kind of complexity. It is not the only one possible. Indian caste society and traditional Australian world-views are two spectacular examples of social and cultural complexity, respectively. Nonetheless, modernity was, in the latter half of the twentieth century, in a uniquely important position; it was hegemonic on the verge of becoming universal. It synchronises and standardises an enormous number of persons, all of them little cogs in a great machinery. It draws on a shared mechanical time-structure, a global medium for economic transactions（money）, a technology of production and destruction based on a shared theoretical science. Modernity coordinates the movements and thoughts of an enormous number of people in ways which are both unknown and unthinkable in non-modern societies. It makes particular individuals superfluous by externalising time, language, economy, memory, morality and knowledge. And it lays the foundation for a nearly infinite social complexity. Forever new millions of people can be drawn into the system through its simple common denominators, without it changing character or needing reorganisation.

发展的标尺

线性时间不是问题的组成部分。我尚未提及对发展的信念。从某种程度上说，这是现代性的典范，一些人——包括悲观主义者和乐天派——都相信我们已经开启了一个真正的后现代时期，因为对发展的普遍信念似乎正在消失。在现代社会的合法化过程中，认为历史变迁向着特定方向推进的观念尤其重要。知识、技术、道德和生活标准——所有这些，都可以看作是进步。当今的数码产品优于往日的电子产品，20 世纪哲学家的理解远比 18 世纪时更深刻。如果把所有的事情都考虑进去，当今的人类要比以前舒适得多。毕竟，如果最后这个假设不正确，适当的矫正能对发展更具有信心，譬如对存在竞争的标签（比如社会主义）来说可能就是如此。

Linear Time Is Not Part Of The Problem

Still I have not even mentioned the faith in progress. To some, this is the very quintessence of modernity, and some both pessimists andoptimists believe that we have initiated a truly postmodern era since the universal faith in progress seems to be disappearing. The idea that historical change moves in a particular direction is important in the legitimation of modern societies. Knowledge, techniques, morality, standards of living, knowledge all of this, it has been assumed, progresses. The electronic gadgets of today are better than yesterday's gadgets, the philosophers of the twentieth century understood more than those working in the eighteenth century, and, all things taken into account, humanity is more at ease with itself today than in earlier periods. If this last assumption should not, after all, prove correct, the proper antidote has been even more faith in progress, possibly of a competing brand （such as socialism）.

　　在对发展的信心方面，线性时间是一个重要的维度。后面将会谈到，在产生时间的专横性方面，线性时间的失败是一个关键的因素。现在，线性时间并非时钟与日历的必然后果。实际上，时钟记录的是暂时的时间，只能持续 12 或 24 个小时。或许，有些读者还记得一个关于有毛病时钟的笑话，它们并非一文不值：一天至少有两次没有问题。相反，给年份和日期编号的日历一直向前，但我们知道的大多数传统日历——从泰国到中美洲——都已经涉及周期性仪式的纪年法，而没有涉及历史变化。时钟、印刷术、科学、工程学、工业生产和资本主义共同构成文化包装，并对发展产生信心。这是一种强有力的包装。然而，我们中间有很多人却有一种不愉快的感受，觉得会有一些事情将恶化。世界并非必然变得更好、更公正、更人道和更容易控制，或者事情并不一定朝着任何特定的方向发展。这种感觉不是由线性时间造成的，而是由对时间的感知造成——感觉时间不再完全是线性的。至于在时间不再存在之前，关于人们可把时间分成多少个碎片还有很多的限制。现存的时间以单一的、狂热的和歇斯底里的时刻存在，而且还在持续地发生改变，但只是指向下一个时刻而已，并没有指向任何更进一步的未来。具有讽刺意味的是，促进线性时间发展并对进步产生信心的力量，在发展的某个特定阶段可能会导致完全相反的结果。

Linear time is an important dimension of the faith in progress, and as will later be shown, its failure is a key factor in creating the tyranny of the moment. Now, linear time is not a necessary consequence of clocks and calendars. The clock actually records temporal cycles lasting for 12 or 24 hours. As the readers will recall, the tired joke about defective clocks notes that they are not entirely worthless: they are correct twice a day. Calendars with numbered years and days, on the contrary, point forward, but most of the traditional calendars we know from Thailand to Central America have referred to cyclical ritual epochs, not to historical change. It is the clock plus printing plus science and engineering plus industrial production plus capitalism that constitutes the cultural package which creates the faith in progress. It is a powerful package. And yet, many of us have an unpleasant feeling that something is about to go terribly wrong; that the world is not necessarily becoming a better, more just, humane and manageable place, or at least that events do not necessarily point in any particular direction. This feeling is not caused by linear time, but by a time perception which is no longer sufficiently linear. There are limits as to how many pieces one can partition time into before it ceases to exist as duration, and the only time in existence is a single, manic, hysterical moment which is continuously changed, but which does not point any further into the future than to the next moment. Ironically, the forces that led to the development of linear time and the faith in progress may, at a particular stage in their development, lead to the exact opposite.

现代社会试图让每个人都更有效率并收获更多，同时加速变迁的内在过程，并使其标准化和一体化，这些事实最终带来了本书所讨论的问题。当今的变化如此之快，以至于不太可能被理性地叙述出来。而且，当一些事情总是在发生，事实上就什么也没有发生。引起这种矛盾处境的主要因素是速度，这是我们现在需要面对的事实。

Perhaps the problem that is taken on in this book is ultimately caused by the fact that modern societies were too successful in their attempts to make everybody more efficient, to achieve more, tostreamline, standardise and accelerate their immanent process of change. Change, or "progress", now takes place so fast that it has become impossible to relate to it sensibly. And when something happens all the time, nothing really happens. Speed is a key factor in bringing this paradoxical situation about, and to that we now turn.

第四章　速　度

这些天一切都变动得很快

不仅仅是时间和到美国的飞机

也不仅仅是汽车、火车和轮船

还有音乐

日本人在录制贝多芬第五交响乐的唱片时

已经把时间减少了四分十五秒

这些都是快节奏的方式

4　Speed

Everything moves so fast these days. Not just time, not just the plane to America, cars, trains and ships, not just music.

 The Japanese have reduced the time to four minutes and fifteen seconds in a recording of Beethoven's fifth symphony.

That's how fast things are.

　　上面引用了挪威很受欢迎的诗人与表演家波勒增的一首小诗。他用幽默诙谐的语调提到了日本的乐队演奏，但讽刺诗与现实相比，有时候就显得苍白无力。奥斯陆国家剧院一位资深的歌剧首席女主角回忆，她参加演出的易卜生名剧《罗斯莫庄》整整持续 4 了个小时。从 1998 年开始，这部戏剧的舞台表演时间却只有 118 分钟。在舞台对话方面，并没有任何大的删减或砍削。

The above is quoted from the popular Norwegian poet and performer Odd Börretzen. His mention of a certain Japanese orchestra is witty, but sometimes satire pales by comparison with reality. An ageing diva at Oslo's national theatre thus recalls a performance of Ibsen's Rosmersholm which lasted a full 4 hours. The most recent staging of the play, from 1998, lasted for 1 hour and 58 minutes. There were no major cuts or deletions in the dialogue.

波勒增提到贝多芬是比较奇怪的,同样 1995 年以来,昆德拉在他那本漂亮的短篇小说《迟缓》中亦是如此。在昆德拉讲述的故事中,有一个具有关键特征的场景,一位捷克籍的科学家,坐在旅馆的房间里,边看着快速更替的新闻报道,边仔细考虑下面这些问题:没有任何特定的次序,也没有能够支配一切的叙述方式,新的碎片如何替换旧的碎片;如果把历史看作一幅挂毯,要将这些一闪而过的新闻碎片编织进去,显然是不太可能的事情;每条一闪而过的新闻出现的时候,总是那样急促和焦躁,因为下一块新闻碎片已经急不可待地等待粉墨登场。他认为当代的历史也是按照这样的方式来叙述, 就像管弦乐队连续演奏贝多芬的 138 首作品,但是每一首只有前面的 8 小节。他推测未来 10 年,管弦乐队可能就只演奏每一首曲子的第一个音符了——而每首曲子都有 138 个音符。他认为再过 20 年,乐队演奏贝多芬的乐曲,全部加在一起可能只是一长串的嘈杂音,就像贝多芬失聪第一天所听到的声音。

It is curious that Börretzen should mention Beethoven; so does Milan Kundera, in his beautiful little novel La Lenteur （Slowness） from 1995. There is a scene where a key character in Kundera's story, a Czech scientist, sits in a hotel room, reflecting over the sheer speed in news broadcasts, mulling over how fragments give way to new fragments without any particular order, without an overarching narrative; how it has become patently impossible to weave those snippets of news that flash by into that large tapestry called History, and how every flash is presented in a breathless and impatient way because the next flash is already eager and waiting in the wings. Contemporary history, he says, is narrated in the same way as a concert where the orchestra plays all of Beethoven's 138 works consecutively, but only the first eight bars of each. In another 10 years, he reflects, they will only play the first note of each piece 138 notes altogether. "And in twenty years, the whole of Beethoven's music would be summed up in a single very long buzzing tone, like the endless sound he heard the first day of his deafness."

昆德拉与贝多芬都没有错。一切事情似乎越来越快。2000年5月一个相对宁静的早晨，我坐在桌旁，匆匆记下本书的一些注释和片段，但三封同时抵达的邮件，内容一样并且都标记了小红旗（表示优先级别高），随后秘书亲自来访，实际上，她过去只是从外面的走廊经过，她敲了门之后进来告诉我，政府警告居民即将面临危险。当我们可以收发电子邮件之后，几乎很难再看到秘书，因此，我们立刻明白了当时局势的严峻程度。

Kundera and Börretzen are right. Everything seems to move faster and faster. As I sat by my desk in relative peace and quiet one morning in May 2000, jotting down notes and fragments for this book, I was interrupted by three simultaneous and identical e-mails marked with red tags （"Priority: High!"）, followed by a physical visit from the secretary, who actually walked around in the corridor, knocking on doors and warning the inhabitants of imminent danger. Since we got email, we hardly see our secretary any more, and so we immediately understood that the situation had to be very serious.

现在，这种不同寻常又引人注目的行为，既不是火灾、大罢工和军队的政变，也不是大学雇员抵制腐朽制度或自动发起又不断升级的自杀风波，而是安装在计算机硬盘上的小小程序——电脑病毒！比如，通过电子邮件附件发送的"爱虫病毒"，包含了一份言辞恳切的请求，要收信人打开附件《我给你的情书》。如果收信人按要求操作——实际上大部分人都会这样做,这完全可以理解,因为邮件正文承诺这是无条件的爱情宣言——爱虫病毒就会开始删除文件,把电脑中的资料搞得乱七八糟,然后通过收信人电子邮箱的通讯录,继续发送电子邮件给那些无辜的计算机用户。在中餐前,很多同事都收到了带有"爱虫病毒"的邮件,而且邮件的来源广泛,许多邮件被反复接收两三次。

Now, the reason for this unusual and dramatic behaviour was neither a fire on the first floor, a general strike, an attempted coup d'état by the military or even an escalating and spontaneous wave of suicides among university employees protesting against the decay of our institution, but a small computer program that had infected many of our hard disks. A virus! The virus program had arrived as an attachment to an email entitled "I LOVE YOU", which contained a plea for the recipient to open the attached "love letter from me to you". If one did and many did, understandably, given that they had been promised an unconditional declaration of love a malign virus would begin deleting files, messing up data and then proceed to move on to other innocent computers via the victim's electronic address list. A surprising number of colleagues received the virus before lunch on that day, generally from different sources, and many got it twice or even three times.

5月3日周三晚上,绰号"爱虫"的病毒首次在香港出现。当天再晚一些时候(美国是周三早晨),美国人起床打开电脑后,"爱虫病毒"开始扩散到全世界,其传播速度非常惊人。接下来的几天,"爱虫病毒"占领了其他许多地方——在哥德堡大学、奥斯陆周刊和挪威国际研究所,并且在周四早上,从我电脑中的三个地方蔓延到整台电脑。当人们在周四下班回家时,反病毒的公司已经开发出了拯救程序,并且上传到互联网供计算机用户自由获取。从一开始"爱虫病毒"就具有致命性和传染性(而其他病毒在变成致命性病毒之前,多年内只处于局部地区,比如黑死病),并且整个传染过程持续了不到3天。在此期间,美国估计有七八成的电脑染上此病毒,只是程度有深有浅。周四晚上,美国有线电视新闻网报道,尽管北欧图片社防范森严，但还是被"爱虫病毒"侵袭，丢失了 4500 张新闻图片。

The virus, which in a matter of hours had been nicknamed "The Love Worm", was first observed in Hong Kong late in the evening on Wednesday, 3 May（local time）. When the population of the USA got out of bed a little while later （and it was Wednesday morning in the US）, the virus began to move across the world with astonishing speed. Within the next couple of days it had reached among many other places the University of Gothenburg, a weekly Oslo newspaper and the Norwegian Institute of International Studies, and arrived from individual computers in all three places at my computer on Thursday morning. As people began to return home from work on that fateful Thursday, the leading anti-virus companies had already developed remedies which were freely available on the web. The virus was virulent and epidemic from the very beginning （other viruses, such as that which carries bubonic plague, may be passive for years before turning vicious）, and the entire epidemic lasted less than three days. Within that span, between 60 per cent and 80 per cent of the computers in the USA were estimated to have been infected to a greater or lesser degree. On Thursday evening, CNN online reported that the Scandinavian photo agency Scanpix had lost 4,500 images, in spite of impeccable security routines.

短短一两天之内，具有传染性的"爱虫病毒"扩散到了全世界，带来了一个突如其来的后果，紧接着全世界新闻媒体都发出了警告信息。一周之后，病毒的始作俑者被菲律宾警方逮捕。

A couple of days' epidemic dissemination all over the world were brought to an abrupt end, following the spread of prominent warnings in virtually all the world's media. A week later, the virus makers were arrested by the Filipino police.

人们不禁会把欧洲历史上更早期的主要传染病与"爱虫病毒"进行比较。其中,最有名又可能后果最严重的莫过于黑死病(1347—1351 年)。这种传染病使欧洲大部分地区出现大面积死亡和政治分裂,持续几年之后于 1349 年传播到了挪威西南部的卑尔根市,次年抵达波罗的海大陆地区。尽管黑死病极具传染性,但是从西西里岛传播到里加还是花了 3 年的工夫。除了与欧洲毗邻的地域(西亚与南非),在欧洲以外没有其他地方感染黑死病。实际上,530 年的大瘟疫更具全球性——这场瘟疫始于东非,给中国、阿拉伯半岛和欧洲带来了浩劫。它的扩散速度与 800 年之后的黑死病旗鼓相当。不管是 6 世纪还是 14 世纪的瘟疫,无论地域空间相隔多远,这些病毒都能很快被消除。

One cannot help comparing this epidemic with earlier major epidemics in European history. The most famous and, possibly, the most consequential was the Black Death （1347—1351). It had already caused mass death and political fragmentation in large parts of Europe for a couple of years when it finally reached Bergen in 1349, arriving in the Baltic lands only the next year. It took the plague three years to make the trip from Sicily to Riga, in spite of the fact that it was extremely contagious. Excepting the immediate neighbouring areas （West Asia and North Africa), no other continents than Europe were affected. Indeed, the great plague of the 530s was more global it started in East Africa and caused havoc in China, Arabia and Europe and it moved just as fast as the plague 800 years later. Whatever was far away in space, in the fourteenth as well as in the sixth century, was also far removed in time.

风驰电掣的历史

我们的历史是一部加速度的历史。有很多可能的理论方法可以通往我们近代的历史,现代史让几代学者与学生忙碌了一个多世纪。有些人关注历史观念,而另外一些人则强调经济或政治。这样行动起来就会完全不同。例如,如果把最近两百年的历史看作一部有关加速度的历史,我们就会很受启发。奇怪的是,在各类有关全球化的作品中,这个维度极不显著。这个维度之所以看起来令人惊讶,原因在于全球化是加速度的一种特殊形式，可以减少空间距离的重要性，而这往往会阻碍全球化。在无线通信时代，持续的时间与距离之间已经不再有联系。维利里奥是最重要的速度理论家，他认为我们现在生活的时代已经不存在延期的问题。

Our History Is The History Of Acceleration

There are many possible theoretical approaches to our near past, and the history of modernity has kept generations of academics and students busy for more than a century. Some concentrate on the history of ideas, while others emphasise economics or politics. It can be done differently. For example, it can be highly illuminating to view the history of the last 200 years as a history of acceleration. Strangely, this dimension is rarely foregrounded in the extensive literature on globalisation. The reason why this is surprising is simply that globalisation is itself tantamount to a particular form of acceleration, which reduces the importance of distance, frequently obliterating it altogether. In the era of wireless communications, there is no longer a connection between duration and distance. As the theorist of speed, Paul Virilio, puts it: we now live in an era with no delays.

维利里奥认为，互联网技术已经发展成了一个家族，这一点并非言过其实。正如读者所认识到的那样，他既不考虑市郊的往返列车，也不考虑市民候车时打电话谈论官僚的琐事。全球化远程通信和其他以卫星为基础的通信方式，实现了即时传送和非固定发送。与网络相连的节点可以在同一个地方，以及世界上不同地方同时存在。实际上，从墨尔本或从隔壁办公室收发邮件，已经没有任何差别；同样，观看在比利时举行的足球比赛现场直播，或者是在基里巴斯举行的新年庆祝仪式现场直播，以及当地电视台传送的现场采访，都与在现场观看没有时间差别。过去被认为可以产生空间距离的时间，已经一去不复返了。

Virilio had the Internet family of technologies in mind, and thus he was not overstating the point. As the reader realises, he was thinking neither of commuter trains nor of citizens waiting to speak to a bureaucrat on the phone. Global telecommunications and other communication based on satellites are placeless and immediate. All the nodes connected through the Net are in reality both in the same place, everywhere and nowhere. In practice, there is no difference between sending and receiving email from Melbourne or from the office next door; or watching a direct transmission from a football game in Belgium, New Year celebrations in Kiribati or an interview transmitted from one's local television studio. Time, regarded as a means to create distance and proximity, is gone.

这些我们熟悉的事实产生了许多意想不到的后果，维利里奥对此进行了分析，他谈到自己研究的领域，就是有关速度与加速度的研究。其中，他对军队的研究最有兴趣。100 年前，入侵类似波兰这样的国家需要数周，战争的速度取决于骑兵的平均推进速度。尽管战马的行进速度很快，但它们需要食物和休息，而且容易受到山川、沼泽与河流的阻碍——更别提那些不愿屈服的乡间村民，还会破坏桥梁并设下陷阱。20 世纪初，坦克与双层甲板的飞机陆续问世，战争的速度在很多方面得到了提升，再加上火炮与中程导弹，好战的国家基本上可以在短时间内，对邻近的国家造成无法形容的损失。

This familiar fact has many unintended consequences, some of which are explored by Virilio, who talks of his own field of study as dromology, the study of speed and acceleration. One of his special fields of interest is the military. A century ago, it would take weeks or months to invade a country like Poland: the speed of war was identical with the average speed of the cavalry. Although horses are fast animals, they need food and rest, and they are further delayed by hills, swamps and rivers not to mention intransigent villagers who destroy bridges and set traps. At the beginning of the last century, the tank and the double-decker airplane were introduced, and suddenly the speed of war was greatly increased. Then came the Spitfires and medium-range missiles, and, today, a warlike state can in principle inflict unspeakable damage on another country in a matter of minutes.

维利里奥灵感的源泉,部分源于媒体理论家麦克卢汉,他最广为人知的乐观主义标语是"地球村",人们可以在其中参与一场规模宏大的社交活动,讨论价值观、美和人类共同的命运。维利里奥更愿意讨论"全球性大城市",其特征是匿名性和非整合性,每一个身居其中的人都可以与别人交往,但是没有任何人——由于前面的原因——与别人真正地交谈。这种"虚拟城市"依靠即时通信技术。换句话说,在我们所处的情景中,时间支配着空间。按照维利里奥的说法,空间距离已经消失,当我们实现了天涯若比邻时,实际上就没有什么重要的事情了。

One of Virilio's sources of inspiration is the media theorist Marshall McLuhan, perhaps most widely known for his optimistic slogan "the global village" where all of humanity participates in a magnificent conversation about values, beauty and its own shared destiny. Virilio prefers to speak of a "global megacity" characterised by anonymity and disintegration, where everybody communicates with everybody else, and where nobody for that very reason really speaks with anyone. This "virtual city" is organised by means of realtime information technology. In other words, we have a situation where time dominates space. Distances vanish, and when that which is far away becomes as close as that which is near, nothing is really near any more, according to Virilio.

维利里奥的悲观情绪接近于 19 世纪后半叶的古典社会学家, 比如滕尼斯和齐美尔,他们对于都市生活的匿名性、个人主义、传统与宗教信仰权威的丧失、实用主义、工业社会中典型的目标导向型行为方式,提出了令人担心或使人陶醉的模式。这是否意味着加速度引发的问题比我们能够想到的问题更古老呢? 当人们提出无法回答的问题时,答案只能与往常一样,只有"是与不是"可以选择。

Virilio's pessimism is close kin to that of the classic sociology of the latter half of the nineteenth century; authors like Ferdinand Tönnies and Georg Simmel wrote in a worried（Tönnies）or fascinated（Simmel）mode about the anonymity of urban life, about individualism and the loss of authority in tradition and religion, and about that pragmatic, goal-oriented style of behaviour that is so typical of industrial society. Does this mean that the problems raised by acceleration are older than we seem to think? The answer is, as usual when one raises unanswerable questions, yes and no.

每一代人都有一种趋势,认为自己所处的时代独一无二,其理由很好:所有的新时代都有自己独特的方式。同时,不妨宣称大部分的新时代都具有新奇性,实际上能够存在很长一段时间——可以始于柏拉图或农业革命，也可以始于马可波罗、哥伦比亚、古腾堡或宗教革命,完全在于你个人的选择。有些人强调喷气式飞机和互联网的独特性,认为当电报、蒸汽机或者快速的两轮战车发明时,世界就发生了最重要的变化,但是如果考虑到速度与加速度,人们就会反对这种看法了。换言之,天底下的新东西很少甚至没有。

Every generation has a tendency to regard its own era as being unique, and with good reason: all epochs are in their way unique. At the same time, it can also be claimed that much of that which is perceived as novel, has in fact existed for quite a while say, since Plato, or since the agricultural revolution, since Marco Polo, Columbus, Gutenberg or the Reformation （take your pick）. Regarding speed and acceleration, one may object, to those who stress the unique aspects of jet planes and the Internet, that the most important changes took place when the telegraph was invented, or the steamship, or for that matter the fast Roman two-wheel chariot. In other words, there is little or nothing new under the sun.

这种争辩有其局限性。尽管电报是一项能够带来巨大影响的发明,但是马可尼认为,互联网也只不过是一个脚注而已。全球实时通信完全不同于以往的技术,它以实时性为基础，创造了人类生活的框架。然而，把电子革命看作早期改革和加速度的直接延伸，也是完全正确的。前一章讨论了西方文化史上一些重大信息的内涵——书写、货币、印刷与时钟。这些都有助于将通信从即时性背景中释放出来，比如书写可使知识积累起来，不受时间的影响；时钟使时间具有机械性和普遍性；货币可使商品的价值具有可比性。无论人们身处堪培拉还是坎普尔，一美元、一小时和一个头条新闻各自都具有相同的含义。虽然环境在不断变化，但公分母将不同地点连在了一起。

This kind of argument has its limitations. Although the telegraph was an invention with enormous consequences, the Internet signifies more than a mere footnote to Marconi. Global telecommunications based on real time create a framework for human existence which differs radically from that of all earlier technologies. Yet it is correct to regard the electronic revolution as a direct extension of earlier innovations and accelerations. The previous chapter discussed the implications of some great informational divides in Western cultural history writing, money, printing, the clock. All these contributed to liberating, as it were, communication from its immediate context; writing made knowledge timeless and cumulative, the clock made time mechanical and universal; money made values comparable. Whether one is in Canberra or in Kanpur, a dollar, an hour and a news headline mean pretty much the same. The circumstances continue to vary, but the common denominators link places together.

工业革命的产物是标准化和节省时间，在工业革命造成的破坏中，时间的专横性建立了它的基础。只有在工业社会，时钟才能够用在一个巨大而复杂的工业生产环境中促进同步化的效率。也正是在这样的时代中，时间与货币才能够紧密耦合。至少从伊拉斯谟时代开始，守时就成了一种美德。但是，节省时间就是获得金钱的观念，却只有在工业大规模取代传统手工艺时，才有可能成为生产领域的指导原则。始于 18 世纪末期的工业革命，在西方社会需要整个 19 世纪才能完成，在引入生产线和打卡机之后达到终点。

Standardisation and time-saving are true-born children of the Industrial Revolution, and it was during the disruptions caused by industrialisation that the foundations for the tyranny of the moment were laid. Only in industrial society could the clock be used to promote synchronised efficiency in a large and complex industrial work setting. It was also in this era that time and money were tightly coupled; punctuality had been a virtue at least since the time of Erasmus, but the notion that time saved is money made became a guiding principle in production only when industry replaced traditional crafts on a large scale. The Industrial Revolution, which began towards the end of the eighteenth century, would need the entire nineteenth century to be completed in the West, culminating in the introduction of assembly lines and time recorders.

这个快速变迁的时代,有些人为之着迷,也有些人担惊受怕。新生产的商品具有可怕的质量;殖民帝国扩张并创造世界经济——就像当今的世界经济一样——主要的基础是从贫穷国家进口原材料,然后把富裕国家生产的商品出口到贫穷的国家。在很大程度上,火车、轮船、电报和电话线在很大程度上促成了世界的收缩,其方式与当今世界的收缩过程并无二致。在 19 世纪,时装业开始以新的步伐发生变化,"巴黎时装模式年"的概念开始出现。

Living in this era of acceleration and fast change, the general public was partly fascinated, partly frightened. New kinds of commodities were produced in frightful quantities; the colonial empires expanded and created a world economy based like today's world economy largely on exports of raw materials from the poor countries and exports of manufactured goods from the rich countries. Trains, steamships, telegraph and telephone lines all contributed in no small measure to the shrinking of the world in ways that must have seemed no less impressive than the current shrinking process. During the nineteenth century, fashion in clothing began to change at a new pace, and the notion of "this year's Paris models" appeared.

时至今日，欧洲与北美的居民也开始关心速度的效应、距离的收缩以及我们称为全球化的东西（实际上，他们通常更关注大西洋西岸，很少注意大西洋东岸）。1824 年，蒸汽机车作为新发明刚一出现，有些富有远见的评论家就立刻意识到这将会改变世界。当时《苏格兰人》杂志的记者写道："当蒸汽机车普及时，当前极快的速度［每小时 10 英里（1 英里 = 1609.34 米。——编者）］是否可以翻番，还没有人敢去预测。"他注意到美国人极其渴望改进蒸汽机车，并开始研究这项新科技，甚至设想将来每小时 20 英里的速度还可以继续翻番。有趣的是，苏格兰的评论员将其与当今普遍使用的技术作了比较，认为"欧洲之旅"（那时包括巴黎与佛罗伦萨）所需的时间，与现今从爱丁堡到伦敦的时间相当。

The inhabitants of Europe and North America were concerned with the effects of speed, the shrinking of distance and what we would today call globalisation, as they are today (and, like today, they were generally more enthusiastic on the western coast of the Atlantic than on the eastern coast). In 1824, the steam railway was a recent invention, and some foresighted commentators immediately realised that it would change the world. "When the steam carriage becomes widespread, it is not particularly daring to predict that the present extreme speed [10 miles an hour] may be doubled", wrote a journalist in The Scotsman. He further notes that the Americans, "with their characteristic eye for improvements", had begun to study this brand-new technology, and envision a future where even the wondrous speed of 20 miles an hour might be doubled. Interestingly, the Scottish commentator draws comparisons of the same kind as those commonly used today when a new, accelerating technology is introduced: he states that "the tour of Europe" (which then included Paris and Florence), soon could be undertaken in the same time as "our grandfathers" had needed to travel from Edinburgh to London.

尽管火车速度越来越快并且试图与飞机竞争,目前,欧洲铁路公司试图将自身重新定位:为匆忙的空中旅行与容易受挫的公路驾驶提供一个既有思考时间又有安静空间的选择。乘坐火车旅行,或许可以享受到标准的时间。有关火车的此类观念——作为过去时代的浪漫遗迹(特别是在火车蒸汽锅炉和坦克引擎的发明地英国,这种怀旧的形式得到了发展)——很快就偏离了最初的意思。特纳在1844年出版的油画《雨水、蒸汽和速度》中,在这方面点出了时代的精神。这幅油画描绘了大西部铁路,它起着横贯伦敦西部的桥梁作用。这幅画表明火车的运行速度太快,以至于人的眼睛很难感知窗外的景色。火车的平均速度为每小时20英里,而在理论上则可以达到每小时50英里。挪威第一条铁路从奥斯陆通往奥斯威德,全长60公里,在1855年正式通车时,平均速度不到每小时20英里。然而当时仍有很多人忧心忡忡。他们认为人们乘坐火车旅行时,蒸汽机车驱动的高速运动不符合自然规律,乘客无法仔细地观赏周围的景色。因此,这对人类感知的自然边界提出了挑战。

In spite of ever faster trains and attempts to compete with air traffic, European railway companies nowadays try to position themselves as offering a contemplative, quiet alternative to the hectic bustle of air travelling and the frustrations of driving. Travelling by train, one may enjoy slow time. This concept of the train as a romantic vestige of a bygone era （a form of nostalgia which is particularly well developed in Britain, the home oftrainspotters and Thomas the Tank Engine） is very far removed from its original significance. Turner's painting Rain, Steam and Speed from 1844 brings out the spirit of the age in this respect. It depicts the Great Western Railway as the train crosses a bridge just west of London. The picture suggests an almost unreal speed, a movement so quick that the human eye has difficulty perceiving it. The train moved at an average velocity of 20 miles an hour, although it could in theory reach all of 50 miles an hour on certain stretches. When the first railway in Norway, from Christiania （Oslo） to Eidsvold some 60 kilometres to the north, was opened in 1855, the average speed was less than 20 miles an hour, and yet many were worried. They felt that the unnaturally high speed of the steam train made it difficult to take in the details of the landscape when one was travelling. It challenged the natural boundaries of human perception, it was said.

随着蒸汽机车的出现，电报线也如雨后春笋般发展——往往沿着铁轨附近架设电报线。这种发明，被称为维多利亚时代的互联网，或许可以代表自古腾堡时代以来，信息技术史上最重要的变化。因为这是首次脱离物理对象提供信息服务，也是首次将急件打包传送时总重量不到 1 克。换句话说，万维网的胚芽早在 1838 年就已经播撒了种子。按照 19 世纪中期的标准，电报线的网络发展极快，1866 年第一条穿越大西洋的海底电报线已经开通。这实际上代表着新的事物。仅仅在十几年前，欧洲和美国之间的通讯需要数周或几个月，而且完全取决于季节和气候条件。到了 19 世纪 30 年代末期，轮船淘汰了帆船，又过了不到 30 年，伦敦与纽约之间也有了电报线。当 20 世纪初无线电报出现时，实际上可以说互联网即将粉墨登场了。对于数百万欧洲移民来说，他们无需再等候数周或数月，才能了解到故乡亲戚的最新消息。当家乡年迈体衰的叔叔过世时，他们可以在同一天收到报丧的电报。1876 年，贝尔申请了电话机的发明专利。尽管到 1927 年才首条横贯大西洋的电话线才开通，但是其后几十年内电话机已经非常普及。因此，19 世纪后半叶，全球贸易迅速扩张（几乎可与 20 世纪 90 年代媲美），当时的大英帝国——技术变迁的动力室——成了世人皆知的日不落殖民帝国。如果按照一种更加乐观的方式来理解，密切整合的全球社会，在 19 世纪 90 年代与 20 世纪 90 年代，扩张规模基本一致。

Literally in parallel with the steam railway, telegraph lines mushroomed they were often built along the railway tracks. This invention, which has been described as the Internet of the Victorian age, perhaps represented the most important change in the history of information technology since Gutenberg. For the first time, messages were severed from physical objects. For the first time, despatches could be sent for many miles in packets with a weight of less than 1 gram. The germ of the WWW was, in other words, sown in 1838. The network of telegraph lines grew extremely rapidly by the standards of the mid-nineteenth century, and the first transatlantic cable was operative already in 1866. This really represented something new. Only a few decades earlier, communication between Europe and the USA had taken weeks or months, depending on the season and weather conditions. Then, towards the end of the 1830s, steamships made sailships obsolete, and less than 30 years later, one could cable messages from London to New York. When the wireless telegraph was launched, just before the last turn of the century, it could indeed be said that mere cosmetics (or, actually, electronics) remained before the Internet was a reality. It was no longer necessary for millions of European migrants to wait for weeks and months to hear the latest news about their ageing relatives. They would receive a cable on the same day that their ailing uncle finally expired. In 1876, Bell patented the telephone, and it became common within a few decades, although one would have to wait until 1927 for the first functioning transatlantic lines. To all this, it must be added that global trade grew enormously in the latter half of the nineteenth century (another parallel to the 1990s), and the British Empire then a powerhouse of technological change became known as the colonial empire where the sun never set. The idea of a tightly integrated global society was, understandably, as widespread in the 1890s as it was in the 1990s, and was generally perceived in a more optimistic way.

随着大城市的发展,可选择的商品日益增多,旅游成了一种日常现象,每周发行的杂志也纷纷涌现,深受各阶层人士的喜欢;各种报纸都在争抢最新的资讯。19世纪晚期,富裕国家已经建立了新社会,当时德国、法国和美国位居前列,其社会面貌与我们当今的生活有很多相同之处。他们的特征是快速变迁、复杂性日益增加、迁徙与技术变革。20世纪全球现代性的图标在1886年就已经启动,早期的广告界就承诺要反对"慢性思维"。1905年,可卡因作为秘方出现,但是当代成千上万的爱好者仍然认为,可口可乐即使不是思维所必要的东西,也是精确抵制缓慢的物品。

The big cities grew, the selection of goods grew, tourism became a mass phenomenon, weekly magazines were established and became popular among all classes, and the newspapers competed ferociously for the latest news: the new society that was established in the late nineteenth century in the richest countries, with Great Britain, France and the United States at the forefront, had a lot in common with the society we live in today. It was characterised by acceleration, growing complexity, a sense of uprootedness and fast technological change. The very icon of global modernity in the twentieth century Coca-Cola was launched in 1886, and early advertisements promised that it countered "slowness of thought". It is true that the cocaine was taken out of the secret recipe in 1905, but millions of contemporary devotees would still agree that what CocaCola does for them is precisely to counteract slowness, if not necessarily of thought.

100 年前，使工作制度发生重要改革的关键人物，是美国工程师泰罗（Frederick W. Taylor, 1856—1915 年）。他虽然不是首位利用工时标定方法监督工人的研究者，但是他开发的方法在工业界留下了深刻的印记。在泰勒看来，通过测算工人每一道工序的持续时间，然后削减浪费的时间——不仅仅是休息时间，还有不太必要的身体运动，能够或者几乎能够一直让生产更有效率。对他提出的方法，有人钦佩，也有人憎恨，人们把这种方法冠名为"泰罗主义"，其副作用是把生产过程切成了许多的组成部分，为流水作业线奠定了基础，使得每个工人反复从事小部分机械性动作。在某种程度上，"泰罗主义"是工业社会对度量公制的反应：它标准化了个人的主观性，阻止和根除了个人的主观性。

A key person in the transformation of work that took place about 100 years ago, was the American engineer Frederick W. Taylor （1856—1915）. He was not the first to use time studies to monitor workers, but he developed a method which would almost immediately leave its deep mark on the industrial world. In Taylor's view, it was always or nearly always possible to make production more efficient by measuring the duration of every act the workers did, and then to eliminate the "wastage" not just the breaks, but also unnecessary bodily movements. His method, admired and detested under the name Taylorism, made it possible, almost as a side-effect, to chop up the productive process into a great number of constituent parts, and thus cleared the ground for assembly line production, where every single worker performs a small number of mechanical, repeated movements. Taylorism is, in a way, the response of industrial society to the metric system of measurement: it standardises, chops up and eradicates subjectivity.

生产过程、通信技术以及 19 世纪后半叶日益增长的消费,具有的共同特征是嘈杂、快速和匿名的生活,并被认为是新鲜事物。当然,并非每个人都对此印象深刻。19 世纪 80 年代,小说家哈姆生在美国工作生活了几年,从一开始就对美国巨大的技术进步记忆犹新。他在给朋友的一封信件中,用一种充满愉悦的方式,描绘了布鲁克林大桥这个庞然大物,桥梁上到处是钢质接头和巨大的螺栓;对于早期出现的电梯,他也采用了一种新奇的描述方式, 将其称为 "跷跷板式的装置"。1889 年,他写作了一篇散文名为《现代美国人的精神生活》,其中的观点与以前迥异。他嘲弄美国人不加批判地接受一切的趋势,认为美国人鄙视传统又精力充沛——在他看来,对发展的乐观主义和天真的信心存在很大的问题。美国人充满活力、坐立不安又能迅速回转的特征,往往让人认为是自由本身已经成了美国国民特性的根基。

The noisy, fast and anonymous life characterising the productive process, communication technology and increasingly the consumption of the second half of the nineteenth century, was perceived as something new. Not everybody was equally impressed. The novelist Knut Hamsun, who lived and worked in the USA for several years in the 1880s, was at the outset impressed by the great technical advances of the country. In a letter to a friend, he described the enormous Brooklyn Bridge, all steel joints and huge bolts, in lyrical terms; and he also included a curious description of an early lift, which he describes as "a seesaw-like device" (et slags Vippeindretning). When, in 1889, he wrote his essay "On the Spiritual Life of Modern America", he had changed his mind. He now poked fun at the American tendency to embrace uncritically anything new, their disdain for tradition and their energetic and in his view quite unjustified optimism and naïve faith in progress. "And the Americans themselves are convinced that all this restlessness and energy and rapid turning-around is a trait that freedom itself has ingrained into the American national character."

在描述美国人对社会变革的典型态度时,哈姆生对托克维尔(他在半个世纪前写了关于美国的有影响力的著作)作出了回应,他与吉卜林一样,预计到当代欧洲人会批评互联网时代。吉卜林年轻时首次访问美国的时间远远少于哈姆生,但是对于技术环境将会施加给个人的风险,他亦表达了同样的看法,认为在这样的情况下,原则几乎没有或只有很少的补偿力。吉卜林的论文发表之后,在美国引起了强烈的反响,他的论文涉及他所看见的英语的普及化与简化。(这里要提一下维多利亚晚期的另一个重要人物王尔德,他认为美国人与大不列颠人除了语言之外,还有很多共同之处。)当然,语言的简化也可以看作一种加速度——或者说经济地谈论艺术。

In describing the "typically American" attitude to change in these terms, Hamsun both echoes Alexis de Tocqueville (who wrote his influential work on America half a century earlier), anticipates contemporary European critics of the "dot com" era, and closely parallels Rudyard Kipling. The young Kipling's first visit to America was much shorter than Hamsun's, but he returned with many of the same views on the perils of letting oneself be sucked up by a technological environment where speed rules with few or no countervailing forces. Kipling, whose essay aroused furious reactions in the US when it was published, was particularly concerned with what he saw as the vulgarisation and simplification of the English language (reminding one of another late Victorian luminary, namely Oscar Wilde, who once wrote of Americans that they and Britons had so much in common, except, of course, language). Linguistic simplification can, of course, be seen as a kind of acceleration the art of speaking economically.

　　商品生产所需的新产能与工业革命引起了 19 世纪的加速发展，其中信息技术起着推波助澜的作用。在 21 世纪的加速发展中，信息技术同时发挥着催化剂作用，它是那些令人梦寐以求的商品及经济动力的源泉。这种仓促而又碎片化的存在，导致了今日许许多多的挫折与时间陷阱。一定程度上，这是哈姆生、吉卜林与 100 多年前的其他作家用讽刺的笔调所描述的旧闻。但是，信息社会为现在的情形增添了一些真实的新特征。速度就有现代的特征，而且现代性至少已经存在了 200 年以上。在本书中，我要明确表达的速度原则，可以采用一般的方法分阶段叙述，但是只与现代社会有关。此外，很多实例可以表明，在现代性的特定阶段——冷战时期与信息时代，的确存在很多独一无二的方面。

Acceleration in the nineteenth century was caused by the Industrial Revolution and new productivity demands in commodity production, aided by information technology. In the acceleration of the twenty-first century, information technology is simultaneously catalyst, source of coveted goods and economic powerhouse. That hurried, fragmented kind of existence which leads to so many frustrations and time traps nowadays is, to a certain extent, old news, satirically depicted by Hamsun, Kipling and others more than 100 years ago; but the information society also adds some genuinely new features to the situation. Speed is modern, and modernity has existed for at least a couple of hundred years. The principles of speed that I shall formulate later in this book are phrased in general ways, butthey are only relevant in modern societies. Furthermore, the examples will indicate that there are indeed aspects of this particular phase in modernity the post-Cold War period, the information age which are unique.

令人上瘾的速度

速度是一剂令人上瘾的麻醉药。在 21 世纪初，这个标题似乎还不太贴切，但却到了该发生的时候了。在 19 世纪，人们观察、评论或偶尔批判的加速发展，时至今日仍在进行，而且能够被更尖锐地感受到。现在的计算机网络和卫星通信将世界更加紧密地联系在一起，这是过去电报或轮船公司苦思冥想也无法实现的。

Speed Is An Addictive Drug

The topic has not properly reached the agenda of the 2000s yet, but it is about time that it did. The acceleration that was observed, commented upon and occasionally criticised by people of the nineteenth century has continued to this day, and it became more acutely felt than ever as computer networks and satellite-based communication linked the world more closely together than any telegraph or steamship company could even contemplate doing.

很久以前，所有的信件都要依靠手写，还要通过缓慢的邮寄服务（马驮、车载或船运等）才能分发出去。写一封信需要很长的时间，而寄送与分发信件则要更长的时间。到了 19 世纪，写信与寄信的速度都提高了：打字机出现数十年之后，火车和轮船相继问世，这些都使信件的寄送与分发更加安全迅速。进入 20 世纪之后数十年，人们就开始用飞机寄送邮件。现在，一对分居澳大利亚和美国的恋人，已经完全没有必要苦等数月才能收到对方的回信了。20 世纪 50 年代，如果运气好的话，被抛弃在欧洲的亲戚甚至只要 3 周的时间，就可以收到从明尼苏达州返回的信件。

A long, long time ago, all letters were written by hand, and they were distributed through slow mail services （horse and carriage, sailing ships, etc.）. Writing a letter took a long time, and distributing it took even longer. In the course of the nineteenth century, it wasn't just the production and distribution of letters that were accelerated: the typewriter appeared, a few decades after trains and steamships had made distribution safer and swifter. A few decades into the twentieth century, aeroplanes also began to be used in the distribution of mail. Now, it was suddenly possible to keep in touch with one's beloved in Australia and America without having to wait for months for them to respond. In the 1950s, abandoned relatives in Europe might even get a return letter from Minnesota in a mere three weeks, with a bit of luck.

现在如何呢？现在，我们用鼠标点击屏幕上的发送按钮之后，就连用 30 秒钟等待回复也很不耐烦了。

And now? Nowadays we start to wait impatiently for the reply about 30 seconds after pressing the "Send" button on the screen.

这种加速形式带来了几方面的后果，虽然还不能说是什么副作用。电子邮件的优势及其固有的用途，在于它能够促进人际交往活动。电子邮件比电话更灵活，因为无论人们正在做什么事情，别人给他发一封电子邮件，并不会使他分心或受干扰。另外，电子邮件还不会丢失，它总能送到收件人的邮箱，而且从不会偷懒。

This form of acceleration has several kinds of consequences, not to say side-effects. The advantage, and purpose, inherent in email is that it facilitates the act of contacting others. In comparison with the telephone, it is also said that it is more tactful, since sending an email does not interrupt and divert people from whatever it is that they are doing. On the other hand, by the very same token, email precludes absence: one can always be reached; one is never simply out to lunch.

过去，当我们还在使用枯树作为通信的原材料时，就已经在信息科技的物质基础中嵌入了一种迟钝性，能够抑制那些不合时宜的纠缠。从不同的角度来看，技术本身阻碍了对不必要的文字的过滤，使写信成了十分费劲的差事。写信本身很耗时间，而且写好之后还要折叠并装入信封，寄信人需要在信封正面写上收信人的姓名与地址，并在右上角贴上邮票，最后还要找到邮筒才能投寄出去。此外，邮局分发信件时还有一些奇怪的特征；比如，今天当地报纸的头版头条新闻就是《邮寄一封信用了 6 天！》电子邮件根本没有这些限制。因此，我们很多人都宁愿使用电子邮件，而不愿意再用过去经常使用的纸质信件。电子邮件在发送方看来是一种祝福，但到了接收方就有可能成了一种诅咒。

In the old days, when we were still using dead trees for most of our correspondence, there was an inbuilt inertia in the material base of the information technology that inhibited untimely pestering.Put differently, the technology itself offered resistance which made the work of writing a letter sufficiently laborious to filter out many unnecessary letters. The writing itself took time, the sheet had to be folded and put into an envelope, one had to write the name and address of sender and addressee on it, glue a stamp in the upper right-hand corner and find a mailbox. Add to this the inherently erratic nature of postal distribution; today's local newspaper runs a front-page headline which reads: "Express letter took six days!" These limitations do not affect E-mail. For that reason, most of us send more e-letters than we used to send cellulose letters. E-mail is a blessing for the sender, but can be hell for the recipient.

速度影响了风格与语法。很多人不会对电子邮件进行校勘。他们在信件开头会用一种非正式且不明朗的词汇"Hi"，甚至对陌生人也是如此，或者干脆没有任何的问候语。（这里面存在很大的文化差异。有一天，我收到了一个日本籍学生的邮件，他在信件中说由于"未经许可"就写信给我，因而非常严肃地向我道歉。）在电子邮件中，经常会有不完整的语句和错误的语法。以这种方法来分析，电子邮件应该介于书面语与口语之间。但是如果它几乎完全代替旧式信件,文化在整体上就会出现亏损。无论在数量上取得了多少,最终都会失去质量。

Speed influences style and syntax. Many do not proofread their electronic correspondence. They start their letters, even to strangers, with an noncommittal, informal "Hi!" or without any initial greeting whatsoever. (There are cultural differences here. The other day, I got an e-letter from a Japanese student, who solemnly apologised for writing to me "without permission".) The letters are often littered with half-baked sentences and bad grammar. Viewed in this way, E-mail can be located somewhere between the written and the oral, but if it more or less entirely replaces the old-fashioned letter, the culture as a whole will end with a deficit; it will have lost in quality whatever it has gained in quantity.

速度对标准的时间也会产生不利的影响。它有可能填平所有的差异。过去,一封回信要寄到初始的发信人那里,需要一周到一个月的时间。这是雷打不动的事情。所以,当一个人把信投入邮筒后,他可以返回来工作,安静地坐下来,并继续从事原来正在做的事情。不过,这个时代已经一去不复返了。现在我们发送的邮件,可以在几小时之内得到回复,而且一天之内还可能会两次发送同样的信息。原因是发件人没有收到回信,会认为第一次邮件没有送达,因而会第二次发送邮件。

Speed also affects slow time adversely. It threatens to fill all the gaps. In the old days, a reply to a letter could take anything from a week to a month to reach the original sender. Nothing abnormal about that. So when one had put the envelope in the mailbox, one could return to work, sit down quietly and continue doing whatever one was doing for quite a while. This era is gone. Nowadays, we are expected to respond within hours, and, not infrequently, the same message is sent twice, perhaps with an interval of a day or less. The writer obviously believes one did not receive it the first time, since one has not yet replied.

这并不意味着夏令时具有单方面的攻击力。速度在正常范围内，可以表现卓越。但它具有传染性，可能带来严重的副作用。除非我们理解了速度的运作机制和增减的内容，否则我们会失去保持必要迟缓的机会。

This is not meant as a one-sided attack on fast time. Speed is excellent where it belongs. But it is contagious, and it has possibly serious side-effects. Unless we understand how speed functions, what it adds and what it removes, we are deprived of the opportunity to retain slowness where it is necessary.

在我们生活的时代，香烟代替了烟斗，玉米片替代了麦片粥，电子邮件正在取代纸质信件，两分钟的新闻影片在新闻界是最热的产品。报纸的文章越来越短，电影镜头的切换更加频繁。按照我们所收邮件的数量，我们每个人回复电子邮件所用的时间，正在成比例地减少。音乐电视引入了不断变化的风格，而且永不停止，这已经成了时代潮流的精确写照。速度是一剂毒药：我们在快进键探索电影中观察自己，公众对于缓慢的运动日益失去兴趣，这相当令人恐惧。就我个人的体会，滑冰与越野滑雪遭遇了严重的问题，很难招募新人，也没有观众的欢呼；观众的注意力转移到了更具爆发性的运动，比如冰球和高山滑翔；当我们在街上行走或等候交通信号灯变化时，我们会使用移动电话来填补间隙；当电车晚点 5 分钟时，我们会谴责市政运输管理部门。过了这么多年，我们还在等待链接更快的计算机与互联网。总之，现在一切正在日益加速变化。

We live in an era when the cigarette has replaced the pipe, cornflakes have replaced porridge, email is replacing paper-based correspondence, and the 2-minute newsreel is one of the hottest products in the media field. The newspaper articles become shorter, the transitions in films more frequent, and the time each of us spends responding to an electronic letter is reduced in proportion to the number of e-letters we receive. The restless and shifting style of communication that was introduced with

MTV has become an accurate image of the spirit of the age. Speed is an addictive drug: horrified, we watch ourselves groping for the fast-forward button in the cinema, the public loses interest in slow-moving sports; in my part of the world, ice skating and cross-country skiing have serious problems of recruitment and audience appeal, as people switch to more explosive sports such as ice hockey and downhill; we fill the slow gaps by talking in mobile phones when walking down a street or waiting for a traffic light to change; we damn the municipal transport authority when the tram is 5 minutes late, and we are still, after all these years, waiting for computers and Internet connections that are sufficiently fast. Everything moves faster now.

要速度，越简单越好

速度导致事情的简化。这一点需要我们注意。在 19 世纪 40 年代以前，人们需要请画师为自己画好一幅像，以便留给自己的子孙后裔。王公贵族与平民百姓一样，都要在画师面前静静地坐上很长一段时间。之后出现了笨重的照相技术——银版照相，由于曝光时间需要近一个小时，因此不太适合描绘小孩、动物和其他移动的物体。然后出现了我们知道的照相技术——令人难以置信的是这种形式几乎一直没有变化，直到数字技术取代普通的摄像术之前。由于凡尔纳发明的暗房、红灯、化学冲洗和晾干的技术一直保留下来，这项技术基本没有多大改变。多年来，人们为了去照相馆拍照需要事先化妆；在市镇上，装饰用品商店出于战略考虑，往往紧挨着照相馆的大门；人们拍完照片之后，还要等候一段时间才能看到结果。后来，艺术照开始普及，作为一家之主的父亲（有时包括母亲），只要碰到合适的机会，就会拍上一张快照，胶卷曝光后几天之内就可以变成照片。二战之后，波拉一步照相机（波拉一步照相机，一种在拍照后立即可以冲洗的照相机，也译作宝丽来照相机或波拉罗伊德照相机。——编者）问世，它能立即显示照片；其后，承诺一小时之内就可取相片的联营企业正式成立。在书写时代，20 世纪 90 年代前期数字拍摄技术开始问世，并最终成为主流产品。从想法到实际影像所需的时间，从数周逐步减少到零。

Speed Leads To Simplification

One might also put it like this. Before the 1840s, one had to contact a portrait painter to have one's face saved for posterity. Royalty and commoners alike had to sit for ages in front of the painter. Then came the first, cumbersome photographic technology, the daguerreotype, which certainly was unsuitable for depictions of children, animals and other moving targets, since the time of exposure could last as long as an hour. Then came photography as we know it incredibly, it has survived almost unchanged in form until it is only now about to be replaced by digital technology. ("Incredibly" because there has always been at least for me more than a hint of Jules Verne about the darkrooms with their red lights, chemical baths and drying lines.) But for many years, people dressed up in order to go to the photographers; in some towns, the outfitters were strategically located next door to the photographer; and afterwards, one waited a good while to see the result. Then the art of photography was democratised, and family fathers (and mothers) could take their "snapshots" whenever it suited them, and exposed films became pictures in a matter of days. After the Second World War, the Polaroid camera was introduced, which automatically developed pictures in a minute; and, somewhat later, the first chains that promised to develop your film in an hour were established. At the time of writing, digital photography, launched in the secondhalf of the 1990s, is finally making major inroads. The time taken to get from idea to image has gradually been reduced from several weeks to zero.

如果孤立地看，我们没有什么理由去担心这些变化。但是，加速与高度压缩几乎无处不在，而且往往会产生意想不到的后果。其中，仿效得比较好的是派森的"竞赛"，其赢者是成功在一分钟内概括普鲁斯特的《追忆似水年华》的人。袖珍杂志《读者文摘》擅长出版一些经过删减与压缩的文章，从这种意义上来讲，它已经领先于 1922 年初次面世的时代。1938 年以来，这本杂志总发行量达到 2800 万册，而且已经出版了系列图书。《读者文摘》一直忠于杂志的理念，对现有书籍进行彻底的压缩，从格里森姆（美国知名畅销小说作家，他的一系列创作富含法庭法律内容的畅销犯罪小说为他赢得了巨大的声誉和财富。——编者）的著作到托尔斯泰的《战争与和平》，都是按照此种方式处理。这些文学作品都被整合到快进的按钮中，为满足信息丰富而鲜有慢节奏的时代，它们不得不作出调整。一些作家甚至声称他们喜欢自己的作品被压缩，并且允许《读者文摘》在市场营销中使用他们的头像。

Seen in isolation, there is little cause to worry about these changes. But acceleration and compression are omnipresent, frequently with unintended consequences. One of the better parodies is Monty Python's "competition" where the winner is the person who best succeeds in summarising Proust's A la recherche du temps perdu in 1 minute. （"And the winner is ... the girl with the biggest tits!"）Reader's Digest, that pocket-sized magazine which specialises in publishing abridged and simplified versions of texts, was in this sense ahead of its time when it was launched in 1922. Since 1938, the magazine, which has a total global circulation of 28 million, has published its own book series. It consists, true to the ideology of the magazine, of radically shortened versions of existing books, ranging from John Grisham's latest blockbuster to Tolstoy's War and Peace. This is literature with an integrated fast forward button, tailored for an era with too much information and too little slow time. Some authors even claim that they enjoy these abridged versions of their own books, and allow the Reader's Digest to use their faces in its marketing programme.

要速度，流水作业是必须

速度产生了流水作业线的效果。1851 年，在伦敦水晶宫举行的首届世界博览会上，工业产品琳琅满目，花样繁多，坚持传统手工艺的人士认为工业品质量很差。他们强调产品质量需要时间和高度发展的个人技术，因此，工业化大生产的形式意味着产品质量的大众化。

Speed Creates Assembly Line Effects

Already at the first World Exhibition at Crystal Palace in London in 1851, where industrially produced goods were displayed in dazzling quantity and variation, the defenders of the traditional crafts objected that industrial goods were inferior. Quality requires time and highly developed personal skills, they argued, implying that the industrial form of mass production （which was still in its infancy） meant a vulgarisation of quality.

这种态度并不罕见；在很多地方都能遇到持这种态度的人，而且他们出于各种动机不断提升这种态度。精英们总是想方设法阻止象征自己身份的符号被泛化。与传统手工艺品相比，工业制品日益便宜，而且越来越容易被普通百姓获得。因此，社会上有些团体几乎会预先声明，由于他们是普通人所以低人一等。从不同角度来看，不管是以环境问题为出发点，还是考虑产品的使用寿命，只要不适用"质量"这个模糊的分类，人们都可以得到同样的结论（也就是对工业制品持批判的态度）。一则关于英美关系的大众轶事与草坪有关。一位没有耐心的美国人问道："我们怎样才能获得一块与你的一样漂亮的草坪呢？"英国人回答说："从四百年前开始就可以了。"许多产品的制造速度越来越快，效率也越来越高，但质量并不一定会变差。塑料水桶与汽车就是两个实例。其他劳动密集型产品发展势头也不错，不仅耐用，而且手感也好。特别值得一提的是缝纫业，对我而言，尤其注重的是另一类人特制的衣服。至于葡萄酒与法国白兰地，生产周期延长可以改善品质，这与许多其他的食物一样，比如啤酒、奶酪和一些肉制品。

This attitude is far from uncommon; it can be encountered in many areas and can also be promoted with a variety of motivations. Elites have always tried to prevent the symbols of their elite status from being democratised. Industrially produced goods are cheaper and more accessible for common people than crafts were; for this very reason, there are groups in society that are virtually preprogrammed to claim that they are inferior merely because they are common. From a different perspective, one may reach the same conclusion （that is, a critical attitude to fast industrial production ofgoods） with environmental concerns as a starting-point, or by referring to the lifespan of products or that rather vaguer category called "quality". A common anecdote about the relationship between the USA and Great Britain is the one about lawns. "How should we go about getting lawns as nice as the ones you have?" asks the impatient American. The Englishman answers, "Start 400 years ago." Many products can be made faster and more efficiently without a necessary deterioration in quality. Plastic buckets and cars may be two examples. Other products are rather better off with labourintensive, slow and thoughtful production they last longer, taste better, sound better or whatever. There is something special about tailor-made clothing, especially adapted to me by another human being. With wine and cognac, slow maturation leads to improved quality, as is the case with many other foodstuffs, including beer,cheese and some kinds of meat.

　　食物的烹饪时间与其质量(比如口感与营养价值)没有必然的联系。有些菜肴需要文火慢炖几个小时,才有特别的味道或有益健康。例如,英国人炖汤与煮羊肉,还有挪威人周日午餐的菜肴,都是按照这样的方式。同样,有些人认为生牡蛎拌上几滴柠檬精油,是世界一流的烹调方式。一般而言,常见数量的食物在烹调时,质量对于慢速的时间要求比较严格。就拿家禽来说,制作肉制品的烘烤机,需要按照汽车生产的工业管理原则来制造,所需平均时间约为一个月。在挪威,为了满足大众对营养价值的追求,1 只毛重 1100 克的家禽,经过宰杀、剔除内脏和烘烤(用盐和辣椒粉调味)等一系列的程序,恰好要用一个月的时间。几年前,人们对奥斯陆一个小镇上的家禽情有独钟,因为那里的人把小鸡自然放养,使得鸡肉的脂肪含量充足，而且汁肥味美。他们开店加工本地出产的家禽，关键在于其烘烤食物的时间达到了慢速制作的时间的两倍。这样，当地的烤鸡价格翻了一番，但与我们习以为常的工业生产烤鸡相比，其口味的确迥然不同。

There is no necessary connection between the duration of the act of cooking and quality （meaning good taste or nutritional value）in food. There are dishes that must simmer for hours before completion without thereby becoming particularly tasty or wholesome; one might think of, for example, certain English stews and a particularly nasty concoction of boiled mutton and cabbage that used to be a common Sunday dinner in Norway. Similarly, some hold the view that raw oysters with a drop of lemon （cooking time = zero）are a world-class culinary treat. Still, as a general rule, quality requires slow time in generous quantities with respect to food. Take poultry as a example. An average broiler in a country which has turned the production of meat into an industrial discipline on a par with car manufacturing, lives on an average a month. In my native country, the broiler will have been fed with growth-promoting nutrients for exactly a month when it reaches a gross weight of 1,100 grams, at which point it is decapitated, plucked and eventually grilled （always seasoned with the same mixture of salt and paprika powder）before being presented to the consumer. A few years ago, some people near a small town in the Oslo area discovered that if they allowed the chickens to lead more normal lives, their fat reserves were more amply developed and the meat, as a result, was juicier and tastier. They set up shop and began to produce chickens that were given regular food and, crucially, were allowed to live twice as long as the standard broiler. The result was a chicken that cost more than twice as much as usual, but which was also endowed with a radically different taste from the grilled industrial broilers most of us had grown up with.

20 世纪 90 年代中期，北美的百威啤酒公司想收购捷克的百威啤酒厂，这个例子同样可以说明前面的道理。收购动机很容易理解：捷克的啤酒厂在欧洲中部地区规模很大,但与美国的百威啤酒公司相比,它只是一个小矮人了,但它拥有在全欧洲署名"百威"商标的权力。因此,没有收购之前,美国百威啤酒公司在欧洲销售时,只能贴"麦芽"的商标。现在,两种品牌的啤酒放在一起,结束了各自用规模衡量复杂程度的历史。美国的百威啤酒看起来像尿液,闻起来有一股碳酸的气味,喝起来有一丝苦味。捷克的百威啤酒则是金黄色,与捷克其他的淡啤酒一样,泡沫丰富且具有芳香气味,但很快它就将被归入全球第一啤酒商的门下(全世界总共只有四个国家的啤酒属于该行列,捷克是其中之一。)。美国百威啤酒公司虽然慷慨大方,但作为买家必须低调。捷克啤酒厂认为如果被并购到美国百威啤酒公司,就要引入美国的生产方法,那么啤酒的质量就会出现灾难性的下降。若要制作出好的啤酒,生产规模与速度无法协调一致。因此,时至今日,全球市场依然存在两种截然不同的百威啤酒—— 一种是快速生产出来的啤酒,适合于那些急于解渴的人饮用;另一种是慢速制作出来的啤酒,室温下就能储存,需要慢慢品尝才够味。

A similar example on a larger scale concerns the North American Budweiser company's attempt to buy the Czech Budweiser brewery in the mid-1990s. The motivation for the takeover bid was easy enough to understand: the Czech brewery, which was large in a Central European context but a dwarf compared to the American beer factories, possessed the rights to the name Budweiser all over Europe. For this reason, the American product had to be sold under the label "Bud" in Europe. Now, the two beers can be placed near either end on a scale measuring complexity in beer. US Budweiser looks like urine and tastes of carbonic acid with a tinge of bitterness added. The Czech namesake (also known as Budvar) is as golden, rich and aromatic as other Czech lagers, meaning that it belongs to the global premier division of beers. (Only about four countries count in the world league of beer; the Czech Republic is one of them.) Despite a generous offer, the American would-be buyers were turned down. The Czechs immediately saw that the production methods that would be introduced if they were to become part of the global Budweiser empire would entail a disastrous decline in quality. The demands for volume and speed were impossible to reconcile with a desire to make good beer. For that reason, there exists to this day two radically different Budweiser beers in the global market a fast one, which is fine for quenching one's thirst in a hurry, and a slow one, which should be imbibed in quiet contemplation, and which can safely be served at room temperature.

有时候，获得的速度与辅助功能远大于损耗，有时候感觉不到有何损失。例如，有一群过分强调获取的人，总是梦想获得早上额外的 10 分钟，甚至用一碗粥代替谷类食物作为早餐。各种食物都有即拆式的小包装，从蒸粗麦粉、墨西哥卷饼、地中海番茄酱到调味汁，都让忙碌工作的人有机会准备可口的饭菜，而且吃起来味道纯正。由于人们很少能有机会用几小时去做一顿大餐，若是没有其他选择，这个概念也不失为一个好主意。如果速度与成本是人们选择产品的主要标准，就会使文化整体丰富性与复杂性产生净损耗。如果大家都不再区分廉价盒装红酒与波尔多葡萄酒之间的差异，不认为新研磨的咖啡豆与雀巢咖啡粉不同，或者感觉不到马勒［马勒（1860—1911 年），杰出的奥地利作曲家及指挥家。——编者］的交响乐比流行音乐更具深度与丰满度，那么文化在整体上就会陷入穷困潦倒的境地。但是，清教徒的习俗毕竟只属于清教徒本身。当我乘坐飞机旅行时，往往很乐意喝上一杯速溶咖啡，尽管我总对这种产品持很深的怀疑态度。事实上，的确没有其他咖啡可供我选择。

Sometimes, the gains of speed and accessibility are greater than the losses, and sometimes the loss is imperceptible. It cannot, for example, be said for certain that there are droves of over-stressed people around who dream of an extra 10 minutes in the morning in order to replace their breakfast cereal with a bowl of porridge. Instant packets of various foodstuffs, from couscous and taco shells to Mediterranean pasta sauces or, for that matter, sauce bé arnaisc, give busy people the opportunity to prepare tasty meals that are nearly the real thing. If the alternative is nothing, because one rarely has the opportunity to spend hours cooking, this concept is far from being a bad idea. If speed and cost were to become the main criteria for choice of products, however, the result would be a net loss of richness and complexity in the culture as a whole. If enough of us stop tasting/smelling the difference between a cheap box wine and a vintage Bordeaux, cease to know that newly ground coffee beansgive an entirely different result from the powder surrogate offered by Nestlé , fail to hear that Mahler's symphonies have a greater depth and richness than the latest pop songs, then the culture as a whole will have been impoverished. But puritanism is only for Puritans. Whenever I travel by air, I take great pleasure in drinking instant coffee although this is a product I normally regard with deep scepticism. The alternative is no coffee.

然而,速度也有自身的成本,有时候(仔细思考一下,信息时代常常如此)除了快速的类型,似乎没有什么最好的选择了。比如说,如果你有 1 个小时的时间可以自由支配,就可以听古典音乐或未删节的交响乐,也可以欣赏 12 首不同风格的 5 分钟浓缩版的交响乐,要做出选择并不会很难。这个实例也不荒诞。许多畅销的经典著作,往往是"摘要"或"集锦"的形式,是一个个没有背景的小片段。当然,这没有某些人所认为的那样新颖。在两次世界大战期间,奥涅格写了一首《圣诞大合唱》,就是把大家熟悉的圣诞歌曲加工成了一锅大杂烩。我们已经听过很多了,时间是稀缺的资源。而且,作曲家与听众都急于求成。

But speed has its costs, and sometimes （to think of it, quite often in the information age）, nothing can be the best alternative to an instant version. If, say, you have an hour at your disposal for listening to classical music, and the alternatives are one full-length symphony and twelve five-minute summaries of various symphonies, the choice ought not to be difficult. The example is notabsurd. Many of the bestselling classical records are "summaries" or "highlights". Decontextualised snippets. And this is not as new as some might believe. In the inter-war years, Arthur Honegger composed his Christmas Cantata, where he cooked up a potpourri of familiar Christmas songs. Much has been heard before, and time is scarce. Composer and listener alike are anxious to hurry on.

速度会使精确度遭受损失

在古代，当人们与外部世界交往时，总是习惯采用书信的形式，往往需要数天或几周的时间。书信往来的节奏非常缓慢，但却体贴人心。一些名人总会在出版的著作中收录那些很好的信件——其中最经典的是马克思与恩格斯的书信来往。王尔德最得意的著作《狱中书》实际上也是一封书信。他用了两个月的时间写成该书，开篇就说："亲爱的波西，在漫长的等待徒劳无获之后，我决定给你写上一封信。"当今时代，要是名人将自己的电子邮件摘选出版，可以想象他一定是疯了，但我也可能是想错了。

Speed Leads To a Loss Of Precision

In the real old days, when contact with the outside world tended to be in the form of letters, correspondence took days or weeks. The rhythm of corresponding was slow and thoughtful. Illustrious individuals had their best letters collected in published works one of our best sources to Marx's thought is his correspondence with Engels. Oscar Wilde's best essay, "De Profundis", was actually a letter. It took Wilde two months to complete, and begins: "Dear Bosie, After a long and fruitless waiting I have determined to write to you myself ...". It is hard to believe that anyone would be crazy enough to publish the "selected email" of a famous man or woman living today, but, naturally, I may be proven wrong.

虽然通信交往中也会有马虎草率，但是加速带来的后果更严重。一般来说，当要求一个人立刻行动时，他做的事情往往在头脑中已经出现。可以说，任何人怒气冲冲地按下红色键或终止关系后，都知道接下来的第二件或第三件事情已得到过很多的提醒。维利里奥区分了加速与不稳定的直接关系。思考决策、讨论并获得长远打算的时间越短，产生灾难性失误的风险就越大。范围变化得越快，缓慢选择的

可行性就越小。对其他方面,我也存有一种预警性的恐惧。媒体、新闻报道、社会与
文化变迁方面的加速度,产生的政治实践缺乏思想意识,媒体在其中掌握了主动
权,因此,社会没有长远的思考和清楚的模式。像海德尔这样的民粹主义者,以及
布莱尔之类的政治家,都有这方面的趋势。缓慢的节奏已经日益淡出人们的视野。

The less slow time that remains to think decisions through, discuss and acquire a
distanced overview, the greater is the risk for disastrous errors. The faster the territory
changes, the less viable are the slow options. I shall leave apocalyptic fears to others.
It is serious enough that acceleration in the media, in news coverage, social
transformations and cultural changes, have resulted in a political practice virtually
devoid of ideology, more dominated by media initiatives than by long-term thinking
and clear models for society. Both populist types like Jörg Haider and designer
politicians like Tony Blair are symptomatic of this trend. The slow ones are going out
of business.

据说 1950 年夏天的某一天, 瑞典传奇首相尔兰德正在摆弄一台磁带录音机
时,从广播节目中得知朝鲜战争爆发。这场战争并非未被预料到,但是很多人担心
它最终会导致第三次世界大战。那么,尔兰德做了什么呢? 他继续摆弄他的收音
机,并通过听磁带记录的战争新闻是否响亮,来测试麦克风的性能。他一个人待在
房间里。尽管尔兰德对于世界引人瞩目的大事反应迟缓,却没有人会批评他优柔
寡断或者未立刻行动。

Sloppiness and superficiality in correspondence notwithstanding, there are more
serious consequences of acceleration. As a general rule, when one is required to act
immediately, one does the first thing that comes to mind. （Anyone who has ever, say,
pressed the red button or terminated a relationship in anger knows that the second or
third thing often has a lot to recommend it.）Paul Virilio identifies a direct connection
between acceleration and uncertainty.

20 世纪 50 年代是一个相对加速发展的十年，事实上，尔兰德对战争的反应被一位记者打断了，他想知道尔兰德当时正在做什么事情。但是，现今一切事物都在日益变快。人们不得不以光速行动，否则就会被下手更快的人挤掉。在全球金融、政治与销售领域，这个原则同样有效。

It is said about the legendary Swedish prime minister Tage Erlander that, one summer day in 1950, he was playing with a tape recorder when he heard on the radio that war had broken out in Korea. The war was not unanticipated, and many feared that it might eventually lead to a Third World War. What did Erlander do? He continued to play with his gadget, testing its microphone by thinking aloud about the war on tape. He was alone in the room. In spite of this slow reaction to a dramatic world event, nobody thought of criticising Erlander for indecision or failing to act immediately.

2000 年冬季，奥地利的一个执政党不乐意与政府合作，在不到 24 个小时之内，所有的欧盟国家就对其执行制裁。如果时间可以跑得更慢一些，有一半的欧盟国家可能会重新考虑制裁的决议，或许还有其他更合适的手段。假如时间的脚步可以再减缓一点，一开始海德尔就可能不会掌权。此外，全球金融市场的多米诺骨牌效应，正在以惊人的速度推进——香港金融界引发的涟漪即刻扩展到了新加坡，在人们尚未来得及眨眼之前，就已经波及伦敦和洛杉矶。

以上只是专横的时间的几个例子。

Even the 1950s was a fairly accelerated decade, and Erlander was, as a matter of fact, interrupted in his reflections by a journalist who wondered what he was going to do. But today everything moves much faster. Decisions have to be taken at the speed of light, otherwise, one is squeezed out by those who act faster. This principle is as valid in the global financial market as in politics or marketing. Since Haider has already been mentioned: it took the governments of all EU states less than 24 hours to implement sanctions against Austria when, in the winter of 2000, a party with an unpleasant smell became a partner in a government coalition there. Suppose time had moved only a bit more slowly: in that case, half the EU governments would presumably have had second thoughts about the sanctions, realising that other means would be more appropriate. （And suppose time had moved even more slowly: in that case, Haider would probably never have been in power in the first place.）The domino effects in the global financial markets, further, now take place at incredible speeds a ripple in Hong Kong reverberates immediately in Singapore, spreading repercussions to LA and London literally before anyone has the time to raise an eyebrow.

These are just some examples of the tyranny of the moment.

我们正在处理的现象远不止"媒体社会"，也非几十年来人们已经耳熟能详的陈词滥调。但是，大众媒体——尤其是电台与广播——是重要的潮流引导者，也是与速度有关的病毒携带者。今天纸张的概念，既是一种象征，也是现代性的标记之一。但是，假如纸张没有流通，那么就没有多大价值。18世纪晚期，报纸发生了重大变化，人们开始使用时钟来监控生产劳动。同一时期，法国与美国的工业改革，把个人自由的理念引入产业革命，并开始改变劳动力。当前有一大批吹毛求疵的人，尤其是在大城市，他们迫切需要赶上时代的潮流。因此。现在的日报都是昙花一现，其寿命仅仅只有一天。

We are dealing with a phenomenon which is much more encompassing than "media society", a cliché that has been around for decades already. But it must also be said that the mass media especially radio and television are important trendsetters and virus carriers concerning speed. Now, journalism has always been a profession characterised by speed. The notion of today's paper is both a symbol and a sign of modernity. It is worth nothing if it is not current. Typically, the newspapers had their major breakthrough in the late eighteenth century, at the same time that clocks began to be used to monitor work; which was also the same period that the French and American Revolutions introduced their individualistic ideals of freedom and the Industrial Revolution began to transform labour. There was now a critical mass of people, especially in the major cities, who felt an acute need to keep up to date with contemporary events. Then, as now, a newspaper was ephemeral. Its lifespan was exactly one day.

其他媒体也在加速变化。电台与报纸任何时候都可以更新内容，其他媒体也可以在数年之内发生突变，比如用电子出版物代替报纸。（在这个领域内，科技变化如此之快，以至于没人能够作出精确的预测，但是值得注意的是，在 2000 年年底，一种前景被人看好的"原型"，有点类似于昔日通俗的小报，却被用户作为电子墨水经常使用。）

Other media are faster. Radio and television can update their content any time, and this is also the case with the media which will probably, within a few years, replace the newspapers, namely electronic publications based on text. (In this field, technological change happens so fast that there is little point in attempting to make accurate predictions, but it is worth noticing that a "promising prototype" in late 2000 had a passing similarity to a tabloid newspaper, but it was being updated as frequently as the user wished with "electronic ink".)

谈论互联网上报纸的生命周期似乎意义不大：任何项目都只在它被更新替换之前存在。这些信息更新得越快，电子报纸的声誉就越好，点击率就越高，赞助商就会越多。在挪威，一流电子报刊的读者——顺便说一下，这个报纸压根就没有纸质版——浏览报纸的平均时间是 45 秒钟。一些新上瘾者会一天数次浏览电子报纸，尤其是在发生重大事件（比如内战、人质危机和足球锦标赛等）时。这些媒体给人灌输一种新的节奏和不安定的情绪——尤其重要的是——新的新闻消费惯例。在挪威的工会与雇主组织进行年度谈判期间，最初作为威胁手段的罢工最终往往会成为现实,只是规模有大有小而已。在这些冗长的谈判期间,我曾经深夜还守候在电脑面前,因为次日一大早就要去另一座城市开会。如果谈判破裂,斯堪的纳维亚航空公司就要罢工,那我的出行计划就会受到明显的影响。因此,我要定期浏览网页报纸,以便了解最新的动态。到了就寝时间,所有的电子报纸都说双方仍未达成协议,谈判还得继续,那些饥渴交加的谈判者已经订了比萨。好啊! 不过这严重干扰了我整晚的工作。如果没有电子报纸,我就要等到第二天早上才可以知道谈判的情况(当然那次压根就没有发生罢工事件),事情也就可能会好得多。

It makes little sense to talk about the lifespan of an Internet newspaper: any item survives only until the staff have managed to update or replace it. The faster they are updated, the better their reputation, the more hits they get, and the more sponsorship. An average reader of the leading electronic newspaper in Norway the only newspaper, incidentally, that does not have a paper version spends 45 seconds browsing the paper. News addicts go there several times a day, especially during dramatic events (civil wars, hostage dramas, football championships...). This kind of media instils a new rhythm and a new restlessness, and importantly new routines in the consumption of news. During the annual negotiations between the trade unions and the employers' organisation, strikes are a threat which often become a reality on a small or large scale in Norway. Once I sat at my computer late at night during these lengthy negotiations, and the next morning I was due to fly to another city for a conference. If the negotiations broke down, SAS personnel would goon strike, with obvious consequences for my immediate plans. I therefore checked the Internet newspapers regularly in order to follow the latest developments. As bedtime approached, all the main electronic newspapers informed me that agreement was still not reached, that the negotiations continued, and that the tired and hungry negotiators had ordered pizza. Fine, but my evening of work had been seriously disrupted. If the electronic newspapers had not existed, the paper I delivered the next day (for there was no strike after all) might have been better.

2000 年，网络公司的领导者在斯堪的纳维亚的记者中制造了一个小小的风波，后者擅自质疑互联网报纸的资料来源及其对质量的控制。她的观点认为，网络记者工作节奏太快，几乎没有时间去检查新闻的来源。因此，这种负担就转给了读者，以便适合信息民主的美好新世界。

The leader of an Internet company created a minor stir among Scandinavian journalists in 2000 when she took the liberty of thinking aloud about quality control and source use in Internet journalism. Her view was that Internet journalists had to work so fast that they rarely had time to check their sources. Therefore, this burden was transferred to the reader, as befits the brave new world of informational democracy.

当人们在信息之路上遭遇垃圾时，很难决定是该大哭还是该冷笑了之。为了揭露北大西洋公约组织种族灭绝的阴谋，记者是否要前往科索沃并准备自掘坟墓呢？因为我对当地网站是否详细报道辣妹维多利亚最近的行踪还存有疑虑，所以我是否要给维多利亚本人挂个私人电话询问呢？我是否需要看完国家队沉闷的足球赛，才能证实每个人都注意到的事实——国家媒体无法提供一种超脱的描述？

When one comes across rubbish of this calibre, it is difficult to know whether to burst into tears or cynical laughter. Does she really mean that I should travel to Kosovo and start digging up graves in order to expose NATO lies about the extent of genocide? Should I personally phone Victoria Beckham to ask her about her recent whereabouts, since I harbour a vague suspicion that my local web site might not have got all the details right? And do I really have to watch all the unspeakably depressing football games of my national team, just to get a confirmation of a fact everyone is aware of, namely that the national media are unable to offer a detached description of them?

在某种意义上说,答案是肯定的,而且现实可以终止任何最初的欢愉。我的一个朋友原来服务于国家一流的互联网报社,后来他离职的主要原因就在于(当然,可能也有薪酬较低和职业理想等原因):每个人都需要始终盯着对手,想方设法让自己的新闻尽可能快地出版。因为,随时都可以修正错误之处,没有需要担心其他事情。

In a sense, the answer is yes, and this is where reality calls a halt to any initial merriness. A friend who used to work for the leading national Internet newspaper says that his main reason for leaving the job (for another, less glamorous and less well-paid position) was exactly this: the only point was to beat the others, to have your news published as fast as possible. Any corrections could be added any time, so don't worry.

拉莫内是一位优秀的主编,负责的月刊《法国外交世界报》总能按期出版。他在一本著作《专横的通讯》中,表达了自己对新闻业加速发展后果的看法,其流露的忧虑态度超过了幽默风趣的成分。他在这本著作的篇首提出,以前的人很少能够获得丰富的资讯,但并不意味着他们消息不灵通。其中一个重要原因是速度,尽管拉莫内也考虑到了所有权与自我审查权。速度,连同一定时间内提供的信息量的增长,导致了彼此竞争的加剧和编辑处理工作的弱化。他列举了著名记者卡普辛基的事例,卡普新基认为编辑人员不能再过分关心故事的真实性,而应该判断故事的是非曲直是否能引起读者的兴趣。从这方面来说,故事是否具有更宽泛的社会关联度,已经不再是判断的一个标准了。很典型的例子是拉莫内在1999年出版的著作写到的全球最大的新闻,包括戴安娜王妃的逝世以及克林顿总统与莱温斯基的绯闻。拉莫内认为,在这些热点新闻中,没有复杂性的生存空间(当然必须提一下吉卜林,他在100年前就谈到过美国人对速度的嗜好)。在新闻记者随意处理的内容中,填满了这种好与坏的简单对比,而其消费群体的数量正日益下降。因此,对卢旺达内战很难给出合适的报道,但是在一些欧洲国家里,对于平民政治的兴趣却与日俱增，这种政治活动不仅口号简单，而且容易操作。

Ignacio Ramonet is chief editor of the excellent, and not least slow, monthly Le Monde Diplomatique. In his book La Tyrannie de la communication, he is inclined towards a more worried than humorous attitude to the consequences of increased speed in journalism. At the outset, he states that never before have people had access to more information, but this does not mean that they have also become better informed. One important cause is speed, although Ramonet also looks at ownership and self-censorship. Speed, combined with increased quantities of information on offer at any given moment, leads both to heightened competition and weakened editorial treatment. He quotes the justly famous journalist Ryszard Kapú scinski, who claims that editors no longer fuss over the "credibility" of a story, but rather judge its merits on whether or not it is sufficiently "interesting". That a story should have a wider societal relevance is not a criterion in this regard, and characteristically, the greatest global news stories in the couple of years preceding Ramonet's book (published in 1999) were the death of Princess Diana and the affair between Bill Clinton and Monica Lewinsky. Ramonet shows that there is no space for complexity in this overheated brand of journalism. (Kipling, it must in all fairness be added, said this a hundred years earlier, referring to the American penchant for speed.) A simple good/bad contrast is all that can be crammed into the decreasing number of consumer seconds journalists have at their disposal. This is a main reason why it was so difficult to give the civil war in Rwanda proper coverage, but it also sheds interesting light on the rise of populist politics in several European countries, with their simple slogans and easy fixes.

对于新闻流通速度而言，接收端时间的稀缺可能是参数之一，但近十年以来，几乎没有任何其他职业(政治家除外)在赢得公众尊重方面能有类似的下滑，这是一种有趣的逻辑。在美国、英国、法国和斯堪的纳维亚半岛，民意测验表明，公众已经不信任新闻记者。数十年前,拉莫内认为,新闻记者需要个人正直、勇敢和无私地追求真理,类似超人、蜘蛛侠和丁丁这样的卡通英雄人物。然而,这些东西在今天已经行不通了。当新闻报道的标准变为立刻呼吁民众和快速出版时,过去的方程式"信息 = 自由 = 民主",就已经很难成立了。

Although the scarcity of time at the receiving end may be an argument for the increased speed of news turnover, there is an interesting dialectic here in that hardly any other profession （apart from politicians）has suffered a similar decline in public esteem in the last couple of decades. In the USA, in Britain, France and Scandinavia, journalists are distrusted by a majority of the people questioned by pollsters. A few decades ago, Ramonet muses, journalism was a profession associated with personal integrity, courage and selfless search for truth; cartoon heroes like Superman（Clark Kent）, Spiderman （Peter Parker）and Tintin are all journalists by profession. This would not have been viable today. The Enlightenment equation information = freedom = democracy is difficult to uphold when the criteria for journalistic coverage are immediate appeal and fast publishing.

要速度,信息全打包

速度需要空间,这是速度最普遍的原则之一。汽车跑得越快,同样数量的汽车所需要的跑道就越多。如果交通工具数量增加,而空间无法拓展,那么速度就一定要下降。信息对空间的要求和汽车不太一样,它对时间的要求却与其类似。对于信息供应商——从广告商到作者——来说,最稀缺的资源是他人的关注。如果供我们使用的时间数量保持相对不变,而信息的数量却一直增长,就不得不把它挤入我们可使用的有限时间里,因此,人们注意的范围就必然减小。电视为此铺平了道路。由于观众习惯接受那些被压得越来越紧的信息,因此信息的压缩程度就会日益上升。早在 20 世纪 90 年代,对加利福尼亚州小学生开展的一项研究揭示,小学生课堂注意力持续的平均时间为 7 分钟。他们已经习惯了电视上商业广告产生的节奏。因此,教育者似乎需要面对一个真实的挑战:如何设计一种教学方法,能满足每隔至多7分钟就休息一次的情况!有些领域可以如此。比如,机械地学习重音节时。但在其他领域,则明显缺乏直接的解决办法。

Speed Demands Space

This is one of the most general principles of speed. The faster cars drive, the more lanes one needs for the same number of cars. When it is impossible to expand the available space and the number of vehicles grows, speed decreases. Information does not require space in the same sense as cars, but it does require time. The great scarce resource for all purveyors of information from advertisers to authors is the attention of others. When an ever increasing amount of information has to be squeezed into the relatively constant amount of time each of us has at our disposal, the span of attention necessarily decreases. Television has paved the way here. As viewers get accustomed to taking in more and more compressed information, it can be compressed even further. Early in the 1990s, a study of California schoolchildren revealed that their attention span in class lasted, on an average, 7 minutes. They were accustomed to the rhythm created by commercial breaks on television. Here, it seems, educators are faced with a real challenge: how to design teaching methods that do not require more than 7 minutes of continuous time between the breaks! In some areas, this could be done. Rote learning of strong verbs, for example. In other areas, the solution must evidently be less straightforward.

因此,要获得一小撮人的注意,就应确保时间可以方便地分割成小段。每个人都能分出8秒的空闲时间,但谁能分出两年的空闲时间呢?(现在可能是理解西方哲学史的时候了。)此外,填充各种间隙还需要相关技巧。借助无线电话的技术,我们在沙滩上、电梯里或在与孩子玩耍时,都可以阅读电子邮件、新闻和公交时刻表。2000年春天,MP3播放器也整合进一种新式的无线电话技术。这意味着一个人无论是在浏览书面的信息还是在打电话时,都可以使用电话机来听音乐。这就可以确保空洞无聊的时间不再出现;间隙和用来自由思考的时间被擦除。或许,无线上网就是这种短暂的时尚产品,而在 2000 年年底的日本,无线手机上网用户已经超过了 1400 万人。《新科学家》注意到,2000 年秋季之后出现了一种新的现象,在阅读信息的一分钟内,至少有 20 个日本人可以获得 1 部无线上网手机。

One way of obtaining a snippet of people's attention thus consists in making certain that time is fast and cut into conveniently short lengths. Everyone has 8 seconds to spare; but who has two years? (This may be the time required to understand the history of Western philosophy.) Another, related technique consists in filling all the gaps. The WAP telephone technology makes it possible to read email, news and bus schedules in the lift, on the beach or while playing soccer with one's children. In the spring of 2000, a new WAP telephone was launched with an integrated MP3 player. This means that in the breaks between scanning written information or talking on the phone, one can use the telephone to listen to music. This ensures that the empty and boring pauses; the gaps, the time that might have been used for free-floating slow thoughts, are eradicated. WAP as such is probably a passing fad, but the Japanese equivalent, i-mode, had an incredible 14 million users in late 2000 a year after its initial launching. New Scientist notes, near the beginning of a feature section from autumn 2000, that at least 20 Japanese acquired an i-mode phone "in the minute it's taken you to read this far".

在不久的未来,无线电话技术可能用来确定用户的准确地点,这将使电话成为一种设备,以便有效填补都市人忙碌生活所留下的间隙。在人们离开车前往超市购物时,仍然有几分钟的空隙。很快,在踏入商场大门时,他就会听到电话中传来的震动声,以及屏幕上突然出现的信息:塞恩斯伯里超市今日特别优惠——新西兰羊羔每只 2.99 英镑,前方 30 英尺向左转。这是加油站与超市手推车上(一年前我注意到,为了留出广告空间,当地超市购物车的手柄突然加宽)广告促销逻辑的延伸。

The cellphone technology of the near future will make it possible to identify the user's exact location. This could turn the phone into a device which efficiently fills the few gaps that are left in a busy urban person's life. There is still a gap of maybe a couple of minutes between leaving the car and entering the first shop in the mall. Soon, one will hear a beep from the cellphone upon approaching the mallentrance, and onscreen information will flash forth: "Special offer today at Sainsbury's: New Zealand lamb ￡2.99, 30 feet ahead and to the left." This is an extension of the logic that has brought us the petrol nozzle ad and the shopping trolley ad (it was only a year ago that I noticed that the trolley handle at my local supermarket had suddenly tripled in width, to make room for advertising).

那些提供信息的人，为了几秒的空隙时间互相竞争。信息贩子越多，用户自己能用的时间就越少。发送信息的人不能使用强制手段，当然现在不是自由的宗教激进主义时代，因此他们必须灵活处理。在 20 世纪 90 年代，还有人质疑信息顾问的数量正在以指数级的方式增长吗？

Those who offer information, and our numbers are on the rise, fight over the vacant seconds in the lives of others. The greater the number of information pedlars, the fewer seconds users have for each of them. The senders certainly cannot use coercion, in this age of libertarian fundamentalism, and so they must be smart. Does anyone still wonder why the number of information consultants grew exponentially during the 1990s?

速度是种传染病

速度具有传染性。这一点在媒体尤为明显。最快速的媒体，比如数字电视节目与互联网报纸,正在被印刷类媒体仿效。文章正日益变短,其承载的信息更清楚,但分析却越来越少。电台里专门的新闻频道吹嘘每小时都会更新新闻,无线上网的手机可以代表当代大众媒体的快速特征。这类设备的屏幕比普通手机大两倍,可以直接与互联网连接。比如,人们能够用它查询股票交易行情、当晚的电影节目、头条新闻和电子邮件,还有不断更新的新闻摘要。过去,人们只有等到晚上,才能从电视上看到最新的消息。

Speed Is Contagious

This holds true in the media, as elsewhere. The fastest media, at the moment television and Internet newspapers, are being imitated by the printed media. The articles become shorter and shorter, with clearer "messages" and less analysis. Dedicated news channels on radio, for their part, boast that they update their news every hour, while the WAP format epitomises everything that is fast in contemporary mass communication. WAP phones and similar devices have a "screen" which is about twice as large as the display of an ordinary mobile phone, as well as direct access to limited sectors of the Internet. One can, for example, check the stock exchange rates, the evening's cinema programme, the news headlines and the email on a WAP telephone, and the super brief news items are updated virtually continuously. In the bad old days, one had to wait until the TV news in the early evening for an update.

这一类技术要得到广泛的传播,并非不可能。在信息过剩的时代,每个人可能都能拿出十秒的空闲时间,但能拥有整整一分钟闲暇时间的人并不多。因此,最快又最紧凑的媒体就有竞争优势。信息革命的一般原则是,同样的事物需要在快慢之间进行"公平与自由"的竞争,结果往往是快者获胜。问题是竞争过程中容易损失什么。若要回答这个问题,需要背景及理解能力。事后产生的想法往往被称为可信性。因此,编辑一份可靠性高的日报并且始终吸引读者,的确是很难的事。但是,正如一位主营单幅海报的资深编辑在街头与我进行快速而零碎的谈话时所言：无线网络报纸的编辑，由于需要不断更新新闻，因此主要靠的是想象！发布新闻之前，编辑没有足够的时间打字，因此需要不断修改。这种情形就是我接下来要谈的问题。

It is not unlikely that this kind of technology will become widespread. In a situation with an information surplus, everyone has 10 seconds to spare, but very few have a whole minute. This gives a competitive edge to the fastest and most compact media. A general rule of the information revolution is that in a "free and fair" competition between a slow and a fast version of "the same thing", the fast version wins. The question is what gets lost on the way. The short answer to this question is context and understanding; the longer one involves credibility. It is hard enough to edit a credible daily newspaper, which, among other things, attracts readers throughbeing first with the latest. But, as a senior editor of a major broadsheet mentioned to me during a fast and fragmentary conversation on a streetcorner: just imagine being managing editor for the WAP edition of a newspaper, which demands continuous updating! One would scarcely have the time to type the news before it was published and therefore in need of revision. This situation is just around the corner as I write this.

拉莫内宣称，过去 30 年生产的信息相当于之前 5000 年的信息总量。他举例说明了这一点："《纽约时报》周末版包含的信息，就比 18 世纪接受过良好教育的人毕生所学的知识还多。"

Ramonet claims that during the last 30 years, more information has been produced than during the previous 5,000 years! He illustrates the point with an example: "A single copy of the Sunday edition of the New York Times contains more information than a cultivated person in the eighteenth century would consume during a lifetime."

今日人们演奏贝多芬的第六交响曲《田园交响曲》，是否比 200 年前演奏得更快，我无法知晓。但是正如前面提到的那样，仅仅在 20 世纪，其演奏速度就明显得到了提高。最近，政治科学家研究了挪威国会每年财政辩论的发展历程，并对1945 至 1995 年间大选演讲的速度进行了比较。研究结果表明，1945 年竞选演讲的平均语速是每分钟 584 个音素。1980 年，每分钟的音素量提高到了 772 个，而1995 年的音素量则为 863 个。换句话说，与 20 世纪 40 年代相比，1995 年的演讲速度提高了近 50%。

I have no way of knowing whether performances of Beethoven's sixth symphony, the idyllic Pastoral symphony, are much faster today than the performances of 200 years ago. But as already mentioned, plays have accelerated very noticeably during the twentieth century. A political scientist recently studied the development of the annual financial debate in the Norwegian parliament, comparing the speed of speech in selected years from 1945 to 1995. He shows that the members of parliament spoke at an average velocity of 584 phonemes per minute in 1945. In 1980, the number of sounds had risen to 772, and in 1995 it had reached 863. In other words, the average politician spoke 50 per cent faster in 1995 than his or her predecessors did in the mid-1940s.

我们不妨举一个这样的例子：有一栋古老珍贵却遭受过轻微毁损的房子，住在里面的人决定粉刷一下洗手间。这人虽然穷一点，但还是想过得更幸福一些。按照联合国的财政预算赤字，他发现厨房实在破败需要修整。于是，他开始拆除旧的厨具设备，并不断地打电话给水管工与泥瓦匠，其过程令人甚为沮丧。几乎与此同时，他发现房屋的墙壁损坏得实在厉害，很有必要对卧室重新粉刷并更换地板。速度的传染性与此类似。

Or one could put it like this: it is as if one lives in an old, venerable but slightly dilapidated house and decides to refurbish the bathroom. Having finally done this, a poorer but hopefully happier person following a budgetary deficit worthy of the United Nations, one discovers for the first time that the kitchen is really quite run-down. So one begins to tear out the old kitchen fittings, and soon enters a new frustrating round of phone calls to plumbers and masons. Then one is bound to discover, almost immediately, how old and worn the hall is, and really, wouldn't it be a terrific idea to give the living room a coat of paint and a new floor? Speed is contagious in an analogous way.

如果一个人习惯了某区域的速度，对速度的渴望会蔓延到新的领域。机场快巴抵达公交站台的速度越快，等待每隔 5 分钟一趟的公交感觉的时间越久。正如计算机网络已经变快一样，许多人已经习惯了网络连接所需的等待时间，实际上，这往往只是很短的时间。即使是我们按下键盘，就能看到网页的内容，我们也不一定满意。期间所需的等待时间——几年前的 10 秒与今日的 2 秒，一样让人们无法接受。

If one gets used to speed in some areas, the desire for speed will tend to spread to new domains. Five minutes spent waiting for the bus lasts longer the faster the airport express train takes you from the terminal to the bus stop. As computer networks have become faster, many of us have grown accustomed to an Internet connection where waiting time is in principle, and often in practice, minimal. Still, we will not rest content until the web pages are accessed the very same moment we press the button. Two seconds of waiting time today is as unacceptable as 10 seconds would have been a couple of years ago.

这个原则具有一般的有效性。坐飞机从奥斯陆到哥本哈根，需要 40 分钟的时间，此时若耽搁 15 分钟就会完全不同。此外，若选择乘坐轮船，穿越斯卡格拉克海峡需要整整一晚的时间,这样,早到或晚到 15 分钟就没有多大的差别,这是由于轮船的速度不利于小气的省时计划。其他的活动可以等待。换句话说,不管是人还是生活领域,快速的时间都具有传染性。

This principle has a general validity. If the plane from Oslo to Copenhagen takes 40 minutes, 15 minutes' delay makes a lot of difference. If, on the other hand, one chooses to take the boat, which takes an evening and a night to cross the Skagerrak, 15 minutes lost or saved makes little difference, since the rhythm of the boat militates against petty time-saving schemes. Other activities can wait. Fast time, in other words, is contagious both between persons and between life domains.

时间的损耗与节省,具有同样的趋势

1965 年,工程师摩尔发现了摩尔定律。他认为微处理器的运行速度,每 18 个月就可以翻一番。(近来,吉尔德定律认为网络宽带传输速度每年可以翻一番。)到目前为止,摩尔定律始终正确。然而,奥斯陆大学的计算机科学家用克努特定律补充摩尔定律,认为摩尔定律是正确的,但计算机软件的复杂性与规模每隔 16 个月就可以翻一番。按照克努特定律,任何计算机执行的日常杂事,都比以前所用的时间更长。

Gains And Losses Tend To Equal Each Other Out

In 1965, the engineer Gordon Moore spelled out the principle that has come to be known as "Moore's Law". It states that the capacity (read: speed) of microprocessors is doubled every 18 months. (Recently, it has been supplemented by "Gilder's Law", which states that the transmission speed bandwidth on the Net is doubled every year.) So far, Moore has been right. However, a computer scientist at my university supplemented Moore with "Knut's Law". It states that Moore's law is correct, but that computer software doubles in complexity and size every 16 months. According to Knut, then, the daily chores performed by any computer nowadays take longer than before.

　　显然，克努特是一个聪明人，其话语有点夸张（实际上，克努特定律使我想起了几年前一份报纸刊载的文章，上面说到跑步有益健康。该文认为那些经常慢跑的人，寿命的确比别人长；一般而言，他们花在慢跑上的时间越多，比普通人的寿命越长）。但在一般意义上来讲，克努特定律是对的。我可以列举苹果计算机的几个实例。文字处理器 MacWrite 于 1984 年面世时，只有 50KB[1KB=1024B，1B 即为 1 字节（1 Byte）。后面 1MB=1024KB，1GB=1024MB。——编者]的磁盘空间（磁盘背面有 400KB 的空间）。我现在写作本书时使用的程序 WriteNow4（1994 年的版本），所占的磁盘空间有 348KB。世界上最新的文字处理器的最新版本，是微软的 Word 软件，需要 5.1MB 的磁盘空间，换句话说是 5000KB。为了使程序合理地运行，还需要一大堆附属处理程序。其中一些是与微软 Excel 和微软 PowerPoint 共享的。微软办公软件程序包所需总空间，已经超出 100 兆字节，而且大部分人都会安装所有的程序。12 年以前，普通硬盘的总容量只有 20MB。我们对此已很满足，觉得有了很大的磁盘空间了，因为我们出生时，计算机压根就没有硬盘！我们可能需要一个文字处理器，诸如 50KB 的 MacWrite；一个简报程序，比如摩尔（More，当时最新最好的版本是 384KB）；还要一个电子制表软件，比如 200KB 的 CricketGraph，这些东西可以与需要 100M 以上空间的微软文字处理软件完成同样的任务。自然的，现在的人需要运行更快的计算机，比我们那时候梦寐以求的更快。

Knut is obviously a witty man, and he exaggerates. (Actually his law reminds me of a newspaper story from a few years back, on the assumed health benefits of jogging. It noted that people who jog do live longer than others on average, exactly as much longer as the time they spend jogging.) But in a general sense, Knut is right. Allow me to illustrate with a few examples from my own computer world, which is called

156

Macintosh. The first version of the word processor MacWrite, launched in 1984, took a little more than 50 KB of disk space （disks back then, remember, took all of 400 KB）. The program I am using to write this book, WriteNow 4 （that is, the 1994 version）, takes 348 KB of disk space. The latest version of the world's most popular word processor, which is Microsoft Word, requires 5.1 MB, in other words well over 5,000 KB. And for the program to function properly, a heap of additions are needed. Some of them are shared with the sister programs Excel and PowerPoint. Altogether, Microsoft's office package requires more than 100 MB, and most people install all programs. In the old days, that is a little over a dozen years ago, the total capacity of an ordinary hard disk was 20 MB. We felt we had a lot of space back then, we who had grown up with computers without hard disks! We might have a word processor such as MacWrite（50 KB）, a presentation program like More（384 KB in the last and best version）and a spreadsheet such as CricketGraph （200 KB）at our disposal, and were able to perform the same tasks that an average user of Microsoft Word now needs more than 100 MB of disk space to perform. Naturally, he or she also needs a much faster computer than we could even dream of at the time.

　　因此,软件一直都在改进提高吗?这完全取决于个人的追求。我个人追求简单稳定的程序。这些东西很容易学会,而且直接与写作有关。尽管每年我都要写好几百页文字,但最低级的 WriteNow 软件所提供的已经足够,我似乎从未需要更多的东西。的确,Word 软件使我们能够制作目录和精致的模板,并且可以通过宏命令自动运行大量的功能;但在我的经历中,随着使用的进行,我们更容易剪裁文档,以适合个人的特别需要。计算机程序越简单,理解程序设计思路并与实际技术关联起来所花的时间就会越少,就可以越专注于手边的任务。相反,计算机程序越复杂越庞大,崩溃和出故障的风险就会越大。近几年来,各种各样恼人的电脑宏病毒已经蔓延到广大的计算机用户,但也只是在 Word 软件的用户中比较普遍。

　　So the software has been improved? That depends on what one is after.

Personally I prefer the simple and stable programs. They are easy to learn and straight forward to relate to, and although I write hundreds of pages every year, I never seem to need more than what humble WriteNow is able to offer. Yes, Word does make it possible to make tables of contents and fancy templates, and to run a number of functions automatically through macros; but in my experience, it is easier to tailor documents to one's special needs as one goes along. The simpler a computer program is, the less time and energy is spent on relating to the actual technology and trying to read the thoughts of the programmers, and more concentration can be expended on the task at hand. The larger and more complex a program is, the greater the risk of crashes and breakdowns. Irritating macro viruses have in recent years become widespread among computer users, but only among Word users.

这与错误类别的复杂性有关。日益增加的速度并不一定让我们更有效——后面还会讲到这一点。多年前，《连线》杂志连载的一个故事，是关于强大的太阳微型系统公司新任首席执行官，故事讲述了他想如何改进员工效率的事情。他想出了几个好主意，其中之一令人惊奇地利用了公司里痴迷电脑的员工所提出的意见。现在，许多员工习惯使用网络上现有的幻灯片模板，在里面添加自己的演示文稿。在公司的公共硬盘里，有幻灯片模板、插图、建议和以前使用过的文本。在制作自己的幻灯片时，员工们总会事先浏览这些文件，寻找合适的模板。首席执行官发现公共硬盘总共有12.9GB的幻灯片材料，于是，他把这些东西删除了。此后，员工们只能自己制作幻灯片了。实际上，他们现在工作效率反倒提高了，而且每张幻灯片的制作时间比以前更短。

This is to do with too much complexity of the wrong kind. Increased speed does not even necessarily make us more efficient a point to which I shall return later. The magazine WIRED ran a story a few years ago about the new CEO of mighty Sun Microsystems, and how he wanted to improve the efficiency of his staff. He came up with several ideas, but one in particular took the computer addicts on the staff by surprise. Now, many of the employees routinely made transparencies for use in external and internal presentations of what they were up to. As an aid, they had loads of templates, illustrations, suggestions and previously used presentations lying around on the shared hard disks of the company. While working on a particular presentation, people would browse these files to look for ideas,suitable templates, etc. The CEO found out that there were altogether12.9 gigabytes of PowerPoint stuff on the servers. He deleted everything. From now on, the staff had to make their own presentations from scratch. And indeed, they now worked more efficiently, and spent less time on each transparency than before.

技术变革的结果你 hold 不住

技术变革会产生不可预料的副作用。所有的技术都有不可预料的后果。无论何时人们获得更多某一类别的技术,结果并不一定都相同。甚至可能出现完全不同的事情。一个明显的事例是单频道电视向多频道遥控电视的过渡。在欧洲大多数国家,自 1980 年左右这种改变就开始了。国家电视台是政府宣传的法宝——换句话说,电视可以创造一种强有力的国家认同。不管观众有没有受过教育,他们都能同时在情感上与电视直接相连。它使无数人同时观看节目,为他们提供反映现实的特别报道——从彼得格勒到海参崴,或者从慕尼黑到基尔。研究表明,20 世纪几个欧洲国家的方言差异正在减少,这得益于国家的电台与电视台——在那里国家承认的语言差异具有主导优势。

Technological Change Leads To Unpredicted Sideeffects

All technology has unintended consequences, and whenever one gets more of a particular kind of technology, the result is not necessarily "more of the same". It could just as well be "something entirely different". One telling example is the transition from single-channel (or, at any rate, two-or three-channel) television to multichannel television operated by a remote control. In most European countries, this change has taken place since around 1980. National television is a fantastic tool for propaganda or, put differently, it can create a very powerful, shared national identity. It communicates directly, simultaneously and emotionally to literates as well as illiterates. It synchronises large segments of the population, and presents a particular version of reality to all from Leningrad to Vladivostok, or from Munich to Kiel. Research has indicated that the dialect variation in several European countries was reduced during the twentieth century thanks to national radio and television, where a few nationally acknowledged variants were dominant.

1983 年，挪威在经历了一代单频道电视之后，开始引进遥控卫星电视。最初，以天空电视台（天空电视台为英国电视台。它是欧洲最大的收费电视台之一，由传媒大亨默多克的新闻集团所控制。——编者）之类的卫星频道为主，由于这个领域当时为数不多，因此在一些欧洲国家，天空电视台的节目主持人拥有超级巨星的地位，有很多的目标群体追随他们。[恐怕很多人都还记得夏普（帕特·夏普，英国广播和电视节目主持人及 DJ。20 世纪 80 年代在欧洲，他作为天空电视台综艺节目主持人之一而知名。——编者）]那时，可选择的东西太少。后来，电视观众可以接收到新的挪威语频道（估计有五六个），另外可选择的卫星频道也越来越多。当然，并非每个人都能看到所有频道的节目，因为有些频道需要收费。尽管如此，根据媒体调查显示，处于老牌垄断地位的 BBC 挪威台，已经失去了部分原有的观众。过去人们聚在电视机前观看晚间新闻的时光已经一去不复返。换句话说，电视台（以及广播电台）具有极大的整合功能，能够在国家层面创造一个共享的话语圈，只有一个或少数几个电视台具有主导作用，这些电视台通常是国家控制的频道。然而，我们获得与电视相关的技术日益增多，突然之间电视台不再创造整合的结果，相反使观众日益分散。

After a generation of single-channel television, satellite TV was introduced in remote Norway in 1983. To begin with, dedicated satellite channels such as Sky and

Super were dominant, and the field was still so scantily populated that certain of Sky's video jockeys were able to achieve megastar status in some European countries, since a large percentage of the target group followed them. (Anyone remember Pat Sharp?) There were only a few alternatives.Eventually, TV viewers got access to new Norwegian channels （around five or six at the latest count）, in addition to a growing selection of satellite channels. Not everyone has access to everything, and many of the channels operate on the basis of subscriptions. Nonetheless, media research shows that the old national monopoly, the Norwegian poor cousin of the BBC, has lost its grip on the population. The good old days when the majority of the population gathered around the screen when the evening news was on, are gone never to return. In other words: television （and radio） functioned in an immensely integrating manner, creating a shared field of discourse on a national level, so long as it was dominated by one or a few, often state-controlled channels. Then we got a little more of the same technology （more channels, and some more, and some more still）, and suddenly television no longer creates integration, but fragmentation.

　　我们只需回顾起初的情形。数字电视使每一个家庭原则上都可以开发自己独特的观看模式。我可以选择观看爵士音乐会和诗歌朗诵会,直到我厌倦为止,而我的邻居可能喜欢经典的西部电影，只有当年轻貌美的主持人播报天气预报时,他才会暂时休息一下。

We have still only seen the beginning. Digital TV, which at the time of writing has graduated from the grapevine to the pipeline, entails that each household can in principle develop its own, unique pattern of viewing. I can watch jazz concerts and poetry recitals until I fall over, while my neighbour can concentrate his attention on classical Westerns, only interrupted by weather reports presented by young and beautiful women.

从文化史中很容易找到实例，可以说明新技术的使用产生的其他后果，这些后果人们压根就未曾料到。我已经说过，一些加速的技术，本来是要促进效率的提高，但可能产生严重的副作用。因此，绝对不能想当然地认为新技术一定可以提高效率。这个主题后面还要讨论，现在先分析其他方面。就拿眼镜为例，尽管我们没法准确给出其起源，但众所周知，首次提及光学透镜是1268年培根的作品。有了眼镜，有学问的人、僧人和其他人士在视力衰退时，依然可以进行阅读。不过，好几个世纪之内，人们只开发出了远视镜，用来帮助患有远视疾病的人。任何年过四十的人，都可能换上此疾。在文艺复兴时期，这个发明具有重要意义；在现代，远视镜的作用也不可低估。有了远视镜的帮助，那些受过良好教育的欧洲人，可以毕生学习并继续扩大自己的研究领域，使其积累的知识量得到很大的提高。

It is easy to find examples from cultural history to indicate that the introduction of new technology has led to consequences other than those anticipated. I have already suggested that some of the technologies of speed, intended to boost efficiency, may have grave sideeffects and that it cannot even be taken for granted that they do boost efficiency. This is going to be a major theme later, and I shall leave it for now. But take eyeglasses, for example. Although their exact origin is unknown, the first known reference to optical lenses is from Roger Bacon, writing in 1268. Spectacles made it possible for learned persons, monks and others, to continue reading for many years after their eyesight had begun to deteriorate. For several centuries, only convex glasses, to aid farsightedness （hyperopia）, existed. This is the common form of eyesight deterioration among people above 40. The importance of this modest invention for the Renaissance and the beginning of the modern era should not be underestimated. The cumulative growth in knowledge was boosted enormously when members of the learned community of Europe could continue to expand their fields of learning throughout their lives.

这个例子不够好？或许还有一些更好的事例，能够表明在主流文化史中，技术变迁可以产生广泛而未曾预料的后果。正如前面所言,时钟最初是用在僧侣的祈祷中,使他们整天的功课有时间的间隔;同样,对于现代人的日常生活来说,工业品和大众传媒已经不可缺少。古腾堡发明活字印刷时,几乎没有人会想到,这项技术能在发展民族主义与民主方面起到决定作用。戴姆勒〔戈特利布·戴姆勒(1834—1900 年),德国工程师和发明家,现代汽车工业的先驱者之一。——编者〕与福特都未预料汽车会使城市中心区衰退,因为有了汽车,人们即使住在郊外,也可以到主干道附近的消费场所或超市去购物。当然,在 20 世纪 30 年代商用客机——富人与权贵的奢侈待遇——刚刚引入时,也没人能够预料到在如今,从富裕国家到贫穷国家,洲际飞行都成了跨国移动的主力军。

Far-fetched example? Perhaps, but there are also excellent examples of wide-ranging unintended consequences of technological change to be found in mainstream cultural history. The clock, as noted earlier, was originally constructed to synchronise prayer times for monks working the fields during the day; today, it is a pillar of the modern way of life, and has become indispensable for industrial production, mass communication and large chunks of people's everyday life everywhere. When movable type was invented by Gutenberg, scarcely anyone thought that it would be decisive in the development of democracy and nationalism. And neither Gottlieb Daimler nor Henry Ford would have expected the car to lead to inner-city decay since it moved residential areas to the suburbs and shops to consumption reservations near major highways. On a minor note, it might be added that nobody would have thought, when commercial air traffic was introduced in a small way in the 1930s as a luxurious treat for the wealthy and powerful that inter-continental flights would be a backbone in the migration process from poor to rich countries.

新技术不可能适用于任何事物,但是该如何使用新技术,人们却永远不可能完全搞明白。无论多么耀眼的技术变革,总要在特定社会中满足特定的需求。同时,他们可能带来微妙又极其重要的副作用。正如前一章所言,书写技术可能削弱人的记忆力。

New technology cannot be used for anything at all, but it is also never known how it will be used. Technological changes, no matter how dazzling, are always put to use by particular societies with particular needs. They also bring subtle, but often highly consequential sideeffects with them. Writing, as mentioned in the previous chapter, impairs the faculty of memory.

在 20 世纪 90 年代,谁能相信最活跃的手机用户会是青少年呢？他们使用手机发送短信,与朋友及时保持联系。根据最新统计[按照作者写作本书的时间,这个统计数字应该是 2000 年年底全世界手机用户发送短消息的数量。——译者],全世界每年通过手机发送的短信数量为 90 亿条,其中光德国就有 10 亿条。在挪威,2000 年 10 月份的手机发送短信数量,相当于 1999 年全年国内所有手机用户发送短信的数量。1980 年,个人电脑首次问世时,消息灵通的记者用相当严肃的笔调写了一篇文章,讨论他们如何用计算机制作购物单,并统计存货的数量。在本书写作的时代背景下,新的通信技术仍然处在试验阶段,无法知道未来三五年甚至 20 年,通信技术会有怎样的用途。尽管如此,还是容易看到一些信息技术的后果:减小距离、缩短时间,并以阶梯式信息填补空隙。与汽车和喷气式飞机一样,新的信息技术可以产生加速度,并使人们对信息产生更多的需求,直到信息持续时间接近零为止。但是,随着复杂程度的增加,新技术的副作用也在增加。例如,大马路上无论有多少条车道,总会被车辆塞得满满当当。一个计算机网络供 1000 人同时发送邮件和打开浏览器,可能没有多大问题;但是,如果是 10000 个用户同时做这些事,恐怕就会出现故障;同样,1000 个用户同时观看高清电视节目的现场直播,也会出现类似的问题。正如上下班高峰期全世界都会出现交通堵塞一样,网络也会出现令人烦恼的延迟与拥挤。

Who would have believed, in the mid-1990s, that the most active users of mobile phones would be adolescents, and that they largely use them to send SMS messages in order to stay in touch with their friends hour by hour?（At the latest count, 9 billion SMS messages are sent annually in the world, a billion of them in Germany alone.）When personal computers were first marketed around 1980, reasonably well-informed journalists wrote in a deeply serious mode how they would be used to make shopping lists and inventories of the contents of the freezer. The new information technology that lurks in the background of this entire book, is still at a trial stage, and there is no way of knowing how it will be put to use in three, five or 20 years. It is nonetheless easy to see some consequences of information technology: it removes distance, shortens time and fills the gaps with cascades of information. Like the car and the jet plane, new information technology leads to acceleration and demands for further information, until time seen as duration approaches zero. But as complexity increases, so do the sideeffects. Roads, for instance, have a curious tendency to be filled by cars, no matter how many lanes they have at their disposal. And a given computer network may function well for 1,000 users who run email software and Netscape/Explorer, but badly for 10,000 users who are up to the same thing; just as it would function badly if the 1,000 users demanded transmissions of high-resolution video film in real time. Just as traffic jams occur worldwide in the rush hour, annoying delays and jams occur on the Net.

若要解决这些问题,合适的建议需要考虑两个方面:我们需要更大的容量和更高的速度,就像长远考虑任何事情一样。但是,我们不该忘记,在获得 20MB 的硬盘作为存储空间时,我们是如何得高兴;我们也不清楚,未来四年之内这些装置是否会被放到博物馆中。

The proposed solutions are the same in both cases: we require more capacity and higher speed, as if that would solve anything in the long run. But let us not forget how happy we were when we finally got hard disks with a storage capacity of all of 20 MB;

at that time, we then had no idea that those devices would be ripe for the museum in less than four years.

速度的传染性和它与效率的亲密关系，在一个众所周知的故事中可以清楚地呈现，这个故事现有多种版本。在海因里希讲述的故事中，一位德国的游客去西班牙旅游，他很惊讶地发现，西班牙人习惯在海滩边的树底下打盹儿。这个德国人向一位渔夫走去，并和他探讨效率的优点。他对渔夫说，如果你现在不浪费时间，而是出去打鱼，可能可以获得比现在多三倍的鱼，并能买一条更好的渔船。然后他继续展开幻想，渔夫就可雇佣员工并开设工厂，最终成为一个大富翁！但是西班牙人回答道："这是为了什么呢？"德国人说："哦，这样你就可以提前退休，依靠公司利润就可舒适地生活，并且可以在海滩上逍遥自在地打盹。"然而，西班牙人翻过身来回答道："我现在就在打盹啊！"

The contagious nature of speed, and its intimate relationship to efficiency as a value in itself, is brought out clearly in a well-known story which exists in many versions. In the variant told by Heinrich Böll, a German tourist visits Spain and discovers, to his horror, a Spaniard dozing in the shade of a tree on the beach. The German approaches the man, a fisherman, and lectures him on the virtues of efficiency: "If you had gone out fishing now instead of wasting your time, he explains, you might have caught three times as much fish and bought yourself a better boat." Eventually, he fantasises, the Spaniard might employ others and build a factory. He could become a rich man! "What for?" Asks the Spaniard. "Well", says the German, "you could have gone into early retirement, living off the profits and spent your days dozing on the beach." "That", says the Spaniard before turning over, "is exactly what I am doing."

有些事情已经失去控制。节省时间的技术使得时间变得比以前更加稀缺。通过信息获取财富并没有让我们更开化，反倒更不开化。在下一章，我会解释这是怎么一回事,并分析这件看起来失控的事情究竟是什么。

Something has run out of control. Time-saving technology has made time more scarce than ever. The wealth of available information has not made most of us more enlightened, but less enlightened. In the next chapter, I shall explain how this can be, and approach the question of what this "something" is that seems to be out of control.

第五章 指数级增长

当我描述德特夫人那晚的情形时,我想起了现在数学教材第一章的著名方程式:速度的级别与遗忘的强度成正比。

——摘自昆德拉的《慢》

5 Exponential Growth

When I described Madame de T.'s night, I recalled the well-known equation from one of the first chapters of the textbook of existential mathematics: the degree of speed is directly proportional to the intensity of forgetting. (Milan Kundera, *Slowness*)

关于发明国际象棋的最著名的神话故事发生在波斯一个遥远偏僻的地区。(广告上说 6 世纪印度发明了国际象棋,这肯定有误。)当时,波斯王已经把手边的游戏玩遍,找不到新的玩法了,于是命令朝廷中最聪明的人发明一种新的游戏,可以超过他所见过的所有游戏。不久,这个人向国王呈献了一种新式的战争游戏,用一张 8×8 的方格纸,交替使用黑白两色,然后将两组图案分别以黑白两色雕刻在木块上。这些木块上面刻有战士与指挥官,有很多的步兵,每一个级别只有两个指挥官,每方有一个国王和一个王后,他们是整个游戏中最为重要的角色。而且,王后的权力比国王还大,但是如果国王被包围,游戏就得结束。

The most famous myth about the invention of chess is located to Persia in a remote and misty era. (It is almost certainly wrong: chess was probably invented in

India in the sixth century AD.）The king of the wealthy Persian empire loved games and intellectual challenges. One day he had exhausted the possibilities inherent in the games at hand, and ordered the sharpest mind of the court to conjure up a new game that would surpass everything he had seen thus far. After a while he was presented with a stylised war game, with a board measuring eight times eight squares in alternating black and white colours, and with two sets of pieces, one in each colour, carved in wood. The pieces depicted soldiers and officers; the infantry（"pawns"）were numerous, but there were only a couple of officers of each rank. Naturally, each warring side had only one king and queen, and they were the most important pieces in the game. For some reason, the queen had a greater range than the king, but it was only when the king was besieged that the game was over.

波斯国王非常高兴,并询问国际象棋的发明者想要多少奖赏。这人非常谦虚地说:"陛下,我不要很多的奖赏,您只要按照下面的方式奖励我——在棋盘的第一格放 1 粒麦子,第二格放 2 粒麦子,第三格放 4 粒麦子,第四格放 8 粒麦子,第五格放 16 粒麦子,依此类推,直到整个棋盘上的 64 个格子都放满麦子。"国王听完后如释重负,很爽快地答应了他的要求,并暗自庆幸他为自己省下了金银宝石。然后,他吩咐手下的谋臣计算,该从仓库里拿出多少麦子赏赐给这个人。

The Persian king was very pleased, and offered the inventor the fee he required. "I will not ask for much, my lord", the man replied modestly, "just one grain of wheat for the first square of the board, two for the second, four for the third, eight for the fourth, sixteen for the fifth and so on, until we reach the sixty-fourth and final square." "That you shall have", said the king in relief, saving his treasury from depletion of gold and brilliant stones; and then his mathematicians began to calculate how much wheat they would have to fetch from the stores.

大臣算完后大吃一惊。这个看似朴实的赏赐似乎非常昂贵。整个波斯帝国十

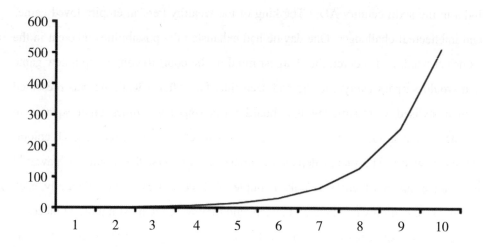

Figure 5-1   Number of wheat grains for the inventor of chess: the first 10 squares

图 5-1   奖给国际象棋发明者的麦粒数量变化趋势（10 个棋盘格）

年的小麦产量，还不够奖赏给这个人。因为计算结果似乎在越来越快地变大——实际上，增长速率从一开始就呈现出来了，但是很快就变大了。每换一个棋盘格子，数量就要增长一倍。到第十个棋盘格子时，需要 512 粒麦子；到第 11 棋盘格，则需要 1024 粒麦子。第 15 个棋盘格里要放 16384 粒麦子，到第 20 个棋盘格子，需要放的麦粒差则超过了 50 万。

They were surprised. For a while, it seemed as if the expense would be very modest for the king. The ten first squares yielded barely enough wheat for a porridge meal for the inventor and his family （see Figure 5-2）. Then, the numbers seemed to grow more rapidly albeit in reality, they continued to grow at the same rate as from the beginning, but they quickly grew very much larger. Twice as large for each new square on the board. The tenth square was worth 512 grains, the eleventh 1024. The fifteenth square was worth 16,384 grains, the twentieth more than half a million （see Figure 5-3）.

The twenty-sixth square was valued at more than 33 million grains of wheat, the

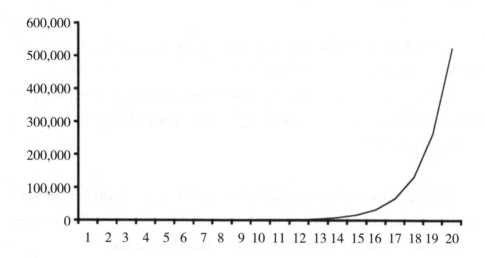

Figure 5-2   Number of wheat grains for the inventor of chess: the first 20 squares

图 5-2   奖给国际象棋发明者的麦粒数(20 个棋盘格)

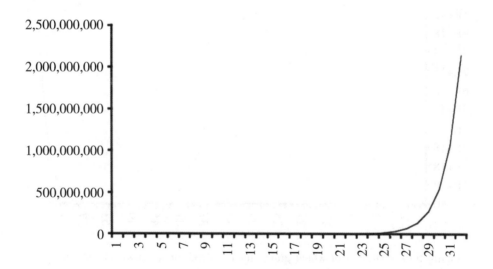

Figure 5-3   Number of wheat grains for the inventor of chess: the first 32 squares

图 5-3   奖给国际象棋发明者的麦粒数量变化趋势(32 个棋盘格)

thirty-first more than a billion（see Figure 5-4）.

依此类推,在第 26 个棋盘格子中需要放入的麦粒数量,已经超过 3300 万;而到了第 31 个棋盘格中,则将超过 10 亿麦粒。

然而不幸的是,事情远没有结束。在威严的数学家们还没有完全计算出应给的麦粒数量之前,他们已经意识到就算把全世界收割的麦粒全部给这个人,国王也还要欠他很多麦子。

It had to end in disaster. Long before the courtly mathematicians had calculated the grain values of all 64 squares of the chess board, they realised that the king owed the inventor of the game many times the world's total wheat harvest.

显然,发明国际象棋的神秘人物,也是指数运算的发明者。指数运算的最普通

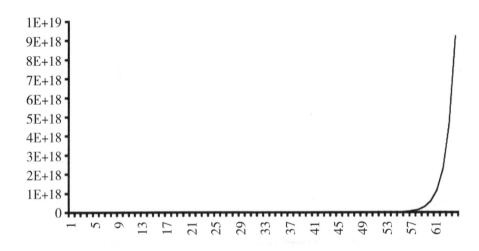

Figure 5-4   Number of wheat grains for the inventor of chess: all 64 squares

图 5-4   奖给国际象棋发明者的麦粒数量变化趋势（64 个棋盘格）

Note: 1E+18 is 1 followed by 18 zeros, etc.

1E+n is 1 followed by n zero: 1E+n 表示 1 后面跟 n 个零。

原则是每一步翻番,或者是在相同时间的间隔后增长一倍。换句话说,在突然增长到顶峰值之前,实际增长率的变化曲线一直比较平坦。正如图 5-1 所示,即使我们看到前 10 个棋盘格麦粒数变化曲线比较陡,但由于其数值很小,看起来就没有多大的害处。当然,如果与第 64 格的麦粒数相比,第 32 个棋盘格的麦粒数——只有 2 147 483 648——也就不算大了。如果全部计算在内,国王欠下的麦粒数量将达到 9 223 372 036 854 780 000 之多。

The mythical inventor of chess was clearly also the inventor of exponential mathematics. The principle of the most common exponential function is doubling for each step or time interval. The actual rate of growth, in other words, is even, but the numerical growth follows a low curve before it suddenly rises towards the ceiling. As Figure 5.1 a d indicates, the growth curve is pretty steep even if we look at the first ten steps, but it still seems harmless since the numbers are so small. Compared with the value for the sixty-fourth and final square, the value for the thirty-second square a mere 2,147,483,648 grains is insignificant. The king's debt for the last square amounted to 9,223,372,036,854,780,000 grains.

用指数增长变化率的粗略曲线图表示当前的发展趋势,容易看出其内在的敏感性。我们不妨先来猜猜以下的数量:二次世界大战以来的航空运输、近两百年来人口的增长量、纳斯达克股票交易市场创立以来的成交量、1995 年以来互联网用户的数量、1991 年以来网络的通信量、1985 年以来微软处理软件的规模、1984 年以来苹果公司系统扩展的平均数量、1950 年以来普通美国青少年从电视节目中看到的谋杀案数量、1950 年以后出版的专业期刊数量、1950 年以来全世界清洁剂的品牌数量、1980 年以来电视频道的数量等。

Many current tendencies seem susceptible to descriptions by way of roughly exponential growth curves with varying rates of doubling. Let me hazard some guesses at the outset: air traffic since the Second World War, global population growth over the last 200 years, the turnover at the NASDAQ stock exchange since its foundation, the number of Internet servers in the world since 1995, the traffic on the Internet since 1991, the size of Microsoft Word since 1985, the average number of system extensions on a Macintosh since 1984, the number of murders an average American teenager has seen on television since 1950, the number of academic journals published since 1950, the number of detergent brands in the world since 1950, the number of television channels since 1980...

在一段时间内并不剧烈的指数增长

与国际象棋发明者的故事类似，下面的事例更接近当代人的生活。

在一个瓶子里放入 2 个细菌。瓶底有一层棕色的黏稠的啤酒液，细菌来自热带国家，喜好 30 摄氏度的环境温度，按照普通的繁殖速度，一分钟内每个细菌可以繁殖出 1 个细菌。1 分钟后，瓶子中就有 4 个细菌；然后下一分钟是 8 个，再下一分钟为 16 个、32 个……当然，还有一些细菌会死亡，这使得计算会变得更加复杂。不过，几个月之后，细菌也只是覆盖住了瓶底。自此之后，细菌数量增长就明显了。当瓶子的 1/8 都装满细菌时，聪明的数学家推算瓶子里的细菌面临"人口爆炸"的危险。有些人对此忧心忡忡。当瓶子里的细菌装满一半时，一些人开始担忧了。他们组织了游行示威和请愿，手拿旗帜，口中呼出发怒的口号，要求当局尽快行动避免这场可怕的灾难。然而警察却说："别担心，还有的是空间。"

Exponential Growth Is Even And
May Seem Undramatic For a Long Time

An example similar to the origin myth of chess, but which is closer to contemporary concerns, is this:

Two bacteria colonised a bottle. They bred at average speed, and a sticky, brown layer of beer covered the bottom of the bottle, which stood in the shade in a tropical country and had a constant temperature of slightly below 30℃ . Under these circumstances, it took the bacteria 1 minute to double in number. When the first minute was gone, there were thus 4 bacteria, then 8, 16, 32 and so on. (Eventually some begin to die, which makes the calculations more complicated.) It took them months just to cover the bottom of the bottle. When this was accomplished, the population growth took off. When an eighth of the bottle was full, the brightest mathematicians among the bacteria had calculated that the bottle was faced with a disastrous population explosion. Not many listened to them. When, a little more than 2 minutes later, the bottle was half full, many began to worry. They organised petitions and demonstrations, carrying banners and shouting angry slogans, demanding the authorities do something to avert a terrible catastrophe. The politicians replied: "Don' t worry, there is plenty of space."

这个寓言与人口激增有关，从 1798 年开始流传，到现在已经有很长的历史了，当时马尔萨斯在他的名著《人口论》中提出了这个问题。在马尔萨斯最初提出人口剧增的观点时，人们尚未意识到未来出现人口爆炸的可能，但人们必须承认马尔萨斯具有前瞻性。按照马尔萨斯的说法，食物生产量按照代数方式增长，也就是从 1 到 2，再依次到 3、4、5 的简单递增。相反，人口的增长趋势是按照几何方式，或者说是指数运算的方式，从 1 到 2，再到 4、8、16，等等。因此，如果人类不放慢人口繁殖的速度，就很有可能面临饥荒。很自然的，身为牧师的马尔萨斯提倡人们节欲。

This allegory of the population explosion has a long prehistory, beginning in 1798, when Thomas Robert Malthus published his An Essay on Population. This was at the very beginning of what would later be seen as a period of explosive population growth, and, whatever one's views on Malthus, one must at least concede that he was ahead of his time. According to Malthus, food production grew arithmetically, that is by simple addition: 1, 2, 3, 4, 5... Population, on the contrary, had a tendency to grow geometrically （or exponentially）, that is 1, 2, 4, 8, 16, etc. For this reason, famine would occur unless one took steps to reduce population growth. Malthus, a cleric, naturally recommended sexual abstinence.

两百年来，马尔萨斯的思想对于政治与科学具有深刻的影响力。达尔文的自然选择理论使马尔萨斯的"自然增长"机制发生了转变，尊崇达尔文的马克思采用极其强烈的措辞，甚至是用他自己的标准批判马尔萨斯。马克思曾经取笑地称马尔萨斯为"狒狒马尔萨斯"。总之，他提出的人口增长模式，依然是关于人口增长国际讨论会的基础，自马克思以来这些参数一直没有发生明显的变化：批评马尔萨斯的人指出，在一定区域范围之内，社会分配与技术因素将影响其可支撑人口的规模。

Malthus's thoughts have been deeply influential in both politics and science for 200 years. Darwin's theory of natural selection hinges on a Malthusian mechanism of "natural growth", while Marx, who admired Darwin, castigated Malthus in extremely strong terms even by his own standards （he once characterised him as "the baboon Malthus"）. In a general way, his model of population growth still underlies international discussions about population growth, and the arguments have not changed significantly since Marx's time: Malthus's detractors point out that social distribution and technological factors influence the population size a given territory can sustain.

按照马尔萨斯的理论，我们可以假设，地球上每一对夫妇平均生育四个小孩。对于简单的指数曲线来说，这是一个必要的数字。我们可以进一步假定每一代人的跨度是 30 年。如果有一个名为布鲁克的小村庄，创立于马尔萨斯提出人口论的 1798 年，而且当时只有两对夫妇。不久之后，假设是 1805 年，这两对夫妇各自有了 4 个小孩。这样，总人口就变为 12 个了。30 年之后，8 个小孩各自结婚生子，每一对夫妇生育 4 个小孩。这样，总人口就是 12+(4×4)=28 个。之后，老人逐渐去世。总人口减少为 24 个。又过了 30 年,也就是 1865 年,第二代人去世,但是他们的 16 个孩子各自都已结婚,而且每对夫妇生育了 4 个小孩。

We may assume, with Malthus, that each couple on earth has on average four children who survive. This is the number necessary for a simple exponential curve. Let us, further, assume that the span from birth to own children lasts on an average 30 years. A certain village, we may call it Filthy Brook, was founded by two couples in 1798, on the same day as Malthus published his theory. Total population: four persons. A little later, let us say in 1805, they each have four children. Total population: twelve. After 30 years, the eight children have married their neighbours, and each couple is bringing up four children each. Total population: 12+(4×4)=28. Then the elderly die. Total population is now reduced to 24. Thirty years later, that is in 1865, the second generation are dead, but their 16 children have married each other and have given birth to four children each.

现在,总人口就是 24−8+(8×4)=48 个。然后,又过了 30 年,祖父母辈的老人去世,新人结婚并生育小孩,到 1895 年布鲁克村庄的人口数量就是 48−8+(16×4)=108 个了。现在,我们来看一下如今这个村庄的情形。最初布鲁克村庄只有一家杂货店和一个邮局。90 年之后,也就是到 1985 年,另外三代老人也先后过世。现在,村庄总人口数量是 896 人。然而,每个人都能很容易看出,这个村庄似乎还不像一个小镇。而且,在此期间邮局也关门了,其原因无需在此讨论。但是,村庄里的数学家可能会说,不妨想象一下 2195 年时村子里的人口数量。到那时,已经有229376 人。这样,我们这个舒适的英国小村庄,或许已经没有什么空间了。

Total population is now 24−8+(8×4)=48. Then another 30 years pass, with loss of grandparents, new marriages and new children, and the population of Filthy Brook in 1895 is 48−8+(16×4)=108. It now begins to look like a village proper. Filthy Brook gets its first grocery and a post office. Ninety years on, in 1985, another three generations have passed. There are now a total of 896 inhabitants. It is easy to support everybody, and the village remains something less than a small town. (The post office is nevertheless closed down in this period, for reasons which will not be discussed here.) But, the mathematicians of the village say, imagine the situation in 2195! We will then have a population of 229,376. Not much will then be left of our cosy English village.

在全球的规模上来看，这种人口增长自然是最后人口拥挤的根源。因此，最终的人口数量变化趋势并不一致，也不好断定地球可承受力的上限如何，人们似乎更愿意集中居住在一起。我们应当注意心理学家的反应。对那些相信马尔萨斯理论的人而言，这些世界似乎还没有他们所担忧的那么拥挤。当前，如果假定每一个人都来威尔士，而且拥有 4 平方米独享的空间。而且，假设现有合理的住宅建设方案可以充分使用空间，那就甚至还可以有一两家小餐厅。

On a global scale, this kind of population growth is naturally a recipe for crowding in the long run. There is nonetheless no agreement regarding what "the long run" should be taken to mean here, that is what is the upper limit for the planet's sustainability, and people in general seem to rather enjoy living close together. Rat psychologists should take notice. The world may still be less crowded than many worried Malthusians believe. At the moment, if we assume that every person alive were brought to Wales, each individual would have 4 square metres at his or her exclusive disposal. Assuming the existence of a reasonable housing scheme with efficient use of space, there might even be space for a café or two.

千百年来，人口增长一直很慢。在农业革命之前，据估计，地球大约可以承载 800 万的人口。这个数字当然存在争议，但是事实上就在农业革命的前夕，全球人口大约只有 500 万。1800 年，全球人口已经超过 10 亿。之后过了 130 年，全球人口就达到了 20 亿；而 30 年之后就已经突破 30 亿；15 年之后的 1975 年，全球人

口已经突破 40 亿。1987 年,全球总共有 50 亿人;就在我们刚刚熟悉这个数字时,
12 年之后全球总人口已经宣称达到了 60 亿,据说第 60 亿位婴孩出生在印度或
中国。如果按照当前的速率增长,世界总人口每隔 40 年就要翻一番。今天的人口
与我出生那年的人口总量相比,已经增长了一倍。这样,到 2040 年全球人口将达
到 120 亿;到 2120 年则将达到 480 亿。在世界上的某些地方,人口翻番的速度要
快得多,比如非洲每 24 年翻番,亚洲则为 34 年。所以,不管任何时候来看,全球人
口增长曲线始终是右边朝上的发展趋势。但是,现在似乎有水平的变化趋势。从
40 亿到 50 亿用了 12 年时间,同样,从 50 亿到 60 亿也用了 12 年时间。

For many thousands of years, humanity grew very slowly. It has been estimated
that the Earth was able to support roughly 8 million people altogether before the
agricultural revolution. This number is certainly subject to debate, but it is a fact that
the global population at the dawn of the agricultural revolution is estimated at about 5
million. The first billion was reached only in 1800. Another 130 years went before the
second billion mark was passed, 30 years between 2 billion and 3 billion, and 15 years
from 3 billion to 4 billion, reached in 1975. In 1987, the global population was 5
billion, and we had only just become accustomed to this figure when, twelve years
later, it was announced that citizen of the world number 6 billion had just been born,
probably in India or China. If the present rate of growth continues, the world's
population will continue to double every 40 years. (There are twice as many people
alive today as when I was born.) In that case, global population will be 12 billion in
2040 and 48 billion in 2120. In some parts of the world, the rate of doubling is much
faster (Africa: 24 years, Asia: 34 years). Almost no matter what time scale is
employed, the growth curve of the global population will tend to point skywards on
the right. But it is beginning to flatten out. The interval between 4 billion and 5 billion
was twelve years; the same as the interval between 5 billion and 6 billion.

这个案例表明,指数曲线似乎在很长一段时间内平缓发展——有时甚至适度

而审慎，然后突然改变特点向上冲。当指数曲线发生这种飞跃时，其内容就要发生质变。在为世人所知之前，小村庄布鲁克只是一个小镇，但很快就成了一个城市。皇宫里谦卑的恶作剧制作者，迅速地变成了一个狡猾的自大狂。

What these examples indicate is that an even development of exponential growth may seem undramatic for quite a while it may even be perceived as modest and wholesome before suddenly changing character and shooting upwards. When this leap takes place, a qualitative change occurs with the content. After a while, the small village Filthy Brook is a small town, and before one knows it, it is a city. The modest games-maker at the King's court is suddenly transformed into a cunning megalomaniac.

指数增长的魔术式拐点

指数增长造成空间的稀缺。本章虽然以一个与国际象棋有关的故事开始，但本意并不在此，也并不是要讨论细菌或人口的增长问题。我冒昧地占用读者几分钟时间，是要通过这些实例，引入一种特别的推理方式。本章的主题是信息的过量和信息获取量不受控制的增长，以及这种趋势带来的后果。前一章谈到人类社会早期信息的不足，而现在却是信息太多。在过去的 30 年里，人类生产的信息总量，已经相当于之前 5000 年里的信息总量，这就是我所说的曲线拐点。

Exponential Growth Creates Scarcity Of Space

This chapter does not really deal with chess games, bacteria or population growth. I took the liberty of appropriating a few minutes of the readers' time on these examples in order to introduce a particular line of reasoning. The topic is the surplus of information and the uncontrolled growth in the available quantity of information, and some of the results of this tendency. In an earlier chapter I wrote that whereas there was formerly a scarcity of information, there is now too much of it. If it is correct that, in the course of the past 30 years, humanity has produced as much information as in the previous 5,000 years, we are talking about a very steep curve.

越来越多的信息正在为日渐缩小的空间而争战。一个很明显的后果,是每个人花在每条信息上的时间正在减少。在挪威,目前发行量最大的报纸是在圣灰星期三(圣灰星期三,也称圣灰节。当天教会会举行涂灰礼,要把去年棕枝主日祝圣过的棕枝烧成灰,在崇拜中涂在教友的额头上,作为悔改的象征。——编者)出版的。不是因为这份报纸的质量高,而仅仅是由于复活节期间连续五天都没有报纸发行。同样,由于电视频道数量减少,人们会采用更平静和连贯的模式观看电视。当专业期刊数量减少时,读者在每篇论文上所花的时间就会增多。当书架上的光盘数量较少时,每张光碟播放的次数就会增加,听者对每首歌曲就会更熟悉。我们还可以列举出很多的实例,当书籍更少时……

A growing number of messages are fighting over forever shrinking vacant spaces. An obvious result is that each of us has to spend a decreasing amount of time on each piece of information. The most widely-read newspaper edition in Norway is the one published on the last Wednesday before Easter. This has nothing to do with quality, but with the simple fact that this country has five consecutive newspaper-free days during Easter. It can also be assumed that when there were fewer television channels, people watched TV in a more calm and continuous mode. When there were fewer professional journals, readers spent more time on each article. When there were fewer CD on the shelf, one played each of them more often and became more familiar with each piece of music. When there were fewer books...

在日益缩短的时间内将信息浓缩,使得信息发送方必须不断变化。例如,现在的电视节目制作方,非常注意观众手中的遥控器,一旦电视节目的热度下降,观众就要准备快速移动到更激烈的频道。1982 年, 特纳启动美国有线电视新闻网络时,想缩短商业广告的时间,以便与两分钟的《头条新闻》节目相称。1971 年,30 秒钟的商业广告刚刚引入时,被认为是最快的广告,但很快就落伍了。特纳雇佣的媒体顾问施瓦茨,将 30 秒的广告缩短为 8 秒,然后是 5 秒。在最近的一次电视采访中,施瓦茨吹嘘自己可以制作 3 秒钟的广告,而且一定可以脱颖而出,成为此类商业广告的典范之作。

The compression of information into decreasing time spans also entails changes on the sender side. The people who make TV programmes nowadays, for example, are perfectly aware that they are making them for a group of spectators armed with a remote control in their right hand, ready to zap to a competing channel as soon the temperature of the programme falls. When Ted Turner launched CNN in 1982, he wanted briefer commercials to match his 2-minute "headline news" programmes. The 30-second commercial, which had been regarded as ultra-fast when it was introduced in 1971, was suddenly sluggish. Turner hired the media consultant Tony Schwartz, who immediately shortened the 30 seconds to 8, then to 5 seconds. In an interview, Schwartz recently boasted that he could make 3-second commercials which would outcompete all of these, and offered examples of such commercials.

很快,观众就习惯了新的节奏。从 20 世纪 50 年代开始的电影,最显著的特点是其令人难以置信的慢节奏——至少对于生活在 21 世纪的人来说是这样, 不仅对话的展开异常缓慢,就连汹涌的波涛与落日的场景也慢得很,人们似乎总要互相对望很久,感觉他们好像没有什么更好的事可做。虽然电影院里的观众手中没有遥控器,也无法按快进键,但是从电视荧幕中获得的期望,还是可以影响电影院观众的节奏:希望尽可能地快,越快越好!

After a while, viewers grow accustomed to the new tempo. One of the most striking aspects of feature films from the 1950s, at least for us who live in the 2000s, is how unbelievably slow they are, with slowly unfolding dialogues, lingering scenes with crashing waves and sunsets, people who seem to be looking at each other for many seconds, seemingly without anything better to do. Even though the audience of a cinema is not equipped with a remote control or a fast forward button, the expectations created by watching the TV screen affect the rhythm of cinema spectatorship: as much as possible ought to happen as fast as possible; the more, the better.

速度不仅具有传染性，还能使人上瘾。（信息的消费几乎不同于任何其他事物，由于影碟机的普及，全球各个电影院里的观众数量都在下降。这是否与影碟机有快进键，而电影院没有快进键有关呢？）同样，促进人们消费比抑制人们消费更容易；增加信息传输的节奏比减缓节奏更容易。

Speed is not just contagious; it is addictive as well. (Unlike nearly everything else to do with consumption of information, cinema attendance is decreasing globally, correlated with the spread of video machines. Does this have anything to do with the presence/absence of the fast forward button?) Just as it is easier to make people increase their consumption than to make them reduce it, it is easier to increase than to reduce the tempo of information transmission. Speed is a narcotic.

速度就像一剂麻醉药

速度就像一剂麻醉药。副作用越来越明显，这是错误的快速发展带来太过复杂的事物。恩格斯是一位工厂主，也是马克思主义者（实际上他是第一个马克思主义者，是马克思的搭档与长期的赞助人）。恩格斯曾经说过量变在一定程度上就会导致质变。在《自然辩证法》这本最受贬损的书中，恩格斯进一步发展了这个原则，并提供了事物质变的理论。这本书出版于作者身故之后的两次大战期间，的确值得一读。一旦将其应用于该使用的地方（而不是物种进化），量变到质变的转化原则就值得再看一看。一个给定的系统生产的同一件产品越来越多，但是突然之间有一些完全不同于以前的产品。然而，人们往往对此不加注意。

Speed Is A Narcotic

This is about too much complexity of the wrong kind. Friedrich Engels, factory manager and Marxist (he was actually the first Marxist, as Karl Marx's long-standing patron and collaborator), once wrote about how quantitative changes are, at particular points, turned into qualitative changes. This principle was developed in one of his most vilified books, the study of "the dialectics of nature" where he offered a theory of change in nature. The book, published posthumously in the inter-war years, is indeed a curious read. But the principle of the transformation of quantity into quality deserves a second look, as long as it is applied where it belongs (which is not the evolution of species). A given system produces more and more and more of the same, but suddenly, one gets something entirely different instead of more of the same. This frequently happens without anybody noticing.

一个人可以同时做 3 件事情，而且都能做好。同样，一个人也可能同时做 6 件事情，而且 6 件事都能做好。甚至，还有人能够同时做 12 件事，而且都能做好。然后，他们接着做第 13 件事时，却完成得非常糟糕。这就是量变到质变的本质。一段时间内的发展可以不产生任何激烈的后果，但是突然抵达临界值时，整个系统就会发生跳跃性变化，产生一些完全不同的事情，其外部特征也会发生彻底的变化。

One may do three things at the same time and do three things well. One may do six things at the same time and do six things well. Some may even do twelve things at the same time and do twelve things well. Then they get a thirteenth task, and suddenly they perform thirteen tasks badly. This is the essence of the transformation of quantity into quality. Even growth takes place for a long while without dramatic consequences, but suddenly a threshold value is reached, and as a result the entire system flips into something different, changing character completely.

在新几内亚高地的策姆加巴人中,"猪的循环"是人类学的一个经典案例。策姆加巴人种植块茎与蔬菜,并饲养猪。猪的数量均衡地增长。妇女与孩童负责饲养猪,为了给猪寻找饲料,他们需要到距离村庄越来越远的地方,往往要冒着被敌人偷袭的风险。另外,猪的增长对庄稼的危害也越来越大。当猪繁殖数代之后,策姆加巴人喂养的猪已经达到饱和,再增加就没有任何优点,反倒会成为负担。于是,他们就地宰杀这些猪,并举行复杂的仪式过程,发动战争并进行调解。(当然,也有更简单的方式,但这不是本书的重点)。

A classic example from anthropology are the "pig cycles" among the Tsembaga of Highland New Guinea. The Tsembaga grow tubers and vegetables, and raise pigs. The porcine population increases evenly. As it grows, women and children （who are responsible for the pigs） must go further and further from the village to herd them, risking assaults from enemy peoples, and at the same time, the pigs do increasing harm to the crops. After a particular number of pig generations, the Tsembaga have reached a point where keeping pigs is no longer an asset but a liability. They then slaughter nearly all of them and enter into a complex ritual process of warfare and resettlement. （There are simpler solutions available, but that is not the point here.）

另外一个案例来自系统论学者贝特森。他用寓言的形式描述了一匹古怪的马。这匹马由顶尖的遗传学思想开发出来,被称为"多倍体马"。无论长宽高,它都是普通马的两倍。

Another example is narrated by the system theorist Gregory Bateson （1904—1980）. His allegory describes a fantastic horse developed by the sharpest minds in genetics, the polyploid horse. This horse was twice as long, twice as wide and twice as tall as a normal horse.

当然，"多倍体马"的重量是普通马的 8 倍。由于它的骨架只有普通马的 4 倍大，因而无法以直立方式支撑其自身的重量。"多倍体马"的内脏器官也濒临被烹饪的局面，因为其皮肤厚度只有普通马的两倍，可是皮肤表面积却是普通马的 4 倍。由于食管与气管都是普通马的 4 倍，而身体重量却是普通马的 8 倍，所以这匹马长期吃不饱，呼吸也很艰难。

Of course, its weight was eight times that of an ordinary horse. It was unable to support its own weight in an upright position, for its skeleton was only four times as thick as that of an ordinary horse. The inner organs were continually on the verge of being cooked, since its skin was twice as thick, while the surface area was only four times that of an ordinary horse. It was also chronically hungry and had difficulty breathing, since the oesophagus and windpipe were only four times the size of those of an ordinary horse, while the body was eight times as heavy.

这个寓言起源于 20 世纪 70 年代末，作者贝特森预见到了基因工程的潜在危险，用这个故事警告人们不要对基因操作持泛滥的热情。我认为这个故事也谈论到了复杂性问题以及量变到质变的转化。

This fable was originally told in the late 1970s as a warning against the widespread enthusiasm for genetic manipulation that Bateson already saw as a danger at that time. But it is also generally about complexity and, I would contend, the transformation of quantity into quality.

此外，这里还有一个更直接相关的案例。在大学里，一个只有 50 个学生的系，只要一个人管理就够了。他还可以兼任秘书，组织学生的考试，做好财政预算，还能给学生提供建议。当系里的学生达到 100 个人时，一两个管理人员就不够了，至少需要 5 个管理人员。因为一个人的心智不再可能照顾到必需的全部知识。系里的运转依赖于书面的惯例、登记和表格。管理不再停留在对学生的了解,还要知道他们的兴趣和已经取得的水准,还有他们的专业背景,等等。因此,专业的学生辅导员需要注意学生的关系。由于财政预算变得更复杂,因此需要专门雇佣一名财务人员。另外,还需要一个人坐在前台,一个信息技术咨询;为了组织员工有序地工作,还要一个办公室管理人员。

Another, more directly relevant example is this. In a university department with 50 students, one administrator is sufficient. He or she can serve as secretary, organise exams, keep the budget balanced and give some student advice. When the department gets 100 students, one will not need two, but five administrators. This is because it no longer is possible for one individual mind to possess all necessary knowledge. The department becomes dependent on written routines, registration and forms. The administration no longer knows each individual student and does not know their interests or the level achieved by them, their academic background and so on. So a professional student counsellor has to take care of the relationship with the students. Budget control also becomes so complicated that a financial consultant has to be employed. One also needs a person on the front desk and an IT consultant and finally, in order to keep the staff organised, an office manager.

一个组织可以在一段时间内成长,外表却没有明显的变化。许多公司都是建立在人际关系、信任和人类记忆的基础之上。如果组织规模很小就容易管理,也能运作得很好。但是,当雇员的数量超过临界点时,人际关系就进入正式化和官僚化。与此有关的一个案例来自世界关注研究委员会。他们为有需要的人(比如有发展前景的研究者、博士生和有才气的独立学者)提供资助与奖学金。当申请者人数较少时,委员会与接受者之间的关系建立在个人的信任之上。管理研究的官员们很容易留意到"他们"的学者们,也能够知道他们该负的责任。随着申请资助的人数增加,他们不得不填写定期的报告,并提交报告陈明下一步需要明确的工作。于是,研究委员会需要雇佣新人管理与报告有关的体系;同时,研究人员需要花费大量的时间，填写各种表格与报告。

An organisation can grow for quite a while without changing noticeably. Many enterprises are based on interpersonal relationships, trust and human memory. This works as long as the organisation is small and easily manageable. When the number of employees passes a critical point, the relationships must be formalised and bureaucratised. An example from my part of the world concerns research councils. They award grants and scholarships to the needy (that is, promising researchers, PhD students, brilliant scholars who do not want an academic job, etc.). When there were few applicants, the relationship between the recipient and the council was based on personal trust. It was easy for the research bureaucrats to keep an eye on "their" scholars; one generally knew what they were up to. As the number of grant recipients has grown, they are increasingly obliged to write regular reports, submit plans for their further work and so on. Thus the research councils have to employ new people to administer the reporting system, at the same time as research fellows spend an increasing amount of time filling in the forms and writing their reports.

各类正在发展的组织对于这种复杂化趋势理应该非常熟悉。他们认为有必要召开的会议数量日益增加，这是组织规模扩大的负效应。大的组织需要更多的会议，才能协调其活动；因此，雇员需要花费更多的工作时间协调彼此的工作，而不是去完成应做的工作。

This kind of complexification should be familiar from experience of all growing organisations. A further sideeffect of growth is the number of meetings that are deemed necessary. Large organisations need many meetings to coordinate their activities; as a result, employees spend an increasing proportion of their working time in meetings coordinating their work instead of doing it.

严格地讲,这些徒劳的会议占用了太多的工作时间。来自另一个领域的案例或许可以说明这一点。这个案例与摩天大楼有关。近来,亚洲与北美国家正在互相竞争,看谁建的大楼能成为世界第一高楼。在本书写作期间,马来西亚处于领先地位。然而,建筑师注意到了一个奇怪的问题,这最终可能会限制未来摩天大楼的高度。这与安全性或交通问题无关(很奇怪,摩天大楼不会倒塌),而是涉及电梯的数量。按照概测法,通常每15层楼就需要4个小电梯,或者是2个大电梯。因此,建筑物越高,电梯占用的建筑面积就越大。如果我们按照这种逻辑结论推理,一栋500层的大楼,除了电梯之外,已经没有其他的建筑空间!

An example taken from a different field may illustrate how it can be that strictly speaking unproductive meetings tend to fill so much working time. The example is about skyscrapers. Lately, a kind of competition in capitalist machismo has involved people in certain Asian and North American countries, competing over who could build the tallest skyscraper. At the time of writing, Malaysia is leading. The architects have nevertheless noticed a curious problem which may eventually limit the maximum height of tall buildings in the future. It has nothing to do with safety（strangely enough, skyscrapers do not fall over）or problems for air traffic, but with the number of lifts. A rule of thumb dictates a set of lifts （usually four small or two big ones）for every 15 floors. The taller the building, therefore, the more of the floor area is taken up by lifts. If we follow this line of reasoning to its logical conclusion, it appears that in a 500-floor building, there will be room for nothing but lifts!

一个组织太过庞大,就完全有可能只开会,不做其他任何事情。我确信有些管理部门已经接近这种状态。例如,我们若把一栋摩天大楼的每100层分成一段,并安装独立的电梯。这样,乘坐电梯时需要不断换乘。当然,要是一个人的工作地点位于第499层楼,那么他在上班的路上,至少可以把整份报纸全部读完。楼层越低,电梯里的人就越多;于是,较低层的电梯需要加快运行速度,其中有些直达电梯中途不停,比如在50层以下都不停。这种处理方法类似于在规模扩大的组织,由于雇员的工作时间和积极性消耗在使人精疲力尽的会议上，他们被迫在下班后继续做工作上的事情。如果把一个大企业分解成相同规模的 5 个部分，就能够让尽可能少的雇员进行内部的协调。大多数国家的大楼依然很低，因此人们乘坐电梯时，只有一点点时间可以阅读小报。由于我们仍然徘徊在学术的象牙塔中，我觉得有必要再举一个例子。与本章其他的事例一样，这个案例依然与失控增长的后果有关。

It is entirely possible to imagine an organisation which has time for nothing but meetings. （I feel confident that there are departments in ministries that approach this stage.）A solution to the lift problem could be decentralisation. For example, one might partition the building into 100-floor segments. Each set of lifts only runs 100 floors. Then one has to get out and change. Too bad, of course, if one works on the 499th floor, but at least one will then be able to read the paper thoroughly on the way to work. The lower segments will be more crowded than the upper ones; therefore the lower lifts will be very fast, and some of them will be express lifts which do not stop until say, the fiftieth floor. This kind of solution is identical to the one proposed for organisations that waste their employees' time and motivation in exhausting meetings, which force them to do their actual work after office hours. One partitions the enterprise into five parts of the same size, and leaves internal coordination to as few employees as possible. Since we are still lingering near the ivory towers of academia （which are still so low in most countries that one only has time to skim a tabloid while taking the lift）, I will offer another example from there. Like all of the examples in this chapter, it is to do with unintended consequences of uncontrolled growth.

1970 年，北欧国家的社会人类学只是很小的学科，可能只有十二三个研究职位。1980 年，这个数字已经翻番；2000 年，研究人员至少是最初的 10 倍。无论什么时候需要设立新的职位，或者撤除旧的职位，都需要指定三到四人的评估委员会。这些委员需要阅读和评估所有的申请表格，包括申请者的简历和简要的陈述——

需要论述申请者最重要的科学工作。很多时候,还有申请者提交的硕士论文、博士论文以及一大摞论文,有时候还包括一些书籍。每一个职位的申请人数都在增加,每个申请者写作的数量同样也在增加,出版的压力越来越大,因此职位空缺的数量也要增加。几年前,我作为评估委员,参加北欧一所小型大学举行的评估委员会,目的是要挑选两名讲师。到大学邮局领取申请人提交的材料时,我意识到应该带个手推车才行。因为包裹的重量达到了 32 千克。显然,面对如此多的材料,任何人也不可能彻底读完。一般地讲,普通表格的重量约为 4.6 克(按照 80 克的纸张计算),大部分材料采用双面打印,委员们收到的材料大约有 10000 页。按照一天200 页的进度,如果要把这些材料读完,至少需要两个月的时间。当然,大家都不可能完全支配自己的时间。老实说,申请专业职位的人的确认真准备了,但却难以得到应有的重视,即便如此研究者不得不用大量的时间,翻阅这些堆积如山的材料,但又无法用到自己的研究中,同时书架上的期刊与书籍却已布满了灰尘,因为他们没有时间去查阅这些文献资料。

In 1970 there were perhaps a dozen research positions in the then tiny discipline of social anthropology in the Nordic countries. In 1980, the number was at least doubled; in 2000 it was at least ten times the original number. Whenever a new position is established, or an old one becomes vacant, an evaluation committee of three or four persons is appointed. They are obliged to read and evaluate all applications, which apart from a CV and a brief statement from the applicant consists of the applicants' most important scientific work. In most cases, this would include an MPhil. dissertation, a PhD thesis and a stack of articles from each applicant; in several cases also a few books. The number of applicants for each position has grown steadily, the amount of writing from each applicant has grown similarly (the pressure to publish has become heavier), and the number of vacancies has grown. A few years ago, I was a member of an evaluation committee for two lecturerships at a small Nordic university. Arriving at the university post office to collect the applications, I realised that I should have brought a wheelbarrow. The parcel weighed in at 32 kilograms （70 pounds）. It goes without saying that it is impossible to read everything thoroughly when one is confronted with this kind of quantity. Reading every gram would have taken about a year the weight of an average sheet is 4.6 grams （assuming 80 gram paper）, and much of the material was printed and therefore two-sided, and so the total amount of material for the committee's perusal may have been about 10,000 pages. At the rate of 200 pages a day, reading everything would take two months of solid work. Needless to add, none of us had that kind of continuous time at our disposal then （nor later）. The result of this is, truth to tell, that applicants for academic position do not get the thorough treatment they deserve, but also that researchers are obliged to spend weeks ploughing through mountains of material that they will never be able to use in their own research, while the latest journals and books are sitting on the shelf collecting dust.

所有的一切都在增加

所有事物的总量都在增加。在 20 世纪最后 10 年中，书籍与期刊的出版数量一直蹒跚增长。在英国，1975 年出版了 35000 种书籍。1985 年，这个数字增加到了 53000 种。在接下来的 10 年间，英国出版的书籍数量翻番，达到了 107000 种，实现了跳跃式发展。作者们采用电子文档的形式提交书稿，并用简单便宜的程序制作页面，比如 PageMaker 或 Quark XPress。1986 年年底，PageMaker 的第一版问世。

There is a Growing Amount Of Everything

While we are at it: the growth of the number of published books and journals has been staggering during the last years of the twentieth century. In Great Britain, a total of 35,000 books were published in 1975. In 1985, the number had grown to 53,000. Then a leap occurs: during the next decade, the number of books published in the country doubled, to 107,000. The explanation must partly be that new computer technology has made it cheaper and easier to produce books. Writers submit their manuscripts in electronic form, and the page layout is done with a simple and inexpensive programme such as PageMaker or Quark XPress. The first version of PageMaker was shipped at the end of 1986.

　　全世界图书出版增长率整体上并不壮观(尽管还没有对数据进行严格比较),但增长趋势明显。1970年,全世界图书总量不到50万。20年之后,总量已经达到84.2万种。如果继续按照这种趋势增长,在我写作本书的时候,总量就将会超过100万种。

The growth rate for the world as a whole is less spectacular (although the figures are not strictly comparable), but the trend is clear. In 1970, the total number of published books was slightly over half a million. Twenty years later, the number was 842,000. If this trend continues, we have already passed the 1 million mark as I write.

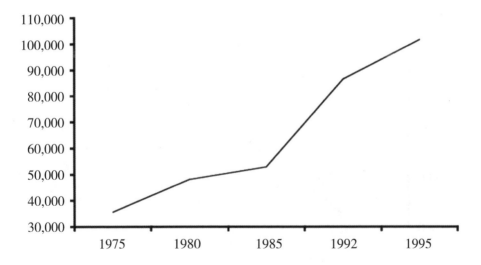

Figure 5–5　Book titles published in the UK, 1975—1996

Source: UNESCO

图 5-5　历年来英国出版的图书类别总量变化趋势(资料来源:UNESCO)

另一个指标是纸张的消耗量。想一想前些年那些预言家对电子计算机化的预测，他们认为无纸化办公即将出现，还提出 20 年后书本将离开人们的视线。可事实并非如此！1975 年，全球印刷用纸为 2800 万吨。到 2000 年，已经上升到 9700 万吨。造纸工业似乎不用担心互联网与数字电视的增长。与信息有关的一切事物都在增长。

Another indicator is paper consumption. Recall how early prophets of computerisation predicted the advent of the paper-free office, and how the death of the book has been announced regularly for 20 years. Well. The amount of paper used for printing was on a global basis 28 million metric tonnes in 1975. In 2000 it had risen to 97 million tonnes. The woodpulp industry seems to have little to fear from the rise of the Internet and digital television. There is growth in everything to do with information.

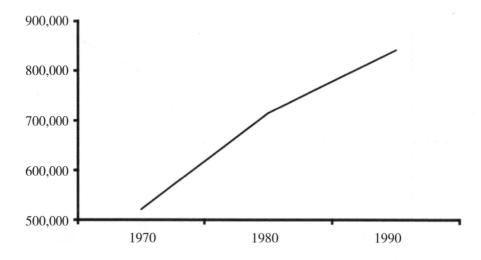

Figure 5–6   Book titles published worldwide, 1970—1990

Source: UNESCO

图 5-6   全世界历年出版的图书类别总量变化趋势（资料来源：UNESCO）

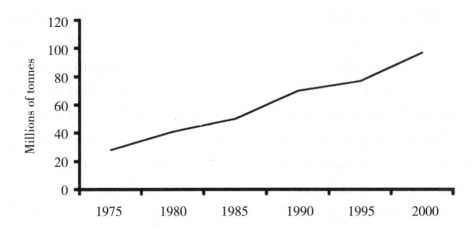

Figure 5-7　Paper consumption in the world, 1975—2000

Source: UNESCO

图5-7　全世界历年消耗的纸张总量变化趋势（资料来源:UNESCO）

这些出版物有很多并非为了阅读而印刷，尽管1970年以来全世界受过教育的人口数量增长很快。大部分出版物是在发达国家印制,这些地区的受教育率一直比较稳定,人口增长也很缓慢。我们并不谈论供巴基斯坦农村妇女使用的图书馆。想一下学术出版物,它们往往被图书馆购入,有时候可以得到国家或研究机构的财政资助,作者需要在简历里提交这些出版物,以期获得一个较好的职位。这些材料似乎只在一个封闭的小圈子内流通,并没有真正的市场和读者群体。专业期刊上的论文被引用的次数表明,在社会科学领域各种公开出版的论文中,过半的论文从未被人引用。于是人们必然会问:"这些文章有没有人读呢?"可能有相当多的论文,只有编辑、文字校对、技术编辑和专业评估委员会成员才会去读一下。这是不是有点夸张和讽刺呢? 或许是吧,但并非完全不切实际。

It seems likely that a lot of these publications are not primarily produced to be read, even if the literate population in the world has also grown immensely since 1970. Most of the growth in publishing has taken place in the rich countries, where literacy rates have been stable and population growth has been slow. We are not talking about the well-stocked libraries of rural Pakistani women here. Regarding academic publications, they are purchased by libraries, sometimes with financial support from the state or a research foundation, and the author depends on being able to place a reasonable number of them on his CV in order to be eligible for a good position. A lot of this material seems to circulate within a closed circuit without a real market or readership. Quotation indexes for academic journals indicate that perhaps more than half of all published journal articles in the social sciences are never quoted. One inevitably ventures to ask: are they ever read? It is likely that a sizeable proportion of published academic work is only read by the publisher's editorial consultants, copy-editors and proofreaders, and members of academic evaluation committees. An exaggerated and cynical description? Possibly, but it is not entirely unrealistic.

与互联网发展有关的最完美的指数增长曲线，是一家公司的年营业额总量变化趋势图。这家公司的主要业务是拓展老式的、以纤维纸张的承载信息。1995 年 7 月，亚马逊网上书店正式开业，在第一个财政年度，其营业额只有 511000 美元，到第二年增长为 15746000 美元。1999 年，营业额增加到 1639839000 美元，2000 年已经超过了 50 亿美元，其中大部分来自于书籍的销售。亚马逊网上书店营业额的增长率非常惊人：在 1999 年第二季度与 2000 年第二季度之间，营业额的增长达 84%。

One of the most perfect exponential growth curves regarding the Internet is, in line with this development, the turnover rate of a company whose main business consists in spreading good oldfashioned, cellulose-based information. The Internet bookshop Amazon.com was launched in July 1995, and during its first fiscal year its turnover was a modest $511,000, which grew to $15,746,000 in the next year. In 1999, the turnover was $1,639,839,000 (more than one and a half billion dollars), and most of this was still book sales. And the growth rate continues to be astonishing: between the second quarter of 1999 and the second quarter of 2000, the turnover grew by 84 per cent!

虽然每个人在谈到互联网或其他类似事情时,都认为在不久的将来这是主要的信息来源,但是出版业依然断定纸浆继续有市场,换句话说,还能够活蹦乱跳。同样,有了电子邮件与传真并不意味着人们在电话上交谈得更少。过去 15 年以来,电话的增长率已经非常明显。当今世界两条最重要的电话线路,是跨越大西洋与太平洋的海底光缆线,都是往返美国的信息渠道。1927 年开始,在技术上就已经可以打越洋电话了,但是直到 20 世纪 70 年代,打一个越洋电话——比如从瑞典的哥德堡打一个电话给西雅图的亲戚——还是件既令人讨厌又昂贵的事。1986年,我在毛里求斯首次从事田野工作,无论何时只要我想让家乡的母亲知道儿子还活着,我就要亲自跑到首都的国家电信中心才能打一个越洋电话。于是,我不得不乘坐发臭的老式公交,然后在烈日下走过 5 条街道,排队等候叫号,轮到之后才能走进一个小房间内,在夹杂着回声与嘈杂音的电话中与母亲交谈,而我口袋中的卢比却正以令人恐惧的速度消失。1999 年秋天,我再次来到毛里求斯,事实上,在任何地方我都可以给家里打电话,我在距离最近小镇比较远的地方,站在海边一棵芒果树的树荫底下给奥斯陆拨了一个电话,听筒里的声音非常清楚,而且话费也不贵。

Publishing which swears by wood pulp is, in other words, alive and kicking, although "everybody" talks of the Internet or something like it as the main source of information in the near future. Similarly, there is little to indicate that people talk less on the telephone since the introduction of email and fax. The growth rate of telephony has been phenomenal over the last 15 years. Two of the most important telephone routes in the world are the clusters of lines that cross the Atlantic and the Pacific oceans, generally channelling calls to and from the USA. It has been technically possible to make transatlantic calls since 1927, but as late as the 1970s, it was cumbersome and expensive to place a long-distance call from, say, Gothenburg to relatives in Seattle. When I did my first ethnographic fieldwork in Mauritius in 1986, I had to make my way physically to the national Telecom centre in the capital, whenever I felt the need to reassure my mother that I was still alive. I had to take an old, smelly bus to town, walk five blocks in the dazing heat, stand in a queue to order the call, wait for my turn, walk into a closet and talk over a poor connection with echo and noise, while my diminishing wad of rupees was depleted at frightening speed. I also spent the autumn of 1999 in Mauritius, and apart from the fact that I could call home from any telephone, I found myself one day in the shadow of a mango tree near the sea, far from the nearest town, making an inexpensive, crystal clear call to Oslo.

从 1986 年到 1996 年，跨越大西洋的电话线路，从十几万条增加到了 1974000 条，增长率接近 2000%。同一期间，穿越太平洋的电话线路，从 41000 条增加到了 1098600 条。1985 年，全世界电信使用总时间（包括电话、传真和数据传输）为 150 亿分钟。10 年之后，这个数字已经增加到了原来的 4 倍，也就是 600 亿分钟。2000 年，全世界电信使用时间估计可达 950 亿分钟。目前，几乎没有哪种传统行业能有这样的增长率。

Between 1986 and 1996, the number of telephone lines across the Atlantic increased from 100,000 to 1,974,000, that is a growth of nearly 2,000 per cent. The corresponding figures for the Pacific were 41,000 in 1986 and 1,098,600 in 1996. In 1985, the total use of telecommunications in the world （telephony, fax, data transmission） added up to 15 billion minutes. Ten years later, the number was quadrupled to 60 billion minutes. The figure for 2000 is estimated at 95 billion minutes. Few traditional industries can match this growth rate.

根据当前的发展趋势，提供这些服务的公司不久后就可以出现指数增长。在 21 世纪的头五年，已经计划发射 1000 多颗远程通信卫星。这类通信方式的主要趋势，正在向无线的、移动的、非嵌入式的方向发展。无论何时何地，人们都可以接收和发送信息。我们现在才看到了最初的阶段，但是发展趋势已经指明了特定的

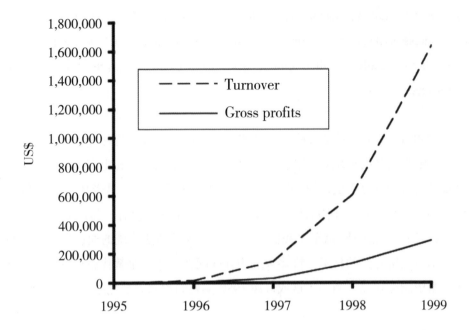

Figure 5-8　amazon.com. 1995—1999

Source: www.amazon.com

图 5-8　亚马逊网上书店 5 年间的营业额与毛利润（资料来源：www.amazon.com）

方向。手机代替固定电话，掌上电脑代替笔记本电脑、备忘录和通讯录，还可以连接互联网；只要公司老总将电脑连接到综合业务数字网，即使居住在遥远的小木屋里，也可以给自己的雇员发号施令。

The suppliers of these services are prepared for exponential growth in the near future, extrapolating from current trends. In the first five years of the twenty-first century, there are plans to send out no less than 1,000 new satellites dedicated to telecommunications. The main tendency is for this kind of communication to become increasingly mobile, wireless, disembedded from place. One can increasingly send and receive information anywhere, anytime. We have still seen only the beginning, but it points in a particular direction. Mobile phones replace stationary phones, PDAs

(Personal Digital Assistants, i.e. handheld computers) replace notebooks, filofaxes and address books, and are already able to connect to the Internet; people have ISDN connections installed in their remote wood cabins and are given laptops by their employers.

1990 年，手机还只是某些职业群体——出租车司机、旅行推销员和其他一些人——随身携带的小玩意。当时，这种手机由汽车上的插座充电。到了 2000 年时，挪威已经有 300 万手机用户（挪威总人口只有 450 万）。芬兰是诺基亚手机的故乡（10 年前是伏特加酒和木质纸浆的故乡），几乎每个儿童都有一部以上的手机。无线通信发展如此迅速，以至于我们相信它可以替代其他传统的通信形式，甚至包括汽车与飞机之类的技术。许多人认为互联网在环境上是替代旅行的合理选择，他们希望能够如此（当然，这或许像 1980 年人们预测无纸化办公时代的到来一

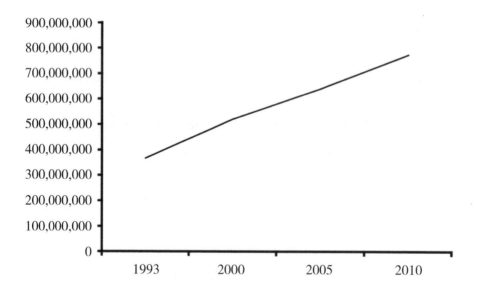

Figure 5–9　Number of air passengers in Europe, 1993—2010

Source: Air Transport Action Group（www.atag.org）

图 5-9　近 20 年欧洲航空旅客总量变化趋势（资料来源：Air Transport Action Group, www.atag.org）

样）。迄今为止，没有什么迹象表明这件事会发生。相反，我们从任何一方得到的东西似乎都在增加。全球的道路与空中交通都在快速发展。

In 1990, mobile phones were still a sort of gadget associated with particular professions taxi drivers, travelling salesmen and perhaps a few others. This generation of mobile phones were powered by the lighter socket in the car and a box that filled half the trunk. At the end of 2000, altogether 3 million mobile phone subscriptions have been sold in Norway (a country with a population of 4.5 million). In Finland, the home of Nokia (ten years ago the home of... well, vodka and wood pulp), children on average possess more than one mobile phone each. Since wireless communication grows so fast, one might perhaps believe that it would replace the other, traditional form of communication, embodied in technology such as cars and planes. Many of those who see the Internet as an environmentally sound alternative to travelling, have been hoping for this to happen (just as some predicted, around 1980, the coming of the paper-free office). So far, nothing indicates that this is about to happen. On the contrary, we seem to get more of everything. Both road and air traffic grow surprisingly fast globally.

20 世纪 90 年代，空中交通的年增长率在 5%~7%之间。2000 年春季，国际航空运输协会（IATA）估计，从 1999 年到 2010 年，航空旅客总量将从 16 亿增长到 23 亿。IATA 还预计，2010 年乘坐飞机抵达美国的旅客总量将达到 2.26 亿人次，而这项数据在 2000 年为 1.21 亿人次，1993 年只有 7900 万人次。如果将这样的增长趋势以曲线的形式画在方格纸上，就难以避免出现接近垂线的情况。这些数字看起来很大，但我们必须记住，它们只是往返美国的旅客数量，其他国家的航空旅客还没有计算在内。比如欧洲，2000 年之后的 15 年内，航空旅客总量预计可翻番。顺便说一句，从 1994 年到 2001 年，空中旅客运输距离估计增长了 50%。

In the 1990s, air traffic grew at a rate of between 5 and 7 per cent a year. In the spring of 2000, the international air traffic association, IATA, estimated that the total number of travellers would grow from 1.6 billion to 2.3 billion between 1999 and 2010. IATA also predicts that the number of passengers arriving in the USA by plane will grow from 79 million （1993）via 121 million （2000）to 226 million in 2010. This growth curve will soon make it difficult to avoid a nearly perfect vertical line when it is transferred to graph paper. And, if these figures sound large, it must be kept in mind that they refer exclusively to travellers to and from the USA; air travel within that country is not included. Regarding Europe, total air traffic is predicted to double in 15 years from 2000. The total number of passenger kilometres, incidentally, is estimated to increase by 50 per cent from 1994 to 2001.

目前,因为这些国际组织直接负责民用航空运输,所以我们需要特别深入地讨论三件事:空中无线电频率的缺乏(航班与移动电话越来越多的结果),航班延误和机场基础设施建设。你该如何设计一个机场,使它在几年内可以轻易地将容

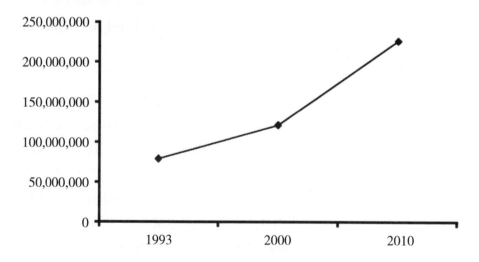

Figure 5-10 Air passengers to and from the USA, 1993—2010

Source: IATA

图 5-10 近 20 年美国出入境航空旅客数量变化趋势(资料来源:IATA)

量扩大一倍,而且不会降低旅客的服务体验和安全度呢? 如果一个人定期乘坐航班出行,换句话说,他就习惯了一个永久性的建筑标志。这不是科幻小说。看过这些图形的研究者,从过去 10 年的发展趋势很简单地推测出了未来的走向。就像其他指数增长曲线一样,这些曲线的增长率相对比较稳定,但是数值却比较大。

For the time being, three issues are discussed particularly intensively by those international organisations that are responsible for civilian air traffic: the lack of vacant radio frequencies (a result of both more planes and more mobile phones), delays and airport architecture how do you design an airport which can easily double its capacity in a few years without compromising passenger services and security? If one travels regularly via busy airports, in other words, one might as well get used to being on a permanent construction site. This is not science fiction. The researchers who reached these figures have simply extrapolated from the trends of the last decades. As is the case with other exponential growth curves, the rate of growth is relatively stable, but the figures are becoming incomprehensibly large.

直到 20 世纪 70 年代, 总体上航空运输依然是一种专用和昂贵的旅行方式。航空运输的大众化过程,与拨打长途电话类似。1960 年,从伦敦拨打纽约的电话,每 3 分钟需要收取 240 美元的费用;2000 年,同样的电话费用是 2 美元(按照1990 年的美元汇率)。航空旅行的费用也在逐渐便宜,没有比旅游业更明显的地方了,因为旅游业成了世界上第三大产业 (仅次于武器与毒品)。根据世界贸易组织(WTO)的统计,旅游业占世界经济的 12%。WTO 进一步估计,2001 年全世界旅游业总收入约为 3.5 万亿美元。自 1950 年以来,旅客人数增长了 20 倍。

Until the late 1970s, air travel was in general an exclusive, expensive way of travelling. It has been democratised, just like remote calls on the telephone net. In 1960, a 3-minute call from London to New York cost the equivalent of $240 (in 1990 dollars). In 2000, the price was $2 (in 1990 dollars). Air travel has become similarly inexpensive, and nowhere is this more evident than in the economic sector which is, perhaps, the third largest in the world （following weapons and drugs）, namely tourism. According to that other organisation called the WTO, the World Tourism Organization, tourism accounts for about 12 per cent of the world economy. The WTO further estimates the total turnover in the tourism industry in 2001 to $3.5 trillion dollars （a trillion is a thousand billions, one followed by twelve zeros.） The number of tourists has grown by a factor of 20 since 1950.

2020 年，预计有 16 亿人将出国旅行。地中海地区仍是北欧游客最中意的目的地，1955 年其接待游客总量为 100000 人；1970 年游客总数为 200 万；1990 年则为 650 万人。发展还在继续。换句话说，一个人从盖特维克到阳光海岸度假，需要从一个永久性建筑转移到另一个永久性建筑物。

In 2020, an estimated 1.6 billion persons will travel abroad. The Mediterranean area, still the most popular foreign destination for North Europeans, received 100,000 tourists annually in 1955. In 1970, the number was 2 million, and in 1990 6.5 million. The development continues. If, in other words, one travels from Gatwick to the Costa del Sol as a tourist, one moves from one permanent construction site to another.

这些图形令人眼花缭乱。增长曲线几乎笔直地往上冲。若从更具包容性的层面上看，1995 年世界总资本的流量估计比 1975 年增长了 100 倍；换句话说，25 年间增长了 10000%。这个曲线图证明，无论全球化谈起来有多么新奇，都要涉及具体而重要的现实。

These figures are dizzying. The growth curves point almost straight upwards. At a more encompassing level, it may be noted that the total flow of capital in the world is estimated to have grown by a factor of 100 since 1975; it has increased, in other words, by 1,000 per cent in 25 years. This figure proves more than anything that

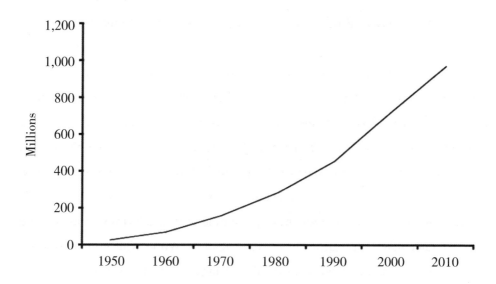

Figure 5-11   Number of tourists in the world, 1950—2010
Source: World Tourist Organization
图 5-11   近 60 年来世界游客总量变化趋势(资料来源：WTO)

however fashionable it may be to talk about globalisation, it does refer to a very tangible and consequential reality.

网络空间的爆炸式扩张

网络空间的增长率超过所有其他的事。本章到目前为止，几乎还没有提及互联网。在我们这个时代，关于指数增长最辉煌的案例，直接与电子信息技术有关，这也是最明显的例子，涉及进入千家万户日常生活的计算机。对于其他信息的传输通道而言，包括报纸与电视在内，互联网是一个厉害的竞争对手。这种变化非常迅速。收音机从发明到 500 万人使用，只用了 38 年的时间。数十年之后，电视机出现，只花了 13 年就达到了与收音机相同的用户数量。而互联网达到这个用户数，仅仅用了 4 年。在 20 世纪，还有谁能怀疑发展是加速变化的过程吗？

The Growth Rates In Cyberspace Surpass Everything Else

Still, I have hardly mentioned the Internet in this chapter. The most spectacular examples of exponential growth in our time are those that relate directly to electronic information technology, and the most obvious examples concern the entry of computers into the everyday life of the world and the appearance of the Internet as a serious competitor to other channels for transmitting information, from newspapers to television. The changes have come about fast. It took the radio 38 years from its invention until it reached 50 million people. In the case of television, some decades later, the same figure was reached in 13 years. With the World Wide Web, it took four years. Is anybody still in doubt as to whether change accelerated during the twentieth century?

在谈论计算机世界的指数增长时，创立于 1975 年的微软公司到现今的发展历程，是一个无法回避的案例。在微软公司经营第一年后，就产生了 16000 美元的盈利。从此，微软公司的发展，就像前面讲到的国际象棋棋盘里麦粒数量的变化趋势。在很长一段时间内，这个盈利在每个转折点都会翻番，但不会让盖茨及其同事变得富裕。到了 20 世纪 80 年代，增长曲线的方向开始发生变化，其拐点出现在 20 世纪 90 年代。增长率基本没变，但现在的数目已经非常巨大，以至于盈利翻番后就可以让股东们挣得盆满钵满。图 5-15 已经显示得非常清楚。

An inevitable example of exponential growth in the computer world is the development of Microsoft from the foundation of the firm in 1975 up to the present. During its first year in business, the company generated $16,000 in surplus. Its growth from that year onwards has followed the same logic as the number of grains of wheat accorded to the mythical inventor of chess. The surplus could for a long time be doubled at each crossroads without making Bill Gates and his companions rich. Towards the end of the 1980s, the direction of the growth curve began to shift, seen from the vantagepoint of the late 1990s. The rate of growth was roughly constant, but the numbers were now so large that a doubling of the surplus entailed rather a lot of money going into the pockets of the shareholders. Figure 5-15 shows this clearly.

微软公司从来没有特别创新的技术，但在开拓市场方面却有娴熟的技巧。然而，他们没有占据主导优势的一个重要市场是服务器市场。服务器是互联网上用于储存、组织、发送和接收信息的一个盒子。不管是电子邮件、网页、非正式信息还是别的东西，网上所有信息的传输都需要经过服务器。在这个领域，美国思科公司无论是硬件还是软件方面都处于领先地位。从 1995 年到 1999 年的 5 年之内，思科公司的营业额从 22 亿美元（这已经是一个不小的数目）增长到 122 亿美元。因此，利润也在快速地增长。

Microsoft has never been particularly innovative technologically, but the company has been incredibly skilful at conquering new markets. One market that they nevertheless do not dominate is the important server market. A server is a box which stores, organises, sends and receives information on the Internet. All information on the Net passes via one or several servers, whether it is email, WWW pages, chat messages or something else. The leading company in this sector, both on the hardware and software side, is Cisco. In five years from 1995 to 1999 their turnover grew from $2.2 billion （which is already a sizeable sum） to $12.2 billion. The profits grew accordingly.

1994 年 7 月，万维网上可搜索到的网站数量是 300 万个，到 2000 年 1 月这个数字已经变为 720 万个。虽然近几年出现了一些暂时的回落，但从互联网上挣钱的前景依然合理。这个数据从最初的白手起家，估计到 2000 年时已经达到 3.77 亿美元，而到 2002 年则将冲破 12 亿美元大关。若有任何人质疑这个乐观的估计，可以看看微软、思科和帝王公司的成长故事。

The number of hosts (web sites) on the WWW grew from 3 million in July 1994 to 72 million in January 2000. The outlook for people seeking to make money from the web is also reasonable, in spite of several temporary backlashes in the last few years. The estimated figure in this respect goes from nearly nothing to $377 million in 2000, and is expected to pass the $1,200 million mark in 2002. If anyone doubts the optimism of this estimate, think of Microsoft, Cisco and the Emperor's grain stores!

电子信息区别于纸质信息和其他具体信息的地方，就是它有令人感兴趣的品质和特性。当信息供应商将信息提供给消费者时，自身的信息总量并不减少。比如说，我用 VISA 信用卡支付 249 美元（只存在于网络空间的虚拟货币），下载我喜欢的最新版网页制作软件，对于提供信息给我的美国服务商而言，其储存的软件信息并不会减少。占有和控制信息的人，在出售信息之后，拥有的信息量没有任何减损。一般来说，信息供应商储存的信息永远不可能倒空。数年前，我在大学为社会科学专业的数百名学生，做了一场有关达尔文主义的演讲，其后我头脑中储存有关达尔文的知识并没有减少。（恰恰相反，通过演讲和与学生互动，我的信息储备量还获得了增长。）最糟糕的事情可能发生在供应商那里，二进制位元、字节和想法已经落伍——这件事发生的概率逐年增加。电子信息作为商品所具有的特性，使其很容易出现指数增长的趋势。迄今为止，几乎没有人认为信息增长会与人口爆炸和工业污染的增长出现一样的势头。现在正是时候思考我们接下来要做的事情！

Information in electronic form has an interesting quality distinguishing it from both paper-based information and all other physical objects. It is not reduced in quantity when one gives it away. If, say, I charge my Visa card with $249 (virtual money; it exists only in cyberspace) to download the latest version of my preferred web design software from a server in the USA, the stocks of the supplier are not reduced by as much as a gram. One possesses information, one sells it, and one has as much left. A supplier of information has stores which can in principle never be emptied. If I give a lecture about Darwinism for a few hundred students in the social sciences （which I do a couple of times a year）, I do not have any less knowledge about Darwin afterwards. （Quite the contrary, as a matter of fact!）The worst thing that could happen to a supplier of bits, bytes and ideas, is that it becomes outmoded and the probability of this happening increases year by year. This quality of electronic （and spoken）information as a commodity, makes it particularly promising as a candidate for exponential growth curves. So far, few have regarded the growth in information as a problem on a par with population growth or growth in industrial pollution. It may be high time that we do.

　　每天各种未经过滤的信息不断填充到我们的生活里,这不只是我个人作为一名学者发出的叹息。信息功能方面的指数增长,在各个地方基本上大同小异。信息可以分割成小块,并找到路径直接进入读者的大脑,占据最后 1 立方厘米的空间。即使读者、观众和听众没有花费半天甚至更多的工夫消费现成的信息字节,他们依然会受此影响。或许,在加油站给汽车加油时,你也可以看到输油管上装饰的广告;或者你会沉迷于手机上的短消息;也可能你会整晚坐在电视机前放松,这些正是加速度下的信息扩散媒介。即使你一天只看一档节目,或者一周只看一档新闻节目,而不接受其他的信息资料,这一档新闻节目并不会因此减缓传输的速度。

This is not merely a personal lament from a scholar who has had his fill of unfiltered information. Exponential growth in information functions in roughly the same way everywhere. Information is partitioned into little pieces, it finds paths to reach the last vacant cubic centimetre in the brain of the reader. Even readers/watchers/listeners who do not spend half their day or more consuming ready-made bits of information are affected by this. Perhaps they fill the tank of their car at a petrol station where the nozzle of the petrol hose is now decorated with an advertisement; perhaps they are addicted to SMS messages; or perhaps they simply spend their evenings trying to relax in front of the television, which is a medium of accelerating

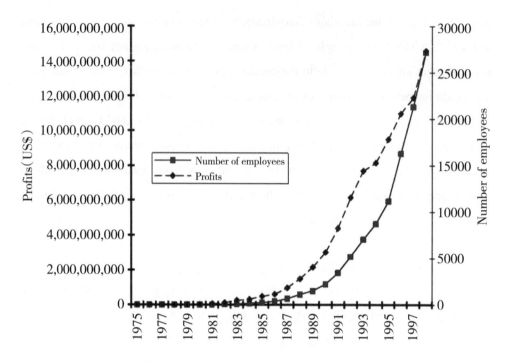

Figure 5-12   Microsoft, 1975—1998

Source: www.microsoft.com

图 5-12　微软公司盈利及雇员数量变化趋势（资料来源：www.microsoft.com）

speed. Even if one watches just one news programme a day, or for that matter a week, and protects oneself against other sources of information, that particular programme does not become any slower for that reason.

指数增长末端的时间无穷短

时间正在归零。本章大部分案例属于普通的指数增长曲线，譬如细菌繁殖的例子和国际象棋发明者索要麦粒数的实例。这些变化曲线的 X 轴代表持续的时间。当曲线出现向上走的陡坡时，就意味着更多的事务被挤压到了有限的时间里。换句话说，这条曲线阐明了被压缩的时间：越来越多的信息、消费、运动和活动被

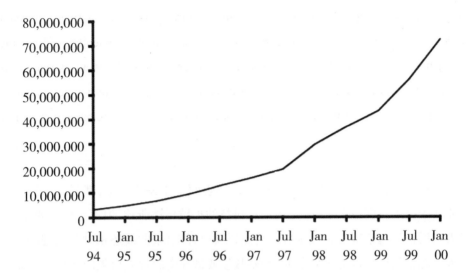

Figure 5-13　Number of WWW hosts in the world, 1994—2000

Source: Internet Software Consortium（www.isc.org）

图 5-13　全世界网站总量变化趋势

压缩到有效的时间里，而且有效的时间保持相对不变（虽然有些精神病人天真地梦想"睡得更有效率"）。当指数增长曲线完全垂直时，时间就不复存在。当然，这是临界的个案，实际上很难想象；只有在新闻突然变得陈旧时，才会发生这种情形，这就像一件时装刚上架就过时了一样。

Time Goes Towards Zero

Most of the examples presented in this chapter belong to the most common kind of exponential curve that is, the case of the bacterial colony, but not the chessboard and the grains of wheat. They are curves where the x axis represents duration. When the curve makes its steep movement upwards on the right-hand side, an implication is that more events are squeezed into the time span in question. They illustrate, in other words, the compression of time: more and more information, consumption, movement and activity is being pushed into the available time, which is relatively constant (although there exist lunatics who earnestly try to "sleep more efficiently"). When the line is perfectly vertical, time has ceased to exist. This, naturally, is an extreme case which is difficult to imagine in practice; it is a state which occurs only when the news is outdated the moment it comes on the air, when fashion clothes are passe just as they hit the shops and so on.

本章的分析表明，我们这个时代的许多表面不相关的现象，都可以用指数增长曲线来描绘。这些现象很多是由信息科技的扩散传播所致，但不是全部如此。全球人口增长看起来很具指数函数的特点，尽管目前这条曲线还相对平坦。此外，世界人口翻番的比率也低于旅游业、网站数量或世界受教育人口数的增长率。简单地讲，读者与作者的数量、游客量、微软视窗操作系统的用户、书籍的出版量和手机的用户数，都比世界人口增长的速度更快。同样，过去十年来，奥斯陆的咖啡馆和印度餐馆的数量、全球的现金流量和世界空中运输总量，也比世界人口增长更快。这些增长趋势之间互相关联，即使现在还不太明显。当某些地方的人口增长后，生存空间就显得更稀缺。当然，这并不意味着上限必须降低，或者人们一定要挨饿，但其中的复杂性会增加。当阅读书写、上学、发送电子邮件、乘坐公交、火车或飞机的人增多时，人们之间关联的网络密度就会加大。那些有吸引力的地方容易受到人们更密集的关注，稀缺性将随着密度的增大而增加——伦敦中心区的地价将远远高于赫布里底群岛。某些特别稀缺的财产，在人们的生活中将会出现真空状态。

As this chapter has shown, growth curves with exponential tendencies can be plotted on to many, apparently unrelated phenomena in our time. Many of them are admittedly caused by the spreading of information technology, but not all. Global population growth continues to look quite exponential, although it is currently about to flatten out. Besides, the world's population doubles less quickly than, say, the number of tourists, the number of web sites or the number of literate persons in the

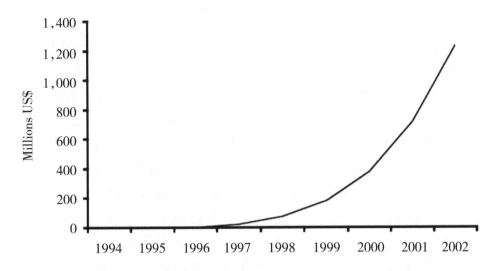

Figure 5-14　Surplus generated by the Internet, 1996—2002

Source: www.nua.ie, 2000

图 5-14　互联网产值变化趋势

world. Briefly put, the number of readers and writers, the number of tourists and users of Microsoft Windows, the numbers of books published and mobile phones grow much more rapidly than the world's population. The same could be said about the number of café s and Indian restaurants in Oslo during the past ten years, global flows of capital and the world's total air traffic. There is a connection between these growth trends, even if it is not self-evident. When the population grows somewhere （in a village, a country or on a planet）, space becomes more scarce. This does not imply that ceiling levels are necessarily reduced or that people will have to go to bed hungry, but that complexity grows. When growing numbers read and write, go to school, send email, travel by bus, train or aeroplane, the networks that connect people become more dense. Attractive plots of land are sought after ever more intensively, and scarcity increases with growing density property is much, much more expensive in central London than in the Hebrides and a kind of property which is particularly scarce, is any vacant moment in people's lives.

毫无疑问，指数增长最终必然改变其过程。这只是早晚的事，问题在于早晚的程度如何。20 世纪 90 年代，埃博拉病毒按照扁平的指数曲线扩展；艾滋病的传播亦是如此；世界人口的增长、热带雨林的消失、最近北欧计算机的年销售量、微软公司的发展等，都是如此。这些指数曲线何时以及如何改变方向，目前不可能回答。在热带雨林的消失过程中，可能在没有热带雨林时，拐点就出现了，也可能会早一点就改变发展的方向。然而，正如本章开头所讲的国际象棋的例子，即使我们把前 10 个或 20 个棋盘格单独拿出来分析，尽管此时离达到世界生产的麦粒总量还有很长一段距离，麦粒数的增长曲线还是以很陡的方式向上变化。如果我们研究 1975 年至 1985 年微软公司的发展历程，就可以绘制一条相当陡峭的增长曲线。或许到 2030 年，分析人士会说 2000 年的航空运输旅客量还比较适中，但是2010 年之后，每年的数字就已经越发令人无法忍受。同样，穿越太平洋的电话线路、旅客乘坐飞机的公里数与网站的数量，在一段时间内还将继续以指数级方式增长，却不会出现被人们视为灾难的临界点。但是，代价的增长已经很明显——按照传统的观点，环境并不一定退化，但时间趋近于零却是事实。每一个空闲的时刻，都被塞得越来越满，间隙已经完全被填平。这种压缩的结果，就是我在下一章里要谈的堆垛。

It goes without saying that exponential growth is eventually bound to alter its course. Sooner or later. The question is, what is sooner and what is later? A flattening of growth curves happened in the case of the Ebola virus in the 1990s, it will happen with AIDS; it has happened to world population growth, and it will happen with the disappearance of the rainforests; it has recently happened to annual computer sales in Scandinavia, and it will happen to Microsoft. Just how and when this change of direction will come about, is impossible to say. In the case of the rainforests, it will occur when there is no more rainforest left, but not necessarily any earlier. However, as the chess example indicates, the growth curve points upwards quite steeply even if we just isolate the first ten or twenty squares, long before the entire world's production of wheat is implied. If one had studied the development of Microsoft during its first ten years, from 1975 to 1985, one would already have been able to plot a pretty steep growth curve. Perhaps in 2030, analysts will say that air passenger traffic was still modest in 2000, but after 2010, the figures became increasingly intolerable. It may well be the case that the number of telephone connections across the Pacific, the number of passenger kilometres travelled by plane and the number of web sites will continue to grow exponentially for a while yet, without a critical mass of people seeing it as a disaster. But the price of this growth is already evident it will not necessarily be environmental degradation in the traditional sense, but the fact that time approaches zero. More and more is squeezed into every free moment, and the gaps are filled. The result of this compression I now propose to discuss in terms of stacking.

第六章　信息的俄罗斯方块:堆垛

"只能如此了,我的意思是和上周一样!"

——在奥斯陆电车上听见一个人对牛仔裤广告的评论

6　Stacking

"This is just so, I mean, like, last week!"（Comment on jeans ad, heard on Oslo tram）

第一部进入北欧市场的美国肥皂剧是《王朝》。1983 年,得益于卫星与光缆传输,这部肥皂剧通过多频道电视吸引了一群好奇和激动的观众。和其他成千上万的观众一样,我与朋友跑到厨房,然后打开那台老式的黑白电视机,观看《王朝》首日的播出,试图发现这部肥皂剧究竟讲什么。数周之后,由于还有其他事要做,我们停止不再看这档节目了,我们相信自己已经明白了这部肥皂剧的意思。6 年之后,我到加勒比海的热带特立尼达拉岛,进行民族志田野调查。在特立尼达拉岛,大部分人正热衷于观看《王朝》这部肥皂剧。尽管当地也有其他的肥皂剧播出,特别是在午饭时有一档电视节目《年轻与骚动不安的一族》非常流行,但人们似乎对《王朝》情有独钟。由于人类学的黄金法则告诫我们,在田野调查时,要尽量与当地人做同样的事,于是我租用了一台电视,并开始观看《王朝》。

The first real American soap opera to hit the Scandinavian markets was Dynasty. It was introduced to a curious and excited audience in the same year as multi-channel viewing appeared in the same countries, thanks to satellite and cable transmissions, namely 1983. Like many thousands of others, my friends and I went into the kitchen and turned on our old black-and-white television on the first evening of Dynasty, to find out what this was. After a few weeks we believed we had understood it, and ceased watching the programme since we had other things to do （chiefly wearing black clothes and staring blankly in front of us in grim concert venues that had been redecorated to look like abandoned factories）. The years went by. Six years later, I travelled to tropical Trinidad in the Caribbean Sea to carry out ethnographic fieldwork. In Trinidad, it turned out, a large part of the population followed Dynasty （although other soap operas, particularly the lunchtime show The Young and the Restless, were even more popular）. I rented a TV set and began to watch Dynasty again, since a golden rule of anthropology admonishes practitioners doing fieldwork to try to do whatever it is that the natives do.

　　我已经6年没看这部肥皂剧了，所以用了6秒钟时间，才重新适应其叙事风格。与其他同类的节目一样，《王朝》也按照多频道格式剪辑。在制作过程中，这部肥皂剧意识到了观众在观看节目时，会不停地用手指按遥控器，一旦节目不合自己的胃口，就会切换电视频道。电视剧每隔7分钟就会穿插一个广告，这样吊人胃口的东西会使观众异常疲劳。而且，这种令人喘不过气来又快速播放的电视剧缺乏连续性。与其他同类的连续剧一样，《王朝》这部肥皂剧的播放速度快得惊人。

I had been absent from the series for six years, and it took me about 30 seconds to get into the narrative again. Like other programmes of the same kind, Dynasty was tailored for the multichannel format. It was being produced in the awareness that the viewers would restlessly finger their remote control while watching, ready to switch channels at the first indication of inertia. It presupposed commercial breaks every seventh minute or so, and so the cliffhangers were overdone and frequent. The cost of this breathless, fast kind of drama is a lack of progression. Like other serials of the same kind, Dynasty was a drama which stood still at enormous speed.

这样的时刻有碍于发展

20 世纪 70 年代后期，大部分欧洲国家只有一两个（最多三个）国家电视频道。许多电视台都是国营性质，而且非商业化运作。直到 20 世纪 70 年代中期，黑白电视节目在许多国家占主导优势。其中，最流行的戏剧系列《阿什顿之家》，乃是根据约翰·芬奇的小说改编而成。这个戏剧用非常严肃的方式叙述了二战期间一个英国家庭的故事，是体现缓慢与累积性的典型。如果观众错过其中的一集，就会丢掉叙述的线索，因为故事的人物及其关系随着故事的展开不断发生改变。这预先假定了在没有许多嘈杂的选择下忠实并具有耐心的观众。这样，电视连续剧的基础是特殊事件产生缓慢反应的节奏，给未来行动的方向留下印记。《王朝》的基础是爆发性瞬间，《阿什顿之家》的基础是线性时间和自然的增长。

The Moment Precludes Development

As late as the 1970s, most European countries had one, two or a maximum of three national television channels. Many were state run and free of commercials. Until the early to mid-1970s, programming in black and white dominated the offering in many countries. One of the most popular drama series at the time was The Ashton Family, based on John Finch's novel. This series, which was a deadly serious narrative about an English family during the Second World War, was typically slow and cumulative. If one had missed just one episode, one lost the narrative thread, since the people and their relationships changed as the story unfolded. It presupposed loyal, patient viewers without a lot of noisy alternatives. In this way, the series could be based on a rhythm where particular events slowly reverberated through the cast, leaving their imprint on the future direction of the action. While Dynasty was based on the explosive moment, The Ashton Family was based on linear time and organic growth.

选择这两个案例，并不是因为它们特别有趣，而是因为它们能够说明我们文化的根本性变迁，其变迁方式是从线性的缓慢走向快速的瞬间。过去 20 年来，电视已经成了比以前更快的媒体，收音机也发生了同样的变化，这些媒体似乎变得更令人兴奋和喘不过气，并提供了更多的频道供人选择。这两个电视剧之间的关系，类似于互联网与书籍的关系。书籍具有连续性。读者可以从第一页开始阅读，还可以按照特定的顺序阅读。作者控制了供读者阅读的文本，因此可以自由建构一个累积性的和线性的情节或论证过程。读者通过阅读书籍，可以抵达一个新的知识或洞察力的平台。不管阅读的速率如何，书籍都可以是一个对阅读艺术的理想描述。

This example was not chosen because it in itself is particularly interesting, but because it illustrates a fundamental change in our culture; from the relatively slow and linear to the fast and momentary. Television has, over the past couple of decades, become an ever faster medium, and the same change has taken place in radio, which generally seems to become more hectic and breathless the more channels one has to choose between. The relationship between the two TV series, further, is analogous to the relationship between the World Wide Web and the book. The book is sequential: you begin with page 1 and read it in a particular order. The writer controls the drift of the reading, and is therefore at liberty to construct a cumulative, linear plot or argument. The reader reaches ever new plateaux of knowledge or insight as she (most readers are women) moves through the text. This, at any rate, is an ideal depiction of the art of reading.

在网站与纸质出版物图书馆之间，存在一些重要差异。最重要的是，网站上的信息未经组织，可能按照字母顺序或其他方式排列。不同的主题与页面按照部分随机的方式连接在一起。网站也没有分出层次：现有的数百万网站，都可以在同一层次上进入。多年来，万维网的积极使用者觉得，这是一个稠密而难以处理的丛林，每天都在变得更黑更密。当人们在网上寻找似乎并不在上面的信息时，很容易使人断定，网络是真实世界的化身，是博尔赫斯哲学故事中所说的巴别塔图书馆。这个神秘的图书馆包含已经写好的书籍以及将要完成的所有作品——也就是字母的各种组合。在那里一切事物都可利用，这些事物以外的其他事物也可利用，其他地方的事物也是如此，所以墨菲定律（墨菲定律是由美国工程师爱德华·墨菲提出的著名论断，其主要内容是：事情如果有变坏的可能，不管这种可能性有多小，它总会发生。——编者）在网上同样可以使用。在正常情况下，我们可以首先发现其他任何事物。正如媒体研究人员所言：网络就像汪洋大海，海里面满是黄金，但是能否找到一小块黄金，全凭个人的运气。网络不具约束性，既大众化又嘈杂。一些事物已经堆在其他事物的上面，但整体的堆码每天都在进行。

There are several crucial differences between the web and a library of paper publications. Above all, information on the web is not organised, be it alphabetically or in any other way. Different themes and pages are linked together in partly random ways. The web is not hierarchical either, the millions of sites in existence are all accessible at the same level. Active users of the WWW have for years felt that it is a dense and cumbersome jungle which grows a little darker and denser every day. When one surfs the web in search of information which seems not to be there (despite 100,000 hits on Alta Vista), it is tempting to conclude that the web is a real-world incarnation of Jorge Luis Borges's philosophical fable about the library of Babel. This mythical library contained, apart from all books that had been written, all the books that could have been written that is, every possible combination of the letters of the alphabet. Everything is available out there, but everything else is also available out there, and like almost everywhere else, Murphy's Law operates on the web as well: under normal circumstances, one will find everything else first. As a media researcher expressed it: the Internet is like the large oceans. They are full of gold, but it costs a fortune to exploit even a tiny fraction of it. The web is uncensored, democratic and chaotic. Everything is already stacked on top of everything else there, but it still grows a little every day.

徒劳的信息过滤器

反对存储碎片的过滤器无法删除碎片。在网上冲浪所需的最重要的工具，既不是拥有大量随机存储空间的超快速计算机，也不是宽带连接器或最新的网络浏览器，而是好的过滤器——尽管前面这些设备都有助于网上冲浪。正如之前多次提及的那样，在信息社会并不存在信息的稀缺。目前的信息已经过多。如果没有机会将信息过滤，人们得不到自己需要的信息，就可能迷失方向，甚至在信息的海洋中淹死。许多人愿意帮助网络用户找到方向，关键是可以从中获利。那些专门研究网络搜索的公司，在网络空间中取得了经济上的巨大成功。第一家这样的公司是雅虎！其中，Alta Vista 是当前最大的公司。有时候，只有这些搜索引擎的主页，能够与受大众欢迎的几家主要色情网站竞争。网络搜索引擎最简单的形式是数字索引。例如，如果你想勾画出近几个月之内萨克斯演奏者莱伯的活动，或想了解科索沃最新的政治局势，抑或是苹果公司最新的操作系统，你只要在搜索引擎上敲入关键词，几秒钟后就可以得到相关网站的链接列表。通常，一份无价值的列表可以容纳数千个链接。然后，你可以缩小搜索的范围，譬如，键入"苹果 OSX 下载"，很快就可以得到一份更容易使用的列表，其链接数目不到 100 个。这样就大大缩小了搜索范围，便于找到你感兴趣的微观细节。在网上冲浪所需的最重要的工具，既不是拥有大量随机存储空间的超快速计算机，也不是宽带连接器或最新的网络浏览器，而是好的过滤器——尽管前面这些设备都有助于网上冲浪。正如之前多次提及的那样，在信息社会并不存在信息的稀缺。目前的信息已经过多。如果没有机会将信息过滤，人们得不到自己需要的信息，就可能迷失方向，甚至在信息的海洋中淹死。

Filters Against Fragmentation Do Not Remove Fragmentation

The most important tool needed to navigate on the web is neither a super fast computer with lots of RAM, nor abroad band connection or the latest news in web browsers （although all of this helps）, but good filters. As mentioned several times already, there is no scarcity of information in information society. There is far too much of it. With no opportunity to filter away that available information which one does not need, one is lost and will literally drown in zeros and ones. Many are willing to help web users to find their way, not least because it can pay off. Several of the greatest economic successes in cyberspace are companies which have specialised in web searches. The first one was Yahoo, and currently the largest one is Alta Vista. It is sometimes said that the homes of these search engines are the only web pages that can rival the major pornographic sites for popularity. In their simplest form, they function as digital indexes. If, for example, you want to map out the movements of saxophonist Didier Malherbe during the last few months, or you want to read about the current political developments in Kosovo or the latest operating system from Apple, you type the keywords, and in a matter of seconds you get a list of links to relevant web sites, normally a useless list containing thousands of links. Then you narrow the search to include, say, "+Apple +OSX +download", and soon you will have a manageable list of less than a hundred hits. You have reduced the universe to that microscopic segment you are interested in.

使用 Alta Vista 或类似的搜索引擎，并不比使用数字电话簿更优越。然而，研究人员正在不断开发信息过滤的新方法，目标可能是帮助网上浏览者阻止那些他们不想看到的或是向他们兜售商品的信息。后面这种情况使用的方法别出心裁，并且很有吸引力。多年来，我登陆亚马逊公司的网站时，和其他上百万的客户一样，总会得到这样的欢迎辞："托马斯您好！我们为您推荐！"接着是各个主题的几个热门标题，这些主题基本上都在我喜好的领域之内，这是根据亚马逊公司开发的软件筛选所得。然而，过滤器的功能往往不够，如果你不觉得世界已经足够嘈杂，我建议你用一个晚上的时间，阅读雅虎公司提供的信息类别，以此作为网上浏览的出发点。

Searching with Alta Vista or a similar engine is not much more advanced than searching a digital phone book. However, new methods for filtering information are continuously being developed, whether the aim is to help frustrated web surfers to protect themselves against unwanted information, or to sell them goods. The methods used in the latter instance are often inventive and seductive. For a few years, I have been greeted by www.amazon.com in the following way like millions of other customers: "Hello Thomas! We have recommendations for you", followed by a few "hot titles" in the subject areas that fall within my fields of interest, according to Amazon's software. Often, however, filters are less than functional. If you feel the world is not chaotic enough, I recommend an evening of reading with Yahoo's categories as a point of departure.

过去，我们很多人容易接受那些提供给我们的信息，不管是日报上的新闻，还是电台的消息。现在，选择已经没有限制。通过网络，我们可以收听美国中西部频道，订购专门的新闻服务——也就是说，我们可以拒绝接受那些与战争及暴力有关的坏消息，可以掌握马来西亚的天气情况或者哈拉雷股票市场每日的成交量，也可以只了解好莱坞的最新进展。这些量身定制的服务可以有几个来源，并采用几种格式（电子邮件、网页和无线设备的信息）。在微软公司的信息里，从商务、健康到天气、体育和旅游，每个人都可以选择自己喜欢的类别；而"美国在线"网页中心的资料，包括了从汽车到研究以及当地新闻等一切事情。其他可提供定制服务的公司包括 UnCover Real，它可以将你感兴趣的期刊目录定期用电子邮件发送给你。

In the old days, most of us tended to accept the information we were offered, whether it was the daily newspaper or the radio news. Today, the freedom of choice is unlimited. Via the web, one can listen to Midwestern C&W channels, subscribe to specialised news services say, one can refuse to take in sad news about war and violence, one can follow Malaysian weather or the Harare stock exchange daily, or one can read everything about the latest offerings from Hollywood and nothing else. These kinds of tailored services are available from several sources and in several formats （email, web, WAP）. At Microsoft News, one may choose one's personal categories from business and health to weather, sports and travel; while America Online has web centres with material on everything from cars to research and local news. Other kinds of services include UnCover Real, which offers to email you the table of contents of your favourite journals regularly.

在前一章，我已经指出为何我们迫切需要这类过滤，同时也证明了如果这类过滤（及其得到改善的版本）充分普及，最终留给国家公共环境的空间将几乎没有。因此，不能保证邻居已经知道政府最新的预算削减计划或坠机事件。可能你忙于紧跟苹果公司开发的软件，处在喜悦的追随之中，丝毫没有注意到国家足球队永久的悲剧。不像那些良好的旧媒体（比如报纸和国家电视频道），网络上的新闻位置不固定，也没有清楚的优先权。基本上任何事情都与其他事物一样重要，而且距离相等，因此，获得《印度人》的电子版，与获得《独立报》的电子版一样容易。

I have already indicated, in the previous chapter, why there is a pressing need for this kind of filtering; it is also evident that if these kinds of filters （and greatly improved versions of them） become sufficiently widespread, there is eventually little left of the national public spheres. There is then no guarantee that the neighbour has heard about the government's latest budget cuts or the latest plane crash. It may even be that he was so busy following software developments at Apple that he is blissfully unaware of the perpetually tragic state of the national English football team. Unlike the good old media （such as newspapers and nationwide television channels）, news on the web is placeless and without clear priorities. Everything is in principle just as important as everything else, and besides, distance is bracketed, which entails that it is no more difficult to access the electronic edition of the Hindu than the corresponding edition of the Independent.

由于一切事情都可以在网络上获得,在区分想要和不想要的信息时也不存在固定的社会分享惯例,因此每个人被迫开发自己的路径,对世界进行自己个性化的砍削(用软件市场的行话表述,就是定制化服务)。当前发展趋势的一个合理想象,是当前流行的数字音乐储存系统 MP3(当读者读到这段文字时,MP3 可能已被 MP4 代替)。尽管很多人还是购买 CD——老式黑胶唱片的直接延伸。与印刷的书籍或报纸一样,CD 也是一个具有开始、中间和结尾的已制作完成的产品。因此,人们无法按照一时的想法剪贴内容。即使他非常痴迷贝多芬的第五交响曲,他也无法用瓦格纳歌剧的序曲予以代替。不管你喜不喜欢,它还是它本身。

Since everything is available on the Web and there exist no fixed, socially shared routines for distinguishing between wanted and unwanted information, each individual is forced to develop their own paths, creating their own, personal cuts of the world. （In software marketing jargon, this is called customisation.） A telling image of the direction current developments are taking, is the currently popular system for digital storage of music, MP3 （which may have been replaced by MP4 by the time this is being read）. Still, most people buy music on CD, which are a direct extension of the old vinyl LP. Like a printed book or newspaper, a CD is a finished, completed product with a beginning, a middle and an end. One cannot cut and paste the content according to whim; even if one is mighty sick of the overexposed first movement in Beethoven's fifth symphony, one cannot replace it by an overture from one of Wagner's operas. One may like it or not, but that is how it is.

MP3 是音乐的电子传输格式。无论是虚拟播放器（只能在电脑上使用），还是实体播放器，都可以播放 MP3 文件，而且可以在网站可以免费下载[大部分歌曲可在有争议的 Napste（Napster 是一款可以在网络中下载自己想要的 MP3 文件的软件，最初是由西恩·帕克创建。它同时能够让自己的机器也成为一台服务器，为其他用户提供下载。——编者）上下载]，当然任何人都可以下载。另外还有一些有偿服务，原则上需要花钱购买，比如贝多芬第五交响曲的 MP3 格式。当你付费后，就可以获得一个密码，然后就能下载一整首交响乐。当你有了 MP3 格式的交响乐时，就可以逃避第一段无聊的乐章，甚至跳过第二段迟缓的乐章，你可以按照自己的想法干自己的工作。不同于一张完整的 CD，MP3 播放列表只包含听者主动选择的曲目，比如绿洲乐队的曲调、马勒第四交响曲的第二乐章、巴托克第二弦乐四重奏曲的第一乐章、摇滚乐队的两首经典曲目、戴维斯和科特兰的老式唱片。然后，你可以把全部的乐曲装在便携式 MP3 播放器中，供汽车或电视机使用。

MP3 is a file format for electronic transmission of music. There are both virtual players （for use on the computer） and physical players of the Walkman kind available, and there are enormous amounts of music on the web, which anyone can download. Following several lawsuits （the most famous of which involved the successful Napster site）, it is likely that people will increasingly have to pay for their music downloads, which so far have been largely free （and legally ambiguous, to say the least）. When one buys Beethoven's fifth, one thus pays for a password which allows a single download of the entire symphony. When one then has the symphony in MP3 format, one can finally evade that tiring first movement, or for that matter the sluggish second movement; one may edit the work just as one wants. Unlike a completed CD, an MP3 playlist contains only pieces which the listener has actively chosen, such as say a tune by Oasis, the second movement of Mahler's fourth, the first movement of Bá rtok's second string quartet, two Beatles classics and an old recording of Miles Davis and John Coltrane. Then one may copy the entire thing on to a portable MP3 player for use in the car or on the tube.

MP3 是网络逻辑的具体案例。原则上，任何事物在网络上都可以获得，每个用户将自己获取的片段汇总在一起。MP3 与 CD 的关系，就像网络与书籍的关系一样。互联网非常适合当前盛行的新自由主义思潮，而且至少在两个方面为这种思潮的产生作出了重要的贡献。万维网（还有多频道电视、MP3 和"弹性工作"）可以提供自由和选择。我们不得不注意，在其他事情中存在的不足，比如内聚力、有意义的环境和迟缓。

MP3 is a concrete example of the logic of the web. In principle, everything is available out there, and each individual user puts together his or her own, personal totality out of the fragments. MP3 relates to the CD as the web relates to the book. The Internet fits perfectly with, and is also in at least two ways an important contributing cause of the prevailing neo-liberal ideology. WWW（and multi-channel television, and MP3, and "flexible work"...）offers freedom and choice by the bucket-load. On the deficit side of the balance, we have to note, among other things, "internal cohesion, meaningful context and slowness".

信息片段取代了整体

片段代替了整体。我们需要缓慢过渡到本章的主要观点上来，但作为序曲，我还要插入对互联网另一面的描述。20 世纪 60 年代，自由理论家麦克卢汉作为媒体理论家名声大振，他曾经描述过视觉文化与触觉文化的差异，并比较了在不同的信息科技领域内，不同感觉在使用方面存在的差异。按照麦克卢汉的说法，前现代的人具有协调的触觉——各种感觉器官作为一个整体单元平等地发挥作用。"听觉—触觉"感知对于经历和知识异常重要。通过学校教育，视觉可以占上风并抑制其他感觉。（想一下柏拉图的洞穴寓言，这似乎已经发生。）人类逐步受到抑制，思想开始变窄。书写使我们的耳朵多了一双眼睛，对麦克卢汉来说，这使一些事情误入歧途。他认为，单纯线性文本是碎裂的、缩减的媒介，会使读者脱离整体的经历，无法完全使用所有的感觉。从电视中，麦克卢汉找到了一个机会，可以在书写进行破坏之前重新创造感觉的整体。麦克卢汉在 20 世纪 60 年代写作最重要的论著时，对这种新媒体提出了乐观的看法——有些人对此会觉得不可思议。

Pieces Replace Totalities

We are slowly moving towards the main point of this chapter, and as a prelude, I shall add yet another facet to the description of the Internet. The literary theorist Marshall McLuhan（1915—1980）, who rose to fame as a media theorist in the 1960s, once wrote about the difference between a haptic and an optic culture, a contrast that refers to varying usage of the senses under different regimes of information technology. Pre-modern people lived, according to McLuhan, in a "haptic harmony" all senses were equal and functioned as a totality, a unity. The "auditive-tactile" senses （hearing and touch）were essential both for experience and for knowledge. With literacy, the visual sense gained the upper hand and suppressed the others. （In Plato, this has already come about; just think about his cave allegory!）Humans thus became increasingly inhibited and narrowminded. Writing gave us "an eye for an ear", and to McLuhan, this entails something of a fall from grace. To him, the pure, linear text is a fragmenting and reductive medium which removes the reader from a total experience with the full use of all his or her senses. In television, McLuhan saw an opportunity to re-create that sensory unity which the advent of writing had destroyed, and he had a great some would say incomprehensible optimism on behalf of this new medium when he wrote his most important books in the 1960s.

麦克卢汉身故 15 年后，《连线》杂志认为他是互联网的守护神。一般说来，他谈论新媒体(尤其是电视)的很多东西，都出人意料地适用于万维网。就我关心的事情而言，我认可麦克卢汉观点的主要趋向，但是我的结论与他恰恰相反。以碎片方式发挥作用的，其实不是书籍，而是电视。书籍与万维网的关系，犹如单频道电视与多频道电视的关系，线性时间是一种贵重的资源，经不起我们的浪费。在此背景下，提出一整套对比说明工业社会向信息社会、国家建设向全球化以及书籍向监控器的过渡，是非常诱人的。例如，可以列出以下的对比：

工业社会	信息社会
CD 和黑胶唱片	MP3
书籍	万维网
单频道电视	多频道电视
书信	电子邮件
固定电话	手机

甚至还可以包括下列内容：

终身一夫一妻制	阶段性一夫一妻制
铁饭碗时代	灵活就业时代
深度	宽度
线性时间	片段化时间
信息不足	信息过量

A decade and a half after his death, McLuhan was launched, by the magazine WIRED, as a patron saint for the Internet. Much of what he said in general about new media (especially television) fits the World Wide Web surprisingly well. I agree with the main thrust of McLuhan's argument, but my conclusion is the exact opposite of his. It is not the book, but television that functions in a fragmenting way. The book relates to the WWW as single-channel television relates to multi-channel television, and linear time is a valuable resource that we cannot afford to waste. In this context, it is tempting to propose a whole series of contrasts that may illustrate the transition from industrial to informational society, from nationbuilding to globalisation, from book to monitor. We may, for example, depict the changes like this:

Industrial society	Informational society
CD/vinyl record	MP3
Book WWW	
Single-channel TV	Multi-channel TV
Letter	E-mail
Stationary telephone	Mobile telephone
... and while we are at it, why not also:	
Lifelong monogamy	Serial monogamy
The era of the gold watch	The era of flexible work
Depth	Breadth
Linear time	Fragmented contemporariness
Scarcity of information	Scarcity of freedom from information

以上所列的最后一点，将在本书末尾一章进行分析。现在，我们集中谈论新信息管理体制的效果。我支持麦克卢汉的重要观点：信息碎片化浪潮是我们这个社会的典型特征，它刺激了一种思维方式，很少令人想起工业社会的精确的、逻辑的和线性的思维方式，而使人更多地想起自由组合、诗性和隐喻性的思维方式，这些是许多非现代社会的特征。信息社会提供的是脱离语境的标记，而不是按照整齐的行列给知识排序，这些脱离语境的标记或多或少都彼此关联。

More about these last points in the final chapters. For now, I shall concentrate on one effect of the new informational regime, and I will give McLuhan my support on a crucial point: the tidal waves of information fragments typical of our kind of society stimulate a style of thought that is less reminiscent of the strict, logical, linear thinking characteristic of industrial society than of the freely associating, poetical, metaphorical thinking that characterised many non-modern societies. Instead of ordering knowledge in tidy rows, information society offers cascades of decontextualised signs more or less randomly connected to each other.

产生这种变化的原因，既不是万维网的引入，也不是多频道电视的出现。相反，根据前一章的分析，与信息有关的每个领域都在迅速地增长，但是用来消化的时间却远远没有以前那么多。

The cause of this change is neither the introduction of the World Wide Web nor multi-channel television as such. It is instead the fact, documented in the previous chapter, that there is rapid growth in every area to do with information, but no more time than formerly available to digest it.

当代文化正在全速运动

加速度与指数增长的裙带关系导致了垂直的堆垛。由于两翼是专门留给具有特殊利益的小群体（比如前卫摇滚、理论物理、社会人类学方法和希腊史诗等），中间部分的堆叠越来越高。把空间隐喻转译成时间维度，意味着没有空余的时间可以传播信息，只好将信息压缩并堆叠，其时间跨度就越来越短。举例来说，就像市中心建高楼大厦，但在市郊到处都是平房。电视剧《王朝》、多频道电视与商业赞助的电视连续剧具有同样的逻辑特征，这种逻辑就是要使最具竞争性的新闻节目日益变短，商业广告的播出时间也要越来越短——下面，我还要举一些例子来说明这一点。

Contemporary Culture Runs At Full Speed Without Moving An Inch

Put differently: the close cousins of acceleration and exponential growth lead to vertical stacking. Since the flanks are reserved for small groups with special interests (e.g. progressive rock, theoretical physics, veteran buses, social anthropological method, Greek poetry), more and more is stacked up in the middle. Translated from the spatial metaphor to the temporal dimension, this means that since there is no vacant time to spread information in, it is compressed and stacked in time spans that become shorter and shorter. High-rise buildings appear in the centre, sprawling bungalows in the suburbs. The logic that characterises Dynasty and similar multi-channel, commercial-financed television series, is the same as that which entails that the most competitive news programmes are shorter than the others, that commercials become shorter and shorter and, yes, I shall offer more examples eventually.

垂直堆垛的概念源于一本讨论前卫摇滚音乐的书籍。20 世纪 70 年代前期，在一些留着长发身穿长外套的披头士中，前卫摇滚非常流行这种音乐风格。当朋克主流的年轻文化遭受不屑一顾的嘲笑时，就没有人敢在舞台上将各种乐器的声音堆叠在一起了，他们差不多都被迫转入地下活动，但却使不能正确使用乐器成了一种美德。20 世纪 90 年代后期，互联网掀起复古的浪潮，和别的事物一样，前卫的摇滚乐再度复苏——有时候不得不承认，这带来了灾难性后果。

The concept of vertical stacking is taken from a book which of all things deals with progressive rock, a musical genre that was particularly popular among long-haired and great-coated boys and men in the first half of the 1970s, and which was forced more or less underground when punk not only made the dominant youth culture jeer dismissively at anyone daring to go on stage with stacks of synthesizers, but which also made it a virtue not to be able to play an instrument properly. Like everything else, progressive rock was re-awakened by Internet-based retro waves in the second half of the 1990s sometimes, it must be conceded, with disastrous results.

北美哲学教授马丁在为自己喜欢的摇滚乐队(包括从 Yes 到 King Crimson 的乐队)辩护时，试图解释近十年来电脑与录音室制作的舞曲有何问题，包括豪斯舞曲、高科技舞曲、鼓和贝司及其他音乐流派——这些实际上都可以称为非线性、重复并有节律的舞曲。在他看来，这些音乐缺乏连续性和方向性，在任何地方都不能占据首位——不像贝多芬、戴维斯和齐柏林飞艇乐队的风格。欣赏这些音乐，通常需要进入一间充满各种音乐的房间里，待在里面不觉得冰冷，才可能进入角色。马丁喜欢线性乐曲，可以陶冶内心——尽管有一部分可能是即兴创作而成。对于新的节奏音乐，马丁这样评价：

The North American philosophy professor Bill Martin has tried, in his broad defence plea for bands he loves （from Yes to King Crimson）, to explain what, to his mind, is wrong with the computer and studio-based dance music of the last decade, including house, techno, drum'n'bass and other genres which have little in common apart from the fact that they can be described as varieties of nonlinear, repetitive, rhythmical dance music. This is music which in his view lacks progression and direction, which unlike, say, Beethoven, Miles Davis and Led Zeppelin is not heading anywhere. Enjoyment of such music is generally undertaken by entering a room full of sound where a great number of aural things are happening, and staying there until it no longer feels cool. Martin's preferred music is linear and has an inner development although it may often be partly improvised. About the new rhythmic music, he has this to say:

至于后现代的建筑艺术，按照堆垛的观点，原则上任何声音都可以与其他声音合拍。然而，即使最折中混杂的建筑物，也必须具有地基，能够与大地牢固地铆合在一起；同样，垂直堆垛的音乐往往取决于持续的拍子。有些舞曲堆垛在其他舞曲的上面，却往往没有太多可整合的音乐风格。马丁怀疑这种音乐是否可以创造任何真正的新事物。"垂直堆叠的方法含蓄地(甚至明确地)接受一种观点，认为音乐(或者更普遍的艺术)只不过是填充网格的复合物。"当然，我个人并不准备支持这种论点，但是在有关专横的时间方面，马丁提供了一个绝佳的案例：堆垛时互相重叠，每一个空隙都被填满，内部几乎没有整合。

As with postmodern architecture, the idea in this stacking is that, in principle, any sound can go with any other sound. Just as, however, even the most eclectic pastiche of a building must all the same have some sort of foundation that anchors it to the ground, vertically stacked music often depends on an insisting beat. There are layers of trance stacked on top of dance, often without much in the way of stylistic integration. Martin doubts that this music will be capable of creating anything really new. "The vertical-stacking approach implicitly (or even explicitly) accepts the idea that music (or art more generally) is now simply a matter of trying out the combinations, filling out the grid." I will not risk my personal friendships with trance adepts by supporting this argument, but instead draw attention to the fact that, inadvertently, Martin offers an excellent description of an aspect of the tyranny of the moment: there are layers upon layers on top of each other, every vacant spot is filled, and there is little by way of internal integration.

堆垛替代了内部的发展

特别有天赋的音乐家和作曲家伊诺，是新式节奏音乐的先锋和教父。早在 20 世纪 70 年代，他就提出了"环境音乐"的概念，这种非线性音乐可以起到听觉壁纸的作用，正如《机场音乐》唱片套上的说明所言，因为容易使人忽略才值得一听。在节奏音乐的领域，很少有人能够超过伊诺。1995 年他开始写日记，第二年就把日记中记录的乐曲出版了（可能经过了编辑）。1995 年 9 月 8 日，由于摇滚乐取得了突破性发展，他勾勒了通俗音乐的发展阶段。他建议将其分为 10 个阶段，并将不久之后的发展阶段定为第 11 个。我们感兴趣的是伊诺所说的第十阶段的内容，也即 1991 年到 1995 年，此时已经进入了书写时代。伊诺给其他时代都贴上了诸如"合成流行乐"或"华丽摇滚"之类的标签，却这样分析 20 世纪 90 年代的特征："参见 1964—1968 年或 1976—1978 年的音乐。"换句话说，没有什么新东西，只不过是把前面的潮流切碎后重新拼凑而已。

Stacking Replaces Internal Development

The exceptionally gifted musician and composer Brian Eno is both godfather and pioneer in much of the new rhythmic music. Already in the 1970s, he developed his concept "Ambient Music", non-linear music which could function as an aural wallpaper, but which was also intended to be "as listenable as it was ignorable", as the liner notes of Music for Airports put it. Few know the field of rhythmic music better than Eno. In 1995 he kept a diary, and published (presumably an edited version of) it the following year. On 8 September, he made a sketch of the "phases" of popular music since the breakthrough of rock'n'roll. He proposes ten phases plus an eleventh one, which he locates to the near future. What is interesting in our context is Eno's category number 10, that is the period 1991—1995, up to the time of writing. While the other eras have labels such as "synth pop, 4th world" or "Glam", he characterises the 1990s like this: "See '64—'68, add '76—'78". In other words nothing new, but re-hashes of former trends.

作为兴趣适中的旁观者,我独特的感想倾向于赞同伊诺的观点:多年来,我们似乎立刻就拥有一切。每一种想象的复古潮流依然存在,同时过去时代的大明星在当下依然出名——比如威尔士的低音歌手琼斯,被那些念旧的人重新唤醒。除了非线性音乐和重复的舞曲,20世纪90年代的流行音乐取得了与甲壳虫乐队大致相同的突破性发展;重金属乐队承担了20世纪70年代中期紫色乐队与齐柏林飞艇乐队留下的挑战;"新迷幻摇滚"乐队从某种程度上类似1968年的软机器乐队或者是1965年的平克·弗洛伊德乐队。同时,还有能够真正保持大牌名气的艺术家,譬如迪伦、滚石乐队和桑塔纳乐队,他们都保持了近40年的生命力。

As a moderately interested bystander, my distinct impression tends to confirm Eno's view: for several years now, we seem to have everything at once. Every imaginable retro trend exists, at the same time as the big names of bygone eras remain big today, or as in the case of the Welsh crooner Tom Jones are being re-awakened by nostalgics. Apart from non-linear, repetitive dance music, the 1990s saw major breakthroughs of pop groups that sounded roughly like The Beatles, heavy metal groups that took up the challenge where Purple and Zeppelin left it in the mid-1970s, "neo-psychedelic" bands that sound somewhat like the Soft Machine of 1968 or the Pink Floyd of 1965 and at the same time, the really big names remain artists like Dylan, the Stones and Santana, who have been around for nearly 40 years.

推动激进的政治家前进的力量是对进步的线性信念—— 一种对发展的强大的道德意识——前卫摇滚音乐（还有其他音乐）对于发展具有内在的信心。音乐家总想把手边的乐曲提升到新的高度，摒弃以往的乐曲，并创造更好的新东西。马丁区分了线性音乐与非线性音乐的差异，认为这类似于现代与后现代的对比，不幸的是，近 100 年来，当代音乐家都创作非线性音乐。无论如何，对于流行音乐趋势的讨论，一般存在两个具有特色（还远远不是典型）的观点，与手边的问题直接有关。

Just as progressive politics is fuelled by a linear faith in progress a strong, moral idea of development progressive rock (and many other kinds of music) had an inbuilt faith in progress. The musicians wanted to take their kind of music to new heights, break with the past, create something new and better. Martin discusses the difference between this concept and the new non-linear music as an instance of the modern/postmodern contrast, which is unfortunate, as modernist contemporary music has been non-linear for nearly a hundred years. Anyway, there are two general points emerging from this idiosyncratic (and far from representative) discussion of trends in popular music that may be linked directly to the issues at hand.

其一，趋势的堆叠表明不存在变迁，只有再循环。摇滚乐和流行乐只是表面现象，但是可以作为晴雨表。当甲壳虫乐队复制绿洲乐队的风格时，老牌的滚石乐队以及菲尔·柯林斯风格毫无疑问是这一领域的大师，这或许是文化无法自我更新的表现。马丁也认为没有真正的创新，只有新组合的连续水流。专横的时间具有填充空隙的特征，这对创新性非常不利，对此我将在本书最后一章进行论述。松弛的时间预算产生空隙，从中会出人意料地产生新事物，而排得满满的时间表则不可能产生新东西。

First, stacking of trends implies that there is no change, but mere recirculation. Rock and pop may be surface phenomena, but they are also barometers. When Beatles clones like Oasis, geriatric groups like the Stones and chubby crooners of the generic Phil Collins type （who would have believed, in 1975, that this man who at his best played the drums like an octopus on speed would turn into Elton John?） are the undisputed masters of the field, this may be symptomatic of a culture unable to renew itself. As Martin expresses it: there is no real creativity, but a continuous stream of new combinations. I shall return to this in the final chapter, to argue that the filling of gaps typical of the tyranny of the moment is seriously detrimental to creativity. The new arises unexpectedly from the gaps created by slack in time budgets, not from crowded schedules.

其二，在摇滚、爵士与新的节奏音乐的听众之间，存在着巨大的差异。节奏音乐一直在向前发展，摇滚和爵士乐则有开端、很长的中间过程（内部发展）和结尾或高潮。有趣的是，印尼的加麦兰乐曲，是重复性乐曲的作曲家产生灵感的重要来源，这些作曲家中最典型的是极简抽象派艺术作曲家里奇。这种音乐是从传统的仪式文化发展而来，没有线性的发展概念。当代文化正在加强本质上非线性的方式，考虑到麦克卢汉针对其后果所提出的观点，与加麦兰音乐的联系并不单调乏味。

Second, the listener's situation is radically different between rock/jazz and the new rhythmic music. The latter goes on and on; the former has a beginning, a long middle （internal development） and an end or climax. Interestingly, Indonesian gamelan music has been a significant source of inspiration to many of those who work with repetitive music, among them the minimalist composer Steve Reich. This is music developed in a traditional, ritualistic culture with no linear concept of development. The link with gamelan music is far from uninteresting, considering McLuhan's （and my） view to the effect that an essentially non-linear way of being in time is being strengthened in contemporary culture.

对于那些不在乎甚至漠不关心加麦兰乐曲、极简派艺术、迷幻舞曲与前卫摇滚音乐之间的关系的读者而言，这个讨论似乎有点深奥难懂。但是，在我们彻底不管这事之前，还有很多要说的东西。在卡斯特有关信息时代的著作中，有些地方对新世纪音乐进行了简短的评论。他将其看作我们这个时代的古典音乐（虽是这是个有争议的断言，但却是对的），并将其描述为供"瞬间与永恒、我与宇宙、自我与网络进行双向参考"的表达式。沙漠的风与海洋潮汐为许多重复性模式创造了背景，这些模式组成新世纪的音乐。这是声音低沉单调、没有分期和拖延的乐曲，它不仅是对日常商业竞争的矫正，而且具有完美的对称性，因为它容纳了时光的流逝。

To readers whose relationship to gamelan music, minimalism, trip-hop and progressive rock is loose, or perhaps even one of indifference, this discussion may seem a bit esoteric. But there is more to say about the matter before we leave it entirely. Somewhere in his enormous work about the information age, Manuel Castells has chosen to include a paragraph about new age music. He regards it as the classical music of our era （a debatable assertion, but all right）, and describes it as an expression for "the double reference to moment and eternity; me and the universe, the self and the net". Desert winds and ocean waves create the backdrop for many of the repetitive patterns that make up new age music. It is a droning, time-less and lingering kind of music; an antidote to the quotidian rat-race, but also perfectly symmetrical to it, since it brackets the passage of time.

可以列举不同的例子来说明：当越来越大的信息量以逐步增加的速度分散时，要创造叙事、秩序和发展顺序，就会日益困难。碎片有成为霸权的威胁。在宽泛的意义上，我们将知识、工作和生活方式联系起来，这是必然的后果。因果关系、内部有机增长、成熟和经验，这些类别都在此情形下承受重压。比如音乐的案例明显是有争议的。(我们许多人在这个问题上都有自己的感情，不是吗？)但主要是用来作为例证。此类现象自然是非常宽泛的，比如新闻业、教育、工作、政治和家庭生活，都受到垂直堆垛的影响。首先，我们可以看一下新闻业的实例。

Put differently: when growing amounts of information are distributed at growing speed, it becomes increasingly difficult to create narratives, orders, developmental sequences. The fragments threaten to become hegemonic. This has consequences for the ways we relate to knowledge, work and lifestyle in a wide sense. Cause and effect, internal organic growth, maturity and experience; such categories are under heavy pressure in this situation. The examples from music, which are clearly debatable. (many of us are passionate in this area, aren't we?) But chiefly meant as illustrations. The phenomenon as such is naturally much more widespread, and journalism, education, work, politics and domestic life, just to mention a few areas, are affected by vertical stacking. Let us take a look at journalism first.

信息世界的报酬递减法则

报酬递减法则具有猛烈的冲击力。关于电视的痛苦，在一本极度悲观的、批评性的手册中，布迪厄提出了一种熟悉的、却不容小觑的论据。他宣称，碎片化的电视瞬间伴随着快速的转换和快节奏的新闻业，创造了公共智力文化，这种文化有助于特定的参与者。布迪厄把他们称为快速的思考者。比利时的卡通英雄卢克非常出名,他画自己的枪比画影子还快,快速思考者是用来描述那些"思考速度比加速的子弹还快的人"。这种人可以在直接传送的数分钟内,解释欧盟的经济政策错在哪里,以及今夏为何要读康德的《纯粹理性批判》,或者解释种族主义伪科学的根源。然而,在一些特殊的事件上,即使最厉害的脑袋也需要时间反省,若要作出精确和足够细致入微的描述,则需要更多的时间(有时候还会多得多)。按照布迪厄的说法,在这个匆忙的时代,这种思考者是无形的,事实上失去了影响力(从平庸的意思上看,布迪厄的看法显然不对。当代没有任何思想家能比布迪厄更具影响力,但很明显他没有把自己定义为快速思考者)。

The Law of Diminishing Returns Strikes With a Vengeance

In a profoundly pessimistic and critical pamphlet about the misery of television, Pierre Bourdieu develops a familiar, but far from unimportant argument. He claims that the fragmented temporality of television, with its swift transitions and fast-paced journalism, creates an intellectual public culture which favours a particular kind of participant. Bourdieu speaks of them as fast-thinkers. Whereas the Belgian cartoon hero Lucky Luke is famous for drawing his gun faster than his own shadow, fast-thinkers are described as "thinkers who think faster than an accelerating bullet". They are the people who are able, in a couple of minutes of direct transmission, to explain what is wrong with the economic policies of the EU, why one ought to read Kant's Critique of Pure Reason this summer, or explain the origins of racist pseudo-science. It is nonetheless a fact that some of the sharpest minds need time to reflect and more time (much more, in some cases) to make an accurate, sufficiently nuanced statement on a particular issue. This kind of thinker becomes invisible and virtually deprived of influence, according to Bourdieu, in this rushed era. (In a banal sense, Bourdieu is obviously wrong. No contemporary thinker is more influential than Bourdieu himself, and obviously he does not define himself as a fast-thinker.)

布迪厄的论点与我们观察到的结果一致，换句话说，媒体吸引力，而不是他们的政治信息或有黏着力的愿景已经成为政治家最重要的资本。这已经不是一种全新的现象；在美国，首次出现此迹象是在肯尼迪打败尼克松，获得总统职位之时。无论如何，按照布迪厄的观点，结果就是那些人讲话像打机关枪，写字采用黑体和大写字母，能够提高影响力和播放率——而不是缓慢行进和讲究系统。

Bourdieu's argument is congruent with the observation that media appeal has become the most important capital of politicians not, in other words, their political message or cohesive vision. This is not an entirely new phenomenon; in the USA, the first indication of this development came with John F. Kennedy's victory over Richard M. Nixon. Anyway, a result, in Bourdieu's view, is that the people who speak like machine-guns, in boldface and capital letters, who are given airtime and influence not the slow and systematic ones.

问题在哪里呢？为何那些拥有快速准确思考天赋的人，却以这种方式被蒙上污名呢？换句话说，快速思考错在哪里？除了只在缓慢模式下才能奏效的思考之外，一些合理的论点只能在连续的方式中发展出来，不允许不耐烦的记者在节目中打断其思路。布迪厄提到一个实例，可供许多专业学者去鉴别。几年前，布迪厄出版了《国家贵族》一书，研究法国教育系统的象征权力与精英构成。20多年里，布迪厄对此领域甚感兴趣，一直在构思这本书。一位记者提议，由布迪厄与大学校友会主席搞一场辩论，后者为正方，布迪厄为反方。这位记者酸溜溜地总结说："至于我为何拒绝，我觉得他压根就不会有思路。"

What is wrong with this? Why should people who have the gift of being able to think fast and accurately, be stigmatised in this way? In a word, what is wrong about thinking fast? Nothing in particular, apart from the fact that some thoughts only function in a slow mode, and that some lines of reasoning can only be developed in a continuous fashion, without the interruptions of an impatient journalist who wants to "move on" （where?） in the programme. Bourdieu mentions an example many academics will be able to identify with. A few years ago, Bourdieu published The State Nobility, a study of symbolic power and elite formation in the French education system. Bourdieu had been actively interested in the field for twenty years, and the book had been long in the making. A journalist proposed a debate between Bourdieu and the president of the alumni organisation of les grandes é coles; the latter would speak "for" and Bourdieu would speak "against". "And", he sums up sourly: "he hadn't a clue as to why I refused."

布迪厄没有明确探讨这个主题，但是他的观点必然导出这个推论，在信息爆炸的时代，媒体的参与也得遵循报酬递减法则。20 世纪 90 年代以前，如果一个人受邀参加电台或电视台的节目，他就要在演播室做好充分的准备。在去参加节目之前，他要刮胡子（即使是参加电台的节目也是如此），还要穿一件刚刚熨过的衬衫，系一条合适的领带，然后带着略微紧张的心情去演播室，并要有决心能够将自己的观点简明清晰地讲述出来。现在，越来越多的人不愿意参加电台或电视直播节目；即使有时候去，也多是三心二意并且缺乏热情。由于电视节目的观众和嘉宾都意识到，随着电视频道的增加，每一个节目的影响力正在减弱，电视频道和脱口秀的数量越多，每一个节目发挥的作用就越小。沃霍尔直接受到麦克卢汉的影响，似乎需要人们有意理解他的观点："未来每个人都可能因为 15 分钟而出名"（若是现在，他可能会说 15 秒钟）。

A topic Bourdieu does not treat explicitly, but which is an evident corollary of his views, is the diminishing returns of media participation following the information explosion. If, before the 1990s, one was invited to contribute to a radio or television programme, one appeared well-prepared in the studio. One might shave （even if the medium was radio）, make certain to wear a freshly ironed shirt and a proper tie, and go into the studio in a slightly nervous state determined to make one's points clearly and concisely. Nowadays, an increasing number of people in the know do not even bother to take part in radio or television transmissions, and if they do, their contributions frequently tend towards the half-hearted and lukewarm. As both viewers and guests on TV shows are aware, each programme has a diminishing impact as the number of channels grow, and the greater the number of channels and talkshows, the less impact each of them has. It is almost as if Andy Warhol was deliberately understating his point when, directly influenced by McLuhan, he said that in "the future", everybody would be famous for 15 minutes. (Today, he might have said seconds.)

在媒体世界中，与堆垛和加速度有关的作用，是新闻日益变短的趋势。有一个笑话说，小报为了吸引读者的注意力互相竞争，当战争最终真正爆发时，报纸的头版只有空间书写"W"这一字母。这个笑话阐明了报酬递减的原则（或者说是边际效益下降原则）。这个原则在加速发展的文化中非常宝贵，在基础经济学课程中，教师们倾向于使用食物和饮料作为范例阐述这个原则：如果你渴了，第一杯碳酸饮料对你来说具有非常高的价值，第二杯也有很高的价值，如果你还感觉很渴，你甚至愿意为第三杯碳酸饮料付钱。但是，你喝完饮料之后，商店里那些剩下的饮料对你来说就突然没有价值了，你绝对不愿意再为那些饮料支付一分钱。另外，如果每个月只允许你享用一次酥软的牛排加上调味品，它们就具有非常高的价值。而当牛排成为日常食物后，其价值就大大降低了。一件商品的边际效益可以被定义为，人们在此商品的最后一个单位的价值上愿意花多少钱、多少时间或多少注意力。尽管到目前为止，这个原则尚未用于我们所做的每一件事上（许多活动，比如吹萨克斯管，人们做得越多报酬就越高），但是，它的确能够为我们提供重要的洞察力，以便理解布迪厄所说的情形——人们如何制作和消费新闻及日益增多的信息？在这方面，很容易看到最终需要的更强的效果，因为公众习惯了速度和爆发性的沟通方式。

A related effect of stacking and acceleration in the media world, is the tendency for news to become shorter and shorter. A tired joke about the competition for attention among tabloids, consists in the remark that when war eventually breaks out for real, the papers will only have space for the "W" on the front page. The joke illustrates the principle of diminishing returns （or falling marginal value）. In basic economics courses, teachers tend to use food and drink as examples to explain this principle, which is invaluable in an accelerating culture: if you are thirsty, the first soda has very high value for you. The second one is also quite valuable, and you may even if your thirst is considerable be willing to pay for the third one. But then, the many soda cans left in the shop suddenly have no value at all to you; you are unwilling to pay a penny for any of them. Tender steaks, further, are highly valuable if you are only allowed to savour them once a month; when steak becomes daily fare, its value decreases dramatically. The marginal value of a commodity is defined as the value of the last unit one is willing to spend money or time and attention on. Although this principle can by no means be applied to everything we do （a lot of activities, such as saxophone playing, become more rewarding the more one carries on）, it can offer important insights into the situation Bourdieu describes how news, and more generally information, is being produced and consumed. In this regard, it is easy to see that stronger effects are needed eventually, because the public becomes accustomed to speed and explosive forms of communication.

　　同时，更重要的是，实际生产新闻和其他信息的人——新闻记者，都在经历本领域内逐渐增加的拥挤程度。读者、听众和观众花在每一小片信息上的时间，已经越来越少。因此，各类出版社的编辑工作（从网络、无线通信到报纸），也在日益削减。我偶尔给出版社写稿子，有时候也作为他们的采访对象，但从未听他们有人抱怨报章杂志的篇幅太短。（自然，他们总梦想："瞧，你做的采访，不能够再短一些吗？我的意思是他不可以说一些其他的事吗？他那些夸夸其谈的言辞，不能写得更好一些吗？为了避免误会，我们应该在报纸上消除愚蠢和不相关的争论。明天中午之前你能再给我一段 100 字的文章吗？"）

At the same time and this is more important here the people who actually produce news and other kinds of information, the journalists that is, experience the increasing crowdedness of their field. Readers, listeners and viewers have less and less time to spare for each information snippet. Thus, editors working in every kind of press (from web and WAP to paper) cut more and more. As an occasional contributor to the press and sometimes an interviewee, I have never heard an editor complain that a particular piece of journalism is too short, to say the least. (One may, naturally, dream: "Look, this interview that you have done, isn't it a bit on the short side? I mean, didn't he say other things as well? He comes through as a man of bombast and one-liners, wouldn't it be better to allow the nuances in his position to come through, in order to avoid his being misunderstood, and then we'll also avoid a stupid and irrelevant controversy in the paper afterwards. Will you give me another hundred lines before lunch tomorrow?")

无线上网设备接收的新闻，处在加速发展的新闻业最时髦的写作时代，所提供的故事长度，使得《镜子》看起来像普鲁斯特的作品。作为补偿，他们每30分钟就更新一次。对那些还不适应这种速度与简洁性的人来说，这种报纸就像一个小虫子，当我们困得打瞌睡时，它就在耳边嗡嗡作响。可以这样比喻，无线上网设备接收的新闻＝赤道非洲的蚊子问题。然而，这种策略显然有起作用的趋势，原因在前面详细阐述过。在一定数量的图像或文字之后，信息的边际效应剧烈下降；在最初的10秒内边际效益相当高，但之后又会如何呢？

News on WAP, at the time of writing the latest vogue in accelerated journalism, offers stories of a length that makes those in the Mirror look like Proust. As a compensation, they can be updated every 30 minutes. To those of us who are not yet accustomed to this speed and brevity, this kind of journalism is like a persistent insect buzzing around the ear as we try to go to sleep. (WAP news = the mosquito problem in equatorial Africa.) Yet there is a marked tendency for such strategies to win, for reasons already elaborated. The marginal value of information falls dramatically after a certain number of images or words; it is pretty high during the first 10 seconds, but then what?

对于这种推理方式最常见的异议，是认为缓慢似乎可以在媒体中复兴，至少在欧洲国家是如此。例如，专用的电台频道一天 24 小时都播放古典音乐，就能将深入得体的推理和提供信息背景的可靠新闻变成人的"感知需求"。在世界范围内，这种情形似乎来自伊斯灵顿，而不是源于弗利特街。大幅印刷广告日益减少，小报（越来越像纸质版的电视）逐步增多。喜欢"缓慢复兴"的群体数量可能被计算到十分位，在这个规模上各处都有略微的增加；喜欢快节奏的群体，则可以大批量地计算。在挪威，电台的节目可以让专业学者谈论 30 分钟，这个节目名为《P2 Academy》，已经坚持播出了 5 年多，内容包括黑洞、青少年犯罪、文化的概念以及类似的权威性问题。听众非常喜欢这档节目。节目主持人与嘉宾同样积极。

The most common objection to this line of reasoning is that slowness seems to be enjoying a renaissance in the media, at least in some European countries. For example, dedicated radio channels play classical music 24 hours a day, and there is a "perceived need"（the pundits claim）for thorough, decent reasoning and solid journalism providing background information. This may well be the case in the world as it appears from Islington, but hardly from Fleet Street. Sales of broadsheets decline, while those of tabloids（which look more and more like printed television）increase. The people enjoying the "slowness renaissance" can be counted in tenths of per cents, and on this scale there may be slight increases here and there; fastness is enjoyed by groups better measured in scores of per cents. In Norway, a radio programme that allowed academics to read out 30-minute talks, called the P2 Academy, has been on the air for more than five years, and it covers black holes, juvenile delinquency, the concept of culture and similar issues authoritatively and well. The listeners love it. Both of them.

被腰斩的连续性

信息的线头破坏了连续性。快速思考者受人喜欢，慢速思考者甚为愠怒，有时候还会被诸如布迪厄文章一类的东西激怒。慢速思考者并不孤单，他对当代新闻业的抨击，是站在社会主义的自豪阵营中，代表保守的知识分子谴责大批量信息生产的庸俗性。这一传统可能始于托克维尔［托克维尔（1805—1859 年），法国历史学家、社会学家。主要代表作有《论美国的民主》第一卷、《论美国的民主》第二卷、《旧制度与大革命》。——编者］，他抨击过实用主义、民主和肤浅的北美殖民文化（柏拉图也说过类似的话）。但是在两次世界大战期间，法兰克福学派达到了顶峰——马尔库斯、霍克海姆以及阿多诺。20 世纪 30 年代，德国犹太人的悲观主义一定有自己的理由。这并不意味着他们错了。当波兹曼写下"现在学生在试卷中已经不使用'因为'这个词"时，他指出的问题与布迪厄讨论的一样，对此前面我已经深入讨论过。当不安定的、闪烁的注视和显著的俏皮话占据主流时，一致连贯与因果关系就消失了。加尔东在他最近的回忆录中，写下了 20 世纪 90 年代他与学生在一起的经历。

Information Lint Destroys Continuity

Fast thinkers are favoured, and the slow thinkers sulk, in some cases reacting through producing essays like Bourdieu's. He is far from alone; his attack on contemporary journalism stands in a proud lineage of socialist and conservative intellectuals decrying the vulgarity of mass-produced information. This tradition may have begun with de Tocqueville's assault on the pragmatic, democratic and superficial North American settler culture （although, if one reads him closely, Plato had something to say on the matter as well）, but reached its zenith with the Frankfurt School of the inter-war years Marcuse, Horkheimer and, especially, Adorno. German Jews in the 1930s certainly had their own reasons for pessimism. This does not mean that they were necessarily wrong. When Neil Postman writes that today's students no longer use the word "because" in their exam papers, he points towards the same problem as Bourdieu discusses, which is further illustrated by the list at p. 109. Coherence and causality slip away when it is restlessness, flickering gazes and striking one-liners that rule the roost. In his recent memoir, Johan Galtung otherwise a relentless optimist writes this about his experiences with students in the 1990s:

长时间接触太多闪烁的图像，这是现实的共时性经历，现实是具有丰富细节的图像，而不是横贯时间、因果链和推理的线索。这两者我们都需要，但现在思考能力正在被缓慢地扼杀，这对视觉、听觉、味觉和触觉有利——然而感觉的放纵留给理智的空间很小。

And far too many suffer from chronic image flicker, a synchronic experience of reality as images rich in details, not as lines across time, causal chains, reasoning. One needs both, but the way it is today, the ability to think is slowly killed, to the advantage of the ability to see and hear, taste and feel an orgy of the senses that gives little space for intellectuality.

在最近一份有关挪威高等教育的报告中，包括了一个与"全日制学生"有关的段落。好像学习已经不是全日制学生的主要活动了！实际上，欧洲的各种理工学校和大学的大部分教师，从 20 世纪 70 年代以来，都经历过这种逐步的变迁。生活成本和消费预期都已经上涨，大部分学生不得不在课外打工兼职。以前，学生主要是在假期里工作，现在周末和晚上兼职的也很普遍，目前给我印象深刻的是学生的兼职与学业衔接似乎天衣无缝，分不清哪一项才是他们最重要的主业。近年来，我给硕士研究生安排的监督会议遭遇越来越多的问题，因为他们有很多时间都在做自己的兼职工作。学习不再是其本身的样子，而是年轻人都市生活的全部经历的入口。自然，这个结果不是学生的问题。和我们一样，他们都是垂直堆垛的受害者。学习竞争的活动范围每学期都在增加。在我们坐下来花 6 个月的时间阅读《精神现象学》之前，往往有一些着急的事情需要先去处理。每一位大学教师都知道，透彻地学习一门复杂的课程，需要很长的一段连续集中精力的时间。由此还会产生失眠和焦虑，以及在很长一段时间内的食欲不振。另外，爱情生活也会出问题。当代大学生还会出现心不在焉和超然离群的现象（在过去，我们还会加上许多高度过滤的咖啡和烟草）。这类学生大有人在，但是很大一部分已经属于不同的另类。当他们出现在教室时，他们都是在从一个地方赶到另一个地方的路上；他们每天都有很多很多的活动，从俱乐部到兼职的场所，不停地调换电视频道、网上冲浪和交朋友等。如果他们想跟上周围环境的节奏，并增加自身的就业机会，就不能不从那种缓慢的修道院式的生活中脱身。在劳动力市场，富有吸引力的申请者的简历，表现了丰富多彩的经历和快节奏的生活。

In a recent report about the state of higher education in Norway, the committee has included a passage about "those students who choose to study full-time". As if studying was not primarily a fulltime activity! As a matter of fact, most teachers at the university or polytechnic level in Europe have experienced a gradual change here since the 1970s. The cost of living and consumption expectations have gone up, and most students are obliged to take wage-work. Formerly, students primarily worked during the vacations, eventually weekend and evening work became more common, and presently it is my impression that work and studies are best seen as a seamless whole where it is difficult to tell which activity is deemed the most important. In recent years, I have had increasing problems arranging supervision meetings with postgraduate students because they have problems getting away from work. Studying is no longer simply what it is that one does, but an entry on the total menu of experiences that composes the life of a young, urban and unattached person. This result is not, naturally, the students' fault. Like all of us, they are victims of vertical stacking. The range of activities that compete with studying grows every semester. There is always something urgent that needs to be done first, before one sits down with The Phenomenology of Spirit for six months or so. As every good academic knows, thorough learning of a complex curriculum requires long, continuous periods of concentration, insomnia and anxiety, reduced appetite for sustained periods, problems in one's love life, absentmindedness and aloofness from contemporary matters. (And in the old days, we would have added: lots of strong filter coffee and tobacco.) This kind of student is still around, but the great majority is of a different kind. When they appear in the lecture room, they are on their way from one place to another; they have a wide spectrum of activities to fill their days with, from clubbing to wage-work, television zapping, web surfing and being with friends. If they want to be abreast with their surroundings and strengthen their career opportunities, they simply cannot disengage themselves for years of a slow, monk-like existence. In the labour market, attractive applicants have CVs which indicate diverse experience and high speed.

学术界的新形势——缓慢获取知识的边际效益正在下降——使我们不再想当然地认为，最聪明的学生一定会从事研究和教学工作。大学要么适应市场（当然很大，英国和北欧也一样）并加快教学的步伐，要么重新将自身定位成反主流文化的状态，体现缓慢、透彻和补充说明。

This new situation in academia the falling marginal value of slowly acquired knowledge also entails that it can no longer be taken for granted that the most brilliant students will be interested in pursuing a career in research and teaching. Universities may either adapt themselves to the market (which is largely what is happening, certainly in the UK and Scandinavia) and speed up their teaching, or they may redefine themselves as countercultural institutions that embody slowness, thoroughness and afterthoughts.

我的处境与学生们类似，尽管我的研究时间没有被外在的谋生需求、看电影、音乐会或镇上的晚会切割成无用的小块，但是会被信息线头的普及分割成碎片。

这些任务包括回复电子邮件、接电话、文件归档、回信、预订机票、阅读不完整的报告和其他官方文件。在最终坐下来忙一些不同事情的时候，总有一些其他的事情需要先去完成。当有很多任务等着我们去完成时，优先考虑的任务应该是首先想到的或实在无法再等的事情。令人惊讶的是，很多学术计划的主要工作从未超出计划初级阶段的范围。专业书籍越来越像糨糊加剪刀制成的拼贴画，里面有一小段是会议的论文，另外一些是期刊论文的摘录。我们可以拿出 5 分钟甚至是半个小时去完成一项任务，但从来不会用 5 年时间去做一件事。由于信息比人口的增长要快很多，涉及我们每一个人的事情必然会更多（尤其是那些被确定为信息交换台的人）。新信息的边际效应几乎为零，因此如果使用日益减小的尺寸包裹信息，就更容易吸引人的注意力。这些摆在一起的小包裹，很容易形成一座纤细而摇摆的塔，高度足以接触月亮。

The students' situation is comparable to my own, although my research time is not chopped up into useless fragments because of a pressing need for external wage-work, cinema and concert attendance, evenings on the town and so on but because of the prevalence of information lint. This includes tasks like replying to email, answering the phone, filing, responding to letters, booking flights, reading half-baked reports and other kinds of bureaucratic documents, and so on. Before one is finally able to sit down with something that might make a difference, there is always something else that needs to be done first. What is given priority in a situation where one has many tasks waiting to be done, is either the first task that comes to mind or that which simply cannot wait. Not unsurprisingly, quite a few academics plan major works that never get beyond the drawing-board. Academic books increasingly look like cut-and-paste collages with snippets of conference papers here and excerpts of journal articles there. We always have 5 minutes to spare for a given task, often even half an hour, but never five years. Since the growth in information is much, much faster than population growth, there is inevitably more to relate to for each of us (in particular, those of us who are positioned as information switchboards). The marginal value of new information is nearly zero, and it is therefore easier to attract a crumb of attention if one wraps the information in packages of ever decreasing size. Little packages that are stacked on top of each other to create wavering, thin towers that are soon tall enough to touch the moon.

用尺寸日益减小的积木灵敏地堆叠，是一项向许多方面扩展的技艺。有节律的舞曲、万维网、多频道电视、新闻业、学习与研究都是本文提到过的案例。按照奇思妙想，人们可以将越来越多的积木组合起来（所以高科技音乐是一个显著的案例）。在一定程度上，这个过程是被量化和证明过的，其结果只能被体验。各种各样的信息日益堆叠在一起，就像巨大的乐高积木塔，砖块毫无共同之处，但事实上却可以彼此契合。速溶这一术语不是因为雀巢咖啡这样的主要产品在全球取得成功才成为理解当今时代的核心概念。"瞬间"或"即刻"是表面的、肤浅的和短暂的。当瞬间（甚至是下一个瞬间）占据所有人时，我们就不再能为"积木"提供建筑的空间，这些积木可以与其他积木一起建成一个或几个立体基阵。现在每一件事都必须与其他事互相交换。入场券不得不廉价销售，最初的投资只能适中。迅捷的变化和无限制的灵活性成了主要的资产。在终审时，任何事物都只剩下单一的、满溢的、被压缩的永恒一刻。不妨假设未来某个时候会达到这一点，过去与未来都能完全抹去，当然我们达到了绝对的极限。想想维利里奥的话："不再有任何延误。"很难设想这件事的发生——许多人类普遍经历只在持续状态下才有意义。然而，在一些领域，时间存在被极度压缩的趋势，其中有一些可能是我们并不想要的，比如消费、工作和个人身份的形成。这是下一章要讨论的话题，是专横的时间在生活方面产生的后果，与互联网、迷幻音乐和加速发展的新闻业没有直接的关系。

The nimble stacking of blocks of decreasing size is a craft which spreads in many directions. Rhythmic dance music, the World Wide Web, multi-channel television, journalism, studies and research are some of the examples that have been mentioned here. One can increasingly combine the blocks according to whim (this is why techno music is such a telling example). This process can only to some extent be quantified and "proved"; its results can only be experienced. More and more of every kind of information is stacked, like gigantic Lego towers where the bricks have nothing in common but the fact that they fit （but they also fit with any other brick）. It is not because of the phenomenal global success of Nestlé 's main coffee product that the term instant is a key concept for an attempt to understand the present age. The moment, or instant, is ephemeral, superficial and intense. When the moment （or even the next moment）dominates our being in time, we no longer have space for building blocks that can only be used for one or a few configurations with other blocks. Everything must be interchangeable with everything else now. The entry ticket has to be cheap, the initial investment modest. Swift changes and unlimited flexibility are main assets. In the last instance, everything that is left is a single, overfilled, compressed, eternal moment. Supposing this point is reached some time in the future, and both past and future are fully erased, we would definitely have reached an absolute limit （recall Virilio: "There are no delays any more"）. It is difficult to imagine this happening there are many universal human experiences that only make sense as duration. However, in several fields, the tendency towards extreme compression of time is evident; some of them perhaps unexpected, such as consumption, work and the very formation of personal identity. That is the topic of the next chapter, which shows some effects of the tyranny of the moment on aspects of life which have no direct relationship to the Internet, trance music or accelerated journalism.

第七章　睡觉都可以工作：乐高积木综合征

工作的完成过程,将会拓展到刚好可以充满全部可以利用的时间。

——帕金森法则(1955 年)

7　The Lego Brick Syndrome

Work expands to fill the time available for its completion （Parkinson's Law, 1955）

在我一生中, 每个典型的工作日都是从我打开办公室的门那一刻开始的,然后启动咖啡机和苹果电脑,播放自动应答电话中的留言,同时记下需要回拨的电话号码。这些事情做完之后,我才会脱下外套挂在衣帽钩上,正式开始一天的工作。我打开电子邮箱,处理早上的第一批电子邮件,然后从我的私人信箱中收取其他的信件。堆积的信件里包含出版社定向发送的广告宣传册,一些讨论会的邀请函以及专业期刊的目录,这些东西必须定期更新。然后,我会登陆 Usenet,参与八到九个所谓的讨论小组,在那里我可以展开与工作有关的全球讨论。其间,我还会阅读几份报纸。

A typical working day in my life begins as I unlock the office, turn on the coffee machine and my Macintosh, playing stored messages from the answering machine as I jot down numbers to be dialled during the day, often before taking off my coat. I then open my electronic mailbox and go through the morning's first batch of email, before collecting the other kind of mail from my pigeon-hole. The stack of mail might contain some direct marketing blurb from publishers, a couple of requests for talks, and a couple of dozen tables of contents from professional journals one ought to read regularly to keep updated. Then on to the Usenet, where I participate in eight or nine so-called discussion groups where global discussions relevant for my work are carried on. In between, I try to read a couple of newspapers.

每天我要发送和接收 3—6 个传真，收发五六个电子邮件，还要接听 10—15 个电话，并写 3—4 封信件。事实上，一天的大部分时间都消耗在这些任务之上。我甚至还来不及思考我最终需要在办公室完成的事情，也就是研究、教学和学科普及化——这些才是我的职业工作。在办公时间，我很少有时间能连续思考两个问题，更别提连续读完两页文章了。为了写一篇比报刊文章更长一点的论文，许多专业研究人员不得不使用周末、假期和晚上的时间——这时候没有电话在身边。

During the day I might send, say, between three and six faxes and receive as many, send and receive about five emails, have ten to fifteen telephone conversations and write three to four letters. As a matter of fact, most of the day is spent on this kind of task. And still I haven't even begun to contemplate doing that which ultimately gives my presence in the office a purpose, namely research, teaching and popularisation in the discipline which is my profession. I rarely find the time to think two thoughts in succession, let alone read two consecutive pages, during office hours. In order to write a longer text than a newspaper article, many academics are forced to use weekends, vacations and late evenings preferably without a telephone line nearby.

这是 1995 年我为报纸所写文章的开头一段。从那时开始，情况已经发生了一些变化。我不再参与 Usenet 的讨论，也不再订购邮件用户清单服务；作为一种反向的补偿，今天我收到了很多很多的电子邮件。但是，我几乎很少再发传真，纸质信件的数量也在减少。除了具体的细节之外，我不能否认以上所作的描述还是十

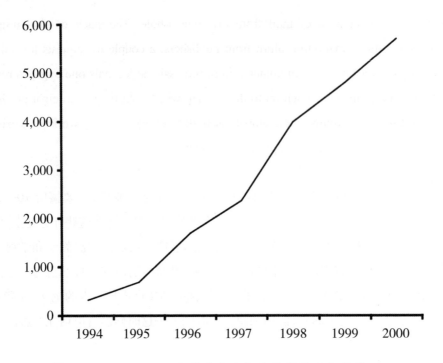

图 7-1 1994—2000 年接受电子邮件的数量变化趋势

Figure 7-1 E-mail received annually by T.H.E., 1994—2000

分裂合今日的情形——不仅仅对我是如此，还包括成千上万的人，他们正以不同方式受到信息社会副作用的影响。我要将这一章献给他们，不仅仅是作为信息的生产与消费者，而且偶尔作为人来讨论这个问题。但是，我要小小的离题一下。

These were the opening paragraphs of a newspaper article I wrote way back in 1995. There have been a few changes since then. I no longer take part in Usenet newsgroups, nor do I subscribe to listservs; as a perverted kind of compensation, I receive much, much more email today. But I hardly send faxes any more, and the amount of cellulose mail has also decreased. Such details apart, I cannot deny that the above description would on the whole be quite appropriate even today and not just for me, but for thousands upon thousands of people who are in varying ways affected by the sideeffects of information society. This chapter is devoted to them （us）, regarded not just as producers and consumers, but also occasionally as persons. But first, a small detour.

生活在公元前 6 世纪埃利亚的芝诺[埃利亚的芝诺(约前 490—前 430 年),古希腊哲学家,他因提出了 4 个关于运动不可能的悖论而知名。他创造这些悖论是为了支持他老师巴门尼德的理论。他认为世界上运动变化着的万物是不真实的,唯一真实的东西是巴门尼德所谓的"唯一不动的存在",所以"存在"是一而不是多,是静不是动。——编者],在那些与哲学家巴门尼德一起住在橄榄园中的学生里,他是最有天赋的一位。巴门尼德教导他"运动只是一种幻觉"——与常识相反,任何事情实际上都在十分安静地站立着——芝诺试图证明巴门尼德是对的,他凭借 4 个悖论做到了这一点,其中最著名的是阿喀琉斯与乌龟的故事。

Zeno of Elea, who lived in the sixth century BC, was one of the most gifted pupils to sit in the olive grove with the philosopher Parmenides. The Master had taught him that movement is really an illusion contrary to common sense, everything actually stood perfectly still and Zeno tried to prove that Parmenides was right. He did so through his four paradoxes, the most famous of which is the story about Achilles and the tortoise.

阿喀琉斯与乌龟举行了一场跑步比赛。乌龟当然爬得很慢,而阿喀琉斯却是参加过奥林匹克运动会的运动员。可是,乌龟的起始位置可以在阿喀琉斯前方几米处。芝诺认为,阿喀琉斯在理论上不可能取胜。首先,他出发后需要一定的时间,才能抵到乌龟最初的地方,但是很快乌龟又会继续往前爬行。这样,他就不可能追上乌龟此时所在的地点。当他到达乌龟前一时刻所在地点时,乌龟又向前爬行了一段距离,如此反复,没有终结。每一次阿喀琉斯到达乌龟刚刚所在的位置时,乌龟总会早一点点离开该处,也就是说乌龟总会在他的前方。随着比赛的进行,两者之间的距离明显在减少——最终接近零。但是在原则上讲,阿喀琉斯永远不可能超越乌龟。

A race had been organised between Achilles and the tortoise. The tortoise was naturally sluggish in its movements, while athletic Achilles was in Olympic form. However, the tortoise was given an initial advantage of a few metres. Therefore, says Zeno, it became theoretically impossible for Achilles to overtake it. First he would have to run to the point where the tortoise was when he started, but by then it would have moved on. Then he would have to run to this point, but again, the tortoise would have crawled on a bit. And so on ad infinitum. Each time Achilles reached the point where the tortoise was a little while earlier, it would have moved a little bit further. The distance was obviously greatly reduced as the race went on it approached zero but Achilles could in principle never overtake the tortoise.

虽然比芝诺晚两个世纪的亚里士多德认为他的观点有误（很容易看出这种观点具有同情心），但是直到柏格森出版首篇论文《时间与自由意志》时，才令人满意地解决了这个悖论，并对时间与空间作了鲜明的区分。柏格森认为时间的持续与空间没有关系，芝诺误解了时间点的含义，结果就产生了这个令人困惑的悖论。按照柏格森的观点，将时间特殊化会使人产生误解。

Although Aristotle, who lived two centuries later, was convinced that Zeno was wrong （and it is easy to regard this point of view with a certain sympathy）, the paradox was not resolved satisfactorily until Henri Bergson, in his first treatise, Time and Free Will, introduced a sharp distinction between time and space. According to Bergson time, regarded as duration, had nothing to do with space, and Zeno's baffling paradoxcs （another famous one is to do with an arrow "which appears to move"） were a result of his misleading creation of "points in time", that is spatialisations of time, which in Bergson's view were misleading.

前面我列举的那些与加速度和堆垛有关的案例,可以视为对芝诺最著名的悖论拐弯抹角(但并非不正当)的注解。芝诺使人们注意到时间与空间的关系。他认为在理论上讲运动是不可能的,因此不得不作为一种错觉。任何人都想知道为何哲学家会因为不接触现实生活而出名。这个结论在这里不太切题,但同时又清楚地体现了通信技术创新,极大地改变了时间与空间的关系。理论家已经提出了奇特的概念以处理这些问题:鲍德里亚谈到了时空轴线的内爆,吉登斯认为时空坐标系已经瓦解,卡斯特认为流动的空间已经代替了固定空间,哈维谈到了时空的压缩,等等。

Many of my earlier examples of acceleration and stacking can be read as oblique (not to say perverse) footnotes to Zeno's most famous paradox. He called attention to the relationship between time and space. His conclusion was that movement was theoretically impossible and therefore had to be an illusion. (Anyone wondering why philosophers have a reputation for being out of touch with real life?) This conclusion is not pertinent here, but, at the same time, it is clear that the relationship between time and space has undergone dramatic changes caused largely by innovations in communication technology. Theoreticians have proposed fancy concepts to deal with this: Jean Baudrillard talks of the implosion of the time/space axis, Anthony Giddens says that there has been a collapse of the time/space coordinates, Manuel Castells writes about how the space of flows has replaced the space of places, David Harvey speaks of time space compression, and so on.

持续一定的时间相应就要通过一定的距离,这种看法已经行不通了。因为在前面几章,我已经阐明延迟、间隙和缓慢正在面临各种各样的威胁。在此背景下,不妨将芝诺的悖论进行更新和再论述,权且作为埃里克森的悖论:如果将时间分割成足够细小的片段,它就不复存在。也就是说,预设任何事件都需要一定的时间,时间分成足够小段之后,就无法持续地存在,但可以作为时刻存在,每一个时刻可以被其下一个时刻赶超。显然,在很多互不相关的领域,也可以看到这样的模式。直到前不久，我们还在面对一个选择——在数量有限的"个人认同包装"里做出选择，这种"个人认同包装"被明确地定义：我要么是这些人中的一员，要么就是另外一群人中的成员。我可以像我的叔叔那样去商店购物，也可以在救世军中找一份有意义的工作。我要么是一个左翼分子，留着长发带着圆形眼镜，对北大西洋公约组织和核电持批判的态度；要么是一个圆滑世故的保守派成员，从育婴、税收到军事问题的一切事物，都支持执政党的观点。

It is no longer viable to pretend that a certain duration corresponds to a certain distance. For this reason, delays, gaps and slowness as such are threatened in ways I have indicated in preceding chapters. Allow me on this background to update and re-phrase Zeno's paradox as Eriksen's paradox: When time is chopped up into sufficiently small units, it ceases to exist . That is to say, it ceases to exist as duration (which presupposes that events take a certain time), but continues to exist as moments about to be overtaken by the next moment. The same pattern can be observed in many, apparently unrelated fields. Until quite recently, we were faced with choices between a limited number of "personal identity packages", which were fairly well defined: either I am one of these, or I am one of those. Either I go into shipping like my uncle, or I find a more meaningful job with the Salvation Army. Either I am a real lefty with long hair, round spectacles and a critical view of NATO and nuclear power, or I am a slick Tory type with navy blue blazers and conformist opinions about everything from child-raising to taxation and military issues.

在这种情况下（这种情况可以贴上"现代"标签），我们这些在自由主义和个人主义国家里的公民，每个人在出生时都会收到一盒色彩斑斓的乐高积木，这种装备具有各种特殊的指令：你可以选择其中的一种！现在（可以贴上"后现代"标签），我们也接受了同一个乐高积木的盒子，但是很遗憾这套指令已经丢失，而且，我们似乎被迫进行重建——至少修改我们每天摇摆的结构。这一定就是吉登斯所想的事情，他在《现代性与自我认同》中，提到了作为事业的自我。它并非一个给定的整体，必须反复地创造。在其他很多不同的领域中，也可以看到具有这种效果的趋势，比如个人认同（我是谁）、工作、职业生涯、家庭生活、消费习惯、口味和政治信念。接下来，我要探讨时刻的固定、堆垛和乐高积木综合征如何影响社会生活、劳动、家庭生活、休闲和消费的中心圈。在加速度、堆垛和指数增长的标题之下，我们已经从不同观点得到描述的模式，体现出了变化的方式，也是当代人生活的支柱。

In this kind of situation (which could, perhaps, be labelled 'modern'), each and every one of us, citizens of liberal, individualist countries, received a box of colourful Lego bricks at birth, furnished with a number of specific instructions for their assembly: choose one! Nowadays (in a situation which could, perhaps, be labelled "postmodern"), it is more as if we receive the same box of Lego bricks, but the sets of instructions alas are long lost, and moreover, we seem to be forced to re-build or at least modify our wavering constructions every day. This must be what Giddens had in mind when, in Modernity and Self-Identity, he spoke of the self as a project: it is not a given entity, it has to be created again and again. Tendencies to this effect can be observed in otherwise very different areas, such as personal identity (who am I really?), work and professional careers, family life, consumer habits, taste and political convictions. I shall now proceed to show how the fixation on the moment, stacking and the Lego brick syndrome influence the central spheres of life in our societies; labour, family life, leisure, consumption. It will be indicated how changes that have bearings on these pillars of contemporary life are expressions of a pattern that has already been described from different points of view, under the headings acceler-ation, stacking and exponential growth.

"弹性"工作的假象

加速变化的职业生活体现了灵活性和不安全性。《职场启示录》是一本重要但最不具影响力的小册子，谈论了新经济以及它对人们生活方式与个人身份的影响；作者斯内特描述了 20 世纪 90 年代新兴经济中的成功人士——灵活、懂得随机应变并掌握技术的人——在生活的中心经历真空的感觉。他没有谈论那些"书呆子"类的人物，按照神话内容，这种人永不结婚，只有很低的社会技能；相反，他谈论的是体面而普通的专业人士，就像美国人所说的，这类人为了过上丰富多彩的生活而奋斗。他们工作的领域包括金融、网络设计、电子商务、广告业、新闻业等，甚至有很多人跻身多个行业。在某种程度上讲，他们工作的公司在十年或二十年前压根就不存在，这些领域因为计算机革命发生了剧烈的变化。当伊芙琳在写作《独家新闻》时（1938 年）驻外记者所做的工作与在数字视频与卫星电视时代的这种工作之间有着巨大的差别。不妨考虑一下 1990 年以前的与现在的通信工程的差异：过去，通信主要依靠电线杆和电缆线。在类似挪威（多山、锯齿形海岸线、人口分散）这样条件艰苦的国家，国有电信公司的工程师往往会吹嘘，他们的电信网络已经覆盖了 99% 的人群，这得益于在贵重的基础实施方面持续的高成本投入。10 年之后，通信行业的人往往谈论互联网的门户网站、以卫星通信为基础的领域、短信、移动电话、互联网和视频会议。从 20 世纪 90 年代中期开始，全球移动电话的销售量已经超过固定电话的数量。在类似中国这样的国家里，为了保证通信覆盖面达到 99%，在国内建设星罗棋布的电线杆与电缆线，绝不可能是一个好的选择。

An Accelerated Professional Life
Offers Flexibility And Removes Security

In an important and influential little book about the new economy and its effects on ways of life and personal identity, The Corrosion of Character, Richard Sennett describes how successful people in the emergent economy of the 1990s flexible, adjustable, technologically capable people experienced a vacuum in the very centre of their lives. He does not talk of the generic "nerd" type who never gets married and who, according to the myth, has underdeveloped social skills, but about decent, ordinary professionals who "struggle to have a life", as they say in the USA. They work within sectors such as finance, web design, e-commerce, advertising, journalism and so on, and there are many of them. To some extent, they work in companies of a kind that did not exist ten or twenty years ago, to some extent in sectors that have been radically transformed because of the computer revolution. There is a major difference between the job of a foreign correspondent today, in the age of digital video and satellite television, and the "same job" say, at the time when Evelyn Waugh wrote Scoop （1938）. Consider also the difference between working in telecommunications before 1990 and today: in the old days, telecommunications were chiefly about telephone poles and cables. The engineers of the state-controlled telecom companies boasted, in the case of difficult countries like Norway （mountainous, with a jagged coastline and scattered population）, that they had achieved a telephone coverage of 99 per cent thanks to costly, but enduring investments in a valuable infrastructure. Ten years later, telecom people talk about web portals, and their field is now based on satellite communication; SMS messages, mobile telephony, Internet and video conferencing. Since the mid-1990s, the number of mobile telephone subscriptions sold globally has exceeded the number of stationary subscriptions. For countries like China, it will never be an option to build a material network of poles and cables criss-crossing the entire country to ensure a coverage of, say, 99 per cent.

　　远程通信的实例非常恰当，因为它在两方面起作用：一方面，这项技术构成了新社会的支柱，在新的劳务市场、新的消费与通信模式等领域发挥决定作用。另一方面，劳务市场突然间被迫适应新形势，因此，新技术本身就是劳动力市场的组成部分，能给从业人员带来显著的影响。在这种背景下，过去拥有丰富的悠久经历的老前辈，自然无法获得很高的市场价值。

The example of telecommunications is apt because it works two ways: on the one hand, this kind of technology makes up the backbone of the new society, and plays a decisive role in the new labour market, the emerging patterns of consumption and communication, and so on. At the same time, it is also itself a part of the labour market that has suddenly been forced to adapt to new circumstances, with obvious consequences for employees. Old-timers with long and varied experience do not have a high market value in this new setting.

斯内特描述的工人，已经脱离了由传送带和计时器支配的单调苦工。他们可以灵活就业，能够游遍天涯海角，并可以收发电子邮件，移动电话一直开机已经成为劳动合同的一部分。很多时候，他们在职业生涯中要数次跳槽（一般来说北美人比挪威人更不习惯固定在一个职业上）。在恒定的压力下，他们需要彻底改造、更新和改变对其现任工作的观点，并迅速调转方向和变化策略。他们的工作鲜有例行公事的味道。仔细研读《职场启示录》可以发现，斯内特说的只是一小撮人，大部分人并不渴望相对稳定的工作和一代之前就可预测的工作情形。他们享受新经济的灵活性和机会（这些机会只局限于少数人，但是每一个人都可以迅速地发展）。然而，在将生活与工作结合在一起时，他们会体验到一些严肃的问题，这些问题并不是一系列不连续的事件和工作调动，等等。

Sennett describes people who have been liberated from the monotonous drudgery of the conveyor belt and the time recorder. They have flexible jobs. They travel extensively, they send and receive lots of email, and as a part of their labour contract, their mobile phone is always turned on. They have in most cases moved several times to advance their career （North Americans in general tend to be less sedentary than Europeans）. They live under constant pressure to reinvent themselves, update and change their perspectives on the job they are doing, turn around quickly and change their strategies. There is little that smacks of routine in their work. Researching the book, Sennett spoke to a handful of people, and most of them did not yearn for the relatively stable, predictable situation that characterised work a generation ago. They enjoy the flexibility and opportunities of the new economy （opportunities that are largely confined to a minority, but one which is growing quickly). Yet they experience serious problems in attempting to make their lives hang together as something other than a discontinuous series of events, career moves and so on.

实际上,有些人不到 35 岁就已经油枯灯灭(顺便说一句,这个隐喻指的是热度除了具有速度之外,什么都没有)。在挪威,从 1999 年到 2000 年,因为亚健康请假的人数占了 12%。按照首相的说法,为了证明 2001 年削减国家财政预算的合理性,如果政府把病休假和临时伤残抚恤金支出降到 1998 年的水平,国家就可以节约大约 10 亿挪威币的资金。别忘了,我们谈论的国家只有 450 万总人口。根据《英国卫报》的报道,40%的美国工人认为他们的工作压力极大。压力并非在于有很多事要做,而是在没有做好其他事之前,无法做自己的工作。在英国,有 30%的劳动力认为他们存在心理健康问题;在德国,有 7%的人因为压力和沮丧提前退休。提早精疲力尽的人已经明确承认了新世纪面临的文明化疾病。

Some of them are virtually burnt out before they are 35. (Burnt out is, incidentally, an excellent metaphor: heat is, physically speaking, nothing but speed.) In Norway, the growth in sick leave from 1999 to 2000 was an unhealthy 12 per cent. According to the Prime Minister, in a bid to justify cuts in the 2001 state budget, the country would have saved the equivalent of nearly £1,000,000,000 if government spending on sick leave and temporary disability benefits were only brought down to the 1998 level! (We are, remember, talking about a country with 4.5 million inhabitants in all!) According to the Guardian, 40 per cent of American workers report that they perceive their job as "very or extremely stressful". Stress is not the same as having a lot to do, but being unable to do one's work before one has to do other things first. In the UK, 30 per cent of the workforce report that they experience mental health problems, and in Germany, 7 per cent take early retirement because they are stressed and depressed. Early burn-out is already in a good position to contend for the title of the civilisational disease of the new century.

从工业到信息经济的重心转移与新技术的出现，表明许多工人实际上在逃避"朝九晚五"的惯例。他们的工作地点可以在家里、飞机上（或者更有可能是在等待延误的航班时）、公园里或汽车上。现身工作场所已经不再是一个必要的条件。他们也许不再需要准时上下班，但是却被要求能够随时在线。

The new technology, and the shift of the gravitational point in the economy from industry to information, imply that many workers actually are in a position to evade the nine-to-five routine. They can work at home, in a plane （or, more likely, in an airport waiting for a delayed plane）, in the park or in the car. Physical presence during working hours is no longer seen as a necessity. They may not need to be on time any more, but instead they are expected to be online.

20 世纪 90 年代，随着新经济的发展，美国人使用的抗压抑药物及相关物质增长显著，斯内特虽然没有明确提到这一点，但他已经注意到了此事。1988 年，美国有 1.31 亿人开过精神刺激类药物的处方；1998 年，这一人数已经上升到 2.33 亿。这一年，光是"氟西汀"这一种药物就有 1000 万患者使用。此外，还有数百万的北美人服用草药和其他非处方的刺激类药物（包括可卡因和安非他命），以便提高个人的安宁状态。精神病学家伦道夫·内瑟推测，美国经济坚定乐观的特征，以及金融冒险现象反常的传播，都与相对便捷的互联网工程有关，最直接的事实是这些物质使人们不再惧怕与焦虑。从 1992 年到现在，氟西汀的效果能够一直延绵不断吗？几乎不太可能，但内瑟的观点并非毫不相关。

工作与休闲的区别正在消失。工作占了上风。20 世纪 90 年代早期，在家里工作和远程工作的概念刚刚出现时，雇主们还担心会失去对工人活动的控制。或许，他们会怀疑员工们不工作，而是躺在沙发上喝啤酒并观看肥皂剧，并认为新的工作机会必然会弱化对员工的直接监管。20 世纪 90 年代晚期，其他方面的焦虑更能切中要害。新的工作方式的确很有灵活性，但不可避免地消除了工作与休闲之间的界限。如果在平等的基础上，最普遍的速度原则表明快者胜过慢者；若在特定的位置，则需要适度的想象能力才能看到劳动胜过休闲。这样，要是人们期待如此或工作性质要求如此，他们就可能实际上一直处在工作状态。

　　Sennett does not mention it, but he might well have: the use of anti-depressant and related substances grew spectacularly in the USA of the 1990s, closely following the development of "the new economy". The number of prescriptions for so-called psycho-active medicines in the US went from 131 million in 1988 to 233 million in 1998. One single product, Prozac, was prescribed to 10 million sufferers in 1998. In addition, millions of North Americans take herbal medicines and other prescription-free stimulants（including cocaine and amphetamines）to improve their sense of well-being. The psychiatrist Randolph Nesse has speculated on the possibility that the strong optimism characterising the US economy, and particularly the exceptionally widespread financial risk-taking associated with rather airy Internet projects, might be directly connected to the fact that these substances neutralise fear and anxiety. Is the continuous boom lasting from 1992 to the present a result of Prozac? Hard, but Nesse's view is also far from irrelevant.

　　The distinction between work and leisure is erased. Work wins. When the notions of working from home and "distance working" were introduced in the early 1990s, employers worried that they might lose control over their workers' activities. Perhaps they suspected that instead of working, their employees would lie on the couch sipping beer and watching soap operas, given new opportunities entailed by weakened direct surveillance. The second half of the 1990s indicated that other anxieties are more to the point. The new flexibility quietly, but inevitably erases the boundary between work and leisure. Since one of the most general principles of speed states that fast time always wins over slow time when they meet on an equal footing, it requires only a modest feat of the imagination to see that labour wins over leisure, and not the other way around, when they meet in a particular site. In this way, people can actually be "at work" always if they so wish, or if the kind of work they do requires it.

希望员工任何时候都处在潜在的工作状态，是目前新工作的重要维度。完全的实用性具有感染力。当某些公司或员工开始这样做时，其他人就不得不紧跟，否则就会失去竞争优势。我的报道人告诉我说，他在公园里看到一个 30 岁左右的男子在与他 6 岁的儿子踢球。这个男子在玩球的半个小时内，耳朵上戴着的移动电话耳塞一直没有摘下来。

The expectation that one should be available as a potentially working person at any time, is an important dimension of new work. Complete availability is contagious. When some firms or individuals begin, others have to follow suit lest they lose their competitive edge. The other day I heard about a man in his thirties, who was being watched by my informant as he kicked a ball in the park with his son, who was around 6. During the half hour the ball game lasted, he did not once remove the cellphone from his right ear.

"金表时代"的远去

新的职业结构也是新经济的重要组成部分。"金表"时代已经远去，也可能不会再回来了。过去（或者说 1985 年以前），许多人从学校毕业后就进入公司。按照资格、功绩与上层的关系的规则，他们在公司的职位变动非常缓慢。在公司忠实地服务 25 年后，员工就能够被合理地安排在金字塔形的等级结构中，公司的常务董事就会从他那巨大的桃花木办公桌后面起身，并授予员工一块金表，上面雕刻着公司的标记。

The Era Of Gold Watches Is Gone

New career structures are also an important part of the new economy. The era of gold watches is gone, and it will probably not return. In the old days (until say, 1985), many would begin to work for a company after completing their education (which could be veryearly in life back then). Then one made one's slow career moves following the rules of seniority, merit and proximity to the powers that be. After 25 years of loyal service to the company, one was reasonably well placed in its pyramidal hierarchy, and the managing director would rise from his enormous mahogany desk and descend to offer a gold watch with the company's insignia engraved on it.

现在，如果一个人数十年干同一个工作，反而或多或少是一个失败者，因为他未能接触到当代的经济。夸张一点讲，那些大半辈子为同一家公司全职工作的人，已经越来越少了。兼职与弹性的工作、自由职业、业务外包、独立的咨询公司和频繁跳槽，已经成了经济结构不可或缺的部分，不仅在美国如此，在北欧和英国亦是如此。

Today, it is instead the case that one is more or less a loser (that terrible American word) out of touch with the contemporary economy if one stays in the same job for more than a couple of years. Exaggerations aside, it is well documented that it is becoming increasingly rare that employees work full-time in the same company for the greater part of their professional life. Part-time and flexitime work, freelancing, outsourcing, independent consultancies and frequent changes of work have become part and parcel of the economy's structure, not just in the USA, but in places like Scandinavia and Britain as well.

从公司的远景来看，公司领导面临的重要挑战，就是想方设法说服优秀的员工留下来。在不断变化的新经济中，如果拥有可供出售的技术，他就可以有很多的选择。灵活性与不安分几乎是一对孪生子。两者总是如影随形。

Seen from the perspective of the company, it has become a crucial challenge for the leadership to find ways of persuading good workers to stay. In the changing new economy, there are many alternatives for people with saleable skills. Restlessness is the Siamese twin of flexibility. They enjoy each other's company.

最后，很多公司似乎已经抹去了短期与长期计划的差别。所有的计划都是短期性的，因为没有人知道未来三五年内，这个世界（市场、目标群体、顾客和毕业生等等）会变成什么样子。

Finally, the distinction between short-term and long-term planning seems to have been eradicated in many companies. All planning has to be short-term, for nobody knows what the world will look like （the markets, the target groups, the clients, the students...）in five or even three years.

这不等于说过去比现在好。不管如何，我都不愿意生活在两次大战期间或20世纪50年代。新工作的灵活性的确创造了真正的选择和自由。传统工业化时代的特征是静态分层的组织模式，现在逐步被新的组织结构替代——虽然难度很大，但必须得承认，后者以网络为基础并以项目为导向的模式，是由手头的任务决定的，而不是取决于公司的组织计划。公司的附属形式多种多样，很多时候既可以由员工的意愿决定，也可以依赖于公司本身的战略。个人主义的价值与选择已经被提到了新的高度，这本身并非一件坏事。

This is not tantamount to saying that things used to be better. By no means. I would not have preferred to live in the inter-war years or the 1950s. The new flexibility of work does create genuine choice and freedom. The hierarchical, static organisational models typical of the classic industrial era are increasingly being replaced with enormous difficulties, it must be conceded by network-based, project-oriented models where the structure of the organisation is determined by the tasks at hand, not by the organisational map. There are a variety of forms of attachment to a company, and this can in many cases depend just as much on the employee's wishes as on the company's own strategies. The values of individualism and choice are taken to new heights, and this is not in itself a bad thing.

然而,新经济会带来很多意想不到的后果,其中一些直接受新经济的影响,还有一些明显令人不悦。首先,新工作使公司与工人一样极其脆弱。变动、动荡和速度的比率,以及不再与计时器和"金表"签订终身劳动合同,能够给个人提供自由,不过需要提醒的是,自由的背后总有可能失去安全性。

Yet the new economy has a number of unintended consequences for those directly affected by it, some of them distinctly unpleasant. First of all, the new work makes firms and workers alike extremely vulnerable. The rate of change, turbulence, speed and freedom from the life-long labour contract with its clocking-in machines and gold watches provide freedom, but also serve as a reminder that the underside of freedom nearly always is loss of security.

其次,现在的工作往往特别注重特殊的人格特质。适应性、开放性、快速的工作作风和机会主义,在经济上和其他方面都可以取得成功。如果有人想知道为何教师职业代表一潭死水(薪水少、社会地位低并且补助微薄),这就是答案所在。教师的工作必定是一个缓慢和累积性的活动,需要依靠一套相对稳定的价值观。教师职业的理念与新时代已经相去甚远。

Second, today's work tends to favour （and boost） a particular set of personality traits. Adaptability, openness, a speedy style of working and opportunism pay off both economically and in other ways. If anyone wonders why the teaching profession has been relegated to a backwater （poor recruitment, low salaries and declining social position）, this is the answer. The work of a teacher is by necessity a slow and cumulative activity based on a relatively stable set of values. Its ideals are far removed from those of the new era.

对于那些全部或部分沉浸在新经济中的人来说，世界不再相互联系可能是最重要的副作用。在不久的将来，能够大行其道的，既不是乐观主义，也不是悲观主义，而似乎是根本性的公开与不稳定。主要的原因在于当下已经发生倾斜，很难将其概念化。可以说在目前的时间内无法出现特定的方向，只能沉迷于自恋和对下一刻的迫切需求。

For those who are wholly or partly immersed in the new economy, the sense that the world is no longer coherently interconnected may be the most important sideeffect. Neither optimism nor pessimism is prevalent in visions of the near future these days; it seems fundamentally open and uncertain. A main cause is that the present is oblique and difficult to conceptualise. It could also be said that no particular direction emerges from this present time, narcissistically obsessed with itself and terrorised by the demands of the next moment.

斯内特感兴趣的是不同生活圈子的关系，尤其是工作圈子与家庭的关系。他的研究对象对他讲："我特别忙，马上就要劳累过度，没有时间照顾家庭，但是这一切很快就能得到改善。"任何管理方面的专家都可以确认这一点，主管们很容易使用他们职业生涯的间隔来说明这一点。然而，并非只有那些忙碌和高薪的主管们拥有现在的这些毛病。许多领域与行业的雇员——新闻记者、学者、销售人员、官员和出版商——觉得快速的工作时间正在拆散私人生活的慢速时间。由于工作被包裹进入那些日益减少的片段（工作营业额、任务和惯例等方面的变化越来越快），而且需要越来越多的单个从业人员，私生活的逻辑已经显得过时并充满问题。尤其是家庭生活需要的一点时间，似乎很难与个人的职业协调关系。无论是在夫妻关系还是父母与小孩的关系中，很容易就能看出这一点。

Sennett is particularly interested in the relationship between different spheres of life, notably work and family. His informants say things like, "I am extremely busy and overworked right now, and I do not have enough time for my family, but this is going to improve very soon." This, any expert on management can confirm, executives are apt to say at brief intervals throughout their careers. These days, however, such difficulties are not the exclusive domain of busy and well-paid executives. Employees in many areas and at many levels journalists, academics, salespeople, bureaucrats, publishers... all feel that the fast time of work is cannibalising the slow time of private life. And as work is being parcelled up into ever decreasing segments along several dimensions （the turnover of jobs, tasks, routines, etc. becomes faster and faster）, and demands growing chunks of the individual employee, the logic of private life becomes dated and problematic. Family life, in particular, seems to demand a kind of time which is difficult to reconcile with professional careers. It is easy enough to see the symptoms of this, both in relationships between spouses and in the child-parent relationship.

对于西欧国家离婚率的增长，这不是一种隐蔽的教化方式。实际上，高离婚率可能是生活质量提高的表现。现在的北欧国家，离婚很容易，也很少有文化方面的处罚，这是对难以忍受的婚姻做出的现实选择。尤其妇女会受益于这方面的变化，男人与小孩则要更少一些。

This is not a covert way of moralising over the growing divorce rates in Western Europe. Indeed, high divorce rates may be anindication of an improved quality of life. When it is easy to get a divorce and there are few cultural sanctions against it, which is now the case in Northern Europe, it becomes a realistic option to get out of unbearable marriages. Women especially seem to have benefited from changes in this field（most divorces are initiated by women）, men and children to a lesser degree.

贝特森对于灵活性的概念非常感兴趣。他在 20 世纪 70 年代早期所写的一篇文章中，坚持认为人类活动能够驾驭的可用能量越多，社会的灵活性就越少。因此，他从人类生态的角度提出了自己的概念，这个观念（可能源于莱斯利·怀特）认为，一个社会的"进化水平"，可以看作其开发可利用能源的效率的函数。按照贝特森的观点，有效开发的结果不是社会取得了多大的进步，而是封堵了多少可能的选择。在农业革命及紧随其后的人口增长之后，已经不可能返回采集狩猎。工业革命及其对钟表时间的依赖性之后，数百万人具有了同步性和能量的高消耗，就很难设想再返回更开放和不固定的农业社会了。

Gregory Bateson was deeply interested in the concept of flexibility. In an essay from the early 1970s, he argues that the more energy that is harnessed for human activities, the less flexible a society is. He thereby turns a notion from human ecology on its head, namely the idea （which stems from Leslie White）that the "evolutionary level" of a society can be seen as a function of its efficiency in exploiting available energy resources. In Bateson's view, the result of efficient exploitation is not so much that society advances, but that possible options are closed off. After the agricultural revolution and its accompanying population growth, there was no possibility of return to hunting and gathering. After the Industrial Revolution and its dependency on clock time, the synchronisation of millions of people and high energy consumption, it is difficult to envision a return to the less temporally disciplined and interdependent agricultural society, and so on.

　　贝特森对灵活性的概念界定，很容易用来解释我们现在讨论的这个主题。时间使用方面的灵活性表明，还有很多空闲时间，尚未被特殊的活动或特定的信息输入来有效地填充。在这些时间内，可以随意地思考，也可以缓慢地活动，既不需要设定目标，也不用考虑持续的时间，只是到处闲逛。欧洲学生的生活在没有塞满兼职、休闲和快速上课之前，还真有可能在藏书楼休闲地徘徊，并发现那些未曾预料的东西。当读书的过程逐渐导向为了应付即将到来（很少距离考试还有很长时间）的考试时，读书的时间就会更稀缺，学生将越来越难以获得独立的发现。课外阅读变得没有多大必要了，因此成了一种奢侈的享受。于是，创造性就此消失。

The Batesonian notion of flexibility can easily be adapted to shed light on the topic at hand. Flexibility in time use implies that there is vacant time, empty time, time available which has not been efficiently filled with specified activities or a specified kind of information input. Time for meandering thoughts, for slow activities with no instrumental aim and no fixed duration, time for just fooling around. Before the life of the European student became crowded with wage-work, leisure and short courses, student life entailed a real possibility of wandering leisurely about in the halls of learning, and discovering the unexpected. When course reading increasingly becomes geared towards the upcoming exams （which are rarely far away）, and time for reading as such becomes more scarce, it is increasingly difficult for a student to make independent discoveries. Extra-curricular reading becomes an unnecessary and therefore unprioritised luxury. Creativity disappears.

贝特森注意到，一个领域内灵活性的增加，会减少另外一个领域的灵活性。如果这是一个普遍的原则，或许就可以用来解释新工作方式为何会减少其他事物的灵活性。这些新工作方式受到商业评论家和社会科学家的吹捧，认为它可以大面积地改善程式化"朝九晚五"的沉闷工作。家庭生活的时间被占用，休闲时间被工作挤占，连空隙时间都被小的任务填充满了。或者，从更普遍的原则来看，可以说当前巨大的灵活性见证了信息传播夺走人们时间的灵活性，人们的时间比以往填充得更满。

Bateson notes that increased flexibility in one area tends to remove flexibility elsewhere. If this could be seen as a general principle, it might explain why it is that the flexibility of "new work" touted by business pundits and some social scientists as a massive improvement on the routine nine-to-five drudgery, takes flexibility away from everything else. Family life is Taylorised, leisure becomes infused with work, the gaps are filled with little tasks. Or, on a more general note, it could be stated that the enormous flexibility currently witnessed in the dissemination of information takes flexibility out of people's time, which becomes more overfilled than ever before.

专横时间中的家庭生活

　　家庭生活天生是慢速的，很难适合当前的时代。专横的时间已经进入亲密的空间，不管人们在道德上如何评定这件事，生活伴侣的频繁更改可以清楚地表明这一点。传统的基督徒坚守"到死也不分离"的信念，这的确是一个重要的安全阀：只有丧偶才能摆脱束缚并自由地再婚。以前，对大部分人来讲，这是一个非常现实的选择。婚姻具有持久性，尤其具有慢速的特性。印度人习惯家庭包办婚姻，也不会轻易离婚，他们经常会说："西方人恋爱达到沸点时就结婚，随后温度逐年下降。我们结婚前互不认识，双方感情相当冷淡。但是结婚之后，夫妻感情就如低热电水壶里的水温一般缓慢上升。"与小说、论文或电视剧一样，婚姻的逻辑表明印度人的模式优于西方人的模式：它需要经过一系列的阶段，每一阶段都要建立在前一阶段的基础之上。无论日子是好是坏，夫妻一起共同面对，最终他们都会变老，出现恼人的怪癖，并且慢慢秃顶变胖，甚至皮肤出现很多皱纹。另一方面，的确可以看见小草越长越绿。然而，当变更配偶的门槛降低时，就会出现很多结果，其中之一是许多人永远无法经历亲密关系的特殊阶段。他们一次又一次地退回起点，不眠之夜带着新冲动、跳动的心和不稳定性；最终，他们会有新的孩子、新配偶的父母、新的住房贷款，以及到宜家家居里挑选家具的啰唆（至少我有过此经历）的路程，并因基督徒的习俗是否合法引发新的争吵，等等。就此而言，一夫一妻制是现存生活趋势的最佳例证，在世纪之交正以很快的速度发生变化。我们乐颠颠地回到起点，经常为自己有能力"保持年轻"而骄傲，成熟已经成了一个古怪的概念。

　　婚姻承受的直接压力来自于专横的时间，它需要未经调停的即时满足，并承诺一直有新鲜的和更激动人心的时刻，这会对与历史、连通性和持续性有关的价值观产生不利的影响。家庭内外都有压力。婚姻的解体是很容易计量的家庭压力的一部分；新工作及与之相连的加速度可能的含义，是将家庭生活贬谪为一个剩余范畴，各种空闲的时间都被手头各类活动填充满了。由于家庭已经"缺乏功能"

（30 年来社会学家一直为此叹息），在新经济范围内，很难理解家庭究竟是为了什么。举一个稍微不同的例子，布里奇特·琼斯与霍恩比式人物特性，——分别是不成熟的男女彼得·潘们，通常要到 30 岁才能逐渐成长起来。

Family Liee Is By Nature Slow And Fits The Current Era Badly

More or less frequent changes of life partners are clear indications of the spread of the tyranny of the moment into the intimate sphere, no matter how one prefers to judge the tendency morally. The classic Christian notion "until death do us part" did contain an important safety valve: one was liberated and free to remarry if the spouse died. In earlier times, this alternative was a realistic one for a lot of people. Yet marriage was considered to be enduring and not least slow. Indians, who generally live in arranged marriages and hesitate to get divorced, may put it like this: "Western marriages begin when love is at the boiling point, and then the temperature goes down gradually, year by year. Our marriages begin when we scarcely know each other, with rather lukewarm emotions on both sides, but then they slowly heat up like a water kettle on low heat." Like a novel, a treatise or a linear television series, the logic of marriage dictates that it should be more like the Indian model than the Western one: it goes through a series of phases, each of which builds on the preceding phase. Couples share "good and bad days" together; both partners eventually grow older, they develop annoying quirks, they become bald, fat or wrinkled, and it must indeed frequently seem that the grass is greener on the other side. However, when the threshold for a change of partner is lowered, one of several results is that a great number of people never get to experience particular phases (or stages) in their intimate relationships. They go back to square one again and again, with new bursts of sleepless nights, beating hearts and uncertainty; eventually with new children, new parents-in-law, new mortgages, new tortuous trips to IKEA (at least in my part of the world), new heated arguments about which Christmas customs are to be considered legitimate and so on.

Seen in this light, serial monogamy is one of the best extant examples of life's tendency to stand still at great speed around the turn of the millennium. We happily return to square one, priding ourselves on our ability to "remain young", and maturity becomes an outlandish concept.Marriages are under direct pressure from the tyranny of the moment, which demands unmediated, instant gratification, which promises ever new and more exciting moments, and which militates against the values associated with history, connectedness and duration. The pressure comes from both within and outside. Dissolved marriages are one easily quantifiable aspect of the pressure on the family; another possible implication of new work and its associated acceleration is the relegation of family life to a residual category, a kind of spare tank of time to be filled or emptied depending on the number of other activities to hand. As the family has been "emptied of functions" (a lament heard from sociologists for 30 years), it becomes increasingly difficult, within the new economy, to understand what it is for. Put slightly differently, the number of Bridget Joneses and characters such as those depicted by Nick Hornby immature and unfixed Peter Pans of both genders, often well into their thirties is clearly on the rise.

在功能上，家庭存在着很多的不固定性，许多父母的主要活动是将家庭时间进行工业化管理。例如，你今天带一个孩子去学小提琴，我带另一个去幼儿园。如果你带他们一起去乡下过周末，我就开始认真处理某些事情，下周就可以由我带他们去我父母那里。今天你待在家里，我就可以出去开会。明天早上我早点上班，你就可以星期四早点上班。好了，一言为定！

The family is riddled with uncertainties regarding its functions. A major preoccupation for many parents is the industrial organisation of family time. It goes like this: if you take X to her violin lesson today, I will go and collect Y at kindergarten. If you take both of them to the country at the weekend so that I can get down to doing something, I'll take them to my parents next weekend. Can you stay at home today, so that I can go to that meeting? If I can leave early for work tomorrow, you can do it on Thursday. Deal!

　　按照这样的方式，家庭生活被安排得井井有条，这需要生产线的管理方式——同时工作的安排日益多样化和苛刻，需要个人履行的承诺也要丰富得多。

In this way, family life is being Taylorised; it acquires the characteristics of assembly line production while working life simultaneously becomes more varied, more demanding and richer in its promises of personal.

　　家庭对时间安排的商议，可以采用无可挑剔的民主方式——至少是在未稀释的竞争上有所进步：从无情的经济斗争到政治妥协，这种方法可以视为旧式家长制的进步。不足的是，很难给家庭生活赋予一种深远的意义；其中，日常时间预算的平衡，已经成了主要的成分。我更相信对于家庭而言，一段较长的持续和缓慢的时间非常重要，因此与其他的社会领域相比，家庭要承受更强的压力。新经济的许多雇主都知道这一点。所以，他们喜欢雇佣单身人士，有需要时就可以劝他们或多或少地加班工作。甚至，他们会为员工配备一个新的手机，并且预存好话费，以便周末还能给员工电话，要求他们立刻与办公室联系。

Family deliberations about the organisation of time can be carried out in impeccably democratic ways which is, at least, an advance over undiluted competition: one moves, as it were, from the ruthless struggles of economics to the compromises of politics; and this method must also be seen as an advance on old-fashioned patriarchy. On the deficit side, it is not easy to invest a profound sense of meaning into family life when balancing the daily time budgets has become a major ingredient. There exists, I am inclined to believe, no other social arena where long duration and slow time are more important, and therefore under stronger pressure, than the family sphere. Many employers in the new economy know this.They therefore prefer to employ single people, who can be persuaded to work more or less all day when necessary. Perhaps they even give their new employees a mobile phone with a fully paid subscription, so that they can phone them on Sunday morning, ordering them to report to the office immediately.

在此背景下，当代家庭的外部框架是瞬间的逻辑，它与家庭的逻辑特点正好相反。家庭生活既非劳动密集型，也非资本密集型，但却是时间密集型。具有嘲讽意味的现象，与孩子待在一起的高质量黄金时间，是忙碌的父母每晚睡前与孩子一起享受的 15 分钟。父母参与严厉和苛刻的劳动力市场，工作与休闲的差别逐渐模糊，同时性别角色也不稳定并具有争议（没有人可以毫不含糊地分清好男人和好女人的意思），因此很难找到一个现有的节奏，使家庭生活具备特殊的质量——缓慢、自然发展和信任，这可以使家庭兴旺繁荣。这些考虑并没有独到之处。然而，家庭作为生活的形式，需要面对由专横的时间造成的其他非理论化问题。

The external framing of contemporary family life in this setting is the logic of the moment, and it is directly opposed to the logic of the family. Family life is neither particularly labour-intensive nor capital-intensive, but it is extremely time-intensive. The parody is that phenomenon which is called "quality time" with the children, where the busy father or mother enjoys 15 minutes of qualitatively outstanding time with the kids every evening at bedtime. In an age when both men and women participate fully in a tight and demanding labour market, and the distinction between work and leisure is becoming blurred, at the same time as gender roles are uncertain and contested （nobody can tell unequivocally what it means to be a good man or a good woman any more）, it is far from easy to find an existential rhythm where the particular qualities of family life slowness, organic growth, trust are allowed to flourish. These considerations are not particularly original. The family as a form of life is nevertheless faced with other, less theorised, problemscaused by the tyranny of the moment.

第一个需要解决的问题是知识的传播。它不仅影响到父母,还会影响从小学到大学各层次的教师。当文化迅速地变迁时,某些人认为过快的速度会使文化失去立足点,这就不容易看到年轻人该从父母一辈那里学什么。父母基于多年生活的经验所积累的智慧,并不一定与年轻人有关。20世纪40年代出生的人,怎么可能教70年代出生的人如何使用电脑呢? 一个40岁的人该怎样苦思冥想,才能向15岁的孩子解释多种族的挑战? 在孩子上大学之前,父母怎么会知道去远东和拉丁美洲旅行的重要性有哪些呢?为何正常的青春期少女不得不每天给朋友们发送短信保持联系而不被社会隔离?认为政治是社会变迁的手段,又有多么愚蠢呢?社会改变得越快,容纳的事情越多,代际之间文化传递的问题就越多。或者还可列举一个不同的例子:儿童与青少年可以逐渐自由地改变自身的价值观以及他们所认为有意义的生活,把不同种类的知识碎片汇总在一起,从学校老师所教导的知识到最新版的任天堂游戏一一排列。持续性和连贯性遭遇失败,自发性与创新性占据上风。正如前面所提到的那样,乐高积木脱离了任何指令系统。不管是好是坏,它自然而然都依赖于内容。只有当人们缺乏价值观或忽视对问题的反思时,才会认真地思考创新本身是否一件好事。可是,毒气室也是一种创新。

The first problem is to do with the transmission of knowledge. It does not just affect parents, but teachers of every kind up to university level. When culture changes quickly, in some people's view so fast that it loses its footing, then it is not easy to see what the young ought to learn from their parental generation. The wisdom of the parents, based on years of experience, is not necessarily perceived as relevant. What could a person born in the 1940s teach someone born in the 1970s about personal computers and their use? How can an older person in their forties even contemplate explaining the challenges of multi-ethnicity to a 15-year-old? And what do mum and dad really know about the importance of travelling to the Far East and Latin America before one goes on to university, or why any healthy teenage girl has to send several SMS messages every day to her friends in order to remain in touch and not be socially isolated; or, for that matter, how idiotic the belief in politics as a means to societal change is? The faster and more encompassing changes are, the more problematic the transmission of culture between the generations becomes. Or, differently put: in this situation, children and adolescents are increasingly free to fashion their own values and their own meaningful lives, pulling together fragments from various sources, ranging from the varied input of schoolteachers to the latest Nintendo game. Duration and continuity lose out; spontaneity and innovation win. The Lego blocks are, as mentioned, liberated from any set of instructions. Whether this is good or bad, naturally depends on the content. Only people who either lack values or who have neglected to reflect on the matter, would seriously hold that innovation is per se good. The gas chambers were an innovation.

谁都想做年轻人

专横的时间引起年轻人的崇拜。与第一个问题关联的第二个问题，是年轻崇拜的极度泛滥。在一些非现代的传统社会中，成年人尤其是中老年人享有很高的社会地位。成年男女结合后产生小孩，既定的职业能够获得劳动成果和安全的自我意识，每个人在社会中获得受信任的地位并顺从他人的命令。欧洲人与非欧洲人的主要差别之一，是非欧洲人退休得早一些，往往 50 岁就回家养老了。这不能归结为非欧洲人的懒惰。第二次世界大战以后，几十年发展的现代性，促使尽可能"保持年轻"成了一种既定的美德。在二战以前的斯堪的纳维亚北部，15 岁的少年人通常可收到象征成年的礼物—— 一个银质香烟盒和一套假牙（一般用鲸鱼的牙齿做成），表明他们的年龄已经足够大了，可以去海边寻找独立的工作，至少在劳动阶级看来，他们已经能够照料自己。他们十多岁就结婚生子，几乎等不及长大成人，就要照料自己的生活。

The Cult Of Youth Is Caused By The Tyranny Of The Moment

The second problem, connected to the first, is the extremely widespread cultivation of youthfulness. In nearly all non-modern societies, adulthood, maturity and even old age are associated with high rank. It is as a grown man or woman with one's own children, an established career in productive work and a secure sense of self that one achieves trusted positions in society and commands the deference of others. A main, understudied difference between Europeans and non-European immigrants is the tendency of the latter to retire at an earlier age, often barely into their fifties. This should not be taken to indicate laziness. In that phase of modernity that developed in the decades after the Second World War, it has become an established virtue to "stay young" as long as possible. Before the Second World War, it was still common in northern Scandinavia for 15-year-olds to receive, as confirmation gifts, a silver cigarette case and a set of false teeth (often made of whale ivory), as symbols of adulthood. They were now old enough to go to sea or find other independent employment, and were generally considered independent persons, at least in the working class. People were barely out of their teens before they married and had children. They could hardly wait to grow up and be in charge of their own lives.

从那以后,生命阶段的边界逐渐变得模糊。青少年时期,作为儿童与成年人之间的中间阶段,已经向两头扩展。上学之后的小孩子,几乎形成了强烈性别取向的流行音乐的一个核心市场,也形成了直到最近仍是青少年专享的衣着风格,而40岁的男人和妇女则被告知,如果能够保持年轻或酷一点,各方面都会好些,因此他们会借助整容手术、植发或吸脂等手段,这些往往不会阻止他们适应周围的环境。因此,他们会持续地感觉到个人身份的不确定与多变性,成为各类生活时尚产品市场的受害者。正如最近有人评论的那样,拉什在《自恋的文化》中,对当代文化的毁灭性批判,在书刚出版时还感觉甚好,现在则成了真实的需要。

Since then, the boundaries between life stages have become increasingly fuzzy. The category of "youth", that intermediate stage between childhood and adulthood, has expanded in both directions. Children who have barely begun school form a core market for strongly sexualised pop music and a style of dress that until recently was the exclusive domain of teenagers, while men and women in their forties are being told from almost every direction that it would be great if they could stay young and cool just a little longer, perhaps helping nature a little bit with a facelift, a hair transplant or some liposuction, and generally make certain not to stop adapting to their surroundings. As a consequence, they continue feeling uncertain and unstable in their personal identity a little longer, and become the grateful victims of all kinds of marketing of lifestyle products. As someone remarked in a conversation recently, Christopher Lasch's devastating critique of contemporary culture, The Culture of Narcissism, was fine when it was published, but it is only now that it is truly needed.

专横的时间具有两个最显著的特征：年轻崇拜和知识传递的危机。这样的文化不重视成年人和长者，也不关心文化的来源，因而显得很没有头绪。

Two of the most serious symptoms of the tyranny of the moment are these: the cult of youth and the crisis in knowledge transmission. A culture that does not value maturity and ageing also does not care where it comes from, and can therefore be quite clueless as to where it is heading.

在每一个社会中，成年人的生活都与责任、可预测性和稳定的承诺有关。一个成年人知道自己是谁，哪一种价值最重要，以及——大部分情况下——必须为孩子与配偶还包括自己的父母亲与姻亲承担明确的责任。相反，当一个人年轻时，总是不固定、迟疑不决并且爱开玩笑，对生活持试验的观点，这意味着他们有机会获取根本的开放性。然而，他们还未使自己承担一个特定的方向。将我们这个时代的陈词滥调翻译过来，就是年轻人具有灵活性，随时准备迎接挑战。有谁愿意忙于这种个体的生活，而不愿意做一个可预测未来的人，去把握自己的优先权呢？

In every society, adult life is associated with responsibility, pre-dictability and stable commitments. An adult knows who he or she is, which values are the most important, and in most cases has clear responsibilities for children and spouse, often in-laws and own parents in addition. When one is young, on the contrary, one is unfixed, uncertain, playful and has an experimental view of life, implying a fundamental openness to the opportunities that might present themselves. One has not yet committed oneself to a particular direction. Translated into the cliché s of our time, this means that the young （or youthful）person is flexible and ready for new challenges. Who would not rather employ this kind of individual than a predictable person who is certain of his priorities?

在新经济中，这可能是对的——至少短期内是这样。我们把青年与价值观联系在一起是成功的秘诀。但是，在另外一些领域——家庭、艺术和个人发展，这却是灾难。在各种文化中，青少年都被视为社会的挑战。恰恰因为我们讨论的这些人夹在两者之间，他们个人往往不太确定自己的身份、责任与权利，同时，他们对社会价值的连续性构成了一种威胁。现在年轻主管的喜好表明，他们对飞逝瞬间的热爱已经超过了对历史的尊重。青年人狂乱的变迁模式已经成了社会的主流。

In the new economy it may be correct at least in the short run that the values we associate with youthfulness are a recipe for success. But in other spheres family, the arts, personal development it is a disaster. In nearly all cultures, adolescence is perceived as a societal challenge. Precisely because the persons in question are "betwixt and between", they are personally uncertain of their identity, their duties and entitlements; and at the same time they represent a threat to the continuity of society's values. The contemporary taste for young executives indicates that love of the flecting moment is currently greater than respect for the long lines of history. The transitional, turbulent mode of youth has become the mainstay of society.

由于各个年龄阶段都被还原为同样的理想，年轻崇拜使分类范畴变得一团糟。当 8 岁的女儿与 42 岁的父亲都认为自己年轻时，就很难建立一种明确的亲子关系了。在我生长的 20 世纪 60 年代末和 70 年代初，母亲还挎着手提袋，并且穿着保守的衣服。十几年前，父亲还穿着经典的风衣，戴着帽子并系了一条领带。周末他们穿牛仔裤也不会出洋相了。年轻崇拜的主要原因，在于文化的加速变迁，这意味着拥有很多自发的能量比个人的积累历史更有意义，而且这很适合新经济，却对家庭产生不利的影响。因此受谴责的对象往往是广告和娱乐业。应当承认，那些年轻貌美的人，拥有高露洁的微笑，在身体恰当的地方填充硅胶，还拥有自信的肢体语言；这些人占领了核心的文化领域，比如流行音乐、广告业、北美电影和电视天气预报。尽管这不彻底，但我还是很容易就能设想出父女之间的对话，最终是以女儿的最后通牒收尾："好了老爸，我会和你去参加菲尔·柯林斯的音乐会，但前提条件是我要在嘴唇上垫一块硅胶。"然而作为一般原则，这个争端是无法避免的。如果说有何区别的话，最近十年以来，流行文化的偶像已经更加年轻（更瘦更敏捷）。但是，如果责备这种表面的现象，就相当于混淆食物的优劣。通俗文化有好坏之分，有些符合传统，也有些具有创新性，但总能体现潜在的模式。在前面的章节里，我已经分析了技术变革产生的副作用，从其他方面来看，这些副作用还会刺激年轻崇拜的观念。顺便说一句，维利里奥在《信息炸弹》里的分析，与这种观点非常相似，轻微的差别在于他把当代文化视为婴儿，而不是青少年。对他而言，"男孩"盖茨利用他那无忧无虑的幻想获得了高级的玩具，这是全球文化精髓的体现，全球文化不加批判地接受了美国文化中的不成熟的方面。

The youth cult makes a mess of categories since every age is reduced to the same ideals. When both the 8-year-old daughter and the 42-year-old father regard themselves as "young people", it is not easy to establish an unambiguous parental relationship. When I grew up in the late 1960s and early 1970s, mothers still carried handbags and wore conservative coats. A short decade earlier, fathers still wore trenchcoats, hats and ties. They would not be caught dead in jeans on a weekday. The main cause of the youth cult is the acceleration in cultural change, which implies that it makes more sense to have a lot of spontaneous energy than a lot of accumulated history in one's portfolio, it fits the new economy perfectly, it affects family life adversely, and the blame is usually put on advertising and the entertainment industry. Admittedly, it is striking how young and beautiful people with Colgate smiles, silicone in the right places and a self-confident body language dominate central cultural arenas such as pop music, advertisements, North American films and televised weather forecasts. (Not entirely though: I can easily envision the conversation between the weary father and the pre-pubescent daughter, ending with the daughter's ultimatum: "All right dad, I will go to that Phil Collins concert with you, but on one condition: I want silicone in my lips first.") As a general description, however, this diagnosis is inevitable. If anything, the icons of popular culture have become younger (and thinner, therefore faster) during the most recent decades. But to blame such surface phenomena is tantamount to confounding the menu with the food. Popular culture can be good or bad, conventional or innovative; but it is always a reflex of underlying patterns. In earlier chapters I have shown how technological change has side-effects that, among other things, stimulate the cult of youth. Incidentally, Paul Virilio, whose analysis in The Information Bomb closely parallels this line of argument, differs slightly in that he sees contemporary culture not primarily as pubescent, but as infantile. To him, the "man-child" Bill Gates with his unworried fascination for advanced toys, is the quintessential embodiment of a global culture which uncritically takes on the childish aspects of American culture.

在此背景下，一个重要的领域与消费有关。社会经济的经典定义将其分成三个体系：生产、分配和消费。最近，西方经济的焦点从生产转移到消费，在伦敦的达克兰（还有很多其他的城市，也有相对应的措施）从工业到商店与公寓的翻修中，这种转移被合适地阐述——实际上进行了总体的再定义。很明显，20世纪后半叶,消费者的角色变得越来越重要。对消费者自由时间和金钱的争夺,在每一个飞逝的瞬间得到了强化。

An essential arena in this context is that of consumption. A classic definition of a society's economy divides it into three institutions: production, distribution and consumption. The recent move from production to consumption as the focal point of Western economies is aptly illustrated in the refurbishing actually total redefinition of areas such as the Docklands in London (and many cities have their equivalents) from industry to shops and flats. It is evident that the role of the consumer has grown in importance during the latter half of the twentieth century, and that the war over the free seconds and pence in the lives of consumers is being intensified every fleeting moment.

消费的堆叠

消费堆叠之后,连贯性就消失了。在 20 世纪后半叶,所有的工业国家都已经提高了物质生活水平,这很容易证明;至于生活质量是否有相应的增长,却是一个还要讨论的问题。我们使用的商品与父母一辈用过的物品大致相似(也有一些例外,比如垃圾邮件、水煮白菜和法兰绒裤子),此外,我们消费的物品越来越多。这个趋势还在继续。现在二十几岁的年轻人非常熟悉电话技术,比他们略大的男人或女人,可能从未接触过这样的东西(手机短信)。在富裕国家,购物已经成了中产阶级日常的活动之一 ——实际上这是一种消遣形式。(许多人——大部分是妇女——非常需要标准的时间,以便在购物中心漫无目的地闲逛,不过这似乎不是不可能的事。)

Consumption Is Stacked, And Coherence Disappears

It is easy to prove that the material standard of living improved in all industrial countries during the last half-century; whether there has been a similar growth in the quality of life, is more open to discussion. Still, we use commodities of roughly the same kind as the parental generation （with some exceptions, such as spam, boiled cabbage and flannel trousers）, and in addition, we consume more, and more, and even more. The tendency continues. People in their twenties are deeply conversant with a telephone technology that slightly older men and women will never become acquainted with （the SMS message）. Shopping has become an everyday activity for the middle classes everywhere in the rich countries virtually a form of recreation. （And it seems far from unlikely that many people, most of them women, acquire some sorely needed hours of slow time by strolling aimlessly around in large shopping centres.）

20 世纪 90 年代以来，世界经济的增长似乎已经达到了前所未有的程度，其先决条件是消费的增长。发现新市场或者使现有消费者增加消费量，都可以达到这种结果。这两种方式都有人使用。在欧洲国家的公路交汇点附近，用不了多久，新的购物中心就会如雨后春笋般涌现，可以预计这将导致商业大街上的商店大规模倒闭。迄今为止，这种事还没有出现。似乎每个人都还有空间，另外新出现的电子购物也才刚刚开始。

Economic growth, which the world has seen to an almost unprecedented degree since the early 1990s, presupposes a growth in consumption. It can either be achieved through finding new markets or by making the already existing consumers intensify their consumption. Both options are being exploited. For a while it was predicted that the new shopping centres that mushroomed near highway junctions in various European countries would lead to mass bankruptcy among high street shops. So far, this has generally not come about. There seems to be room for everyone, in addition to the new e-shops, which are still only just beginning.

为了让人消费得更多,他们要么更频繁地更替现有的产品,要么使顾客可挑选的商品更加多样化。这个领域与其他地方一样,两种情况都有发生。服装与生产资料的使用寿命都在缩短,此外,一个家庭在 2001 年容纳的物品远比 20 年前要多得多。每个地方的选择都在增加,不仅仅在信息领域。不久以前,出现了各种各样的绿色番茄酱。生产商还在寻思制造蓝色的番茄酱,但调查试验结果显示儿童不喜欢这种颜色。几乎在每一个地方,都可以看到这种多样化:早餐麦片、庭院家具、衬衫、灯泡、塔可酱、薯条、牛奶、洗涤剂和度假目的地,当然也有例外,比如微软和可口可乐这样成功垄断市场的公司, 他们的产品可选择的范围可能在减小,甚至比马克思所猜想的还要少。

For people to be able to consume more, they must either replace their existing items more frequently or diversify their selection of commodities. In this field, as in other areas, it is correct to state that both things are happening. Both clothes and capital goods have decreasing lifespans, and besides, a home in 2001 contains many more objects than a similar home would have in 1981. The selection grows everywhere, not just within the field of information. A while ago, a green variety of ketchup was introduced. The producer was also contemplating a blue variety, but the children in the test panel disliked it. This kind of diversification can be observed nearly everywhere: breakfast cereals, garden furniture, shirts, light bulbs, taco sauces, potato crisps, milk, detergents, holiday destinations... the exceptions, such as when the selection range is reduced because mighty companies like Microsoft and Coca-Cola successfully achieve near-monopolies with their products, are fewer than Marx might have guessed.

20 世纪 60 年代末,瑞典经济学家林德对此现象做过研究,然后出版了一本名为《匆忙的有闲阶级》的著作。林德对消费文化持保守的批评态度,认为资本主义发展的内在需求,是每一个居民都要更有效率地生产,还要更密集地消费。这两者都要维持“一个健康的增长率”。就我所知,这个观点很简单,也无可厚非。其后不久，社会学家贝尔在回忆录中阐述了著名的格言，他在《资本主义的文化反驳》中，把清教徒的工作伦理与快乐消费的道德规范结合在一起，以反驳资本主义。然而，林德最初的推断与现在讨论的问题有关。高消费水平对刺激生产很有必要，而且增加生产量对于达到经济增长的总体目标也是必要的。因此，他说需要在越来越短的时间内，消费得越来越多。休闲时间日益被匆忙的疯狂消费挤占。

The Swedish economist Staffan Linder made a study of this phenomenon in the late 1960s, entitled The Harried Leisure Class. Linder, a conservative critic of consumer culture, held that the inbuilt demands for growth in capitalism made it necessary for each inhabitant to produce more efficiently and to consume more intensively. Both were necessary to maintain a "healthy growth rate". The idea is simple and, as far as I know, uncontroversial. It is actually reminiscent of the sociologist Daniel Bell's famous dictum in a slightly later book, The Cultural Contradictions of Capitalism, according to which capitalism contradicts itself through a combination of a puritan work ethic and a hedonistic ethic of consumption. Linder nevertheless makes some original inferences which are relevant for the issues at hand. A high level of consumption is necessary to stimulate production, and increased production is necessary to reach the overarching goal of economic growth. As a result it becomes necessary, he says, to consume more and more in less and less time. Leisure time is increasingly turned into a mad rush for intensified consumption.

显然，对于 20 世纪 60 年代美国的趋势，林德有着特别的观点，他在写作时已经有先见之明。在偏僻和人口稀疏的挪威，只有到了 20 世纪 80 年代，市郊大型购物中心才有沥青路环绕。周末上午人们将车停在超市前面，然后花上几个小时集中有效地消费；在以前这样消费要耗去更多的时间，因为商店分散，而且每个人的消费要求不一样。十几年后，电子商务将进一步增加消费的效率。

It is clear that Linder, who wrote with a particular view to tendencies in the USA of the 1960s, was far-sighted in this respect. In remote, underpopulated Norway, the large suburban shopping malls surrounded by enormous tarmac deserts arrived only in the 1980s. Here, one may park the car on a Saturday morning and spend a few hours consuming efficiently and intensively; much more so than in the old days, when shops were scattered and slow, dependent as they were on paying personal, individual attention to customers' needs. A couple of decades later, e-commerce contributes further to increasing efficiency of consumption.

本章开头我讲到的休闲时间，也会有类似的处境。激光唱片、书籍和服装的销售总量，都在加速地增长。挪威一家大型读书俱乐部，主要依靠消极优先购买权的观念赢利，并将其与月份的选择连接在一起，最近它推介第 18 个月的消费（但没有通知会员；大部分人可能从未注意此事）。人们通过健身室的辅助课程保持健康，而不是在自然环境中长时间地散步；人们习惯把现成的饭菜放到微波炉里加热，以便一边看电视一边吃，这在许多富裕国家已经非常普遍。顺便说一句，目前在挪威最流行的一道菜，是冰冻的比萨。前面章节中详细描述的堆垛原则，说明每一项活动可用的时间变少了。对我们大多数人来说，最明显的替代选择是减少每项活动花费的时间，也可以同时做好几件事。我有好几次都是一边打电话，一边在电脑上点击鼠标，甚至电话线的那一端都可以听到点击鼠标的声音。不管人们选择哪一种方式，留给缓慢和连续的时间都越来越少。而且，边际效应的价值继续在下降。1995 年，一个信息片段可以吸引人们 15 秒钟的注意力，现在可能已经不超过 5 秒钟了。生产商追逐市场的需要，不断对信息进行删减和压缩。

Leisure time begins to resemble the work situation I described at the outset of this chapter. The turnover in CDs, books and clothes takes place at an accelerating pace. A major Norwegian book club, basing its profits on the negative option concept linked with a selection of the month, recently introduced its eighteenth book of the month in one year （without informing the members, most of whom probably never noticed）. People stay fit through intensive programmes in health studios instead of travelling to more natural surroundings, and ready-made dishes to be heated in the microwave oven, making it possible to eat while watching television, have become common in most rich countries. In Norway, incidentally, the most popular dinner by far is the frozen pizza. The principle of stacking, described at length in the previous chapter, implies that there is less time available for each activity. The most obvious alternative for most of us would then consist in reducing the time used for each activity, and/or doing several things simultaneously. (I have several times been caught red-handed clicking with my computer mouse while talking on the phone, by perceptive conversation partners who recognized the sound.) No matter which alternative one chooses, there is less slow, continuous time left. And the marginal value continues to decrease. An information snippet worth 15 seconds of someone's attention in 1995, may not be valued at more than 5 seconds today. The producers chase the "market" and cut, abbreviate, compress and tailor.

时间可以点点滴滴地节省出来。即使是一个高效率的消费者,在晚上看电视时,趁着换频道的空隙,也能迅速地浏览报纸、发送手机短信、喝啤酒、嚼薯条或抽一支低焦油的香烟,其效率无疑也变得越来越高了。但是,这还没有达到边界。在一天中,可能还很容易消费其他更多的东西,(对经济生产的)挑战存在于发现这些消费方式的过程中。对市民(不仅仅是消费者)而言,最终的目标可能恰好相反。

Time can always be economised a little bit more. Even a highly efficient consumer, who spends the evening zapping in front of the box while at the same time leafing through the paper, sending SMS messages, drinking beer, crunching crisps and smoking a low-tar cigarette, can no doubt become even more efficient. The boundary has not yet been reached. It is still easily possible to consume more during the day; the challenge (to the production side of the economy) consists in finding ways to make it happen. To citizens (who are not merely consumers), the goal may ultimately be the direct opposite.

问题不在于每一项活动的孤立变化。毫无疑问，新型种类的选择发展迅速，这与前一章描述的堆垛原则一致：回到黯淡遥远的 20 世纪 70 年代，我的家乡只出产奶酪、洋葱和红椒这三种东西。现在，可选择的类别数量已经翻了好几番，传统的东西被当作"经典"进行销售。尽管在鲜活品市场，多样化给人留下深刻的印象，目前细分化并适应消费人群的鲜活产品，可能与过去奶酪、洋葱和薯条的食用方式一样多，但是，这种行为却处在完全不同的语义世界中，充满了相互矛盾的标志。举个不同的例子，从 1993 年到 2001 年，我担任一家文化刊物的编辑，在我接管这项工作之前，这份名为《当今时代》的刊物至少已经存在了 103 年。虽然多年来刊物不断变化主题，但依然在本质上保留了 1890 年格哈德教授兼评论员创刊时的风格。这个刊物与其他文化类期刊一样，亦如它的标题，包含了大量的访谈、评论文章、辩论、新闻剖析和通俗科学等，探究的主题包括生物学、文化、民族主义、多民族社会、文学、人权、新技术及其副作用、生态学和伦理学。在 20 世纪 70 年代，斯堪的纳维亚的学术期刊数量适中，很容易调查公共空间，因此善于阅读的人只要跟踪两三份一般性质的期刊，就可以正确地检验自己是否能与当前的问题同步（挪威的报纸比较糟糕，由此突出了学术期刊的重要性）。目前，只要稍微瞄一眼琳琅满目的报刊杂志货架——甚至没有必要去互联网浏览——就可以理解当今形势已经完全不一样。与以前相比，《当今时代》的发行量没有发生大的变化，但是它所处的信息生态环境已经发生了天翻地覆的变化。一些期刊认为它们不再能在共享的公共空间内设定议程表，而不得不与其他期刊一起分享读者的注意力。所有的期刊都在振臂高呼。每一种出版物，不管是报纸还是期刊书籍，都日渐成为无休无止的信息乐高积木园里色彩斑斓的砖块、碎片和马赛克的颗粒。这一切显得非常不可思议，展示了当今时代民主与多元的维度。当然，还有很多其他的东西……

The point is not that each activity changes that much, seen in isolation. There can be no doubt that the selection of crisp varieties has grown enormously, in accordance with the logic of stacking described in an earlier chapter: back in the dim and remote

1970s, there were in my country three varieties generally available: original, cheese and onion, and paprika. Today, the selection has grown many times over, and the traditional types are thus marketed as "classic". In spite of this impressive diversification in the crisp market, today's niche-oriented and consumer-adapted crisps are presumably eaten pretty much in the same way as that bag of cheese and onion crisps one was munching in the old days without doing anything else (except, perhaps, attempting to look one's spotty teenage girlfriend deep in the eyes between munches), but the act is surrounded by an entirely different semantic universe, crowded by competing signs.Put differently: from 1993 to 2001, I was editor of a cultural journal that had existed for no less than 103 years when I took it over, called Samtiden (Norwegian for "Contemporary times"). In spite of many facelifts and thematic shifts over the years, it remains today essentially the same journal as the one started by the professor and essayist Gerhard Gran in 1890. Like other cultural journals worthy of the label, it contains a varied menu of interviews, review essays, articles, polemics, analytical journalism, popular science and so on, delving into topics such as biology and culture, nationalism and multi-ethnic society, literature and human rights, new technology and its side-effects, ecology and moral philosophy. As late as the 1970s, the number of journals was so modest in Scandinavia, and the public sphere so easily surveyable, that a reading person could rightly feel that he or she kept apace with current issues and concerns by following two or three general-purpose journals (newspapers are generally dreadful in Norway, hence the importance of the cultural journals). Today, it is sufficient just to a glance at the journal racks of a well-stocked newsagent one does not even have to venture into the Internet to understand that the contemporary situation is completely different. The circulation of Samtiden is neither much higher nor much lower than it was in the past, but it is part of a very different informational ecology than before. A single journal can no longer suppose that it sets the agenda in a shared public sphere, but has to reconcile itself with sharing the stage, and the attention of the readers, with many others, all of which are shouting at the top of their voices. Each particular publication, be it a newspaper, a journal or a book, becomes neither less nor more than a fragment, a little speck in the grand mosaic, a colourful building block in an endless Legoland of information. This is all in all marvellous, it showcases the democratic and pluralistic dimensions of the present age. And yet...

工作、消费、家庭生活和公共空间的破碎，把我们带进了一个现有"身份包装"之外的世界。在脱节的碎片以外，每个人都要创造自己的完整的连贯性。与此相关的问题是，能否完成这一任务，或者生活是否必然要更像拼图，填满各种事件、印象、任意性、自发性以及短期的选择，而不是明确的方向，也即生活是否要变成霸权的快速模式，而非快慢模式的混合。许多人认为这恰恰在很多地方发生，从工作到伦理均是如此，这种一般的暗示性的转变被描述为从现代性到后现代性。著名社会学家齐格蒙·鲍曼的最新力作名为《生活在碎片中》，当然远不止他一个人会用这个标题出版书籍。有人已经证明了信息社会意味着一整套不可预料的后果，其中最重要的是将碎片暂时汇总在一起，时间被分割为日益变小的单元，接着便会失去互相之间的连贯性。这种效应的症状可以是任何事物，从基要主义（对世界无限复杂性的自动排除）到极端机会主义或职业生涯的精疲力尽。缺乏想象的政治是另一种症状，或许这是对所有人最少的鼓励。

The fragmentation of work, consumption, family life and the public sphere brings us to a world beyond ready-made "identity packages". Each must create their own coherent totality out of the disjointed fragments. A far from irrelevant question is whether such a task is at all manageable, or whether life is inevitably becoming more collage-like and filled with singular events and impressions, arbitrariness and spontaneity, short-term choices rather than some over-arching direction that is, of a hegemonic fast mode rather than a mix between fast and slow modes. Many hold the view that this is exactly what happens in a lot of areas, from work to ethics,and commonly, the suggested shift is described as a transition from modernity to post modernity. The influential sociologist Zygmunt Bauman named one of his recent books Life in Fragments, and he is far from alone in publishing books with this kind of title. Information society has already been proven to imply a whole range of unintended consequences, and one of the most important may tentatively be summed up as fragmentation, the dividing of time into ever decreasing units, and the ensuing loss of internal coherence. Symptoms of this effect could be anything from fundamentalism （voluntary exclusion of the world's infinite complexity） to extreme opportunism or burn-outs in professional life. Politics devoid of vision is another symptom, perhaps the most discouraging of all.

效率的罗生门

信息革命真的可以提高效率吗？在考虑该做些什么才能缓和加速发展与堆垛的副作用之前，我还要提请读者注意信息革命可能带来的最后一种副作用。对于那些期待崇高目标的人来说，在学术研究、教育和商业领域内的技术变迁，可以带来效率的增加。但是我们能确定信息管理大规模流线化与计算机一定会增加效率吗？答案可能有三种：其一，答案是肯定的，因为效率增加会促使经济的发展；其二，答案是肯定的，但是令人不安，因为极度追求效率可能会使我们忘记真正的价值；其三，答案实际上是否定的，因为存在自相矛盾的地方，技术发展的趋势与效率的增加恰恰背道而驰。

Does The Information Revolution Actually Increase Efficiency?

Before moving to a consideration of what can be done to mitigate the adverse effects of acceleration and stacking, I shall call attention to a final possible side-effect of the information revolution. For want of other, loftier aims, technologically driven changes within research, education and business enterprises are defended with reference to increased efficiency. But can we be certain that the streamlining of information management and the massive implementation of computerised routines do lead to increased efficiency? There are three possible answers:

（1）Yes, and it is great, because increased efficiency leads to economic growth.

（2）Yes, but it is worrying, since the extreme fetishisation of efficiency makes us forget real values.

（3）Actually no, paradoxically there is a tendency for technology that should presumably increase efficiency to work in an exact opposite way.

第三种观点最有趣，也是我想讨论的问题，尽管前两种观点的关系还有很多可以讲的地方。那么是否可以认为这是信息革命最根本的副作用呢？甚至可以认为信息革命无法提高效率呢？本书已经讨论了信息变革带来的始料未及的后果，这些后果往往不容易看出来。例如，我们需要很多的想象，才能理解一种称为"伟哥"的壮阳药，可以增加全世界的妓女需求量。另一个更不明显的事例是传真，欧洲人在传真发明很久之后才开始普遍使用，原始的传真方式实际上与电报机存在的时间一样长。只是到了20世纪80年代英国邮政工人罢工时，才开始使用传真技术。

Option （3） is the most interesting one and the one I shall explore, although naturally a lot could also be said about the relationship between （1） and （2） as well. Suppose this was the most fundamental side-effect of the information revolution? That it does not even increase efficiency? Several unintended consequences of technological change have already been discussed in this book, and they are frequently easy to see. It does not, for example, require a lot of imagination to understand that the introduction of that male potency technology called Viagra would lead to increased demand for prostitutes all over the world. A little less obvious is the fact that the telefax came into common use in Europe a long time after its invention; primitive faxes had actually existed almost as long as the telegraph. It happened during a major postal strike in Britain during the mid-1980s.

空间污染

维利里奥在谈到"灰色生态"时,认为空间污染是另一种更微妙的副作用。当欧洲到美国的主要交通方式从轮船变为喷气式飞机时,他指出大西洋将不复存在。若要发现这种副作用,我们需要一种历史的思维框架:人们需要知道或记得过去是什么样子。对于那些面临专横的时间的人来说,这是他们需要面对的最令人气馁的任务。

Pollution of Space

A more subtle kind of side-effect is the one Paul Virilio calls attention to when he speaks of "grey ecology", that is the pollution of space. When the jet plane replaced the passenger ship as the means of transportation from Europe to the USA, he points out, the Atlantic Ocean ceased to exist. In order to discover side-effects of this kind, a historical frame of mind is required: one must remember or learn what it used to be like. This is one of the most daunting tasks faced by people subjected to the tyranny of the moment. It is primarily in this sense that the loss of a sense of history is dangerous.

信息技术伴随着许多副作用。所谓时间管理者都是用这种方式建构,大部分用户需要很多时间发现合理利用时间的方式。众所周知,其提供的课程主要是教人如何区分不同的水准和入门系统。有了先进的计算机程序,这种情形就是可比较的,通常也会更糟糕。这些电脑程序刺激用户深入钻研程序本身的秘密,而不是在工作中简单地使用这些程序,用户还要花费大量的金钱去学习程序的运行。(当用户们最终熟悉了软件的用法时,新的软件已经代替了原来的软件。)移动电话和电子邮件也有古怪的副作用。这两项技术使用户比以前更灵活机动,而且无论何时何地都可以发送和接收信息。换句话说,这些技术似乎使时间得到了解放,让用户更加灵活主动,可以更自如地控制自己的时间预算。然而,正如前面章节里直接论述的那样,结果往往适得其反。电子邮件与移动电话创造了一种灵活性,使得人们期待随时都能联系到别人。在一定意义上讲,"不在上班"的说法就永远无法成立了。假如我上了一天班,返回家里后打开电脑,收到雪片般的电子邮件。其中一些邮件结尾是令人头疼的语句"下午1点半给我电话"。此外,过去乘坐地铁或开车去上班途中的空隙,也会突然之间消失得无影无踪。人们即使在公共汽车站候车,也一样可以工作。这种污染方式与马尾藻海被污染的方式一样。

Many side-effects are associated with information technology. Socalled time-managers (including Filofaxes) are constructed in such a way that most users will need a lot of time to find out how to utilise them rationally. As is well known, courses are offered to teach people how to distinguish between their different levels and entry systems. With advanced computer programs, the situation is comparable and often worse. They stimulate the user to dive deeply into the mysteries of the programs themselves, instead of simply using them to do their job, and are sent on costly courses just to learn their functioning. (And when the user is finally conversant with the software, it is replaced by the next generation of applications.) Mobile telephony and email also have curious side-effects. Both of these technologies render the user more mobile and flexible than before; one can send and reply to messages anytime, anywhere. These technologies seem, in other words, to liberate time, making the users flexible and in greater command of their own time budgets. However, as indicated indirectly in the previous chapters, the outcome has been the exact opposite. E-mail and mobile telephony creates a kind of flexibility entailing that one is expected to be accessible at any time. One is, in a sense, never properly out of the office. Suppose I have been physically out of the office for a day; I return, turn on the computer, and receive an avalanche of e-mails. Several of them end on the ominous note: "Call me before 1:30 this afternoon." Furthermore, those valuable gaps that occur as one drivesor takes the tube to work, are suddenly gone. One is reachable, and is able to work, while standing at a bus stop. These spaces are being polluted in the same way as the Sargasso Sea.

当电子邮件与电话很少时，这些技术无疑可以释放出时间。如果收到的信息数量超过一定的临界值，同样技术的功能就会突然间走向反面。最初，它们只是监禁用户、填充空隙、消除一切空当以及那些对创造性和无方向思考异常重要的缓慢时期。热情支持私家车发展的人，崇拜汽车使人变快的能力，认为汽车在任何时候都不受阻碍。但是，现在的汽车数量已经高得无法想象，以至于汽车降到了自行车的速度（同时儿童与青少年因为汽车尾气污染，很容易患上呼吸道疾病）。即使是最热情的汽车迷，恐怕也得考虑将汽车换成自行车，或乘坐电车上下班了。可以说，新的信息技术与此没有什么差别。

When there is only a little email and few calls, such technologies are doubtless liberating. When the number of incoming messages exceeds a certain threshold, the functioning of the very same technologies suddenly flips into its opposite. They begin to imprison the users, fill the gaps and kill those empty, slow periods that are so important for creativity and directionless thinking. Enthusiastic supporters of the private car worship it for making it possible to move fast and without delay at any time. But when the number of cars becomes so great that the average speed drops down to that of a bicycle （while children and adults alike collapse due to respiratory diseases）, even the most enthusiastic driver might seriously consider converting to tram or bicycle. It should be no different in the case of the new information technologies.

人们很少能料想到利用省时技术之后，时间会变得更快更稀缺。然而，事实却又的确如此。这种洞察力萌生的答案可以解决第五章提出的问题，也就是指数增长曲线用何种方式变平。

Hardly anyone had expected time to move faster and become more scarce as a result of introducing time-saving technology. This is nevertheless just what has happened. In this insight lies, perhaps, the germ of an answer to the question raised at the end of Chapter 5, namely how it can be that exponential growth curves sooner or later flatten out.

即使在技术加速发展的一般框架内，任何事物也会变得越来越快。航空旅行是一个明显的案例：当前欧洲各个主要城市之间的航班，有一半以上要延误。伦敦与米兰之间的空中航线堵塞得最厉害。最著名的事例还是空中交通的堂兄妹——路上交通。从 1970 年到 2000 年，美国家用轿车的数量已经增加了两倍——但是投在公路、立交桥、高速公路和建设上的费用只有数十亿美元，因此交通速度只能逐年下降。在曼哈顿区，平均车速只有每小时 11 公里。在其他主要的大城市，情况还要更糟糕。例如泰国曼谷，每天上下班高峰时刻，人们需要花去大量的时间，甚至要在汽车上安装厕所才能解决内急之需。1994 年，洛杉矶因为交通堵塞损失的时间，估计达到了 230 万人时。公路虽然越来越宽，但以很神秘的方式继续堵塞。每天都有几小时，公路就像一个巨大的停车场，而不像表面上有效率的交通大动脉。在华盛顿特区，每个司机一年因为堵车损失的时间达 71 个小时。

It is far from everything that moves faster and faster, even within the general framework of the technologies of acceleration. Air travel is an obvious example: about half of the flights connecting major European cities are currently delayed. The sky over the London Milan axis is heavily congested. The most famous example is still the close cousin of air traffic, namely road traffic. It grows quickly between 1970 and 2000 it trebled in the home of the car, that is the USA but although billions are spent on highways, flyovers and turnpikes, speed decreases year by year. The average speed for a moving car in Manhattan is now 11 kilometres per hour. There are other major cities which are even worse off. Take Bangkok, for example, where some have installed lavatories in their cars as a consequence of spending a large part of their day in rush hour queues. It is estimated that 2.3 million person hours were lost in traffic delays in Los Angeles in 1994. The highways become wider, but in mysterious ways they continue to be filled up. For several hours every day they look more like giant car parks than superefficient transport arteries. The average driver in Washington, DC loses 71 hours a year in traffic jams.

人们在等待电话接听时耗去的平均时间，恐怕也是相当高的数字，尽管我没有找到这个领域的统计数字，但考虑到语音电话的巨幅增量，这方面的增长可能会相当惊人。通过"请等待"的电话提示音，了解每年有多少人力损失在等待电话接听中，可能是一件很有趣的事。或者，因为等待电话接通而浪费的时间，耽搁了多少个傍晚的闲庭信步、与孩子一起玩耍足球、阅读小说或夕阳下漫步的时间。

The average number of minutes used waiting to get through on the telephone is probably also pretty high, and, although I have not found statistics in the field, it is likely to have grown considerably, given the enormous growth of speech telephony. It would be interesting to know how many man-labour years were lost annually through the "please hold" syndrome. Or how many lazy afternoons on the terrace, football games with the kids, novel readings or walks in the sun, for that matter.

另一个相关的案例是奥斯陆与小卫星城镇（卫星城镇是在大城市郊区或其以外附近地区，为分散中心城市的人口和工业而新建或扩建的具有相对独立性的城镇。因其围绕中心城市像卫星一样，故得名。卫星城镇概念产生于英国，美国的泰勒正式提出并使用"卫星城镇"这一形象性的概念。——编者）利勒斯特罗姆之间的铁路隧道。1999 年这条铁路正式通车，接着而来的是其令人无法相信的高额预算和其他丑闻，这段隧道将两个城镇之间的旅行时间减少了 14 分钟。新机场铁路的延伸端，是从奥斯陆到城北 55 公里之外的加勒穆恩。之前，这一段路是从奥斯陆经特隆赫姆到加勒穆恩的铁路——但改造延伸段的成本花了 100 亿挪威币（约合 8 亿英镑），其中 90%的资金是净亏损。如果对包括旅行在内的所有时间，都用金钱来衡量，也许可以计算出这个投资是有价值的，并且最终可以得到回报。然而，我依然有我自己的疑虑，不仅仅是因为加勒穆恩铁路的预算赤字已经相当于未来 31 年内票额的预期总收入。而是显然这节省下来的 14 分钟，立马就被各种等待——在机场排队等待安检或等候延迟的航班，等待地铁或电车，或者在交通高峰期等待出租车等——蚕食掉了。在利勒斯特罗姆与奥斯陆之间节省下来的时间，很快被周围其他活动缓慢而更不可控的时间消耗殆尽。

A related example is this: a new railway tunnel connects Oslo with the small satellite town Lillestrøm. When it was finally opened in August 1999, following an incredible series of budgetary and other scandals, the tunnel reduced the travel time on the stretch with 14 minutes. The stretch is part of the new airport railway leading from Oslo to its new airport at Gardermoen, 55 kilometres north of the city. There was a train connection before the important railway from Oslo to Trondheim went past Gardermoen but the stretch was improved at a cost of 10 billion kroner (£800 million), 90 per cent of which was pure loss. If all kinds of time, including travel time, can be measured in money, it may still be possible to calculate that this investment was worthwhile and will eventually pay off. Nevertheless, I have my doubts, and not just because the budget deficit on the Gardermoen railway is equal to the total expected ticket sales for the next 31 years. It is obvious that great chunks of those 14 saved minutes are immediately eaten up; waiting in queues at the airport or simply waiting for a delayed flight, waiting for the tube or tram, while the taxi is waiting at traffic lights and so on. The extremely fast time connecting Lillestrøm with Oslo is quickly consumed by the slow and less controllable time characteristics of the surrounding links.

在奥斯陆与欧洲其他城市之间的飞行时间如此之短，以至于人们容易认为去哥本哈根只要 45 分钟，去伦敦也只要一个半小时的时间。但是，还有很多准备和"后续"活动，排队进行安检和出入境检查，当交通拥堵时还要等待分配起飞的时间空当。另外，还有从皮卡迪利大街开车进城（几乎与挪威到伦敦的飞行时间相当），或者搭乘出租车时极度苦恼的体验。离家时还要预留额外的时间，等等。专横的时间带来的副作用特点是急躁，这是快慢模式之间突然转换的一种因变量。

The flight time itself between Oslo and other European cities is so short that one is tempted to believe that Copenhagen is only 45 minutes away, London an hour and a half. But then there is all the preparatory and "postparatory" activity, the queues at check-in, security and immigration; the waiting to have a time slot allocated when there is much traffic in the air. The ride on the Piccadilly line into town （which could take nearly as long as the flight from Oslo）, or the excruciating drive into town by taxi. The extra margin one has to allow when leaving home, and so on. Impatience, that characteristic side-effect of the tyranny of the moment, is a function of sudden shifts between fast and slow modes.

此外，不能想当然地认为所有的旅行时间都可以用金钱来衡量。现在，火车——维多利亚时代速度与效率的象征，作为飞机与汽车的替代物，如今是一个值得思考的领域，是人们可以寻求内心平和的地方，可以读一本书或喝一杯咖啡，也可以在目睹窗外的农村景色时，仔细品味生活中好奇的方面。

In addition, it cannot be taken for granted that all travel time can be meaningfully measured in money. The train is nowadays presented as a quiet alternative to the plane and the car; the train the very symbol of speed and efficiency in Victorian times is now a site of contemplation, a place where one may seek inner peace, read a book chapter, drink a cup of coffee, and ruminate over the curious aspects of life while gazing at the passing countryside.

同时，这些强制执行的缓慢环境也有被速度占据的威胁。信息技术有助于填充空隙。便携式电脑和掌上电脑日益扩大的市场，直接与人们在机场等待的时间量有关。如果要说交通高峰与移动电话的普及没有直接的关系，我将感到异常惊讶。在北欧国家,边打电话边开车是如此普遍,以至于需要立法强制司机在驾驶时使用免提设备。现在,很多区间车都装有电视显示器,包括从阿兰达机场到斯德哥尔摩市的特快列车都使用电视屏幕发布当地新闻和天气预报。人们用这种方式是否可以更有效地填充空隙,这是另一个问题。越来越多的人承认,为了做一些重要的事,他们不得不离开办公室,在家里或者偏僻的小屋里工作。

At the same time, speed threatens to dominate even such enforced slow contexts. Information technology helps to fill the gaps. The growing market for portable computers and PDAs （palmtops） is directly connected to the amount of time people spend waiting at airports, and it would surprise me if there were not a connection between rush traffic and the spread of the mobile phone. In the Scandinavian countries, the combination driving/talking on the phone is so common that legislation has been passed which makes it mandatory to use handsfree accessories when talking on the phone in the car. A number of local trains are now equipped with TV monitors, and several, including the new airport express train from Arlanda airport to Stockholm city, use them to send current news and weather forecasts. Whether one becomes more efficient by filling the gaps in this way, is another question. More and more people concede that, in order to get something substantial done, they have to get out of the office and work at home or even in a remote cabin.

使用计算机产生的后果如此之多,以至于需要一本书才能叙述完。有一些前面已经提到过,这里还有另一个问题:对于任何写作的人来讲,连续集中的注意力都是一份不可分割的财富。当一位作家在选择计算机时,需要计算的恰恰就是键盘与显示器。我用的第一台电脑是最古老的型号(个人电脑里的骨灰级别),当时只能接入一种应用程序。换句话说,这使作者在需要写作时就必须写作。如果有人被不受欢迎的来访者打断,那就不是计算机的过错了。现在,作家们可以在尤朵拉(尤朵拉,一个 Windows 和 Mac OS 上的电子邮件客户端软件。——编者)、网景(网景,即网页浏览器 Netscape Navigator。——编者)、电子日记和文字处理器之间自由选择，很多时候还可以享受游戏与音乐。每一个时刻都被下一个时刻所干扰。现存最好的文字处理器，可能是 1987 年至 1990 年间的 Macintosh SE。这种机器的显示器很小，只有黑白两色，而且色彩鲜明。它的键盘也很舒服。硬盘的空间几乎没有什么限制性条款，但是不可以用作很多其他的事情。它的价位也适中，很长时间内一个人不能同时申请购买两台以上 Macintosh SE。20 世纪 90 年代早期，就我个人而言，从未再有那样集中精力的模式进行写作了。

The unintended consequences of computer use are so many that they would deserve an entire book. Some have already been mentioned; here is another: to anyone who writes, continuous concentration is an indispensable asset. What counts when a writing person chooses a computer, is really just the keyboard and the monitor. My first computers were primitive creations (the trilobites of personal computing), where it was only possible to access one application at the time. In other words, they made it necessary to write when one was supposed to do so. If one were distracted by unwelcome intrusions from the outside world, that was not the computer's fault. Today, the writer's gaze flicks between Eudora, Netscape, the electronic diary and the word processor; in many cases games and music as well. Every moment is being disturbed by the next. The best word processing machine that was ever made, may have been the Macintosh SE, which existed from 1987 to 1990. The monitor was small and in black and white, but sharp. The keyboard was comfortable. The hard disk had space for a nearly unlimited number of articles and treatises, but not for a lot of other things. The memory was modest, and for a long time it was impossible to keep more than one application open at the time. Personally, I have never since written in a similarly concentrated mode as during those years in the early 1990s when I was working on this kind of computer.

我们必须理解技术带来的这些副作用，不是为了将计算机和移动电话降低为历史的垃圾（这是勒德分子的误解），而是为了以明智的方式使用它们。下一章我还要继续分析，如何正确理解形成我们现在处境的结构性压力，但这远远不够。就其本身而言，好的心愿是免费的和超前的，最后无影无踪。

It is necessary to understand these side-effects of technology, not in order to relegate computers and mobile phones to the scrapyard of history（the Luddite mistake）, but in order to be able to use them in sensible ways. As the next chapter will make clear, a proper understanding of the structural forces shaping our situation helps, but it is far from enough. Good intentions are free and lead, in themselves, to nothing.

第八章　慢时的乐趣

只有一件事情比缺少时间更糟糕。那就是不缺时间。

——给奥斯卡·王尔德的致歉

8　The Pleasures of Slow Time

There is only one thing that is worse than being short of time. That is not being short of time.

（T.H.E., with apologies to Oscar Wilde）

费加罗先生是一个偏僻小镇上的美发师。他喜欢自己的工作和朋友,每天听听音乐并照顾自己的老母亲,下午去看一个患有慢性病的妇女。然而,他经常会觉得内心空荡荡并流露出难过的神情。一天,他接待了一个前来拜访的男子,并从他那里得到一个使生活变好的秘方。这个男人一身灰白色打扮,口里叼着一支灰色的雪茄,声称自己是时间储蓄银行的业务代表。他向费加罗展示节省时间的方法,以便让他变成一个更幸福的人。他告诉费加罗:将你的老母亲放到老人福利院,不要再去探访那个无用的残疾人,别再与你的顾客闲聊,浪费宝贵的时间——这样你的营业额就能翻番——而且最重要的是,不要把珍贵的时间用于唱歌、阅读以及与你那些所谓的朋友的亲密交往。费加罗接受了这个建议。他变得沉默寡言并且很有效率。然而,无论他节省下多少时间,他总感觉没有空闲的时间,这些时间以神秘的方式消失了。在他意识到之前,已经过去另一个星期、另一个月和另一年,如此反复地一年又一年。美发师不是时间储蓄银行灰色职员的唯一受害者。整个小镇上的人似乎都在这家银行开户了。诸如"从生活中得到更多——节约时间"之类的口号出现在墙壁上，工厂与政府机构里面到处张贴的公告，内容包括"时间很宝贵——不要浪费"或者"时间就是金钱——省着点花"。

我抑制不住要透露故事的结尾了，不过读者可以试着用一个下午阅读一下恩德所写的这篇小小说《卯卯》。我可以保证，这个时间值得花费。

Mister Figaro was a hairdresser in a remote town. He enjoyed his work and his friends, he played music, looked after his old mother and paid a chronically ill woman a visit every afternoon. Yet he often felt empty and sad. One day he got a call from a man who offered a recipe for a better life. The man, dressed in grey from top to toe and smoking a small grey cigar, represented the Time Savings Bank. He showed Figaro how he could save time in order to become a happier person. Place your mother in an institution for the elderly, stop visiting that useless invalid, stop wasting precious time chatting with your customers then you will double your turnover and "above all, don't squander so much of your precious time on singing, reading and hobnobbing with your so-called friends". Figaro followed the advice. He became taciturn and efficient. And yet: "No matter how much time he saved, he never had any to spare; in some mysterious way, it simply vanished. (...) Almost before he knew it, another week had gone by, and another month, and another year, and another and another." The hairdresser was not the only victim of the grey functionaries of the Time Savings Bank. The whole town seemed to have opened accounts with them. Slogans such as "Get more out of life save time!" appeared on the walls, and notices that were placed in factories and office buildings might read, "Time is precious don't waste it!" or even "Time is money save it!" The end of the story I shall refrain from revealing; the reader might instead take an afternoon off to read Michael Ende's little novel *Momo*. It is time well spent, that much I promise.

目前，对于我的分析最明显的异议是类似这样的话："大部分人都没有这样的生活体验。他们平和安静地生活,不需要不停地从网页跳到电子邮件,不必为了那些会议文件匆匆忙忙,以免错过最后期限。他们灵活、开放和年轻的生活感觉不到压力。他们有很多的时间,可以坐在摇椅上边看小说边抽烟,或者在大自然中悠闲地散步,并且可以按照自己的节奏享受生活。你写的只是其中小部分的人,不要假装你知道其他人。"

The most obvious objection to my analysis so far goes like this: "Most people do not have this experience of their life. They lead their lives in peace and quiet, they do not run incessantly from web pages to email to heaps of documents to meetings to rush-hour queues to deadlines. They do not feel a constant pressure to be flexible, open and youthful. They have plenty of time to sit down in an easy chair with a pipe and a novel, or they take leisurely walks in the country, and are able to enjoy life at their own pace. The people you write about belong to a small minority, don't pretend otherwise!"

说到点子上了。但是,这是否意味着富裕国家的大部分居民从不看电视、从不用手机或电子邮件、从不读小报、从不申请需要熟悉信息技术的工作、从不因为还有其他事情需要先做而觉得自己没有足够的时间做事?也从不因为需要等待紧迫的新任务而无法适当地集中注意力做任何事呢?

Point taken. But does this then mean that a majority of the inhabitants of rich countries never watch television, never talk over the mobile phone or write email, never read tabloids, have never applied for a job where familiarity with IT is an essential requirement, and never feel that they do not have enough time for things that really matter because there is always something else they have to do first? And never feel that they cannot concentrate properly on whatever they are doing because new urgent tasks are waiting?

显然，信息时代的副作用将不同程度地影响人们。并非每一个人都能感觉到时间正在加速。甚至在当今世界变化最快的社会中，也只有少数人能够体会到快速时间是一种稀缺资源。不妨以失业的人为例，也可以看看监狱中的囚犯，或是北美都市贫民窟里穷人和数百万处于边缘社会的人。这是不得不考虑的事。然而，在前几章的基础上，我要直截了当地提出以下观点。

首先，破碎和匆忙的瞬间在富裕国家的人口中越来越典型。

其次，加速度影响知识的生产和当代文化的思维模式，因此它关乎每一个人。即使一个失业的人拥有很多的时间，在他打开电视或报纸的时候，也会受到加速发展的副作用影响。

It is obvious that the side-effects of the information age affect people to varying degrees. Not everybody has the feeling that time is accelerating. Quite a few people, even in the most fast-moving societies in the world, have the experience that fast time is a scarce resource. Take unemployed people, for example. Or prison inmates. Or the impoverished and marginalised millions of people in North American urban slums. This has to be taken into account. Yet, I would, on the basis of the previous chapters, state categorically that:

(1)A fragmented and rushed temporality is typical of a growing majority of the population in the rich countries.

(2)Acceleration affects both the production of knowledge and the very mode of thought in contemporary culture, and therefore concerns everybody. Even an unemployed person with aeons of "time to kill", is sucked up by the side-effects of acceleration the moment he or she turns on the TV or opens the newspaper.

显然在这种情形下，工作与休闲时间都被切碎了，间隔变得越来越窄，越来越多的事件被挤进日益减少的时间空当中，而人们对此并未达成一致的意见。虽然那些最强势的人希望掌控自己的时间，但他们仍会抱怨（而且超过其他任何人）自己的行程过于紧凑，妨碍了晚上观看电影和阅读小说等事情。他们与其他人一样，成了时钟的奴隶。学者亨利克是前挪威首相之子，他告诉新闻记者，最近他发现政治职业不可能与家庭生活保持一致，因为现在的文山会海已经远远胜于从前。

Obviously this situation, where both working time and leisure time are cut into pieces, where the intervals become smaller and smaller, where a growing number of events are squeezed into decreasing time slots, is not arrived at by general consensus in the population. Even the most powerful people, who might be expected to be in control of their own time, complain （generally more than anybody else）that their tight schedules preclude evenings in the theatre, reading novels and so on. They are just as much slaves of the clock as anybody else. The son of a former Norwegian prime minister, the academic Henrik Syse, told the press recently that he saw a political career as impossible to reconcile with a functioning family life, because "the pressure created by piles of documents and meetings is much tougher nowadays than it used to be".

在提出建议之前，我先将此书的主要观点作一个简单的总结。

其一，当信息既不剩余也不缺乏时，其包容程度与信息数量的增长成正比。出于对知识的考虑，不得不限制一个人的信息。通常，学生们对于自己最不熟悉的主题，可以写出最好的作文；这迫使他们组织材料，并尽力证明自己能比平常表现得更出色，而且主要的论据并不会离题。再举一个不同的事例：当你在外国待上 6 个月，就可以写一本书了。如果待上 10 年，你只能写一篇论文。因为你知道得越多，就会发现不知道的东西也越多。这个普遍性原则是当今信息社会中人类境况的一部分。我们知道得越来越多，同时也会发现知道的东西少之又少。

Before moving towards some recommendations, I shall sum up the main points developed in this book.

When there is a surplus, and no scarcity, of information, the degree of comprehension falls in proportion with the growth in amount of information. One has to limit one's information out of consideration for one's knowledge. Often, students write their best papers about the topics they are least familiar with; this forces them to structure, justify and argue better than they usually do, and the main argument does not drown in details and digressions. Put differently: after spending six months in a foreign country, you can write a book. After ten years, you can write an article. The more you know, the more you do not know. This general principle is part of the human condition in information society. We know more and more, and therefore we know less and less.

其二，在信息社会中，对于任何商品的供应商而言，主要的稀缺资源是他人的注意力。无论是广告、会谈、科普文章和知识，还是我们提供给外部世界的实物商品，为了获得目标群体时间预算的空位，它们总会发生激烈的竞争。这些空闲的瞬间变得越来越短，因为目标群体中的人都被寄予厚望，供应商认为他们会腾出空间，以便在生活中留下更多的印象、商品、经历和信息碎片。不过，后一个印象会以加速的方式抹杀前一个印象。

The main scarce resource for suppliers of any commodity in the information society is the attention of others. Whether it is advertisements, talks, scientific articles, knowledge or simply physical commodities that we offer the outside world, there is an intensified competition for the vacant slots in the time budgets of the target groups. These vacant moments become fewer and shorter, since the people in question are subjected to powerful expectations that they should squeeze ever more impressions, commodities, experiences and pieces of information into their lives. The next impression kills the previous one at an accelerating speed.

其三，对于信息社会的居民来说，主要的稀缺资源是功能齐备的过滤器。这个观点与前一章一样，区别只在于需要从接收者的角度来分析具体情况。电子邮件对发送者是祝福，但对接收者来说就可能是噩梦。如果一个人收到的电子邮件多

314

于发送的邮件,可能说明他无法掌控自己的信息总量。我们短缺的商品在父母一辈可能闻所未闻。当前信息的缺乏才是特有的稀缺资源。

The main scarce resource for inhabitants of the information society is well-functioning filters. This point is identical with the previous point, differing only in that it sees the situation from the recipient's perspective. E-mail is a blessing for senders, a nightmare for receivers. If one receives more e-letters than one sends, it may indicate that one is not in charge of one's total flow of information. We are short of commodities that our grandparents had never heard of; one typical scarce resource today is lack of information.

其四,加速发展消除了距离、空间和时间。从前,这是对蒸汽机车主要的批评——旅客无法享受美景,他们的心智正在以不健康的方式变得匆忙。现在,批评的对象换成了喷气式飞机、互联网和移动通信。当过去遥远的地方现在变得不再遥远时,以往近在身边的地方也就不再那么近了。

Acceleration removes distance, space and time. This was once the main criticism against the steam train the passengers lose the ability to enjoy the landscape, and their mind becomes hurriedin an unhealthy way. Today, the criticism is levelled against the jet plane, the Internet and mobile telecommunications. When that which used to be remote no longer is remote, that which used to be near is no longer near either.

其五,当快慢时间相遇时,快速的时间获胜。因为总有一些别的事情需要首先完成,所以一个人就不会有重要的事情要做。自然,我们总要先完成最急迫的任务。按照这种方式,缓慢和长期的活动就会败下阵来。当我们所处的时代消除了工作与休闲的差别时,效率似乎是经济、政治和研究的唯一价值,对于透彻和有远见的工作、游戏和长久的恋爱关系而言,这是真正的坏消息。

When fast and slow time meet, fast time wins. This is why one never gets the important things done because there is always something else one has to do first. Naturally, we will always tend to do the most urgent tasks first. In this way, the slow and long-term activities lose out. In an age when the distinctions between work and leisure are being erased, and efficiency seems to be the only value in economics, politics and research, this is really bad news for things like thorough, far-sighted work, play and long-term love relationships.

其六,在生活中的非工作领域,灵活的工作带来了灵活性的损失。这是因为快速时间征服慢速时间具有普遍的趋势。如果灵活性是未被开发的潜能,工作就可以潜在地填平每一个空隙,消除其他地方的灵活性,这会造成严重的后果,并影响创造性、家庭生活和人们内心的幸福。

Flexible work creates a loss of flexibility in the non-work areas of life. This is because of the general tendency for fast time to conquer slow time. If flexibility is defined as unexploited potential, jobs that potentially fill every gap remove flexibility elsewhere, with serious consequences, affecting creativity, family life and people's mental well-being.

最后,当时间被分得足够微小时,作为持续的时间最终就不复存在了。最后剩下的只是令人惊叹的时间碎片包,它以可怕的速度将各个瞬间包裹在一起。

When time is partitioned into sufficiently small pieces, it eventually ceases to exist as duration. All that is ultimately left, is a screaming, packed moment which stands still at a frightful speed.

完全消极的批评只能导致无奈与焦虑。因此,一些积极的建议很有必要。现在我们需要转到主题之上。由于我们还有大量的时间,我们不妨先绕道休闲地漫步走进学术的象牙塔里。

许多人担心事情的状态。的确,很多从国家拿薪水的知识分子对此一直忧心忡忡(社会科学认为这是焦虑的普遍化)。一些人在谈到那些对此不够忧虑的同事时,总会采用一种挖苦和具有优越感的语调。近来,社会学家吉登斯(布莱尔首相的顾问)和卡斯特(全球科技经济专家)成了这一内部整顿的一部分受害者。

Entirely negative criticism can only lead to shrugs alternating with anxiety. For this reason, some positive suggestions are necessary, and to them we now move. I shall nevertheless first make a leisurely detour to the ivory tower of academia, since we still have plenty of time.Many are worried about the state of things.

Indeed, a sizeable number of intellectuals are even paid by the state to keep such worries going （the raison-d'ê tre of the social sciences: generalised anxiety）. Some of them adopt a sarcastic and condescending tone of voice when they address colleagues who are not sufficiently worried. Lately, some of the victims of this internal policing have been the sociologists Anthony Giddens （adviser to Tony Blair）and Manuel Castells （specialist on the global technoeconomy）.

有趣的是,过去几十年来,具有影响力的学者因为焦虑发出的叹息已经有所变化。直到 20 世纪 70 年代末期到 80 年代早期,大部分人只关心资本主义造成的压抑、对工人阶级的剥削和第三世界的新帝国主义;亚群体的主要忧虑是核威胁和全球人口增长,尤其是环境问题。近来,学者们关注的行业重心已经转向了与认同有关的问题,我坚持认为这是一个加速变迁的问题。吉登斯新近出版的著作《失控的世界》就是一个实例,该书讨论的问题与全球化认同有关;在美国的忧虑的学者看来,一个充满前景的行业是全球化和多元文化社会(或者叫做后多种族社会,这是传统学术界胜人一筹的学者提出的概念)中的认同。诸如鲍曼与贝克之类的社会学家,因为其工作的风险、不稳定和矛盾心态,已经成了有名无实的领袖。一般地说,在这个躁动的时代,很难开发出具有内聚力并可信赖的世界观。法国一些具有影响力的知识分子,看到了内聚力的缺乏,将其视为民主与自由价值遭受的特别重要的威胁——布迪厄在这方面似乎已经改变了他的优先权，速度理论家维利里奥就为一主题写作了长达 30 年，最近已进入了法国第一流的思想家队伍中，在美国他的名声（作为标志的学术头衔）也正逐步扩大。在意大利，埃科也有同样的地位，他在美国和德国同样足以被人视为代表。关键是我把这些现象归在加速发展、指数增长和堆垛——专横的时间——的标题之下，这些现象已经成了很多学者认真思考的对象，离开这一点他们鲜有共同性。他们的主题既宽泛也狭窄——一些人谈论新闻和晦涩的全球经济，另外一些人讨论新经济产生的脆弱性，还有人分析闪烁的新闻产生的混乱效果。

Interestingly, the laments of influential academic worriers have changed during the past couple of decades. Until the late 1970s or early 1980s, most of them were chiefly concerned with the oppression caused by capitalist production, the exploitation of the working class and neo-imperialism in the Third World; sub-groups directed their considerable worrying power towards the nuclear threat and/or global population growth, patriarchy and environmental problems. Lately, the centre of gravity of the academic anxiety industry has moved towards questions to do with identity and I would argue an accelerated rate of change. One of the exMarxist Giddens's latest books is called Runaway World and is to do with the identity aspect of globalisation; a very promising growth industry among American academic worriers has been globalisation and identity in multicultural societies （or post-multi-ethnic society, a concept generated by conventional academic one-upmanship）; sociologists like Zygmunt Bauman and Ulrich Beck have become figureheads for their work on risk, uncertainty, ambivalence and more generally difficulties of developing a cohesive, trustworthy world-view in this turbulent era. Some of the most influential French intellectuals see the lack of coherence and overview as a particularly important threat to democracy and liberating values Bourdieu seems to have changed his priorities in this direction, and Paul Virilio, who has written about the theory of speed for thirty years, has recently entered the Premier Division of French thinkers, and his reputation in the USA (a certain indication of academic rank) is growing. In Italy, Umberto Eco represents a similar position, which is also amply represented in Germany and the USA. The point is that the phenomena I have grouped under the sub-headings acceleration, exponential growth and stacking the tyranny of the moment are now taken deadly seriously by a great number of scholars who otherwise have little in common. Their topics are both wide and narrow some write about the new, opaque global economy, others about the vulnerability created by new technology, and yet others about thc confusing effects of flickering news.

最近从许多不同思想家的离散性分析中提炼出的评价，具有一些共同特点。很显然，没有谁提出该做什么。卡斯特用谨慎的警告结束了关于信息时代的三大卷著作，提醒人们反对在他年轻时代非常普遍的摩天大楼（摩天大楼虽然始于神秘的 20 世纪 60 年代，但按年代主要是在 70 年代才开始大范围修建）。吉登斯雄辩而流畅地谈到新的民主规则（民主对话），认为这种民主可能代表每一个人，但是近十年来，他的作品标记恰恰是缺乏有形的物质——可能它们在其他方面才重要。布迪厄是极度悲观主义者。他似乎建议"停机键"，而鲍德里亚则在黑色的幽默中逃走了。对于信息过载和加速发展造成的问题，维利里奥认真地宣布他还没有看到解决的办法。

The current diagnoses represented in the discrete analyses of many very different thinkers, have much in common. Tellingly, few of them has a word to say about what ought to be done. Castells ends his three-volume work on the information age with a cautious warning against building castles in the air as was common when he was a young man (that is, in the mythical 1960s, which chronologically largely took place in the 1970s). Giddens talks eloquently and fluently about a new democratic order (of "dialogic democracy") where everybody should supposedly be represented, but tangible substance has not exactly been the trademark of his writings from the last decade important as they may still be in other ways. Bourdieu is deeply pessimistic.

He seems to propose turning to the "Off" button, while Baudrillard escapes through dark humour and Virilio earnestly declares that he does not see a solution to the problems caused by acceleration and information overload.

　　对于那些非学术读者而言，如此多的一流思想家对这些问题表现出无力和虚弱的态度，似乎是一件很奇怪的事情，而按照这些思想家的观点，这些问题在我们的文化中具有压倒一切的重要性。主要的原因在于它们在社会中的位置，可以作为启迪与教化的承担者，并形成缓慢的、线性的、累积性的和具有凝聚力的知识。他们属于中产阶级知识分子中模糊的少数派，在过去他们拥有海量的休闲时间，可以阅读和写作长篇大论，并为那些有充足闲暇时间、知识库并对权威肃然起敬的读者写一些不需要那么复杂的文章。如今，他们的时代已经远去，而且永远不会再返回最初的形式。早在 1961 年，哈贝马斯就在《公共空间的结构变迁》中对此作了预言。现在，当人们看到这本厚重而晦涩的学术著作时，只有受虐者才会流露出感激之情。信息已经太多，而不是太少。无论什么都可以用快速的方式沟通，也必须使用快速的方式交流。遵守这个原则就是对读者的尊重。只有当他们可以为读者带来重要的、必须缓慢理解的超复杂见解时，才有权利要求读者付出几周的时间。其他人应当记住，无论自己写什么东西，都要与其他的信息资源竞争。这是近年来学术界知识分子社会（经济）地位下降的原因之一。我们必须在信息生态中找到我们自己的位置，首先应该找到解决加速发展副作用的可行性方法。

To non-academic readers, it may seem odd that so many sharp thinkers take such an anaemic and impotent stance towards a family of problems which, in their view, is overwhelmingly important in our culture. It may be that the main reason is their position in society, as carriers of enlightenment, Bildung: slow, linear, cumulative, cohesive knowledge. They belong to an obscure minority of bourgeois intellectuals who, in the old days, had oceans of leisurely time to think and read, and to write heavy, voluminous and often unnecessarily complicated texts for readers who had plenty of time to spare, a good dictionary and considerable fear of authority. Their time is probably gone, never to return in its original form. Habermas prophesied that much already in 1961, in his *Strukturwandeln der Öffentlichkeit* （The Structural Transformation of the Public Sphere）. Nowadays, it is only masochists who can feel gratitude welling up as they are presented with thick, dense and dry academic texts. There is too much, not too little information. Whatever can be communicated fast, should thus be communicated fast. Adhering to this principle attests to respect for one's readers. Only those who are bringers of unusually important, necessarily slow and complicated insights, have the right to claim weeks of their readers' time. Others should keep in mind that whatever it is that they write competes with other sources of information. This is one of several causes for the declining social （and economic） rank of academic intellectuals in recent years. We must find our place in the new ecology of information, and the first step must consist in proposing viable solutions to the side-effects of acceleration.

一切事情都要迅速地完成，这就会使一切事情无法再缓慢进行。因此，缓慢的进程正在质变为快速的过程。20世纪90年代中期，贾德的《苏菲的世界》取得的世界性成功，明显可以追溯到这种嬗变。哲学史的形成早期具有滚雪球般的运气，对大部分人来说，它的存在毕竟可以作为人格形成的要素之一。但这个过程笨重缓慢，耗时又令人厌烦。青少年喜欢适度娱乐和构思巧妙的小说，而对2500年的哲学史，没有人会多加注意。甚至对于那些被未答复的电子邮件、肥皂剧、紧密的会议日程和上下班交通堵塞包围的人来说，用这种方式就可以奔赴幼儿园与项目工作组开晚会之间获取亚里士多德与黑格尔的生动话语。那么出了什么问题呢？快餐总比没有食物要好得多。正如前面所说，无论何时搭乘飞机，我总是喝同一种咖啡，因为没有其他类别可供选择，只有速溶咖啡是唯一可以马上喝的饮品。

Everything that can be done quickly, threatens to do away with everything that must be done slowly. As a result, slow processes are transmuted into fast ones. The fully deserved world success of Jostein Gaarder's Sophie's World in the mid-1990s can obviously be traced to such a transmutation. The history of philosophy in its old shape had a snowball's chance in hell of surviving as an element in the personality formation of the majority. It was too heavy, slow, time consuming and boring. Enter a mildly entertaining and cunningly composed novel for adolescents, which whirls through the high points of 2,500 years of philosophy without the engaged reader even noticing it. In this way it becomes possible, even for people who are otherwise hemmed in by unanswered email, soap operas, packed meeting schedules and rush-hour traffic jams, to grab between collecting in kindergarten and that evening meeting in the project group some juicy mouthfuls about this Aristotle gentleman and that Hegel foghead. And what is wrong with that? Fast food is incomparably better than no food. Whenever I travel by plane, as mentioned earlier, I drink a kind of coffee I would otherwise categorise as undrinkable, which carries the prefix instant. Simply because it is the only coffee available.

  对于这个问题,有三种答案。其一,普遍来说,学者们希望每个人都与自己一样,认为速溶咖啡和普世哲学比什么都没有更糟。宁愿无知也不要《太阳报》和《世界报》。其二,其他人士回应认为,有一些总比什么都没有要强。这种观点很适合当前的情形,看起来具有开明大度的特点,比其他观点更具吸引力。你可以拥有蛋糕并尽情享用,也可以享受非常丰富的生活,如果足够努力还可以有时间做任何事。乐观主义的特点固然很好,但不能对现实进行最好的描述。我们可能面临多种选择,可以走马观花地浏览 10 本书,也可以专门地阅读一本书,而且此时获得的回报可能最好。但是,可以肯定只有一种选择是对的。因此,我们这个时代最典型的情感特征之一是矛盾的心态,就不足为奇了。其三,第三种态度认为效率的增加总是一件好事。有很多不成熟的乐观主义者,认为慢速时间的损失不会导致其他后果,只会使我们能比上一代人做更多的事情。英国电信公司研究室主任彼得·科克兰认为,计算机可以算作"他的第三个脑半球":他的父亲毕生工作了 10 万小时,而他只要用 1 万小时就可以完成这些工作,他的儿子将来只要 1000 小时就够了。但是工作环境是否和原来一样呢? 显然已经完全不一样了,但是如果整个文化的基础是极快的速度以及用特别商定的测量效率的方式,那么反对的意见就会消失在学术与高端文化的黑洞之中,因为它很难再赶得上,进而不可能确保有很多人会注意到这些差异。虽然科克兰和其他人代表着乐观主义,但是快慢时间的差异对于我们大部分人仍有很丰富的意义。快慢时间在现代社会(或后现代社会)都有存在的必要,虽然可以说速度与效率都是稀缺品,可是我们很难坚守这个观点。附带说一句,我个人的立场介于前两种观点之间,这是唯一合理的位置。

There are three kinds of answers to this kind of problem. First, academics who, as a matter of principle, would prefer that everybody strives to be like themselves, would most likely hold that instant coffee and popularised philosophy are worse than nothing. Rather illiteracy than the Sun; Die Welt or nothing. A second response would claim that anything is better than nothing. This is a point of view which fits current sensibilities well, which seems open-minded and generous, and which clearly has a wider appeal than the other view. You can eat your cake and have it, you can have an immensely rich life, and you will have time for everything if you try hard enough. Optimism is a fine quality, but it does not always lead to the best description of reality. It may well be that, confronted with the choice of skimming ten books or reading one of them properly, one will be best rewarded by the last alternative. （One must only make certain that one chooses the right one. No wonder ambivalence is one of the defining sentiments of our time!） The third kind of attitude entails that increased efficiency is always for the better. There exist a considerable number of unreformed optimists who do not think that the loss of slow time will have any consequences other than making it possible for us to do more than earlier generations were able to. Peter Cochrane, research director at British Telecom, has declared that he already thinks of the computer as "my third brain hemisphere": "My father had a working life of 100,000 hours. I could do everything he did in 10,000 hours and my son will be able to do it in 1,000." But would the content of the work still remain the same? Obviously not, but if the entire culture is based on extreme speed and particular, agreed-upon ways of measuring efficiency, and the opposition disappears into the dark holes of academia and high culture because it is unable to catch up, then it is in no way certain that a lot of people would notice the difference. In spite of the optimism represented in the view of Cochrane and others, the distinction between fast and slow time is still meaningful to many of us; and, although both may be necessary in a modern (or postmodern) society, it is difficult to defend the view that speed and efficiency are scarce. My own position, incidentally, is conveniently wedged in the gap between the first and second alternatives, and it is the only sound position.

下面的建议预设认为，缓慢与迟钝——而不是快速——将面临威胁（任何人若对此有异议，都可以给我发电子邮件……不，给我写信，最好是手写的信件）。我针对个人的标准提出以下建议——接下来会有政治家与商业领袖从各个方向发出一些挑战。

The recommendations that follow below presuppose that it is slowness, not speed, that is threatened. (Anyone not in agreement with this, may send me an email... no, send me a letter, preferably handwritten.) I begin with some suggestions aimed at the personal level what you and I can do followed by a few challenges thrown in the general direction of politicians and business leaders.

首先，可以迅速完成的事情，就应该快速地完成。如果运用得当，快速的时间效果极好。（但在不熟练者的手里，快速的时间却是一个危险的工具）。在过去的历史上，从来没有这么多人有机会像现在这样，留下如此多的印象与经历。当批评人士不喜欢这些机会（从游客数量的增长到互联网的迅速扩展）时，他们完全忽视以下事实：令人愉悦的计算机游戏、在偏僻村寨度过令人激动的时光、漫无目的地调换电视频道或者观看短暂的新闻汇集，这些经历对用户有很高的价值，而且总比什么都没有要好。有些事情变化快，有些事则发展缓慢。在浪漫的晚餐里，没有人能够注意到中间人的存在。即使在一本大部头的理论著作中，有一些见解可以被迅速发掘，但有另外一些精辟的观点则要经过多年才能被发现。逻辑学家可能在30岁之前就能达到顶峰，而形而上学者在50岁还无法出版任何有价值的著述。20世纪最伟大的社会人类学家列维·施特劳斯在1949年出版的一本书可以彻底改变我们对亲属关系的思考方式，他花了4年的时间思考一些问题，比如"为何印度的种姓制度看起来像是澳大利亚的亲属体系的镜像？"20世纪90年代晚期，施特劳斯得到了一家大型研究委员会的资助。因为没有取得文献上的进展，在完成研究工作之前的很长时间内，他可能会失去资助。每一件事都有成本，知识生产中的效率意味着死亡与拯救，这取决于个人寻求的知识种类。

What can be done quickly, should be done quickly. Fast time is splendid when it is used appropriately（but a dangerous tool in the hands of the unskilled）. Never before in history have as many people had the opportunity to take in as many impressions and experiences as today. When critics abhor these opportunities（ranging from the growth of tourism to the mushrooming of Internet connections）, they entirely disregard the fact that exhilarating computer games, exciting, event-packed holidays in remote places, aimless zapping or short newsreels may be deeply valued by the users, and are probably better than nothing （which is often the alternative）. Some things move fast, others move slowly. Nobody watches the second hand during a romantic dinner. Even in heavy theoretical work, there are insights that come quickly and others that can only be developed over years. A logician may peak in his career before he is 30, while few metaphysicians have published anything of lasting value before their fifties. The greatest social anthropological thinker of the twentieth century, Claude Lévi-Strauss, took quite a long time. Before he published a book that revolutionised our thinking about kinship in 1949, he had spent four years reflecting on issues like "How can it be that the Indian caste system seems to be a mirrorinversion of Australian kinship systems?" Had he been funded by a major research council in the late 1990s, he would have lost his grant long before completing his work, due to lack of documented progress. Everything has its cost, and efficiency in the production of knowledge may imply both death and salvation, depending on the kind of knowledge one searches for.

凭着良心尤其是惯例，可以快速地做很多事情。人们快速地调整和执行一些消费。如果缓慢地仔细地聆听流行音乐，或者在一家全球连锁店中缓慢体会汉堡包的风味，就只能得到相对少的收获。相反，如果有些人试图从斯蒂芬·金或布兰妮小甜甜的作品中获取方法应用到自己的工作，对这样的消费者来说，普鲁斯特和马勒显然毫无价值。

A lot of things can be done fast in good conscience, especially routine things. Some kinds of consumption are also tailored to be carried out fast; there is relatively little to be gained by slow, careful listening to pop singles or slow savouring of hamburgers from aglobal chain. Conversely, Proust and Mahler offer naught to a consumer who tries to apply methods taken from the consumption of Stephen King or Britney Spears to their work.

我们所做的很多事情，都是快慢掺杂的复合活动。因此，富有经验的演讲者可能会说，准备一场特别的演讲需要的时间，在 10 分钟到 30 年之间。另外，有时我们会把一些活动与速度联系在一起，如果将这些活动重新定义为缓慢的活动，可能会更有利。例如，每天上下班搭乘公交。一个很明显的建议：带上一本平装书。在上下班途中，与呆板地盯住公交时间表相比，阅读书籍或听听音乐更不容易患上胃溃疡等疾病。缓慢的时间不等于有很多很多的时间。阅读和理解一首一般复杂程度的小诗，只要几分钟就行，但是也可以缓慢地做这件事。速度是一项很有用的技巧，可以用来激发一个人去仔细地进行过滤和筛选，在浩如烟海的文本中寻找一个特定的段落。但是，当他拿到一本新的小说时，就会本能地寻找主题索引，很自然地，这会发生严重的碰撞损失。

A lot of what we do are hybrid activities that mix speed with slowness. An experienced lecturer may well say, therefore, that the preparations for a particular lecture has taken her somewhere between 10 minutes and 30 years. Moreover, there are activities we usually associate with speed (or desired speed), that could profitably be redefined as slow ones, commuting, for example. (Obvious advice: bring a paperback.) Those who read or listen to music are less susceptible to ulcers than those who stare stiffly at the bus schedules.Slow time is not the same thing as a great amount of time. It takes only a few minutes to read and understand a poem of average complexity, but it has to be done slowly. Speed reading is a blessed skill when one uses it to activate one's carefully honed filters in skimming large masses of text in search of a particular passage or fact (such as during a Web search), but those who instinctively look for the subject index when they get a new novel, are naturally already severely damaged.

在谈论速度的章节里，我分析了 19 世纪的加速发展，并且谈到了其他的事情——电报、蒸汽机车以及克努特·哈姆生（克努特·哈姆生，挪威著名作家，因其里程碑作品《土地的生长》而在 1920 年获诺贝尔文学奖。——编者）从美国写来的信件。在写作本书的最初计划里，我不想在这些案例上花去大量的注意力，其中有些案例以简单的形式出现，因为 2000 年 6 月的一天早上，我突然间有一个小时的空当。我去商店更换一个有缺陷的灯泡，发现挪威奥斯陆有一些地方自己竟然从未去过。由于我自己的管理失误，我的第一个会面在一个多小时以后，而且是在镇上的同一个地方。我没有无线上网设备，也不迷恋手机。因此，我在太阳底下沿着郊区美丽的大道信步闲逛，很想舔一口色彩鲜艳的冰棍。当我到达会面地点附近的十字路口时，我在一家大学图书馆墙壁上看到一条横幅，上面写道："速度1800—1900。"自然而然的，我就朝着这栋建筑物走去，就像苍蝇飞向一张粘蝇纸一样。图书馆有一个虽小但与我讨论的主题相关的优秀展会，回溯了 100 多年来的历史。如果那天早上我没有信步闲逛，恐怕永远也不会了解到那次展会的事情。

Dawdling is a virtue as long as nobody gets hurt. In the chapter about speed, I wrote about acceleration in the nineteenth century, and spoke about among other things the telegraph, the steam train and Knut Hamsun's letters from America. In the initial plans for this book, I had no intention of paying so much attention to these examples. Some of them are included in their present form simply because, one morning in June 2000, I was suddenly given an hour of empty time. I had delivered a defective lamp to the shop and found myself in a part of Oslo which I rarely visit. Due to an administrative slip on my part, my first meeting was more than an hour off, and it was going to be in the same part of town. I do not have a WAP telephone, and I am not yet addicted to the mobile. Therefore, I strolled leisurely down the beautiful main street of the suburb （called Bygdøy Allé） in the sun, pensively licking a brightly coloured ice lolly. As I reached the main roundabout near the venue of my meeting, my eye caught an enormous banner covering a large part of the front of the old University Library. "Speed 1800—1900", it said. Naturally I was drawn towards the building like a fly towards flypaper, and quite right: the library featured a small, but excellent exhibition about my topic, displaced about a hundred years back in history. Had I not been fooling around aimlessly that morning, I should never have even heard about the exhibition.

几星期之后,我在等待电车时,只有十分钟的空闲时间,但我还是在国家剧院附近的一家大型报刊经销商那里用掉这点时间。我花了几分钟随机地浏览书架,然后在一本名为《电子商务》的杂志上停留了数秒。斯堪的纳维亚的技术爱好者也是美国爱好者,他们倾向于用美式英语表达最夸张的话语,因此当读到封面上的标题《法西斯残留》时,我是唯一对这个消息感到惊讶的人。我马上买了这本杂志。难道信息技术能够发现美元和日元之外的其他价值吗? 在电车上,我拿出杂志慢慢阅读,很快发现自己最初的解释只是一个口误。实际上,杂志的标题是《最快者生存》。这个具有特色的故事说明,信息技术界的人员流动现在已经接近人们可忍受的极限。如果有可能,我要回到计算机旁,以加固我的信念,证明我对这个主题的选择完全正确。此外,除非我一直在浪费时间,否则这个具有鼓励作用的片段不会让我坚定地朝一个方向走下去。换句话说，创新，直接由这些空隙产生。

A few weeks later, I only had about 10 minutes to spare waiting for my tram, but I spent them in a large newsagent's near the National Theatre. After a couple of minutes of random scanning among the shelves, my gaze fell for a couple of continuous seconds on a new magazine about "e-business". Scandinavian technophiles are also Americophiles and tend to make their most pompous statements in US English, and so I was only surprised by the message （not by the linguistic medium） when I read, in enormous types: "SURVIVAL OF THE FASCISTS", on the cover. I picked up the magazine. Had the IT business finally discovered other values than dollars and yen? On the tram, I began to read, and quickly discovered that my initial interpretation must have been a Freudian slip. The actual heading read: "SURVIVAL OF THE FASTEST". The feature story indicated that the turnover speed in the IT business now began to approach the limits of human tolerance. If anything, I returned to my computer reinforced in my belief that my choice of topic had been the correct one. Again, this snippet of encouragement would not have come my way unless I had been wasting time. Creativity, in other words, is directly produced by the gaps.

需要保护慢速的时间。一位寻求政治庇护的人士提出的血泪申请，往往会遭到掌权者的拒绝。这需要公众的支持、社会福利和它所能得到的配额。速度如果控制得好，没有什么可以比过它。人们可以依赖个人和职业的位置，在个人层面上用不同方式保护慢速；但是为了不被速度生吞活剥，有必要自觉地加以选择。例如，可以做出这样的决策：

只在周一早上回复电子邮件。

周二去一个秘密的地方钓鱼，别人找不到自己。

每天上下班需要驾驶60英里（60英里约合96.6公里。——编者），一个人在车上时，电话和收音机全部关掉。

周二与周三阅读专业期刊，不读报纸。

不设立自动留言电话，当自己不在办公室时，不用管那些未接的电话。

在用无线上网设备阅读新闻之前，总会阅读一首诗和两条注解。

在下午四点半到晚上八点半之间，与自己的家人待在一起，不接触外界的事情。

每隔一周的星期三去听音乐会，或者去听管弦乐作品，不受干扰也从不间断。

只要现在这一刻适合自己，就要拒绝下一刻的打扰。

Slowness needs protection. It is an asylum-seeker whose tear-stained application is often turned down by the powers that be. It needs all the public support, social benefits, subsidies and quotas it can get. Speed manages perfectly well on its own, there is nothing more competitive than speed. Depending on one's personal and professional situation, one may on an individual level protect slowness in different ways; but it must be chosen consciously in order not to be eaten alive by speed. Such decisions may, for example, look like this:

·I respond to email on Monday mornings only.

·Every Tuesday I am unavailable, since I am fishing at a secret place.

·I commute 60 miles every day. Driving to and from work, I am alone in the car, with the mobile phone and the radio turned off.

·On Tuesdays and Thursdays I read journals instead of newspapers.

·I have no answering machine. When I am not in, I am not in.

·Before I read the news on WAP, I always read a poem and two footnotes.

·Between 4.30 and 8.30 p.m. I am with my family, and am therefore not available for the outside world.

·I go to the Concert House every second Wednesday to listen to orchestral works without distractions or interruptions.

·I live in the present moment whenever it suits me, and refuse to be interrupted by the next moment.

其次，延迟是伪装的祝福。它们会为事后的想法产生空隙，人们不得不了解如何利用它们。说比做更容易吗？当然，但是每一次人们因为会议延期而觉得宽慰时，就开始意识到这一点。

Delays are blessings in disguise. They create gaps for afterthoughts, one just has to know how to exploit them. Easier said than done? Certainly, but every time one feels relief because a meeting has been postponed, one has begun to realise it.

第三，小木屋的逻辑值得在全球范围内推广。在北欧国家（包括芬兰），小别墅或木屋的概念具有特殊的含义。只有一半的北欧人可以轻易地接近小别墅，但每个人都明白其深层的意义。当人们抵达那些小别墅时，会发现它们要么位于偏僻和荒芜的山间，要么就在海岸线附近的荒滩上（因为各种原因，丹麦除外），此时缓慢的瞬间接管了一切。人们把手表放在抽屉里，等到返回城市后才把它取出来。对于别墅是否需要电视、电话和互联网，很多家庭都发生过激烈的讨论——尽管这些设备可以带来方便，人们却羞于承认这一点。尤其是在挪威，许多人甚至拒绝在别墅中使用电。在这种环境下，产生压力的不是管理活动的时钟，而是管理时间组织的活动。孩子们上床睡觉会比平常晚一个小时，晚餐是因为饥肠辘辘，只要你喜欢就可以随意采摘浆果或钓鱼，等等。具有讽刺意味的是，在这种情况下，许多人的想象特别丰富，下一刻似乎永远不会到来，不需要越过这一刻去看它，把它放到一边去。（这几行文字的写作地点就是——你猜测一下——在我们的小屋里！）目前，现代社会很少有市民会梦想永久地返回到这种令人喜悦的时刻。我们对其他种类的乐趣知道得太多，也非常理解我们当前社会的复杂性，知道回归天然的梦想确实非常具有吸引力。然而，我们别忘了别墅的状态完全不同于碎片化的匆忙情形，可是通常后者却管理了我们的大部分生活。我认为在别墅里的时间里，安排许多不同的活动会很有利，不过其前提条件是，这些活动不需要仔细准确的合作。（在这方面，似乎北部的人在处理专横的时间时，具有相对的优势：在挪威，与此最密切的等价物似乎是板球，但事实上并非同一种事物。）

The logic of the wood cabin deserves to be globalised. In the Scandinavian countries （including Finland in this respect）, the notion of the cottage or cabin, hytta （N） or stugan （S） or sommerhuset （DK）, has special connotations. Only about half of the Scandinavian population have easy access to such cottages, but everybody is aware of their deeper significance. When one arrives at the cottage, which is located either in a remote and barren place in the mountains or on a deserted strip of coastline （Denmark is an exception here, for obvious reasons）, the temporality of slowness takes over. One puts the watch in a drawer, leaving it there until it is time to return to the city. Many families have violent discussions about whether to have TV, telephone and Internet connectivity in the cottage although many do have these conveniences, they are ashamed to admit it. Many people, especially Norwegians, even refuse to have electricity in their cottages. In this context, it is not the pressure of the clock that regulates activities, but the activities that regulate the organisation of time. The children go to bed at a later hour than usual, dinner is served as a result of mounting hunger, berry picking and fishing last as long as one feels like it, and so on. The irony is that many people are fantastically prolific in such an environment, where the next moment is not looking over the shoulder of the present, asking it to step aside. （These lines are being written you guessed it in our cottage!） Now, very few citizens in modern societies dream of a permanent return to such a state of blissful peace. We know too much about other kinds of pleasures, and understand the complexities of our present society too well for that kind of regressive dream to be truly attractive. Yet we should not forget that the temporal regime of the cottage differs radically from that fragmented, rushed regime which regulates so much of our lives in general. I should think that cottage time could profitably be applied to a wide range of activities, if not to activities that by default need to be carefully and accurately coordinated. （In this area, it seems as if Northerners have a comparative advantage in handling the time tyranny: the closest equivalent in Britain seems to be cricket, and it is really not the same thing.）

　　第四,所有的决策会排斥其所包括的事物。长时间的重大新闻节目以及很长一段时间待在偏僻的地域,可能会比其他的短暂选择更好一些;问题在于人们花时间做的每一件事,都需要寄生于其他事情之上,而后者可能也要花费他的时间。当我被其他不太苛刻和互相不太排斥的活动压住时,我怎样才能确定,用一学期阅读康德的著作和待在一个节奏缓慢的泰式小渔村里,哪种使用时间的方式比较明智呢?如果我按照优先顺序进行处理,又该采用什么标准呢?因为缺乏不证自明的标准,很多人试图找时间做一切的事。结果是每一件事或每一个活动都痛苦不堪。这恰恰就是问题之所在。

All decisions exclude as much as they include. Long, profound news programmes and long periods in remote areas may be preferable to their short alternatives; the problem is only that everything one spends time on is parasitical on something else that one might also want to spend time on. And how can I be so certain that it is sensible time use to spend a semester reading Kant or staying in a slowmoving Thai fishing village, when I am overwhelmed by other, less demanding and less mutually excluding activities? If I have to prioritise, what criteria can I apply? For want of self-evident criteria, many try to find time for everything. As a result, each single event or activity suffers. That is exactly the problem.

　　如果你有钱,可以不带薪休假,暂停工作和学习,并把孩子放到乡下友善的亲戚那里,让自己用上半年的时间搞一些有意义的活动。建议你首先考虑下列活动:
　　学习弹爵士钢琴。
　　在巴黎待上 6 个月正确地学习法语。
　　在最新版的模拟城市游戏中,真正熟练地建构一座虚拟城市。
　　熟悉符号逻辑。
　　读一下《尤利西斯》这本小说。

照顾家庭并成为一个更好的厨师。

与朋友在咖啡馆或电影院玩个痛快。

在热带沙滩的吊床里悠闲地度过尽可能多的时间。

Suppose you have spent money, taken unpaid leave from your job or studies, sent your children off to kind relations in the country, and have allowed yourself half a year earmarked for some truly fulfilling activity. Suppose, further, that the following activities are the first to come to mind:

·Learn to play jazz piano.

·Spend six months in Paris to learn French properly.

·Become really skilful at building virtual cities in the latest version of SimCity.

·Get acquainted with symbolic logic.

·Read Ulysses.

·Look after your family and become a better cook.

·Have a good time in cafés and cinemas with your friends.

·Spend as much time as possible in a hammock on a tropical beach.

这些都是值得赞赏的好主意,但是自然不可能同时实现。可以把两三个主意合并在一起,但是计划中捆绑的主意太多,就会把事情搞砸。在这方面,我们这一代人有机会经历17次的概念,而对我们的祖父母那一辈人来说,必定有所保留。报酬递减的原则和堆垛作用十分强势。

All good and laudable intentions in their way, but all of them cannot, naturally, be implemented at the same time. Two or three alternatives may be combined, but a more packed schedule would ruin everything. It is in this light that the notion that our generation has the opportunity to experience 17 times as much as our great grandparents, must be taken with a pinch of salt. The laws of diminishing returns and stacking apply with full force.

在前面的章节里,我提到有些人具有不同寻常的能量与精力,可以同时做 12 件事,而且都做得很好。然后在做第 13 件事时,突然间就会做得一塌糊涂,或者会因为病症发作而精力衰竭。与任何悲观主义或新勒德分子关于使用"停机键"的建议相比,这种见解是一个更有成效的起点。速度是一份巨大的礼物,直到它失控为止。与其他许多人类学家一样,我在田野工作期间也住在一个热带村庄里。村庄的日常生活根本没有我们想要的那样缓慢。对于大部分居民而言,时间不是一种可以测量的稀缺资源。生活以悠闲的节奏继续向前。自然地,数月之后我感觉非常厌烦。有趣的是,这也是许多村民的感受,尤其是年轻的男子和女子。他们从出生以后,似乎一直在等待生活的加速,因为他们生活在现代的边缘,接触的是大城市快速变化的电影与故事。

In an earlier chapter, I mentioned that certain people, with unusual capacities and energies, are able to do twelve things simultaneously and well. Then they get a thirteenth task, and suddenly they do thirteen things badly, or else they collapse and drift away on sick leave based on diffuse symptoms. This insight is a more fruitful starting-point than any pessimistic or neo-Luddite suggestion about using the "Off" button. Speed is a great gift until it gets out of hand. Like thousands of other anthropologists, I have lived in a tropical village during fieldwork. Everyday life in the village was not exactly wanting in slowness. Time was, to most of the inhabitants, not a measurable, scarce resource. Life rolled on at a leisurely rhythm. After a few months, naturally, I was bored out of my wits. Interestingly, this was also the case with many of the villagers, particularly the young men and women. They had, it seemed, been waiting for life to speed up since they were born, living as they did on the fringes of modernity, exposed to fast-moving films and stories from big cities.

换句话说,他们不需要浪漫而无限缓慢的时间。现代就是速度。同时,埃科的"超现代性"的主要内涵,应该就是超速发展。

There is no need, in other words, to romanticise limitless slowness. Modernity is speed. At the moment, however, it is going too fast, a fact which is a main connotation of Umberto Eco's term "hypermodernity".

第五，有必要在快与慢的时间之间有意识地进行转换。近来，坐立不安成了个人的一种特性，这种特性正在茁壮成长。一般来说，这种心理特征的出现，往往是缓慢时间遇上了对快速时间的期待。上下班高峰期和延迟的航班就是最好的例证。《明镜周刊》的一篇老文章（准确地说是在 1989 年的文章），援引了一个 9 岁小孩的话语："我的老师比保姆雅达利说话慢，有的时候慢得让我发疯。我在想快点，让我回家去找雅达利。她能更快地告诉我这些事情。"

It is necessary to switch consciously between fast and slow time. Restlessness is a personal quality which thrives these days. Generally, this state of mind arises when slow time meets an expectation of fast time. Rush-hour traffic and delayed flights are paradigmatic examples. In an old article from Der Spiegel （from 1989, to be accurate）, a 9-year-old is quoted as saying: "My teachers talk more slowly than my Atari, so slowly that it sometimes drives me crazy. I think: Come on, that will do. Let me go home to my Atari. It is able to tell me things more quickly."

然而，1999 年在联合国对小孩教育的调查研究中，一个 5 岁的小孩接受访谈时说："我从来不去玩。因为总有人说快点，我讨厌匆匆忙忙。"总的看来，这两个案例表明了当今同时存在的两种对立趋势：别人的缓慢引起的坐立不安，以及外部对速度和效率的需求造成的挫折感。

However, a 5-year-old who was interviewed in a UN study about education for small children, stated in 1999: "I never get to play. Always, it is just 'Hurry up! Hurry up!' I hate hurrying up." Together, these two quotations reveal that both opposing （or complementary) tendencies exist side by side: a restlessness caused by the slowness of others, and frustration over external demands for speed and efficiency.

两个小孩的观点之间的差别,自然已经被包括在这样一个事实之中,德国的9岁男孩(不过现在已经是一名大学生了)能够按照键盘调整自己的速度,而5岁男孩的节奏则完全由外界决定。解决方案是有意识地管理自己节奏的变化。很多事情人们永远也不需要知道。如果人们一天有几次能够做一些有趣的事,就会对自己更满意;大多数事情人们无需了解,即使是极好的东西。在这种背景下,比其他任何事情更重要的是,给自己的口味、价值观、兴趣和直觉装上健全而有效的过滤器。顺便说一句,这些东西只能够缓慢地获得。

The difference between the two statements naturally consists in the fact that the German 9-year-old（who is already a university student by now）regulates his own speed at the keyboard, while the tempo of the 5-year-old is entirely directed from outside. The solution consists in taking conscious charge of one's own rhythmic changes. Most things one will never need to know about. Some of us would be better off saying to ourselves, perhaps several times a day, that people are up to a lot of funny things; most of it you do not have to know about, even if it might be great stuff. What matters more than anything else in this context, is to equip oneself with sturdy, efficient filters which consist of taste, values, interests and intuition. They, incidentally, can only be acquired slowly.

为了让慢速的时间留存下来,不仅仅需要这些个人训练的项目,还需要政府、贸易组织、雇主组织、政治家和非政府组织的支持——必须将其嵌入社会的结构之中。仅仅呼吁每个人具有良好的心愿,还远远不够。好的愿望不守约束也无法托付给他人,迟早都会被制度系统埋没。人们很容易而且可以自由地伸出食指,说现在自己离线的时间多,很少看乏味的电视剧,读了一些好的老式期刊,不再写很多电子邮件,关掉了手机,乘坐火车而不是飞机去旅行,与小孩和老人待上足够长的时间。虽然这方面的警告具有比打印过程的成本稍高的价值，但很明显它们也是有限的。如果要从根本上限制信息社会的副作用，就需要社会优先权。要是政治家、官员和企业主能够意识到，我们目前有一个黄金机会，可以从快慢两个世界中获得最好的东西——如果我们只看到其中一个，那么我们将失去无法估量的价值，这是非常重要的事情。

Slowness needs much more than this kind of personal training programme in order to survive; it needs support from the state, trade unions and employers' organisations, politicians and NGOs it must be embedded in the structure of society. It is far from sufficient to appeal to the good intentions of every individual. Good intentions are free and uncommitting, and are sooner or later caught up with by the system. It is easy, and not least free, to raise one's index finger to state that now we'd better spend more time offline, watch less stupid television and read good old-fashioned journals instead, stop writing so much email and turn off the mobile phone, travel by train rather than by plane and give ourselves ample time whenever we are with children or elderly people. Even if certain admonitions of this kind may have a slightly higher value than the cost of the print run, they are clearly limited. If it is going to be at all possible to limit the side-effects of information society, societal priorities are required. If would help significantly if politicians, bureaucrats and business leaders realised that currently we have a golden chance to get the best from both worlds the fast and the slow and that immeasurable values are lost if we end up only seeing one of them. Just as the nineteenth-century working class had to fight patiently and militantly to make industrialism serve some of their ends (and not just those of the capitalists), the struggle over our era's scarce resource slowness is going to lead to major confrontations. Probably, in this struggle, technocrats (including many social democrats) and big money will be on the wrong side; they share an almost religious belief in efficiency as a value in itself.

正像 19 世纪工人阶级为了使工业制度能为末端服务（不仅仅是为资本家服务）而不得不耐心并强硬地斗争一样，我们这个时代的斗争是为了稀缺的资源——慢速，这将导致更大的对抗。可能因为技术专家（包括许多社会民主主义者）和大笔的金钱都处在错误的一方，他们在效率上共享一个价值体系，几乎将其视为一种宗教信仰。让社会慢下来，如果社会引入刹车机制，并将其作为社会结构的组成要素之一，就可以有效地抵制专横的时间。

Just as the nineteenth-century working class had to fight patiently and militantly to make industrialism serve some of their ends （and not just those of the capitalists）, the struggle over our era's scarce resource slowness is going to lead to major confrontations. Probably, in this struggle, technocrats （including many social democrats）and big money will be on the wrong side; they share an almost religious belief in efficiency as a value in itself. The tyranny of the moment can only be resisted efficiently if society introduces brakes as an integral element in its structure.

那么，我们该如何做呢?

本书大部分内容是在讨论变化带来的不可预料的后果或副作用。在某些情况下，副作用如此之多，以至于损益几乎相抵。一个标准的案例是世界上高人口密度的大城市里的汽车运输。不妨把交通问题作为一个隐喻性的出发点，用来分析信息问题。当自行车成为一种比汽车快的交通工具时，汽车的边际价值就在下降，并最终趋向于零。当信息浪潮使用户更困惑、消息更不灵通时，信息获取的边际价值会下降并趋向于零。当连续时刻的转换太迅速，以至于人们关心的是下一刻而不是现在时，活在当下的边际价值也会下降并趋向于零。

How?

A major portion of this book has dealt with unintended consequences or side-effects of change. In some cases, the side-effects are so considerable that losses and gains equal each other out. A standard example is car traffic in the densest urban areas in the world. Let traffic problems serve as a metaphoric starting-point for a look at information problems. The marginal value of driving falls towards zero when the bicycle becomes a faster means of transportation. The marginal value of information acquisition falls towards zero when the user becomes more confused and not better informed （or more entertained） by the waves of information. The marginal value of living in the here and now falls towards zero when the succession of moments is so swift that people are more concerned with the next moment than with the present one.

交通堵塞从字面上理解，就是在驾驶时总在刹车，但是必须承认，迄今为止，它还没有让人们都改成骑自行车出门。信息的不和谐声音也许不会令人沮丧，反而使人上瘾。因此，印象的输入和脱离语境的碎片，实际上是否成了身体的需要呢？这是一种不可忽视的可能性。接下来的几年里，宽频与数字化电视将普及，而且会无处不在，诸如蓝牙芯片——一个数字通信的控制中心，可以把几种已知的技术融入一个无缝的系统之中——之类的无线信息技术，可能会给从北欧到美国的技术爱好者造成主要的影响。国家采取限制宽带和网络接入的策略，属于古老的极权主义管理体制。显然，这是认为大众传媒能调节缓慢和速度，而不是建立一套内部引导机制来达此目的。因此，这是我在社会学层面上的第一点建议。

The traffic jam literally puts brakes on driving, but it has to be conceded that so far, this, has not made a lot of people convert to cycling. It may also be the case that the cacophony of information does not discourage people, but on the contrary leads to addiction. A constant flow input of impressions and decontextualised fragments thus becomes virtually a bodily need. This is a possibility not to be disregarded. Over the coming years, both broadband and digital TV will become widespread, and omnipresent, wireless information technologies such as the Bluetooth chip a "command centre of digital communication" fusing several known technologies into a seamless system may also make a major impact in rich, technophile countries from Scandinavia to the USA. State restrictions on bandwidth and net access is a strategy that properly belongs to old-fashioned totalitarian regimes. Suppose, then, that the mass media instead established an internal set of guidelines to regulate the relationship between slowness and speed? Let this, therefore, be my first proposal at the societal level.

一套与缓慢有关的规则正在拓展媒体的道德指南。在大多数欧洲国家,媒体或多或少已经建立了有效规范,用来调节其他的道德原则,这种延伸需要建立在每一个国家现有的框架上。无论采用什么方法,慢速当然都需要一些材料(主要的灾难、科技新闻和国际预算的详情)。如果遗传研究的处理方式与流行音乐领域的最新消息具有一样的形式,那肯定违反了原则。这就需要应用制裁原则。

Ethical guidelines for the press should be extended to include a set of rules regarding slowness. In most European countries, press organisations have established more or less efficient norms regulating other ethical principles, and such an extension would simply build on existing frameworks in each country. Material which by its nature demands slowness （e.g. major tragedies, science news, details about the national budget） should be transmitted slowly, no matter the medium. It would be a breach of the rules if, say, genetic research was dealt with in the same form as the latest news from the world of pop music. Sanctions would apply.

接下来的建议直接与知识的生产有关,也与堆垛产生的令人遗憾的副作用有关。总之,至少在发达国家,正在生产的文本太多太多。在特定社会中,当真空吸尘器与烤箱的生产量增加时,幸福的总和可能也在增长;但是数量与质量之间的关系相当复杂,而且这一点在信息领域尤其明显。

The next proposal is also directly linked to the production of knowledge, and is to do with the unfortunate side-effects of stacking. In sum, too much text is being produced, at least in the rich countries. It may be the case that the total sum of happiness in a given society grows as it increases its production of vacuum cleaners and toasters, but the relationship between quantity and quality is acomplex one, and nowhere is this more evident than in the field of information.

建议将"物以稀为贵"的原则作为信息供应的基本准则。如果 A 文章的长度是 B 文章的两倍，那么它的复杂程度也应该是 B 的两倍。应该鼓励拿月薪的多产作家减少产量，而提高文章的质量。例如，现有的著作众多的教授应该受到鼓励保持 5 年的安静，然后提出一点有影响力的东西（我的一个熟人建议所有的作家都要设定 500 页的最大配额。如果他们超过了这个限度，就必须撤掉之前的作品）。这就需要评估质量，而不是继续统计出版的数量。

The principle of "less is more" should be established as a norm among suppliers of information. If article A is twice as long as article B, it should also be twice as complex. Prolific writers on a monthly salary should be offered incentives to reduce their productivity, in so far as it implies improved quality. For example, established professors who write a lot might be encouraged to keep quiet for five years, provided they then came up with a piece that made a difference. (An acquaintance of mine once suggested that all writers should have a maximum quota of 500 pages. If they exceeded that limit, they would have to withdraw some of their earlier work.) This would entail a need to evaluate quality rather than simply counting number of publications.

另一个建议与电子邮件和手机通信有关。只有少数人渴望石器时代的技术，我们虽然对此鲜有所闻，但有权生活在这两种技术都真正可用的社会。众所周知，在一个不断增长的连线世界中，"难以获得"是一种十分稀缺的资源。所有的雇员都有权一个月离线 1 次，一年休假 1 次。这项权利应该载入劳动合同之中，而且要说明任何人在工作时间之外，没有回复电子邮件的义务。办公用的计算机应该在电脑屏幕下方标示"除非万不得已，不要发送电子邮件！"公共场所——餐厅、银行、公共汽车和电梯——都不可以使用手机。只要在一些地方安装噪音传输器，就很容易实现这一点（这意味着不采用封闭式的视频监控器，人们在互不连接的情况下无需监控）。如果碰到紧急情况，比如站台之间的电车停运两个小时，噪音传输器就可以关闭。还可以建议电话公司一起合作，设定一个全国范围内无手机的日子，采用环保主义者的姿态，类似于石油公司支持热带雨林的举动。

The next proposals deal with email and mobile telecommunications. Only a minority long for that technological stone age when we had hardly heard about any of these, but we also have the right to live in a society where both kinds of technology (which are about to merge) are genuinely useful. Being unavailable is, as is well known, a very scarce resource in an increasingly wired world. All employees should have the right to be offline for one month a year outside of vacations. This right should be embedded in the labour contract, where it should also be stated that nobody is obliged to respond to email outside office hours. Office computers should have the following message engraved on the monitor: "Send email only when you have to." Public spaces restaurants, banks, buses, lifts should be mobile-free zones. This can easily be implemented by mounting noise transmitters in discreet places (in a sense, this represents the opposite of closed-circuit video monitoring people are delinked instead of being under surveillance). In cases of emergency, as when the tube stops for two hours between stations, the noise transmitters may be turned off. An additional suggestion could be that the telephone companies join forces to establish a national mobile-free day an environmentalist gesture similar to oil companies' support of rainforests.

在其他方面也可以采用刹车的方式。例如：第一，政府在上班时间内引入两个小时的公共休假，比如从上午十一点到下午两点。2000年6月7日，挪威行动小组为"缓慢"执行了这个主意，鼓励工人关门后，与同事一起享受几小时缓慢的时间。这是一个相当大的成功。孤立地看，这种首创性似乎没有意义，但是恰恰是这点缀慢的时间，可以用来刺激人们在更广的范围内，反思自己实际处理时间的方式。一天中 3 个小时的空当，可以提供一个非常必要的机会，去思考两个甚至三个想法，直到得出合乎逻辑的结论。其结果可能是我们发现即使我们长时间散步而不与别人通过电脑或电话联系，世界也还在运行。第二，需要披露开会的真正目的——作为一种接口，去与同事一起享受几小时或几天的缓慢时间。每个人都知道，会议最重要的部分是晚上的和喝咖啡时间内的对话——负责安排计划的人必须记住这一点，并合理地安排计划。甚至可以对在开会期间电话铃声不断的人实施罚款。第三，公司要在工作时间内，为慢速设定日常的机会，比如非结构式的小组会谈。为了给员工时间，让他们参与这种反会议的会谈，管理层应该确保减少官方文件的数量以及其他草率发布的信息，使其达到绝对的最小值。

There are other ways of putting the brakes on as well. For example: The authorities introduce two half public holidays embedded in office hours, e.g. from 11 a.m. to 2 p.m. This idea was implemented by a Norwegian action group for slowness on 7 June 2000. Workers were encouraged to leave their offices and enjoy a few slow hours with colleagues. It was a considerable success. Seen in isolation, this kind of initiative may seem meaningless, but it is exactly these glimpses of slow time that may be what is needed to stimulate a broad reflection regarding what people actually do with their time. Three empty hours in the middle of the day may offer a sorely needed opportunity to think two, or even three, thoughts through to their logical conclusion. It might even turn out that some of us discover that the world goes on, even if we are taking a long walk instead of being chained to the computer or telephone. The real purpose of conferences is revealed, namely as pretexts for enjoying some hours or days of slow time with colleagues. As everybody knows, the most important parts of conferences are the conversations that take place during coffee breaks and in the evenings the people in charge of the schedules must keep this in mind, and compose the programme accordingly. One might even fine those participants whose cellphones ring during the conference (this is already in force in a company of my acquaintance).

Companies establish routine opportunities for slowness during working hours, such as unstructured group talks. In order to give the employees time to take part in this kind of anti-meeting, the management also undertakes to reduce the amount of bureaucratic paper and other thoughtlessly distributed information, to an absolute minimum.

　　第四,城市的规划需要直接面向慢速的建筑。开放的广场、狭窄的道路和弯曲的大街,当然,还有漂亮的建筑物,能鼓励路人驻足的设施享有优先权。先考虑慢速的交通,再考虑快速的交通。第五,贸易组织应该将慢速提上议事日程。很多人认为贸易组织与欧洲劳动者风马牛不相及。这是因为贸易组织虽然发展壮大了,但却仍然体现工业革命时的经济。如果贸易组织要继续存在,就必须痛改前非。假设他们在明年的五一劳动节时,把要求慢速的时间和连贯性的口号标在旗帜上,他们就还有机会。或者也可以这样:2000年10月,我作为嘉宾,参加挪威西部卑尔根市举行的国家工作环境会议,并在会上发言。在巨大的葛利格大厅一楼,有一个展览会,很多公司可以在这个展览会上营销自己的方案,以解决工作引起的环境问题。头盔、靴子、通风系统、人体工程学鼠标和设计滑稽的椅子,都有足够的机会展出。我一直徒劳地寻找一家这样的公司,可以提供诸如缓慢、连贯和精巧的设计,使人们自动消除日程表上不必要的会议。时间和空间的污染比空气和水源污染更难以量化,这种污染不仅仅在于环境接口。

Urban planning is directed towards the architecture of slowness. Open squares, narrow pathways, winding streets and naturally beautiful buildings, which encourage passers-by to stop, are prioritised. Slow traffic before fast traffic. Trade unions must put slowness on the agenda. The trade unions are seen as irrelevant by growing proportions of European wage-workers. This is partly because they grew out of, and still embody, the economy of the Industrial Revolution. If trade unions are going to survive, they badly need revitalisation. If they would put slogans demanding slow time and coherence on their banners next May Day, they might still have a chance. Or, let me put it like this: in October 2000, I was a guest speaker at the national Work

Environment Conference in Bergen, western Norway. On the ground floor of the enormous Grieg Hall, there was an exhibition where a large number of companies were allowed to market their solutions to various environmental problems arising at work. Helmets, boots, ventilation systems, ergonomic mice and funny-looking design chairs were amply represented. I kept looking in vain for a company that offered aids such as slowness, coherence and contraptions that would automatically erase unnecessary meetings from people's schedules. The pollution of time and space, more difficult to quantify than the pollution of air and water, is not yet on the environmental agenda.

一方面是极度活跃的、过载的、加速发展的时间，另一方面是平静的、累积性的、有机发展的时间，我们不需要在两者之间进行选择。为了可预知的未来，信息技术在我们的社会中依然具有支配性地位，并将影响所有人——除了少数激进主义者。最后这几页的计划，以一种非常老套并具实验性的方式概述，它们必须找到一种平衡，以便产生一个足够宽广的世界，提供的空间可以兼收并蓄，同时也能反对保守派的原则。我猜想，未来某个时候，人们在临终之际反思自己的生活，将不会后悔用了太少的时间去打移动电话、写电子邮件、参加会议、追无止境的肥皂剧以及从 A 地方到 B 地方——不管是乘坐汽车、飞机、出租车还是通过网络，或者这四者兼有。当民意测验者询问欧洲人，什么让他们的生活最有意义时，他们很少回答这些事情。他们甚至不谈论无忧无虑的假期。很多人会回答说，"花时间与亲密的朋友待在一起、看孩子慢慢长大"以及"为别人做些事"，甚至还有"好食物"或"艺术"。这些答案不太可能是虚假的，我相信应该根据表面的价值来判断它们。本书的分析已经表明，为何很难在实践中获得这些价值。但是还有希望的是，本书也提出，我们完全有可能拥有自己的蛋糕，并可以很好地享受这块蛋糕！

We are not facing a choice between, on the one hand, the hyperactive, overfilled, accelerated temporality of the moment and, on the other hand, a serene, cumulative, "organic" temporality. Information technology will for the foreseeable future have a dominant place in our kind of society, and it will affect all with the possible exception of a small fringe of fundamentalists (that is, people whose identity hinges entirely on what they are against). The project which has been sketched in tentative and doubtless banal ways in these final pages, must consist in finding a balance, that is creating a world which is spacious enough to give room for a wide, inclusive bothand (as opposed to that Protestant principle, either or). I suspect that, reflecting on their lives on their deathbed some time in the future (whether it is one year or 60 years from now), readers will not regret having spent too little time talking in the mobile phone, writing e-mails, attending meetings, following endless soap operas and moving from A to B whether by car, plane, taxi or in cyberspace (or, characteristically, all four). When Europeans are asked by pollsters what gives their lives the most meaning, they rarely mention any of these. They do not even talk about vacations in the sun. Most would say "spending time with close friends", "watching my children grow up", "being able to do something for others" or even "good food" or "art". Such answers are not likely to be hypocritical; I believe they should be taken at face value. This book has shown why such values can be so difficult to achieve in practice. Hopefully, it has also indicated that it is entirely possible to have one's cake and eat it too.

注 释

第一章

尽管本书在准备写作时,间接使用了斯堪的纳维亚语出版的书籍、访谈材料和其他文本,但我一般没有在文中用脚注标明,因为大部分读者几乎不可能接触到这些文献。然而,我需要在此提及一些给予我灵感的重要文献来源。奥斯陆大学法学教授乔恩·宾是一名科幻小说的作家,对挪威30年来的信息时代做了最富想象力的点评;在很大程度上,他点燃了最初我对计算机的兴趣。富有想法的历史学家埃里克森和人类学家、媒体研究者约翰逊,以不同的方式启迪我对时间的思考。丹麦著名科学杂志记者托尔,通过对信息和隐含信息的创新性比较,提出了非常重要的见解;瑞典大学物理学教授波迪在1999年出版了一本小册子《与时间有关的10个想法》,还有丹麦社会理论家施密特,他们对重要问题的主要观点以非常不同的方式与我汇聚在一起。

第二章

托夫勒的《未来的冲击》和《第三次浪潮》,对信息扮演日益增多的经济角色进行了阐述——前者讨论当前的处境,后者探讨不久的将来——分别在多伦多的贝腾出版社(1970年)和纽约威廉莫罗出版社(1980年)出版。1988年,亚当斯出版《蒂克詹特里的侦探事务所》;1994年,霍布斯鲍姆在牛津大学出版社出版了他的著作《短暂的20世纪:1914—1991年》。鲍德里亚在《海湾战争从未发生》一书中进行了评述。上线人数的统计资料来源于www.nua.ie。在本书出版时,在线人数无疑再次更新。在博尔赫斯、奥坎波和卡萨雷斯主编的《想象之书》中,刊载了布林思维德的短篇故事《收集 1973 年 9 月 1 日的人》。在挪威,他的著作由奥斯陆居伦达尔出版公司以挪威文出版。2000 年春季,挪威国家图书馆推出一场名为"19 世纪的速度"的展出,有关马林的 Writing Ball 与尼采与书写技术的关系详情被编入了这次展览会的目录。与各种信息技术有关的全球性增长,在联合国教科文组织的年度统计报告中有详细的记录;在 www.unesco.org.网站上有与这个主题相关的最新信息。引用马克思的话语来自《哲学的不幸》,这本书是他唯一使用法文写作的著作,他在书中反对法国无政府主义者蒲鲁东及其著作《不幸的哲学》。曼德森在其著作《计算机如何破坏散文》中,对苹果机用户和个人电脑用户进行了比较,并引用了 1990 年特拉华州出版的《大学计算机》发布的研究成果。图 2-2 中的赫尔德等人,是指大卫·赫尔德等人编写了《全球政治、经济和文化变迁》。卡斯特的例子引自《千禧年的终结》一书。

第三章

　　本章参考的资料多达百卷,其中,对于文化史的概述很少没有争议。是否可以按照主要的分水岭或分界线给人类历史分出各个阶段,目前还有很大的争论。尽管如此,我个人还是从古迪对国家与教养的研究中受益匪浅,其中最容易理解的是《原始思维的教化》和《犁、剑与书:人类历史的结构》。1994 年,劳特利奇公司重印了麦克卢汉的《理解媒体》,这是一部非常出众且充满火花的作品,讨论了书写及其他感官的延伸。在爪哇的人类学家是指卑尔根大学的奥拉夫。1997 年,柏格森的博士学位论文《时间与自由意志》以英文出版。1907 年,齐美尔的《货币哲学》首次出版,目前仍是有关金钱的交际意义的最佳研究。我的同事拉尔森首先提请我注意乐谱的重要性。各个领域的学者公认为,印刷机是近两千年以来最重要的发明,具体可以参见网站 www.edge.com 或者布洛克曼的著作《过去两千年最伟大的发明》。对伊丽莎白时代以来受教育人数的估计,引自斯科菲尔德(R.S. Schofield)的文章《英国工业革命以前读写能力的测算》。

第四章

波勒曾的案例，引自泰登 1995 发行的一张名为《有时候正确》的激光唱片。正受热议的歌剧红伶温彻，在挪威最著名的人中可能可以排在第五位。公元 530 年的大瘟疫，可以参见戴维·基斯的《现代世界起源的调查》。实际上，维利里奥所有的著作都是速度研究的典范。尤其，他在 2000 年出版的《信息炸弹》，更是谈论目前问题时不可缺少的著作。对滕尼斯、齐美尔和其他社会学家的一般性介绍，到处都能找得到；一般的教材有吉登斯编著的《社会学》。本章引用了苏格兰记者的事例，源于 1999 年 12 月《经济学家》对千禧年问题的讨论。格莱克的著作《更快：一切都在加速》，是可口可乐公司标语的来源地。吉普林的文集《美国札记》在 1891 年首次出版。维利里奥在几个地方谈到摄影、电影和时间，可以参见他的《维摩视觉》。政治学者讲述有关尔兰德的故事，出自 2000 年 4 月的瑞典期刊《摩登时代》。1999 年拉姆内特的著作在巴黎出版，书中第 60—61 页讲述了新闻记者可信度的损失，第 184 页谈到了信息的增长率。关注政治演讲加速度的政治科学家是乌尔夫·托格森。2000 年 10 月 21 日出版的《新政治家》谈到了现在携带电话的特点以及未来的其他电子通信。

第五章

马尔萨斯的《人口论》有很多版本，在他一生中就修订过 6 次。我用的是 1993 年牛津大学出版社的版本。施瓦茨的事例出自格莱克的《更快：一切都在加速》第 188 页，而本章摩天大楼的例子来自该书的第 24 页。恩格斯在他未完成的著作中介绍了自然辩证法，他逝世多年后，这本书以《自然辩证法》的名字出版。拉帕波特的著作《献给祖先的猪》，使得策姆巴加人声名远播。贝特森在《心智与自然：一个必要的整体》中讲述了多倍体马的故事。出版物和纸张消耗的数据资料，来源于联合国教科文组织 1999 年的年度统计报告。亚马逊公司网站可以提供该公司的年度报告，具体可以查询的网址是 www.amazon.com。洲际电话线路增长的资料数据，出自赫尔德等人编著的《全球变迁》一书第 343 页,该书第 170 页也透露了横跨大西洋电话线的成本。全球电信消耗的总时长资料,源自拉姆内特的著作《专横的通讯》第 176—177 页。挪威手机用户统计数字,来自挪威最大的国家电信公司——挪威电信。国际航空业的发展数据,采自国际航空运输协会的网站 www.iata.com。地中海旅游观光的数据资料,出自奥瓦的著作《在度假:假期的历史》第 251 页。

第六章

博尔赫斯有关巴比伦图书馆的寓言,刊载在 1971 年出版的小说集中。麦克卢汉在 1962 年出版了《古腾堡星系》,但他最有名的著作是《理解媒体》。在别人无法理解的那些乐观主义者中,我们应该加上一些重要的媒体批判家,包括克洛克、鲍德里亚和维利里奥。本章引用的事例,来自马丁的《聆听未来:1968—1978 的前卫摇滚时代》第 290、292 页。

第七章

本章的问题首推理论家鲍德里亚的作品《最后的幻想》,吉登斯的《社会的构成》和《现代性的结果》。《英国卫报》关于工作与压力的报道,引自 2000 年 10 月 26 日至 11 月 1 日的《卫报周刊》。有关神经药物的文章是伦道夫写的《氟西汀热销?》(可以参见网址 www.edge.org/3rd_culture/story/100.html.)。有关灵活性问题,贝特森写了大量的文章,其中大部分收集在《生态学的步伐》之中。拉斯奇的著作《自恋的文化》初版于 1978 年,在 20 世纪 80 年代受到广泛阅读和讨论。关于美国汽车文化快与慢的资料,来源于格莱克的著作《更快:一切都在加速》第 124 页。

第八章

1973 年,恩德用德文出版了他的著作《卯卯》,1974 年以标题《灰色的绅士》出版了英文版,1984 年标题重新变为《卯卯》。吉登斯的《失控的世界》(实际上是 6

篇电台演讲稿)于 1999 年在伦敦出版，对他乐观的"第三条道路"的思想，布迪厄和华康德进行了异乎寻常的抨击。哈贝马斯的《公共空间的结构转变》于 1989 年被翻译成英文，并于 1992 年出版平装本。科克伦及其两个孩子的事例，引自《千禧年的迷幻摇滚》。本章还引用了列维·斯特劳斯的《结构主义人类学》。

参考文献

Anthony Giddens. 1997. Sociology. Cambridge: Polity. 1989a.

Anthony Giddens. 1984. The Constitution of Society. Cambridge: Polity.

Anthony Giddens. 1990. The Consequences of Modernity. Cambridge: Polity.

Bateson. 1979. Mind and Nature: A Necessary Unity. London: Wildwood. pp. 66-67.

Bateson. 1972. Steps to an Ecology of Mind. New York: Bantam.

Baudrillard. 1995. The Gulf War Never Took Place. London: Power Books.

Bauman. 1995. Life in Fragments. NewYork: Blackwell.

Benedict Anderson. 1991. Imagined Communities. London: Verso. 2nd edition.

Bill Martin. Listening to the Future: The Time of Progressive Rock 1968—1978. Chicago: Feedback 1997.

Borges. 1970. Labyrinths. London: Penguin.

Bourdieu. 1998. On Television, London: Pluto.

Bringsværd. 1990. The Man Who Collected the First of September 1973. London: Black Swan

Castells Manuel. 1997. End of Millennium: The Information Age: Economy, Society, and Culture Volume III. Oxford: Blackwell. pp. 336.

Castells. 1996. The Rise of the Network Society. Oxford: Blackwell. pp. 463.

Daniel Bell. 1978. The Cultural Contradictions of Capitalism. New York: Basic Books

David Held et al., 1999. Global Transformations: Politics, Economics and Culture. Cambridge: Polity.

David Keys. 2000. Catastrophe: An Investigation into the Origins of the Modern World. London: Arrow.

Douglas Adams. 1988. Dirk Gently's Holistic Detective Agency. Pan.

Edward Mendelson. 1990. How computers can destroy prose. New York Review of Books.

Engels. 1940. ed. The Dialectics of Nature, New York: International Publishers.

Eno. 1996. A Year With Swollen Appendices. London: Faber.

Ernest Gellner. 1988. Plough, Sword and Book: The Structure of Human History. London: Collins.

Galtung. 2000. Johan with no land. Oslo: Aschehoug.

Georg Simmel 1978. Philosophy of Money. London: Routledge.

Georg Simmel. 1989. Philosophie des Geldes. Frankfurt: Suhrkamp.

Giddens. 1999. A Runaway World. London: Profile.

Habermas. 1992. The Structural Transformation of the Public Sphere. Polity 1989a.

Hamsun. 1969. The Cultural Life of Modern America. Mass.: Harvard University Press.

Henri Bergson. 1997., Time and Free Will, Kessinger.

Hobsbawm. 1994. Age of Extremes: The Short Twentieth Century 1914—1991. Oxford University Press.

Jack Goody. 1977. The Domestication of the Savage Mind. Cambridge: Cambridge University Press.

James Gleick. 1999. Faster: The Acceleration of Just About Everything. New York: Pantheon. pp. 50.

Jean Baudrillard. 1994. The Illusion of the End. Cambridge: Polity.

John Brockman, ed. 2000. The Greatest Inventions of the Past 2000 Years.New York: Simon & Schuster.

Jostein Gripsrud. 1995. The Dynasty Years: Hollywood Television and Critical Media Studies. London: Routledge.

Kundera. 1996. Slowness. London: Faber.

Lasch. 1978. The Culture of Narcissism: American Life in an Age of Diminishing Expectations. Washington: Norton.

Lé vi-Strauss. 1969. Les structures é lé mentaires de la parenté . Paris: PUF 1949a

Linder. 1970. The Harried Leisure Class. New York: Columbia University Press.

Manuel Castells. 1996. The Rise of the Network Society. Oxford: Blackwell.

Marshall McLuhan. 1962. The Gutenberg Galaxy. Toronto: Toronto University Press.

Marshall McLuhan. 1994. Understanding Media. London: Routledge. 1964a.

Orvar Löfgren. 1999. On Holiday: A History of Vacationing. Berkeley: University of California Press. pp. 251.

Paul Virilio. 2000. From Modernism to Hypermodernism and Beyond. in John Armitage. ed. London: SAGE.

R. S. Schofield. 1968. The Measurement of Literacy in Pre-Industrial England. in Jack Goody, ed.Literacy in Traditional Societies. Cambridge: Cambridge University Press.

Ramonet. 1999. La tyrannie de la communication. Paris: Galilé e.

Roy Rappaport. 1967. Pigs for the Ancestors. New Haven: Yale University Press.

Sennett. 1998. The Corrosion of Character: The Personal Consequences of Work in the New Capitalism. New York: Norton.

Ulrich Beck. 2000. The Brave New World of Work. Cambridge: Polity Press.

Virilio Paul 2000. The Information Bomb. Verso.

Virilio Paul. 1994. The Vision Machine.Bloomington: Indiana University Press. 1988a.

Virilio Paul. 1996. Cybermonde: La politique du pire Paris: Textuel.